DISCOURSE AND PRACTICE IN INTERNATIONAL COMMERCIAL ARBITRATION

Law, Language and Communication

Series Editors
Anne Wagner, Université du Littoral Côte d'Opale, France and
Vijay Kumar Bhatia, City University of Hong Kong

This series encourages innovative and integrated perspectives within and across the boundaries of law, language and communication, with particular emphasis on issues of communication in specialized socio-legal and professional contexts. It seeks to bring together a range of diverse yet cumulative research traditions related to these fields in order to identify and encourage interdisciplinary research.

The series welcomes proposals – both edited collections as well as single-authored monographs – emphasizing critical approaches to law, language and communication, identifying and discussing issues, proposing solutions to problems, offering analyses in areas such as legal construction, interpretation, translation and de-codification.

Discourse and Practice in International Commercial Arbitration

Issues, Challenges and Prospects

Edited by

VIJAY K. BHATIA

City University of Hong Kong, Hong Kong

CHRISTOPHER N. CANDLIN

Macquarie University, Sydney, Australia

and

MAURIZIO GOTTI

University of Bergamo, Italy

Routledge

Taylor & Francis Group

LONDON AND NEW YORK

First published 2012 by Ashgate Publishing

Published 2016 by Routledge
2 Park Square, Milton Park, Abingdon, Oxfordshire OX14 4RN
711 Third Avenue, New York, NY 10017, USA

First issued in paperback 2016

Routledge is an imprint of the Taylor & Francis Group, an informa business

British Library Cataloguing in Publication Data
Discourse and practice in international commercial
arbitration : issues, challenges and prospects. --
(Law, language and communication)
1. Arbitration and award, International. 2. Arbitration and
award, International--Terminology. 3. Arbitration and
award--Cross-cultural studies. 4. Dispute resolution (Law)
I. Series II. Bhatia, V.K. (Vijay Kumar), 1942-
III. Candlin, Christopher. IV. Gotti, Maurizio.
341.5'22'014-dc22

Library of Congress Cataloging-in-Publication Data
Bhatia, V. K. (Vijay Kumar), 1942-
Discourse and practice in international commercial arbitration : issues, challenges and prospects / by Vijay Bhatia,
Christopher N. Candlin and Maurizio Gotti.
p. cm. -- (Law, language and communication)
Includes bibliographical references and index.
ISBN 978-1-4094-3231-9 (hbk)
1. Arbitration and award, International. I Candlin, Christopher. II. Gotti, Maurizio. III. Title.
K2400.B547 2011
347'.09--dc23

2011030406

ISBN 13: 978-1-138-26939-2 (pbk)
ISBN 13: 978-1-4094-3231-9 (hbk)

Contents

List of Figures

List of Tables

Preface

The more I try to understand how people – individuals and communities – have managed their disputes, the more I am convinced that the answers to my questions must be sought in different disciplines and that the method must be comparative. That conviction has already been reinforced by the insights that have come from trying to work out why processes in different times and places are so alike, or sometimes different.

Comparative research is richer and has more colour if it is viewed not through the monocular microscope of any one discipline: law, history, anthropology, psychology or even language. How much more we can learn if we bring together the tools and experience of all those and other sciences! And how much more rigorously shall we be able to test the results of one another's work!

This book is comprised of chapters written by researchers who cooperated in the second stage of a project coordinated by Vijay K. Bhatia and Christopher N. Candlin, whose stated aim was to focus on 'the actuality of arbitration practices in a grounded and contextualized manner across linguistic, socio-cultural, political and legal boundaries'. This collection is evidence of their success.

To review each chapter would test everybody's patience. Readers want to get at the substance for themselves. I will be happy to do no more than describe what has been accomplished and make an outsider's tentative suggestions for what may be considered as the next steps.

I see the results of all this work as providing the foundations of a bridge. They are great solid rocks, not all of which fit together and some of which in the future may lie submerged, but they are there now. They will not need to be shifted, let alone replaced. Attention now needs to be given to new topics and challenges, though some developments move so fast that the results of worthwhile and considered research are almost certainly doomed to be out-of-date by the time they are published, for example, on On-Line Dispute Resolution.

The bridge still needs to be built. It will span the gulf which now separates the scientist from the practitioner. Though some of the best contributions to the science have come from practitioners, even they have not always been able to transfer their insights into general practice. The architecture has already been sketched and largely determined by the pioneering work of Vijay K. Bhatia and Christopher N. Candlin and their younger collaborators. That, too, need not be done again. Ways need to be found to propagate the new understandings – for example of the extent to which litigation concepts and processes have 'colonized' arbitration. Everyone knew the anecdotal approximations to knowledge. The work presented here is enough to force the professions to face up to the facts as disclosed by the science.

The most devastating hypothesis that has emerged in the last few years is that arbitration is, like litigation, soon to be overwhelmed by mediation as the mode of dispute resolution already preferred by many and soon to be by most parties. That raises, for those of us whose interests include interdisciplinary studies in law and language, a preliminary task: to dispel the confusion in nomenclature – some would claim definition – of the terms 'mediation' and 'conciliation'. Too many assumptions are made: that there is only one relevant language, English; that for our purposes we can assume that there is only one form of English; and that the meaning of the terms is not affected by the users' culture. Whoever takes on this task may like to consider two or three jurisdictions – say North and South Korea and the United States – before drawing general conclusions.

Though the prevailing culture which warps objectivity is usually Anglo-American or at least the cultures of North America and Western Europe, we must be alert to detect influences which work the other way, for example, that arbitration is of its nature an 'amicable' rather than 'adversarial' process. There is no evidence for that in most jurisdictions. The important distinction is between processes which depend on the allocation of rights – litigation and arbitration – and those which are concerned to bring about a peaceful resolution by sharing value – mediation (whatever it is called in any language).

If future research is to be beneficial quickly, it will have to change its emphasis from arbitration to mediation. This volume reinforces the evidence shown in the pioneer studies that it is possible to get a worthwhile corpus of text on arbitration practice. The same should be possible for mediation. Mediators are a different professional group from arbitrators. Though many individuals offer both services, when they are thinking like mediators they are both more open and more positive. Because they want to sell their services and promote their practice generally, access to them as individuals and interest groups should be easier.

Therefore the next steps will depend on the choice of questions which still need to be answered. They will include both the practical and the theoretical. Perhaps these tentative suggestions may be allowed:

1. What needs to be done to transfer the results of completed research into practice?
2. Having shown that arbitration is becoming more like litigation in some jurisdictions, is that a bad thing? What should be done about it?
3. If the language of research is to be English, how do we guard against importing assumptions of cultural universality?
4. Can the results of research into arbitration practice be replicated in mediation?
5. How can research into present practices and future developments in alternative methods of dispute resolution best be managed?

To read these chapters has been a pleasure as well as an education in itself. The editors and authors are to be congratulated on their contributions to knowledge, dependable foundations on which the bridges can be built; for there are at least two: between disciplines and between science and practice.

Derek Roebuck
Oxford

Acknowledgements

The work presented in this volume draws primarily from an international research initiative supported by a Competitive Earmarked Research Grant (CERG) from the Research Grants Council of the Government of HKSAR [Project No. 9041191 (CityU 1501/06H)] entitled *International Commercial Arbitration Practice: A Discourse Analytical Study*.

As the principal investigator of the project, I would like to express my gratitude to all the co-investigators, especially the international collaborators, who have stood by me and have supported me in the last few years to participate in this important international research project. I do not think it would have been possible to demystify some of the dynamics of international commercial arbitration practices without their collaborative efforts and support, which has been exciting, informative and insightful.

I am particularly thankful to Professor Christopher N. Candlin for participating in all the activities of the project, right from the designing of the proposal through to the publishing of the results. I would also like to especially mention the contributions of my friend and colleague Rajesh Sharma from the School of Law, City University of Hong Kong, not only for suggesting international commercial arbitration as the focus of this investigation, but also for providing his perceptive observations and comments as a specialist informant, making this project a successful one. I am also indebted to Professor Maurizio Gotti, from the University of Bergamo, who has always given his unstinted support for all aspects of the research project, including the publication of several volumes of findings, and in particular, for taking the leadership role in the Italian team, which became a real asset for the project.

I would also like to acknowledge the support given to the project by a number of international arbitration centres, in particular by the Hong Kong International Arbitration Centre, the Singapore International Arbitration Centre, the Kuala Lumpur Regional Centre for Arbitration, and the Milan Chamber of Arbitration. Finally, I would also like to express my gratitude to Dr Patrizia Anesa for compiling the thematic index included in this volume.

Last but not least, I am also thankful to all the arbitration and legal professionals who have at various times enriched our understanding of the arbitration practice by sharing with me and the other project members their insightful perceptions as specialist informants.

Vijay K. Bhatia
City University of Hong Kong, Hong Kong

PART I
Issues and Challenges

Chapter 1

International Commercial Arbitration Practice: A Discourse-based Perspective

Vijay K. Bhatia, Christopher N. Candlin and Maurizio Gotti

International commercial arbitration (ICA), as originally proposed by the United Nations Commission on International Trade Law (UNCITRAL), and established by the United Nations General Assembly by its Resolution 2205 (XXI) of 17 December 1966 was meant to promote the harmonization and unification of international trade law. The UNCITRAL also prepared a model law on international commercial arbitration, which was adopted by the United Nations General Assembly on 21 June 1985, and was recommended for adoption as the UNCITRAL Model Law on International Commercial Arbitration. Although the Model Law (ML) was not binding, the United Nations (UN) recommended its adoption and incorporation into the domestic law of individual member states. The main objective of promoting international arbitration was to provide an 'alternative' to litigation to resolve commercial disputes in cross-border contexts.

Today, international arbitration is the most widely used alternative dispute resolution (ADR) method to resolve commercial disputes between parties. International commercial arbitration is considered a consequence of party agreement as it crucially depends on the parties' agreement to resolve disputes through private adjudication by a single arbitrator, or a tribunal consisting of more than one, appointed in accordance with rules of a specific arbitration institution that the parties themselves have agreed to adopt, usually by including an arbitration clause in their contract. The practice of international arbitration has thus developed in a manner to allow parties from different linguistic, legal and cultural backgrounds to resolve their disputes with minimum interference from the courts.

In arbitration, parties or their representatives, often legal counsels, present a dispute to an impartial single arbitrator or an arbitration tribunal to issue an award, which is binding for the disputing parties. The award is generally non-appealable in a court of law. In arbitration, the parties at dispute have considerable input in the selection of the arbitration tribunal, and also in the choice of processes and procedures they would like the tribunal to follow, including the choice of language, the seat of arbitration, as well as the arbitration rules according to which the resolution is negotiated.

Arbitration is thus one of the most appropriate alternative dispute resolution mechanisms when the disputing parties fail to resolve their dispute on their own, and want a third party to resolve their dispute. Their main objective is to avoid the time and expense of litigation where they have absolutely no control over the decision-making process. As mentioned earlier, the decision of the arbitration tribunal is enforceable, and cannot be challenged in a court of law, except on procedural grounds under a very restricted set of conditions. So the main advantage of arbitration is that it is like litigation in effect, in that it is decided by a neutral arbitrator or arbitration tribunal, but unlike litigation, it is informal, expedient, economical, private and confidential in nature, and at the same time, gives sufficient voice and freedom to disputing parties in the way it is actually conducted.

However, it has been recently observed that arbitration as a non-legal practice is being increasingly influenced by litigation practice, a development which seems to be contrary to the spirit of arbitration to resolve disputes outside of the courts. In order to investigate the extent to which the 'integrity' of arbitration principles is maintained in international commercial arbitration practice, a group of discourse analysts in Hong Kong designed an international research initiative, drawing on discourse-based data (narrative, documentary and interactional) to explore the motivations for such an inter-discursive process which appears to be leading to increasing 'colonization' of arbitration practice by litigative processes and procedures.

This study has built on a previous international research project which investigated 'The generic integrity of legal discourse in international commercial arbitration in multilingual and multicultural contexts' by providing discourse- and genre-based analyses of arbitration laws from a number of countries and jurisdictions, by means of pooling research from a number of teams of specialists in discourse analysis drawn from more than 12 countries. This previous research project was based on the understanding that although most of the national arbitration laws followed the spirit of the UNCITRAL Model Law, they were nonetheless formulated and applied differently in different countries, and were often constrained by variations in the languages used, the specific legal systems they were grounded in, and, in addition, the socio-political factors that operated in specific contexts. The project established a network of collaboration from a multidisciplinary group consisting of more than 30 researchers from 13 different countries, which included Brazil, the People's Republic of China, the Czech Republic, Croatia, Denmark, Finland, France, Germany, India, Italy, Japan, and Malaysia. In terms of outcomes, the project has disseminated its findings through several edited volumes together with a special issue of an international journal, in addition to two international conferences organized by the project (see references below). Relying on the degree of interest created in the overall theme, the international collaboration, and the excellent research opportunities for interdisciplinary and international teamwork provided by this initial project, the research teams decided to carry this research forward by focusing on the actuality of arbitration practices in a grounded and contextualized manner across linguistic, socio-cultural, political and legal boundaries.

The main objective of this second project is to analyze *arbitration in action* by undertaking a textual, narratological and discourse-based analysis of primary and secondary data drawn from arbitration practice. Its applied purpose is to explore the degree of *integrity of arbitration practice* in international contexts. Arbitration practice, in this context, is viewed as a professional process which lies at different points on a professional and discursive continuum from *mediation–arbitration–litigation*, and which offers a range of critical moments and sites where law and language intersect, offering the project teams a range of research foci.

Taken together, the outcomes from this subsequent project were to contribute to the strengthening of international commercial arbitration as a non-litigative practice for handling commercial disputes, and to enhance the satisfaction of the involved parties from different cultures, linguistic and socio-political backgrounds and legal systems.

The present volume of edited chapters is meant to showcase some of the findings from international arbitration practitioners from law as well as from arbitration and academic scholars from discourse analysis based on their research during the last few years. Each of the chapters in the volume contains a specific aspect of international commercial arbitration practice. The volume opens with the identification of some of the general issues and challenges, and gradually moves on to issues specific to certain contexts and jurisdictions. Some of the main issues addressed in the volume include ambivalence of international arbitration, witness-examination, evidence, enforcement of awards across jurisdictions and territorial boundaries, language and power in arbitration proceedings, analysis of concurring and dissenting opinions, accountability and voices in arbitration awards, cross-national comparisons of arbitration with other forms of alternative dispute resolution mechanisms, arbitrators' neutrality in arbitration process, confidentiality and publicity in arbitration in the public sphere, and the general issue of 'colonization' of arbitration by litigation, a theme which runs right through most of the chapters. The final chapter then identifies and offers a perspective on the general issue of 'contested identities' in international commercial arbitration practice, seen primarily through the viewing glass of interdiscursive exploitation of disciplinary and professional space.

Research Project Publications

Bhatia, Vijay K., Candlin, Christopher N., Engberg, Jan and Trosborg, Anna (Eds) (2003): *Multilingual and Multicultural Contexts of Legislation: An International Perspective.* Frankfurt am Main, Peter Lang.

Bhatia, Vijay K., Candlin, Christopher N. and Gotti, Maurizio (Eds) (2003): *Arbitration in Europe: Legal Discourse in a Multilingual and Multicultural Context*. Bern, Peter Lang.

Bhatia, Vijay K. and Engberg, Jan (Eds) (2004): *HERMES, Journal of Linguistics*, a special issue, Vol. 32.

Bhatia, Vijay K., Engberg, Jan, Gotti, Maurizio and Dorothee, Heller (Eds) (2005): *Vagueness in Normative Texts*. Bern, Peter Lang.
Bhatia, Vijay K., Candlin, Christopher. N. and Engberg, Jan (Eds) (2008): *Legal Discourse Across Cultures and Systems*. Hong Kong, Hong Kong University Press.
Bhatia, Vijay K., Candlin, Christopher. N. and Evangelisti, Paola (Eds) (2008): *Language and Legal Concepts Across Systems and Cultures*. Bern, Peter Lang.
Bhatia, Vijay K., Candlin, Christopher. N. and Gotti, Maurizio (Eds) (2010): *The Discourses of Dispute Resolution*. Bern, Peter Lang.
Bhatia, Vijay K. (Ed.) (2011): Interdiscursive Colonisation of International Commercial Arbitration Practice, *World Englishes*, Vol. 30, No.1 (76–80).

Research Team

Principal Investigator

Vijay K. Bhatia, City University of Hong Kong

Co-Investigators

Christopher N. Candlin, Macquarie University, Australia
Rajesh Sharma, City University of Hong Kong
Christopher To, Hong Kong Arbitration Centre

International Collaborators

Australia
Luke Nottage, Sydney Law, Australia

Brazil
Celina Frade, Rural University of Rio de Janeiro, Brazil

Brunei/Singapore
Paroo Nihalani, Universiti Brunei Darussalam
Sujata Kathpalia, Nanyang Technological University, Singapore
Colin Y.C. Ong, Colin Ong Legal Services in Brunei Darussalam

Croatia
Susan Šarčević, Faculty of Law, University of Rijeka, Croatia

Denmark
Jan Engberg, Aarhus School of Business, Denmark

Finland
Tarja Salmi-Tolonen, University of Joensuu, Finland

France
Anne Wagner, Université du Littoral Côte d'Opale, France

Hong Kong
Christoph Hafner, City University of Hong Kong

Italy
Maurizio Gotti, Ulisse Belotti, Stefania Maci, Michele Sala, Patrizia Anesa, Larissa D'Angelo, University of Bergamo, Italy
Giuliana Garzone, Paola Catenaccio, Chiara Degano, University of Milan, Italy
Paola Evangelisti, University of Rome for Sport & Movement, Italy
Girolamo Tessuto, Seconda Università degli Studi di Napoli, Italy

India
Gajender Kumar, Advocate, New Delhi, India

Ireland/France
Sophie Cacciaguidi-Fahy, The National University of Ireland, Ireland

Japan
Yasunobu Sato, University of Tokyo, Japan
Iwase, Maomi, University of Hyogo, Japan
Ric Powell, Nihon University, Tokyo, Japan

Macau
Jane Lung, Macao Polytechnic Institute, Macau

Malaysia
Azirah Hashim, University of Malaya, Malaysia

Peoples Republic of China
Wang Wenying, Arbitration Research Institute, China
Yu Jianlong, CIETAC, China

Poland
Joanna Jemielniak, Kozminski Business School, Warsaw, Poland

Spain
Ignacio Vazquez Orta, Rosa Lorés, Isabel Corona, University of Zaragoza, Spain
David J.A. Cairns, Partner in Dispute Resolution, B. Cremades y Asociados

United Kingdom
Janet Cotterill, Cardiff University, United Kingdom
John Jarvis, Advocate and Arbitrator, London, United Kingdom

PhD Students

Han Zhengrui, City University of Hong Kong
Patrizia Anesa, University of Bergamo, Italy
Larissa D'Angelo, University of Bergamo, Italy
Chiara Degano, University of Milan, Italy
Laura Martínez Escudero, University of Zaragoza, Spain
Diana Giner, University of Zaragoza, Spain

PART II
Analyses and Evidence

Chapter 2
Addressing International Arbitration's Ambivalence: Hard Lessons from Australia*

Luke Nottage

Big Costs and Big Law Firms in International Arbitration

Much recent empirical research and even more anecdotal evidence identifies growing costs and delays as a major problem in international arbitration. This may sound familiar. Similar complaints emerged over the 1980s and early 1990s regarding international commercial arbitration (ICA). They were partly confirmed thanks to pathbreaking surveys and some interviews concluded in 1994 by Christian Buehring-Uhle (CBU) – albeit on a small scale – as part of his doctoral research under Professor William Park.[1] Professors Yves Dezalay and Bryant Garth complemented this research with more wide-ranging interviews of arbitrators. They uncovered how the field was developed initially by a few 'grand old men' (mostly professors from continental Europe) serving as arbitrators over the 1950s and 1960s, to resolve otherwise intractable North–South and East–West investment and trade disputes; but then from the 1970s by growing numbers of lawyers from US and then British law firms, making inroads into this new market.[2]

By the turn of the twenty-first century, however, it seemed that the arbitral world had managed to address excessive over-formalization of ICA. The major arbitral institutions revised their Arbitration Rules in the late 1990s to encourage greater time-efficiencies as well as the capacity of the parties and arbitrators to tailor the arbitral process to their particular needs. Some arbitrators, notably Professor Karl-Heinz Boeckstiegel, were celebrated for deploying 'chess-clock' and other

---

* This chapter is based also on research for the project entitled 'Fostering a Common Culture in Cross-Border Dispute Resolution: Australia, Japan and the Asia-Pacific', supported by the Commonwealth of Australia through the Australia–Japan Foundation, which is part of the Department of Foreign Affairs and Trade.

1 Bühring-Uhle, Christian et al. (1996): *Arbitration and Mediation in International Business: Designing Procedures for Effective Conflict Management*, The Hague, Kluwer Law International.

2 Dezalay, Yves and Garth, Bryant (1996): *Dealing in Virtue: International Commercial Arbitration and the Construction of a Transnational Legal Order*, Chicago, IL, University of Chicago Press.

techniques for minimizing delays. International and domestic legislatures began reviewing arbitration legislation to re-emphasize party autonomy and the capacity to follow more streamlined processes.[3] Settled norms and practices were also challenged as Asian parties started to become prominent in ICA cases, although Asian arbitrators were initially slower in gaining work despite the establishment or revival of arbitration institutions in Asia.[4]

By the mid-2000s, however, concerns began to re-emerge particularly about the costs of ICA. In hindsight, perhaps this is not too surprising. Civil procedure reforms in national courts had shown how faster processes do not necessarily lead to lower costs, as everyone tends to front-load preparations and therefore expenses.[5] CBU's follow-up surveys over 2001–2, for example, confirmed persistent difficulties in encouraging settlement during arbitral proceedings (ARB-MED), with attitudes and experiences moreover still varying depending on arbitrators' legal background.[6] Shahla Ali found only somewhat more openness to such techniques, which may well lead to both faster and more cost-effective resolution of commercial disputes, among arbitrators with a significant practice in Asia who were subjected to her larger-scale (but still non-random) surveys and interviews carried out over 2006–7.[7] She also found, 15 years after CBU's study focused instead on practitioners based in the West, even greater convergence regarding the perceived advantages of ICA over cross-border litigation.[8]

---

3 Nottage, Luke (2000): The Vicissitudes of Transnational Commercial Arbitration and the Lex Mercatoria: A View from the Periphery, *Arbitration International*, Vol. 16, No. 1, 53–78; Nottage, Luke (2006): The Procedural Lex Mercatoria: The Past, Present and Future of International Commercial Arbitration, Vol. 6, No. 51, *Sydney Law School Research Paper*. Online at <http://ssrn.com/abstract=838028> accessed 27 August 2011.

4 Pryles, Michael, (Ed) (2006): *Dispute Resolution in Asia*, The Hague, Kluwer Law International; Kim GL (2007): East Asian Cultural Influences. In Pryles, Michael and Moser, Michael, (Eds) *The Asian Leading Arbitrators' Guide to International Arbitration*, New York, Juris, 17.

5 See for example Zander, Michael (1997): The Woolf Report: Forward or Backwards for the New Lord Chancellor?, Vol. 16 (July) *Civil Justice Quarterly* 208.

6 Those from the German law tradition remained open to more intense forms of ARB-MED: Bühring-Uhle, Christian et al. (2005): *Arbitration and Mediation in International Business: Designing Procedures for Effective Conflict Management*, 2nd edition, The Hague, Kluwer Law International, 122.

7 Ali, Shahla (2010): Barricades and Checkered Flags: Comparing Views on Roadblocks and Facilitators of Settlement Among Arbitration Practitioners in East Asia and the West, *Pacific Rim Law & Policy Journal*, Vol. 18, No. 2, 244–278. A large proportion of her respondents appear to be active particularly in mainland China and Hong Kong, although the breakdown is unclear from her published data.

8 Adapted from Ali, Shahla (2009): Approaching the Global Arbitration Table: Comparing the Advantages of Arbitration as seen by Practitioners in East Asia and the West, *Review of Litigation*, Vol. 28, No. 4, 799–844, 833.

Table 2.1 Advantages of ICA over cross-border litigation ('east' v. 'west')

Response – 'highly relevant' or 'significant'	**Region of Practice**	
	East (Ali study)	**West (CBU study)**
Forum's neutrality	88 (%)	78 (%)
Forum's expertise	83	76
Results more predictable	36	42
Voluntary compliance*	42	24
Treaties ensure compliance abroad	85	69
Confidential procedure*	76	56
Limited discovery	47	56
No appeal	64	58
Procedure less costly	36	20
Less time consuming*	57	35
More amicable	52	35

Note: * Statistically significant at 99 per cent confidence level. Multiple responses possible, in percentages.

In particular, comparing practitioners in the West originally (20 per cent) and the East recently (36 per cent), there was no statistically significant difference in ranking lowly the supposed advantage of ICA proceedings being 'less costly'. This is despite the fact that ICA still tends to be much cheaper when conducted particularly in China, as noted later in her study.[9] Other recent survey and interview research directed by Lukas Mistelis also finds ongoing concerns about the cost of ICA.[10] Indeed, these now extend to investor–state arbitration, the latest growth area following the liberalization of Foreign Direct Investment (FDI) regimes in the 1990s and the proliferation of investment treaties that increasingly allow investors to bring full arbitration claims directly against host states.[11] The present book and

9 Ibid, 840–41. More generally, across all questions we would expect more respondents from the East to perceive advantages than those from the West because of the greater relative disadvantages of courts and civil proceedings in Asia, especially in more developing countries.

10 Mistelis, Lukas (2004): International Arbitration – Corporate Attitudes and Practices – 12 Perceptions Tested: Myths, Data and Analysis Research Report, *American Review of International Arbitration*, Vol. 15, Nos 3–4, 525, especially Parts II.B and II.J; and online at <http://www.pwc.co.uk/eng/publications/international_arbitration_2008.html>, accessed 27 June 2010.

11 See, for example, Nottage, Luke and Miles, Kate (2010): Revising Rules in Australia and Japan for Public Interests. In Nottage, Luke and Garnett, Richard, (Eds) *International Arbitration in Australia*, Sydney, Federation Press (based on their 2009 article in *Journal of International Arbitration*, Vol. 26, No. 1); and Nottage, Luke and Weeramantry, Romesh (2009): Investment Arbitration in Asia: Five Perspectives on Law and Practice, *Arbitration International* (forthcoming, with an earlier draft at <http://

its overarching project[12] also identify persistent cost issues afflicting ICA and international arbitration more generally.

This chapter explores one possible root cause of this affliction. The starting point is that although many commentators and even policy-makers talk about the cost- and time-efficiencies of ICA, this is far from a major factor. Table 2.1 bears out the reality that parties negotiate arbitration agreements and then follow through with proceedings primarily because national courts lack sufficient neutrality and enforceability of outcomes. Thus, as intimated by CBU himself,[13] parties must either give up (or settle even with strong cases) or persevere with arbitration – cost what that may, almost. Furthermore, to elaborate a point going back to Dezalay and Garth, we must bear in mind the growing impact of lawyers in the ICA field. In particular, the last 10–15 years have seen dramatic growth in big international law firms, increasingly dominating the field and overwhelmingly operating on a time-charge basis. Their typically highly regimented 'billable hours' system, in lieu of charging fixed rates (for example based on the amount in dispute), tends to create upwards pressures on costs. For instance, as an illustration of the financial pressures preventing settlement during ICA proceedings, Ali reports this comment by a Western junior partner working in an international law firm's branch in Hong Kong:[14]

> When I was a new partner involved in several arbitrations in which I could easily see a settlement option early on I suggested to the other partners that this case could easily settle. The partners didn't say anything, but the unspoken message was that such a suggestion was not acceptable because their billable hour requirements were contingent on the prolongation of the arbitration. This was the key to their annual bonus.

sydney.edu.au/law/scil/documents/2010/SCILWP21_NottageWeeramantry_updated.pdf>, accessed 9 September 2011), both with extensive further references. Some quantitative studies downplay the costs involved, for example Franck, Susan (2007): Empirically Evaluating Claims About Investment Treaty Arbitration, *North Carolina Law Review*, Vol. 86, No. 1, 1. However, her studies rely on generalizations from very small sample sizes, on reported awards (excluding for example the disputes resolved earlier, which well may be very costly), and on arbitral and sometimes lawyer costs (but not for example all the time spent by governments trying to resolve these disputes).

12 The international research project funded by the Research Grants Council of the Government of HKSAR [Project No. 9041191 (CityU 1501/06H)] entitled *International Commercial Arbitration Practices: A Discourse Analytical Study*. Online at <http://www.english.cityu.edu.hk/arbitration/>, accessed 9 September 2011.

13 Above n. 6, 128: 'In the eyes of the parties [ICA] is not an "alternative" type of process but merely a litigation procedure that *works* in an international context. As litigation, arbitration can occasion tremendous costs which keep accruing as the procedure unfolds and have led to a sense of crisis international arbitration circles'.

14 Above n. 7, 268. I thank Dr Ali for confirming from her interview notes that this individual worked in a large international law firm in Hong Kong.

Admittedly, it is an ambitious argument for this chapter to link the worldwide emergence of large law firms and the billable hour business model to the latest round of hand-wringing about ballooning costs in ICA. There are jurisdictions, like Japan, where large law firms have emerged over the last decade – first domestic, then international firms – yet the persistent paucity of ICA cases probably has more important causes.[15] Indeed, in the shorter term these firms and their ICA specialists may play important roles in establishing an arbitration culture. However, in the medium to longer term the typical business model of large commercial law firms generally leads to cost escalation, undermining the attractiveness of ICA in those venues. That certainly becomes less likely where those specialists are highly competitive and/or so overwhelmed with work that they wish to settle cases and otherwise minimize delays and costs in order to move on quickly to their next cases. Yet those situations are more likely to arise in the established and still 'core' venues such as Paris, London or New York, or perhaps now Hong Kong or Singapore, rather than countries like Japan or Australia that are still trying desperately to achieve critical mass in ICA work.

Conversely, there are admittedly jurisdictions, like Hong Kong itself, where large law firms operating on a billable hours model co-exist with growing ICA caseloads. However, a closer comparative analysis suggests that this particular expansion was linked to the decline of arbitrations going to mainland China from around the late 1990s. That was arguably linked to greater awareness among non-Chinese parties and their legal advisors about the possibility of obtaining agreement of Chinese counterparts to arbitration instead of in Hong Kong. Similarly, although Singapore has achieved large increases in ICA cases particularly since 2008 and this coincides with a growing presence of international law firms, the latter phenomenon seems more like a consequence (rather than a cause) of Singapore's ICA caseload. The latter, in turn, appears to be linked more to the boom in the China trade as well as India's emergence in recent years.

Overall, it therefore does seem plausible that the entrenchment of large law firms and the billable hours model tends to undermine the attractiveness of venues that they come to dominate. This may explain why quantitative analysis shows little increase in ICA caseloads by countries that have adopted the 1985 UNCITRAL (United Nations Commission on International Trade Law) Model Law on International Commercial Arbitration (ML), including many in Australasia, as a modern template for arbitration legislation.[16] However, due to a

15 Including comparatively weak government support for promoting ICA, see Nottage, Luke (2004): Japan's New Arbitration Law: Domestication Reinforcing Internationalisation?, *International Arbitration Law Review*, Vol. 7, No. 2, 54–60. Also, it appears that at least the large Japanese law firms do not have as strong a billable hours culture as the international firms have, especially outside Japan.

16 Drahozal, Christopher (2004): Regulatory Competition and the Location of International Arbitration Proceedings, *International Review of Law & Economics*, Vol. 24, No. 3, 371.

lack of good quantitative data about the emergence of law firms and in particular their billing practices in the region, this chapter adopts a case study approach focused on developments in Australia.

The next part of this chapter looks at how the nation has struggled to develop domestic arbitration and to attract ICA cases to its shores, despite adopting the ML in 1989. It notes the parallel emergence of very large law firms, particularly over the 1980s and 1990s,[17] and escalating concerns about the 'billable hours' approach to resolving commercial disputes more generally.[18] From this perspective, Australia's adoption in June 2010 of the 2006 revisions to the ML as well as various other amendments seem unlikely to be sufficient to generate a major change in attitude and practices, reflected in increased ICA caseloads. Commercial imperatives in large law firms may even explain why the 2010 amendments are much less ambitious than those recommended by an array of other stakeholders. After all, any amendments are better than none in terms of 'competing' with the now more established venues like Singapore or Hong Kong, and indeed in preparing Australian lawyers for practice abroad.

Lessons from the second part of the chapter should have a broader resonance for other jurisdictions, especially those which may have adopted the original ML yet be considering further revisions because ICA caseloads remain low. A key variable may be the role of large law firms in that jurisdiction, especially those operating in the arbitration field. Likewise, some more normative recommendations derived from the Australian experience, elaborated in the third part of this chapter, should be relevant for other jurisdictions. More ambitious changes to the regulatory regime, including arbitration laws (such as provisions on ARB-MED) but also more generally, may be needed to expand ICA. Arbitration institutions should be prepared to innovate when running conferences, appointing arbitrators and publishing information – even some redacted awards disclosing arbitrators' names. Parties and in-house counsel should negotiate more flexible arrangements with both outside lawyers and arbitrators. Without such reforms, we will continue to hear complaints about costs and delays in international arbitration. That situation raises both efficiency and legitimacy concerns because it impedes access to justice and it maintains high direct and indirect transaction costs, restricting cross-border trade and investment.[19]

---

17 Aronson, Bruce (2007): Elite Law Firm Mergers and Reputational Competition: Is Bigger Really Better? An International Comparison, *Vanderbilt Journal of Transnational Law*, Vol. 40, No. 3, 763.

18 See for example Mark, Stephen (2004): The Cost of Justice or Justice in Costs – The Experience of the OLSC in Handling Costs Complaints, *UNSW Law Journal*, Vol. 27, No. 1, 225 (referring also to New South Wales Chief Justice Spigelman's criticism of billable hours as encouraging inefficiencies); and Chief Justice Wayne Martin's speech launching the Australian Law Week on 17 May 2010, 'Billable Hours – Past Their Use-by Date', online at <http://www.lawsocietywa.asn.au/AnnouncementRetrieve.aspx?ID=32465>, accessed 5 July 2010.

19 More generally, see Spigelman, JJ (2006): Transaction Costs and International Litigation, *Australian Law Journal*, Vol. 80, No. 7, 438.

Addressing Australia's Own Arbitration Ambivalence[20]

Background to the 2010 Reforms

The *International Arbitration Amendment Act 2010* (Cth), federal legislation of the Commonwealth of Australia enacted on 7 July 2010, is supposed to offer a new dawn for ICA in Australia. The nation had long tended to exhibit quite an ambivalent attitude towards arbitration, both domestic and international. As a federation of former British colonies, Australia inherited elaborate arbitration legislation from England.[21] This supported some use of arbitration to resolve disputes through binding decisions issued by private arbitrators rather than the courts, in certain narrow fields such as the construction industry.[22]

However, that inherited English tradition involved extensive court supervision of arbitral processes and outcomes. In the UK itself, that may have been linked to the large numbers of lay arbitrators (with minimal legal training) appointed from among business people in specific spheres (such as global commodity trades) to resolve disputes that often involved primarily issues of fact rather than law.[23] But judicial supervision also fitted the English system of barristers often being appointed to arbitrate (the more legalistic) disputes, then being appointed judges, who may have liked to 'keep their hands in' so as to be able to present themselves more credibly as arbitrators again upon retirement from the Bench. Indeed, as the Chief Justice of New South Wales (NSW) and the then President of the Court of Appeal pointed out in *Raguz v. Sullivan*, in the nineteenth century there was an even more direct incentive for English judges to keep a wary eye on arbitration: it diverted cases away from the courts, which in those days were much more dependent on court user fees than on general government grants.[24]

---

20 This Part is abridged, with kind permission of the co-author and publisher, from Part II of Nottage, Luke and Garnett, Richard (2010): Introduction. In Nottage, Luke and Garnett, Richard, (Eds) (2010): *International Arbitration in Australia*, Sydney, Federation Press, 1–37.

21 More 'home-grown' was the use of arbitration (and conciliation) to resolve certain industrial disputes: see, for example, Owens, R.J. and Riley, Joellen (2007): *The Law of Work*, South Melbourne, Oxford University Press, Chapter 3 (with a 2nd edition in preparation). However, such innovations did not lead to much cross-fertilisation for arbitration of commercial disputes, the primary focus of this book.

22 Even here, however, private and now statute-based ('adjudication') expert determination schemes have become popular: see, for example, Davenport, Philip (2004): *Adjudication in the Building Industry*, 2nd edition, Annadale, NSW, Federation Press.

23 Such 'look-sniff arbitration' was and is much less prevalent in Australia, far from the world's commodities markets, despite its vast exports of natural resources and primary produce.

24 See *Angela Raguz v. Rebecca Sullivan & Ors* [2000] NSWCA 240 at [47] per Spigelman, C.J. and Mason, P., drawing on Mason, Keith (1999): Changing Attitudes in the

The *Raguz* case, a sports arbitration appeal during the 2000 Sydney Olympics,[25] arose in the context of NSW's *Commercial Arbitration Act 1985* (CAA). This was 'uniform' legislation enacted throughout Australia's states and territories in the mid-1980s and influenced by the English *Arbitration Act* of 1980. Both sets of legislation broke new ground in allowing parties to agree through arbitration clauses to exclude appeals to the courts for arbitrators' errors of law, but only for *international* arbitrations. The Court in *Raguz* followed the understanding, now widely held worldwide, that an international arbitration generally signified one where the 'seat' chosen by the parties is located abroad (in that case, Switzerland, the location of the 'Court' of Arbitration for Sport that administers major international sports arbitrations), even if some or all of the hearings take place locally (in this case, Sydney).

However, more potential for parties seeking greater speediness and finality of proceedings to opt-out of court supervision, in respect of arbitrators' errors of law, remained unavailable for *domestic* arbitrations. Australia's uniform CAAs did not lead to significantly greater use of arbitration to resolve domestic disputes. Arbitrators were often challenged in Australian courts for 'technical misconduct', for example, under the CAAs.[26] Indeed, even or perhaps especially in the field of construction disputes, concerns that arbitration was becoming too much like 'litigation without wigs' led to the expansion of privately-supplied mediation and other alternative dispute resolution (ADR) services from the late 1980s.[27]

In developing its legislative framework focused more specifically on ICA, Australia has also tended to exhibit some ambivalence. On the one hand, it was comparatively slow in adopting the 1958 New York Convention on the Recognition and Enforcement of Foreign Arbitral Awards (the NYC), given effect by the *International Arbitration Act 1974* (Cth) (IAA).[28] The NYC was aimed

---

Common Law's Response to International Commercial Arbitration, *The Arbitrator* [now: *The Arbitrator and Mediator*], Vol. 18, No. 2, 73.

25 See also Sturzaker, Damian and Godhard, Kate (2001): The Olympic Legal Legacy, *Melbourne Journal of International Law*, Vol. 2, No. 1, 241 and more generally Holmes, Malcolm (2005): The CAS: A Case Study of an International Arbitration Institution, *Australian Bar Review*, Vol. 27, No. 1, 56.

26 See Donnenberg, Vicki (2008): Judicial Review of Arbitral Awards under the Commercial Arbitration Acts, *Australian Bar Review*, Vol. 30, No. 2, 177.

27 On the development of ADR more generally in Australia, see Nottage, Luke (2009): Comparing ADR in Australia and New Zealand: Introduction and Update, 22 *SCIL Working Paper*. Available at: http://sydney.edu.au/law/scil/documents/2009/SCILWP22_Nottage.pdf [accessed 27 June 2010]. On formalization of construction dispute resolution in the UK, see, for example, Flood, John and Caiger, Andrew (1992): Lawyers and Arbitration: The Juridification of Construction Disputes, *Modern Law Review*, Vol. 56, No. 3, 412.

28 For a table of showing adoption dates (and reservations) world-wide for the NYC, as well as its text, see: http://www.uncitral.org [accessed 27 June 2010]. The text of the

primarily to support enforcement of foreign awards once issued (under Art. V), namely the last major stage in the arbitral process; but it also added support for foreign arbitration proceedings at the initial stage, by requiring local courts to stay judicial proceedings except in listed circumstances (NYC Art. II).

On the other hand, in 1989 Australia was comparatively quick off the mark in incorporating into the IAA the UNCITRAL ML. The United Nations Commission on International Trade Law published the ML in 1985 (and revised it in 2006) as a template of an arbitral procedural law for jurisdictions enacting legislation to further support the conduct of international arbitration within their borders. The ML was agreed among representatives from a large variety of jurisdictions, including many within, or influenced by the continental European civil law tradition, and it incorporated more respect for party autonomy along with less scope for judicial intervention than in the English law tradition. For example, errors of law by arbitrators (even serious ones) were not included among the grounds listed (in Art. 34) for local courts to set aside awards in international arbitrations (defined in Art. 1 to include, for example, situations where the parties have their places of business in different states). Initially, however, Australia's IAA did allow the parties to opt out of the ML and into the CAA regime. This did leave some scope for courts to review serious errors even in international disputes – unless the parties had then further agreed to exclude that particular possibility, as in the *Raguz* case.[29] That system did respect party autonomy, consistently with the ML approach, but it also made it easier for Australian policy-makers to accept the ML's incorporation into the IAA in 1989.

As with many other jurisdictions quick to adopt the ML in order to modernize and streamline their arbitration legislation, such as Hong Kong (which also adopted the ML in 1989) and Singapore (albeit only in 1994), Australia aimed to attract more ICA cases to its shores. That promised to bring in not only increased professional fees – for Australian arbitrators, lawyers and arbitral institutions – but also follow-on benefits for related services such as hospitality and travel. The Australian Centre for International Commercial Arbitration (ACICA) had already been established in 1985, initially centred in Melbourne, although in its formative

IAA (and the CAAs, along with much Australian case law) is freely available via Austlii. Available at: http://www.austlii.edu.au [accessed 27 June 2010].

29 Above n. 24. Some Australian (and Singaporean) case law readily allowed implied opting-out of the ML: see Garnett, Richard (2010): The Legal Framework for International Arbitration in Australia: The Old and the New. In Nottage, Luke and Garnett, Richard, (Eds) *International Arbitration in Australia*, Sydney, Federation Press, Part III.B. Australia has belatedly, and quite crudely, addressed this problem, in the IAA amendments in 2010, simply by excluding any opting-out whatsoever – at least for arbitration agreements concluded from 6 July 2010 onwards (but leaving a 'black hole' as outlined in the text below). Compare also Nottage, Luke and Garnett, Richard (2010): The Top Twenty Things to Change In or Around Australia's International Arbitration Act, in ibid (Eds), Part IV.A.

era it also administered some domestic disputes.[30] More generally, in 1990 and as very large nation-wide law firms began to form in Australia, the Government also established the International Legal Services Advisory Council (ILSAC) within the Attorney General's Department (AGD, effectively Australia's Justice Ministry) in order 'to enhance the international presence and … performance of Australia's legal and related services'.[31] ILSAC's members, drawn from private and public sectors, have focused attention on international commercial dispute resolution as well as global legal services and market access, international legal cooperation, and international legal education and training.

However, enacting legislation more tailored to international arbitrations – even the ML – is only a necessary, not sufficient, condition for attracting more ICA business in that jurisdiction.[32] Part of the problem lies in the ML itself. Its emphasis on party autonomy certainly creates the *potential* to craft arbitration agreements and to implement flexible arbitral proceedings that better meet the expectations of most within the business community, as well as the government and legal system as a whole. For commercial disputes parties normally seek a dispute resolution system underpinned by some minimal standards of fairness, but generating expeditious, cost-effective and final outcomes.[33]

Yet the ML still needed to set out many provisions, even when expressly or impliedly phrased as 'default rules' subject to contrary party agreement, on various issues that had generated significant differences in legislation or practice worldwide. Jurisdictions adopting the ML, including Australia, typically added some further or different provisions as well.[34] Laying down greater detail in turn opens up scope for more formal legal reasoning, beloved of legal professionals everywhere but particularly within the English (and hence Australian) legal tradition.[35] This window opens further when lawyers work with clients to draft

30 See generally: <http://www.acica.org.au> [accessed 27 June 2010].

31 See: <http://www.ilsac.gov.au/> [accessed 27 June 2010].

32 See also, for example, Drahozal, above n. 16.

33 See, for example, Rubino-Sammartano, Mauro and Kantor, Mark (2006): Is Full Armor Absolutely Necessary to the Arbitration Process?, *American Review of International Arbitration*, Vol. 17, No. 4, 615; many of the presentations in the Clayton Utz/University of Sydney International Arbitration lecture series since 2002 (available at: http://www.ialecture.com [accessed 27 June 2010]); and the empirical studies led by researchers respectively at the University of London regarding users' attitudes (above n 10) and at the City University of Hong Kong regarding ICA discourse and practices more broadly (Online at: <http://www1.english.cityu.edu.hk/arbitration> [accessed 27 June 2010]).

34 See generally, Sanders, Pieter (2004): *The Work of UNCITRAL on Arbitration and Conciliation*, 2nd edition, The Hague, London, Kluwer Law International.

35 See generally, Atiyah, Patrick and Summers, Robert (1987): *Form and Substance in Anglo-American Law: A Comparative Study of Legal Reasoning, Legal Theory, and Legal Institutions*, Oxford, Oxford University Press, extended for example in Nottage, Luke (2000): Practical and Theoretical Implications of the Lex Mercatoria for Japan: CENTRAL's Empirical Study on the Use of Transnational Law, *Vindobona Journal of International*

and negotiate different agreements with their counterparts, which later may end up being scrutinized by the courts.

In addition, even the ML – albeit in quite general terms – insists on basic norms of procedural justice, such as the opportunity for all parties to be equally heard in arbitral proceedings (Art. 18). The government and legal system demand such minimum standards to maintain general public trust in a regime that benefits from public support in various ways, including an enforcement regime more favourable than that provided for other contract-based relationships.

Hence, whether a jurisdiction adopting the ML will in fact attract more ICA cases will depend on many other factors. One is how the courts interpret its provisions. That may be difficult to predict, if the jurisdiction (such as Australia) faces the Catch-22 situation of never really having had many ICA cases in that seat – let alone court challenges and judgments related to such cases. Such a jurisdiction also faces a greater risk of the earlier law or understandings reasserting themselves – even indirectly – and thus leading interpretations of the ML regime away from those widely held elsewhere. These jurisdictions will also tend to generate disproportionate numbers of ICA cases that involve instead the attempted enforcement of agreements to arbitrate abroad or of foreign awards.[36] A broader parochialism may then come into play as well.[37] Courts in such jurisdictions will need to send a consistent message that they support the autonomy of parties and arbitrators, locally and abroad, as much as possible – and as much as in other jurisdictions incorporating both the ML and the NYC.

If the courts do fall short, as happened arguably in Australia over the 1990s and still sometime into the twenty-first century,[38] the legislature must be prepared

Commercial Law and Arbitration, Vol. 4, No. 2, 132, and Nottage, Luke (2007): Changing Contract Lenses: Unexpected Supervening Events in English, New Zealand, US, Japanese, and International Sales Law and Practice, *Indiana Journal of Global Legal Studies*, Vol. 14, No. 2, 385.

36 The number of reported judgments dealing with the IAA each has increased quite significantly, especially in the last decade, but these overwhelmingly do still involve enforcement actions. See Sanig, Michael (2009): Exclusive Jurisdiction – A Matter of National Interest, *Australian ADR Reporter (Chartered Institute of Arbitrators Australia)*, Vols 10–11, 18. His preliminary empirical study found 55 separate cases involving a judgment rendered from 2000 to mid-2009 (with 40 per cent in the Federal Courts, 33 per cent in the Supreme Court of NSW and 18 per cent in the Victorian Supreme Court; compared to 20 over 1990–9.

37 More generally, see also Crawford, James (2009): International Law in the House of Lords and the High Court of Australia 1996–2008: A Comparison, *Australian Yearbook of International Law*, Vol. 28, 1 (earlier available at: http://law.anu.edu.au/Cipl/Lectures&Seminars/2008/KirbyLecture_Crawford.pdf [accessed 27 June 2010]) and Volume 27 of that Yearbook.

38 See Garnett, Richard (1999): The Current Status of International Arbitration Agreements in Australia, *Journal of Contract Law*, Vol. 15, No. 1, 29; and some subsequent case law introduced in Nottage and Garnett, above n. 29.

to intervene promptly. The government can also help minimize the allure of earlier traditions, especially for domestic disputes, by reviewing and revising that other legislative framework. Both Hong Kong and Singapore have been relatively quick in aligning their legislation for domestic arbitration more closely to the ML regime, and Singapore demonstrated particular alacrity in reversing two wayward court judgments regarding its own statutory provisions dealing with opting out from the ML.[39] Legislative correction is often needed to cut through precedent and the complexity built up gradually by courts and lawyers, often with the best of intentions, and often this facility also characterizes the finest common law judges.[40] Yet the risks of over-formalization are often compounded when international instruments are involved, generated painstakingly by lawmakers overseas and then still interpreted by diverse national courts rather than a supranational judiciary.[41]

It is also a conceit of jurists to assume too readily that 'the black letter law' – treaties, statutes and case law – necessarily strongly determine commercial decisions anyway, including where to arbitrate cross-border disputes. The People's Republic of China is the third jurisdiction in the Asia–Pacific that has witnessed a rapid increase in ICA cases, through the China International Economic and Trade Arbitration Commission (CIETAC). Yet it implemented arbitration law reform quite late and without modelling it directly on the ML, and Chinese case law remains difficult to access and to assess from abroad.[42] The expansion in CIETAC's caseload reflects many other factors. One is the Chinese Government's encouragement of State-owned enterprises and other firms to press for CIETAC arbitration, combined with persistent problems within the court system. Another reason for the expanded caseload is simply the enormous growth of cross-border trade and investment – and hence, inevitably, disputes – after China reopened to the West in 1979. Singapore and especially Hong Kong have also benefited from this belated 'China boom', compared to countries like Australia that have traditionally developed relationships with a more diverse array of economic partners. Singapore, in particular, has also enjoyed relatively

39 Above n. 29.

40 See, for example, Rishworth, Paul (1997): *The Struggle for Simplicity in the Law: Essays for Lord Cooke of Thorndon*, Wellington, Butterworths.

41 For a more general critique of international commercial law making, see Stephan, Paul (1999): The Futility of Unification and Harmonisation in International Commercial Law, *Virginia International Law Journal*, Vol. 39, 743 (earlier version available at: http://papers.ssrn.com/sol3/papers.cfm?abstract_id=169209 [accessed 27 June 2010]).

42 See, for example, Wang, Sheng Chang and Hilmer, Sarah (2006): China Arbitration Law v. UNCITRAL Model Law, *International Arbitration Law Review*, Vol. 9, No. 1, 1; Peerenboom, Randall (2001): Seek Truth from Facts: An Empirical Study of Enforcement of Arbitral Awards in the PRC, *American Journal of Comparative Law*, Vol. 49, No. 2, 249. For more information on comparative ICA caseloads, see the figures later in this chapter.

strong government support for its Singapore International Arbitration Centre (SIAC, established in 1991).[43]

These three Asian jurisdictions have further benefited, somewhat paradoxically, from Australia's efforts to collaborate throughout the region in encouraging business people to choose and conduct arbitration closer to home, rather than with the seat (at least) in the traditional but distant 'core' of the arbitration world in Europe and then the US. From the late 1990s, assisted by Australia having adopted a similar (ML-based) legislative framework for ICA as in many other Asia–Pacific jurisdictions,[44] a few Australian arbitrators became very active in proceedings with seats throughout the region. These were administered either by newer institutions such as SIAC or by 'core' institutions such as the International Chamber of Commerce (ICC), which recently sought to further expand its Asian clientele by establishing offices in both Hong Kong and Singapore.[45] For example, as the longstanding Chairman of ACICA, Dr Michael Pryles served as arbitrator in many venues, including SIAC, before being appointed as its Chairman in 2009. He also prompted ACICA to take a leading role in establishing, at a meeting in Sydney in 2004, the Asia–Pacific Regional Arbitration Group (APRAG).[46] This is a regional federation of (now 30) arbitration institutions and associations that aims to improve standards and knowledge of international arbitration, primarily through annual conferences held around the region, and to make submissions on behalf of the region to national and international organizations.[47]

Such initiatives, along with those of individual institutions and governments as well as the Asia Pacific Economic Cooperation (APEC) programme,[48] have certainly helped consolidate and further stimulate a dramatic increase in ICA activity throughout Asia. Apparent already a decade ago,[49] the expansion needed

---

43 See, for example, the 'Maxwell Chambers' facility inaugurated in 2008. Available at: http://www.maxwell-chambers.com/ [accessed 27 June 2010].

44 See further Secomb, Matthew (2000): Shades of Delocalisation: Diversity in the Adoption of the UNCITRAL Model Law in Australia, Hong Kong and Singapore, *Journal of International Arbitration*, Vol. 17, No. 5, 123.

45 See: http://www.iccwbo.org/index.html?id=34530 [accessed 27 June 2010]; and Greenberg, Simon, ICC Arbitrations and Australia. In Nottage, Luke and Garnett, Richard, (Eds), (2010): *International Arbitration in Australia*, Sydney, Federation Press, 122–36. A study of ICC arbitrations filed over 2000–2005 had found that East Asian states, as the seat and (relatedly) the background of the arbitrators, were underrepresented compared to the increasing proportions of East Asian parties: Kim, above n. 4, 33–6.

46 See Pryles, Michael (2004): The Asia Pacific Regional Arbitration Group, *American Review of International Arbitration*, Vol. 15, No. 2, 311.

47 See: http://www.aprag.org/ [accessed 27 June 2010].

48 See APEC's various capacity-building programs in cross-border dispute resolution. Available at: http://www.apec.org/Groups/Committee-on-Trade-and-Investment/Investment-Experts-Group.aspx [accessed 9 September 2011].

49 See, for example, Pryles, Michael (1997): *Dispute Resolution in Asia*, The Hague, Boston, Kluwer Law International (with the latest third edition was published in 2006). See

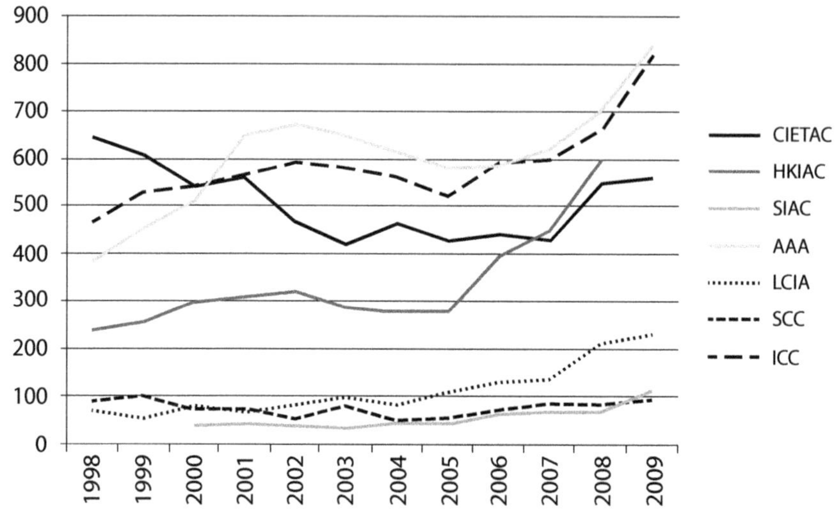

Figure 2.1 Numbers of ICA cases administered by the world's major arbitral institutions

Note: AAA = American Arbitration Association; LCIA = London Court of International Arbitration; SCC = Stockholm Chamber of Commerce.

efforts and improvements on the 'supply side' to match (and perhaps even stimulate) the demand for cross-border dispute resolution services underpinned by the enormous economic growth in the region. Indeed, ICA case filings increased to new levels a few years after the Asian Financial Crisis in 1997 and the consequent (but quite short-lived) stagnation in the real economy, and we should expect the same following the Global Financial Crisis of 2008.[50] Yet weaning Australasian parties and legal professionals off arbitration in Europe or the US resulted in disproportionate increases in ICA caseloads particularly for CIETAC, SIAC and the Hong Kong International Arbitration Centre (HKIAC).[51] These three venues

also Thirgood, Russell (2004): International Arbitration: The Justice Business, *Journal of International Arbitration*, Vol. 21, No. 4, 341.

50 Interestingly, although other factors are probably also involved, SIAC was handling 160 cases as of 31 December 2009, 132 of which were administered by SIAC representing a 64 per cent increase over 2008. Also, the Korean Commercial Arbitration Board (KCAB) handled 78 international arbitration cases (and 215 domestic) cases in 2009, compared to 47 (215 domestic) cases in 2008. See APRAG, *Regional Arbitration Updates* (May 2010), 5 and 9, available at: http://www.aprag.org/ [accessed 25 June 2010].

51 See Appendix I to Nottage, Luke and Garnett, Richard, above n. 19, 32–3, also accessible via Nottage, Luke, 'International Commercial Arbitration Reform in Australia, Japan and Beyond' (12 July 2010), online at <http://blogs.usyd.edu.au/japaneselaw/2010/07/international_commercial_arbit.html>, accessed 17 March 2011. See also Greenberg, Simon, Kee, Christopher and Weeramantry, Romesh (2011): *International*

have also benefited not just in the absolute numbers of ICA cases they have received each year over the last decade or so, but also generally in their year-on-year growth rates (see Figure 2.1).

However, some other Australasian arbitral institutions (such as the Korean Commercial Arbitration Board and the Kuala Lumpur Regional Centre for Arbitration) are also beginning to see significant caseload increases – albeit off much lower baselines. Unfortunately, rather like the Japan Commercial Arbitration Association so far ACICA has not been one of them. Even adding cases administered under other institutions (such as the ICC)[52] and ad hoc arbitrations (for which there is almost never any comprehensive data available), there would still not be more than a dozen ICA cases underway each year with the seat in Australia.

The composition of Australia's trade flows may be a further explanatory factor. High-volume and often high-value exports of natural resources and other commodities (along with related investments) often take place among 'repeat players' with longstanding relationships and norms of behaviour (including, perhaps, arbitration as an ultimate backstop – albeit still in more traditional venues such as London). However, new players are rapidly emerging even in these fields, Australia exports many other types of goods and services that generate ICA cases in other venues, and of course it imports a very diverse range of products.[53]

Anyway, many active venues (such as Singapore or Hong Kong, but also, for example, Switzerland and France) attract ICA activity that does not even involve their own firms. Parties from third countries chose those jurisdictions, in part, precisely for their neutrality. Particularly in those situations, alongside force of habit and broader economic trends like the China boom, geographical convenience becomes another important factor. Australia suffers undeniably in this respect, but the problem does not seem insurmountable. It could be a convenient (or at least mutually inconvenient) venue for parties from East Asia and Chile, for example, or New Zealand and South-East Asia. And especially for smaller-value or less complex disputes, there is always the possibility for parties to dispense with oral hearings anyway or nowadays to use videoconferencing.

Persistently low levels of ICA activity, or 'Australia passing', have therefore attracted increasing concern particularly among Australian policy-makers and legal professionals. Indirectly, as already indicated, the growth of ICA in other parts of the region can benefit Australian arbitrators. It can also benefit Australian lawyers (advising and representing their typically Australian clients in arbitrations outside Australia) and educators (training these Australian professionals, or those

---

Commercial Arbitration: An Asia-Pacific Perspective, Melbourne, Cambridge University Press, especially Chapter 1 on the growth of arbitration in Asia.

52 See Greenberg, above n. 45.

53 For an overview of Australia's cross-border trade and investment, see: http://www.dfat.gov.au/aib/trade_investment.html [accessed 27 June 2010].

from abroad who can learn about core international instruments that their home countries also often have adopted). However, Australia is still missing out on professional fees and broader arbitration-related services revenue. It also risks a 'brain drain' of capable practitioners – although many who go off to practice ICA in Europe, the US or now to Asia do often boomerang back to Australia, even if that means having to shift the focus of their practice upon their return. Australia also ends up with fewer incentives and therefore opportunities to use ICA best practice to improve domestic arbitration, other ADR systems and practices, investor–state dispute resolution (particularly pursuant to investment treaties),[54] and even civil litigation processes.

Early in the twenty-first century, therefore, the AGD set up an informal group to begin discussing possible legislative reforms to the ML-based IAA. This met quite infrequently, however, and it was effectively suspended after UNCITRAL decided to commence formal international discussions about amending the 1985 ML.[55] The AGD sent officials to represent Australia at most UNCITRAL meetings in Vienna and New York, but also sometimes relied on participation from private practitioners. Greater salience and awareness of the ML regime then helped suspend revisions to the CAAs, based instead on the English *Arbitration Act 1996* and its subsequent (quite tortuous) case law developments,[56] which had progressed to the stage of amendments drafted by officials in Victoria and NSW. After UNCITRAL obtained international agreement to revise the ML in 2006, and countries like New Zealand promptly decided to adopt those amendments to update their arbitration legislation,[57] pressure to 'Act' re-emerged on the federal Government in Australia.

Lateral pressure had also developed due to initiatives from the private sector. Australia's six largest law firms agreed to promote Sydney as an arbitral venue, and an attractive website was unveiled.[58] ACICA effectively moved its head office from Melbourne to Sydney (albeit still without dedicated facilities, until

54 More generally, see Bath, Vivienne and Nottage, Luke, (Eds) (2011): *Investment Law and Dispute Resolution Law and Practice in Asia*, London, Routledge.

55 See generally Sorieul, Renaud (2000): Update on Recent Developments and Future Work by UNCITRAL in the Field of International Commercial Arbitration, *Journal of International Arbitration*, Vol. 17, Part 3, 163. See also: <http://www.uncitral.org/uncitral/en/commission/working_groups/2Arbitration.html>, accessed 27 June 2010.

56 For critiques of developments in England, see, for example, Marriott, Arthur (2006): Breaking the Dispute Deadlock, *Arbitration International*, Vol. 22, No. 3, 411.

57 See Nottage, Luke (2008): Reforming International Commercial Arbitration (ICA) Law: The UN, New Zealand – Why Not Australia?, *Australian ADR Reporter*, Vol. 7, 15. Online at: <http://sydney.edu.au/law/scil/documents/2009/SCILWP6Finalised.pdf>, accessed 27 June 2010.

58 See: <http://www.sydneyarbitration.com/> (including some rather tongue-in-cheek elements, such as the comparative prices of oysters!); and more generally: <http://www.acica.org.au/sydney_arbitration.html>, both accessed 9 September 2011.

2010) and opened a branch in Perth. It also began to collaborate more closely with other arbitration associations, especially the Chartered Institute of Arbitrators – Australian Branch (CIArb).[59] ACICA brought in new Special Associates from 2004 to help constitute a Rules Committee that produced what became the ACICA Arbitration Rules in 2005.[60] The AGD provided some limited financial support mainly to help publicize those Rules. They also formed the basis for the ACICA Expedited Arbitration Rules of 2008, designed for smaller or simpler disputes. Those, in turn, were adopted as the core for arbitrations conducted by the Australian Maritime and Transport Arbitration Commission (AMTAC), established within ACICA in 2007 to provide specialist services in resolving shipping and transport disputes especially in the Asia–Pacific.[61]

A broader generational shift had also got underway in Australia, as well as in many parts of Asia. A new generation of arbitration experts, including talented younger practitioners and professors, had already begun to emerge in Europe – where ICA had developed earlier – and then in the US. The ICC and other core arbitration institutions began setting up 'Young Arbitrator' groups, offering more informal and interactive opportunities to share and build up experiences in ICA. Australia-based experts familiar with such initiatives, often through periods practicing or researching in Europe or the US, joined with others to establish in 2004 the Australasian Forum for International Arbitration (AFIA). It too holds informal workshops or events, as well as occasionally making Submissions on arbitration issues of public interest.[62] Many members have considerable experience in ICA through actual arbitration proceedings (albeit mostly conducted outside Australia) or mock proceedings in the Vis Moots or other arbitration competitions

59 Many ACICA members also belong to the CIArb, for example, or contribute to its new quarterly journal: the *Australian ADR Reporter* (see <http://www.ciarb.org/branches/australasia/australia-branch/>, accessed 9 September 2011). The CIArb has traditionally had more of focus on domestic arbitration (like the Institute of Arbitrators and Mediators of Australia, IAMA. See: <http://www.iama.org.au>, accessed 27 June 2010). Unlike ACICA, the CIArb does not administer arbitrations.

60 Until then, ACICA had administered ICA cases using the 1976 UNCITRAL Arbitration Rules. The 2005 ACICA Arbitration Rules are still based on those UNCITRAL Rules, but are now under review. See Greenberg, Simon, Nottage, Luke and Weeramantry, Romesh, ACICA's Arbitration Rules of 2005 – Revisited. In Nottage, Luke and Garnett, Richard, (Eds) (2010): *International Arbitration in Australia*, Sydney, Federation Press. However, the Committee (which I have served on since 2004) also discussed and drafted some other provisions that envisaged the possibility of ACICA someday taking an even more active role in administering arbitration cases.

61 See: <http://www.acica.org.au/amtac.html>, accessed 9 September 2011.

62 See: <http://afia.asia/>, accessed 17 March 2011. AFIA events are mostly hosted at large law firms (but once at Sydney Law School) and in Sydney or Melbourne (but increasingly also before or after larger events taking place throughout the wider Australasian region).

for students.[63] All this is underpinned by arbitration courses, research and other initiatives undertaken by universities throughout Australia.[64]

The Legislative History: An Overview

In the 2007 General Election, a coalition led by Kevin Rudd and the Labour Party wrested control of the House of Representatives from a conservative coalition headed by John Howard, who had served as Prime Minister of Australia since 1996. Rudd's new Attorney-General, Robert McClelland, initiated several reviews aimed at reducing complexities, costs and delays in dispute resolution both in and out of court.[65] On 21 November 2008 he announced a formal Review of the IAA, and the AGD released a Discussion Paper (DP) calling for Submissions within a tight deadline. The Review's aim was to consider whether the Act should be amended to:

- ensure it provides a comprehensive and clear framework governing international arbitration in Australia;
- improve the effectiveness and efficiency of the arbitral process while respecting the fundamental consensual basis of arbitration; and
- consider whether to adopt 'best-practice' developments in national arbitral law from overseas.

The DP specifically mentioned the hope that a revised IAA would make Australia a more attractive venue for ICA, especially within the Asia–Pacific region. Thirty Submissions were received over the Australian summer period from individuals (including the editors of this volume), organizations (such as ACICA, AFIA and the CIArb) and other groups (including the judiciary).[66]

---

63 See <http://www.cisg.law.pace.edu/vis.html>, accessed 27 June 2010 (in Vienna since 1993) and <http://www.cisgmoot.org/>, accessed 27 June 2010 (in Hong Kong since 2003), and generally Nottage, Luke (1999): Educating Transnational Commercial Lawyers for the 21st Century: Towards the Vis Arbitration Moot in 2000: Part Two, *Hosei Kenkyu [Kyushu University]*, Vol. 66, No. 1, F1. As one of many newer mooting opportunities to develop ICA skills, where Australians have also played a leading role, see, for example, <http://sydney.edu.au/law/anjel/content/anjel_teaching_comp.html>, accessed 27 June 2010.

64 See Nottage, Luke (2007): International Arbitration and Commercial Law Education for an International World. In Deguchi, Masa and Storme, Marcel, (Eds) *The Reception and Transmission of Civil Procedural Law in the Global Society*, Antwerp/Apeldoorn, Maklu, 71–80 (also at <http://ssrn.com/abstract=838030>).

65 See <http://www.attorneygeneral.gov.au/>, accessed 27 June 2010; and for example, Nottage, Luke and Green, Stephen (2011): Who Defends Japan? Government Lawyers and Judicial System Reform. In Wolff, Leon, Nottage, Luke and Anderson, Kent, (Eds) *Who Judges Japan? Popular Participation in the Japanese Legal Process*, Cheltenham, Edward Elgar (on reducing legal costs for the government).

66 Most are available, along with the DP, at <http://www.ag.gov.au/internationalarbitration>, accessed 27 June 2010. See also the summary of most of those, at

At a speech in Sydney on 2 February 2009, the (then) Chief Justice of NSW added his voice to the chorus expressing broader concerns about Australia's regime for commercial arbitration:[67]

> The focus on commercial arbitration as a form of commercial dispute resolution has always offered, but rarely delivered, a more cost effective mode of resolution of disputes. Our uniform legislative scheme for domestic arbitration is now hopelessly out of date and requires a complete rewrite. The national scheme implemented in 1984 has not been adjusted in accordance with changes in international best practice. Of course, in our federation, agreement on technical matters such as this in multiple jurisdictions is always subject to delay. The delay with respect to the reform of the Commercial Arbitration Acts is now embarrassing. This is not an area in which harmonisation based on the lowest common denominator principle is appropriate.
>
> In my opinion, the way out of the impasse is to adopt the UNCITRAL ML as the domestic Australian arbitration law. It is a workable regime, itself now subject to review at the Commonwealth level. Its adoption as the domestic Australian arbitration law would send a clear signal to the international commercial arbitration community that Australia is serious about a role as a centre for international arbitration. Our competitors in this regard, such as Hong Kong or Singapore, do not create a rigid barrier between their domestic and international arbitration systems. Nor should we.

At its meeting over 16–17 April 2009, Australia's Standing Committee of Attorney Generals (SCAG) responded to such entreaties by agreeing on precisely this course:[68]

> Ministers agreed to the drafting of new uniform commercial arbitration legislation based on the UNCITRAL ML on International Commercial Arbitration, supplemented by any additional provisions as are necessary or appropriate for the domestic scheme. The aim of the draft model Bill is to give effect to the overriding purpose of commercial arbitration, which is to provide a method of finally resolving disputes that is *quicker, cheaper and less formal*

<http://sydney.edu.au/law/scil/documents/2009/ArbitrationTableSummary_Nottage.pdf>, accessed 9 September 2011.

67 See <http://www.lawlink.nsw.gov.au/lawlink/Supreme_Court/ll_sc.nsf/vwFiles/Spigelman020209.pdf/$file/Spigelman020209.pdf>, accessed 27 June 2010 (18–19).

68 See its Summary of Decisions (April 2009), available via <http://www.scag.gov.au/lawlink/SCAG/ll_scag.nsf/pages/scag_meetingoutcomes>, accessed 27 June 2010 (emphasis added). Following a Consultation Draft dated 15 October 2009 (available via <http://www.scag.gov.au/lawlink/SCAG/ll_scag.nsf/pages/scag_pastconsultations>, accessed 27 June 2010), on 7 May 2010 SCAG announced agreement on the content of the draft Commercial Arbitration Bill.

> than litigation. Adoption of the draft model Bill by jurisdictions will be subject to consultation with stakeholders.

On 25 November 2009, the Attorney-General introduced into the House of Representatives the *International Arbitration Amendment Bill* (the Bill). His accompanying ('Second Reading') speech argued that the reforms 'will ensure the Act remains at the forefront of international arbitration best practice', and concluded that: 'This Bill will not only assist Australian businesses in resolving their disputes but will ensure Australia is an attractive venue for parties from around the world to resolve their disputes'. The Attorney-General emphasized that confusion would be reduced by preventing international arbitrations from taking place except under the ML regime; that the Bill would add new optional provisions for parties as well as adopting UNCITRAL's 2006 revisions to the ML; and that further new interpretive provisions were:[69]

> intended to emphasise the importance of *speed, fairness and cost-effectiveness* in international arbitration, while clearly defining and limiting the role of the courts in international arbitration without compromising the important protective function that the courts exercise.

Soon afterwards, on 4 December 2009 at ACICA's conference entitled 'International Commercial Arbitration: Efficient, Effective, Economical?' held in Melbourne, the Attorney-General's keynote address reiterated similar points before calling for a broader 'cultural change':[70]

> [...] legislative change is only one part of what is required to build a truly Australian brand of international commercial arbitration. What is needed – and what I hope the legislative reforms contained in the Bill will spark – is cultural reform as to how arbitration is conducted in Australia.
>
> This isn't something the Government can legislate for – though the Bill gives a pretty good idea of what the Government has in mind. The Bill states that in using or interpreting the Act and the ML, a court must have regard to the fact that arbitration is an efficient, impartial, enforceable and timely method by which to resolve commercial disputes. This is a clear statement of the Government's expectations for international arbitration.

---

69 This Speech (emphasis added), along with the initial text of the Bill and its Explanatory Memorandum, are available via <http://parlinfo.aph.gov.au/parlInfo/search/display/display.w3p;adv=;db=;group=;holdingType=;id=;orderBy=;page=;query=Id%3A%22legislation%2Fbillhome%2Fr4261%22;querytype=;rec=0;resCount=>, accessed 27 June 2010.

70 'International Commercial Arbitration in Australia: More Effective and Certain', via <http://www.attorneygeneral.gov.au/www/ministers/mcclelland.nsf/Page/Speeches_2009_FourthQuarter_4December2009-InternationalCommercialArbitrationinAustraliaMoreEffectiveandCertain>, accessed 27 June 2010.

> As the title of this conference suggests there is a real question mark as to whether international arbitration as currently practiced in this country lives up to that statement. Arbitrators need to stop thinking of themselves as common law judges without robes and start thinking of themselves as service providers. Similarly, courts need to respect this essential aspect of arbitration.
>
> If Australia is to ever emerge as an arbitration centre we need our arbitrators to provide a service that is not available in those seats – something that is more than 'litigation-lite'. We need to invent a form of arbitration that is tailored to the needs of the parties – to the needs of business. A form of arbitration that is prepared to do away with unnecessary formalities and get on with identifying and solving the problem that exists between the parties. A form of arbitration that delivers swift and cost-competitive outcomes. A form of arbitration that is innovative and creative and allows the undoubted talents that exist in the arbitration community to flourish. We need to be able to put ourselves forward as the place you come to when you want your problem fixed, and fixed fast and fairly. The Act – once it has been amended by the Bill – will provide a strong legal framework to support that approach.

Unfortunately, but not uncommonly in Australian federal Government practice, the Bill was not referred to any specialist parliamentary committee for public inquiry. It was referred instead to the 'Main Committee', resulting in various individuals and organizations approaching the Attorney-General separately and privately to voice concerns about various provisions in the Bill. In partial response, on 17 March 2010 he introduced revisions to the Bill on behalf of the Government. The Main Committee agreed to the revised Bill on 13 May, so it was introduced into the Senate on 15 June, with the Attorney-General tabling the same Second Reading speech as submitted to the House of Representatives for the original Bill. The Senate agreed to the revised Bill on its third and final Reading on 17 June, with the Shadow Attorney-General (George Brandis) adding a short speech indicating the Opposition's support for the Bill. He mentioned that arbitration was the primary means of resolving disputes without resorting to national courts, typically providing for a process formulated to the parties' requirements and 'therefore more likely to preserve the relationship for them'; and that this legislation sought to 'increase the attractiveness of Australia as a venue for international commercial arbitration … a high-value service in which Australia should enjoy a particular competitive advantage'. The revised Bill, as agreed by both Houses of Parliament, then received the Governor-General's Royal Assent on 28 June 2010, and the IAA as amended basically applies to international arbitrations commenced or underway after that date.[71]

---

71 For a few exceptions and more details, see Garnett, above n. 29, Chapter 2 Part VII. The complete legislative history and documentation is available online via the Parliament's website, above n. 69 (including a 'Revised Explanatory Memorandum' that combines the original Bill's 'Explanatory Memorandum' and the 'Supplementary Explanatory Memorandum' that accompanied the Government's revised Bill).

Much attention has turned to amendments to the uniform CAAs, which take the revised IAA and the ML as their new core. The *Commercial Arbitration Amendment Bill 2009* (NSW), based largely on the ML but now covering only domestic arbitrations, was introduced into the Legislative Council of NSW on 12 May 2009, passed the Council (with a few amendments) on 10 June 2010 and was introduced that day into the Legislative Assembly, where it was passed on 22 June 2010. In his Second Reading speech introducing the Bill, the (then) NSW Attorney-General, John Hatzistergos, echoed some of Chief Justice Spigelman's sentiments in his lecture of 2009:[72]

> New South Wales took the lead in developing this model bill and will be the first jurisdiction to introduce legislation based on the model bill and provide business with up-to-date domestic arbitration laws. The reform of domestic arbitration legislation is particularly timely when one has regard to developments in international arbitration. The regularity and certainty that is conducive to efficient commerce are fostered by uniform national laws that reflect accepted international practice. In addition, the ability of Australian courts to deal with international arbitration is based on their experience with domestic arbitration.
>
> Notably, the jurisdictions with which we compete for international arbitration work do not have different national and international arbitration laws, and nor should we.

Pursuant to the Bill, when implementing Regulations were enacted on 1 October 2010, the old CAA (NSW) was repealed and replaced by the *Commercial Arbitration Act 2010* (NSW), which now basically applies to domestic arbitration proceedings and arbitration agreements formed before as well as after that date. Yet, as of March 2011, no other states had yet enacted parallel legislation, despite the SCAG commitment in April 2009.

Already, however, some recent case law under the old CAA framework may have anticipated a closer alignment between the CAA and ML regimes.[73]

72 See <http://www.parliament.nsw.gov.au/prod/parlment/nswbills.nsf/V3BillsHome>, accessed 27 June 2010.

73 See *Gordian Runoff Ltd v. Westport Insurance Corp* [2010] NSWCA 57, where the NSWCA held (per Allsop P., with Spigelman, C.J. and Macfarlan, J.A. concurring) that under the CAA (NSW) a lesser standing of reasoning was required of arbitrators – similar to that under the ML – than that envisaged by the Court of Appeal of Victoria in interpreting the CAA (Vic) in *Oil Basins Ltd v. BHP Billiton Ltd* [2007] VSCA 255. These conflicting approaches have resulted in Special Leave being granted to appeal the *Gordian* judgment to the High Court of Australia: see *Westport Insurance Corporation & Ors v. Gordian Runoff Limited* [2010] HCATrans 233 at <http://www.austlii.edu.au/au/other/HCATrans/2010/233.html>, accessed 17 March 2011. See further Part III.J in Deboos, Jonathan., Croft, Clyde, Gehle, Bjorn and Garnett, Richard, ACICA's Expedited Arbitration Rules of 2008. In Nottage, L. and Garnett, R., (Eds) *International Arbitration in Australia*, Sydney, Federation Press; Nottage and Garnett, above n. 29, Part IV.F.

Meanwhile, on 3 March 2010 the federal Attorney-General and his NSW counterpart, John Hatzistergos, announced that AU$600,000 would be provided (jointly with ACICA and the Australian Commercial Disputes Centre) to fit out a new 'Australian International Disputes Centre' in a prime location in Sydney, with premises opening from mid-year.[74] This initiative goes back to the NSW Attorney-General's *Blueprint for Alternative Dispute Resolution in NSW – Discussion Paper*, released in May 2009, which had tried to respond to SIAC's improved caseload and physical infrastructure with:[75]

> Proposal 11: Establish a single Sydney International Arbitration Centre that has the physical space, organisational facilities, secretarial, computer and research support in the one location, to position Sydney better as a centre for international commercial arbitration.

Hard Lessons from Australia

Clearly, policy-makers have been 'talking the talk' over the last few years, acknowledging concerns that ICA in Australia had stagnated while taking off worldwide and particularly in the Asia–Pacific. They have also linked this to over-formalization: costs, delays and old ways of approaching commercial dispute resolution drawn from domestic arbitration – and even litigation. But are they 'walking the walk' – have policy-makers done enough to secure the holy grail of greater ICA caseloads, or even the more disparate benefits of a vibrant arbitration culture? Arguably not, and not just because Singapore, Hong Kong and China are already so far ahead, with Korea also now developing critical mass. Another major issue remains present and largely unaddressed in this context: the dominance of large law firms, with their strong emphasis on billable hours, in Australia's ICA world.

The Chief Justice of Western Australia (WA) has recently explained how the notion of recording lawyers' work in tenth of an hour (six-minute) increments, first recommended in the US literature in the 1940s as a cost accounting tool, came to be promoted by management consultants there in the 1950s and 1960s as a client billing system. It then took root in Australia from the mid- to late-1970s.[76]

74 See <http://www.lawlink.nsw.gov.au/lawlink/Special_Projects/ll_splprojects.nsf/pages/aidc_index>, accessed 27 June 2010. The Centre was duly opened on 3 August 2010: see <http://www.disputescentre.com.au/>, accessed 17 March 2011. Compare the magnificent 'Maxwell Chambers' facilities, opened in 2008 presumably with much greater financial support from the Singaporean government: above n. 43.

75 See <http://www.lawlink.nsw.gov.au/lawlink/Corporate/ll_corporate.nsf/vwFiles/ADR_Blueprint.doc/$file/ADR_Blueprint.doc>, accessed 27 June 2010.

76 Chief Justice Wayne Martin, 'Billable Hours – Past their Use-by Date', Address to the Perth Press on the Launch of Law Week 2010, Kings Park, 17 May 2010, available

Advantages – for law firms – included administrative efficiencies, a relationship between price and cost (albeit with variation in mark-ups), better comparability between competitors (at least in theory), and the transfer of risk to the clients. But already by 1999, the Law Reform Commission of WA (chaired by Chief Justice Martin) criticized the incentive that time billing provided for the undertaking of unnecessary work and maintenance of inefficient practices. It urged the legal profession and courts to develop more appropriate ways of billing, reducing the prominence of billable hours systems. This was not done in WA until early 2010, however, when agreement was reached on a scale of fees for certain non-contentious tasks. The Chief Justice went on to elaborate the many and growing disadvantages that have been identified with the time billing system:

- conflict of interest;
- clients bear all the risk;
- no upfront price;
- high levels of complaints;
- focuses on hours, not value;
- fosters a production mentality;
- encourages over-servicing;
- discourages project management or case planning;
- discourages cost–benefit analysis;
- penalizes technological advances;
- creates bureaucracy;
- prices by reference to service and not the consumer;
- cross-subsidization among clients;
- discourages communication between lawyer and client;
- report mechanical functions not real progress;
- encourages boosting profits by boosting targets;
- encourages time-sheet padding;
- rates are not based on cost;
- discourages professionalism (such as mentoring, participation in professional bodies);
- distorts assessment;
- diminishes collegiality;
- encourages hoarding of hours;
- discourages *pro bono* work;
- reduces quality of life;
- insulates lawyers from community and family.

Chief Justice Martin concluded by recommended various alternatives:

---

via <http://www.lawsocietywa.asn.au/AnnouncementRetrieve.aspx?ID=32465>, accessed 6 July 2010.

- a focus on value;
- event billing (fixed fees for completing various stages in litigation, for example, as the Commonwealth Government is now more interested in);
- fixed fees;
- blended billing rates (with a single hourly rate irrespective of lawyer level, reducing incentives to have low-level work done by more experienced and pricier lawyers);
- contingency fees (with 'uplifts' on success now generally allowed in Australia);
- hybrid methods (combining variants of all the above).

What this otherwise hard-hitting speech does not really address is that the billable hours system is now particularly entrenched in Australia's larger law firms, although it is also widespread among smaller firms and among barristers. Big firms rely heavily on the system as a management tool, with junior lawyers and even partners expected to meet minimum hours each year to secure promotions or bonuses. It should also be noted that the 1970s saw the emergence of these large firms, accelerating over the 1980s and 1990s, just as the 1960s witnessed the growth of both large firms and billable hours systems in US law firms.[77]

Of course, other factors were at work in Australia, as in other jurisdictions that have seen the rise of large corporate law firms. Client businesses became national, as barriers to interstate commerce declined and broader deregulation occurred from the 1980s. As 'first-tier' law firms grew, particularly through mergers, others followed suit to preserve reputation as well as to secure similar gains from greater scale. But by around 2005, Australia had 12–15 nationwide 'elite firms' (including six first-tier firms), employing 25.9 per cent of 32,300 solicitors – a much higher proportion compared to total lawyer numbers than in the US, UK, Japan (ranging from 5.6–7.3 per cent) and Germany (2.9 per cent).[78] It is only since the turn of the century that this expansion seems to have levelled off, as Australian firms instead emphasize profitability. This has been achieved through increased leverage (more associates per partner), longer partnership tracks (reportedly around 12 years by 2006, rather than eight to ten years a few years

77 See generally Galanter, Mark and Palay, Thomas (1991): *Tournament of Lawyers: The Transformation of the Big Law Firm*, Chicago, IL, University of Chicago Press.

78 Aronson, above n. 17, 805. He also suggests (807) that these big Australian firms have considerably lower billing rates than US and UK firms, suggesting low profitability, which has constrained interest in large foreign firms in making further inroads into the Australian market. But these rates have to be compared to cost of living indices, absolute profitability does not seem very low (over AU$1 million per annum for a top-tier firm partner even in 2006), and (in addition to DLA Piper linking with Phillips Fox in 2006) Norton Rose as well as Allen & Overy have recently expanded into Australia: see 'Allen & Overy to Open Australia Offices, Target Deals (Update1)', Bloomberg, 8 February 2010, <http://www.businessweek.com/news/2010-02-08/allen-overy-to-open-australia-offices-target-mining-mergers.html>, accessed 7 July 2010.

previously), more emphasis on productivity (but involving pressures to increase billable hours), increased competition for quality associates, firm restructurings and an active lateral market.[79]

This remarkable expansion in large firm presence and the entrenchment of the billable hours system, perhaps especially over the 1990s, coincides with a period during which Australia was conspicuously unable to attract ICA cases to its shores or to develop a new arbitration culture more generally. Instead, Australia experienced rapid growth in privately supplied mediation services as the preferred alternative to court litigation when resolving commercial disputes.[80] These mediators did generally charge by the hour (or by the day) as well, lawyers quite often participated along with the parties, and there was no guarantee of a binding resolution. Yet mediator fees (and even lawyer fees) were often small compared to the amounts in dispute, especially if the dispute could be resolved through early intervention. For international disputes, commercial parties were more easily persuaded to agree to arbitration venues outside Australia where costly big law firms and the billable hour system were less dominant – or at least similar – but which also enjoyed other comparative advantages, such as Singapore or China.

This broader context may help explain not only why ICA never really took off from the 1990s, but also the delays in initiating amendments to the IAA, as well as the subsequent legislative process and specific outcomes. Although ACICA and many other bodies did publically press for law reform, many of their leaders come from large law firms. And such firms also benefit financially from an arbitral regime containing significant uncertainties and complexity, particularly when it comes to contesting (in Australia courts, on billable hours basis) the enforcement of foreign arbitral awards or arbitration agreements specifying a seat outside Australia. In addition, compared to other stakeholders with broader interests in the ICA regime, such as professors teaching and practicing part-time in arbitration, big firms may have had more incentive to see at least some amendments passed. After all, any form of enactment allows them to report 'progress' to clients and overseas practitioners, through their increasingly elaborate publicity programmes.

Lessons for Legislators

From this perspective, various conclusions can be drawn from Australia's experience for all countries where large law firms (and others) operate increasingly on a strict billable hours system, including within the arbitration field. First, regarding legislative reform, all stakeholders and especially the government must be proactive, persistent and transparent. Australia was not only comparatively slow in amending its IAA. In addition, the process was eventually initiated by the AGD releasing a DP that involved quite limited prior consultation. This is the government's prerogative, of course, and a discussion document is designed to elicit

79 Ibid, 807–8.

80 Nottage, above n. 27.

further views and public debate. But the DP focused attention on relatively clear-cut areas for legislative amendment, it was released in November 2008 (shortly before the Australian summer vacation period) with a tight deadline for responses, and initially there was no facility for those Submissions to be shared publically online. No formal forums took place over 2009, where stakeholders could have discussed the many additional reform proposals that nonetheless emerged from the Submissions.[81] The Government simply introduced the Amendment Bill, and then did not refer it to a specialized parliamentary committee, which centralizes and renders more transparent the process of subsequent discussion and any amendments to bills.[82] Consequently, as mentioned above in the second part of this chapter. stakeholders disappointed with the initial Bill needed to write directly to the Federal Attorney-General. This process favours those with the loudest voices or greatest resources available to access ministers, including the large law firms or the professional organizations with which they are closely involved.

Arguably related to inadequate public consultation, the amendments enacted in July 2010 are disappointing in many respects. They omitted or watered down many suggested reforms that would have promoted greater informality and hence potential cost or time savings in ICA. For example:[83]

- Although the drafting is obscure, so we are forced back on the general statutory presumption against retrospective effect for this interpretation, it appears that the amendments in Part III of IAA only apply to arbitration agreements concluded from 6 July 2010 onwards.[84] Thus, we will probably have to wait for several years (until disputes arise under newly concluded

81 See *AGD's Review of the International Arbitration Act — Comparison of 24 Submissions (as of 13 March 2009)* Sydney Centre for International Law <http://sydney.edu.au/law/scil/documents/2009/ArbitrationTableSummary_Nottage.pdf>, accessed 7 July 2010.

82 Compare, for example, the Senate Committee Inquiries into the 'Australian Consumer Law' reforms implemented by two amendments to the *Trade Practices Act 1974* (Cth), which states had also previously agreed to 'apply' (or copy out) as state legislation once enacted at the federal level. See <http://acren.wordpress.com>, accessed 27 June 2010 (with further references) and more generally Nottage, L. (2009): Consumer Law Reform in Australia: Contemporary and Comparative Constructive Criticism, *QUT Law and Justice Journal*, Vol. 9, No. 2, 111. This means that Submissions are made public on the Senate's website, linked to that showing the progress of the Bill through Parliament, and that Committees often call Evidence from among those providing Submissions which are recorded under parliamentary privilege and later published online and in Hansard. See, for example, <http://www.aph.gov.au/senate/committee/economics_ctte/tpa_consumer_law_10/index.htm>, accessed 27 June 2010.

83 See Nottage and Garnett, above n. 29 (based on our 2009 Submission and subsequent article published in *Asian International Arbitration Journal* (2010), Vol. 6, No. 1, 1–43), especially Parts II.B, II.E, III.C, IV.A, IV.E, IV.F, IV.G and V.A.

84 See Nottage and Garnett, above n. 20, 27–28; Garnett, above n. 29, Part VII.

agreements) before those reforms that did get into the 2010 amendments can actually benefit those conducting arbitrations with the seat in Australia. By then the 'novelty effect' and educational impact of the reforms may well have dissipated, and other 'regional competitors' will probably have updated their own arbitration legislation – making them even more attractive as arbitral venues.[85]

- There also appears to be a major drafting error in the statutory reform package. Specifically, a 'legislative black hole' arises for international arbitral agreements concluded before 6 July 2010 where parties (for example, in different countries) have agreed that the seat should be Sydney, but have excluded the ML (as was possible under the old s21 of the IAA). That would normally mean that the CAA (NSW) applies, but the old one has been repealed, and the new CAA 2010 (NSW) does not apply to such 'international' arbitration agreements.[86] If and when a case arises in New South Wales courts contesting such an arbitration agreement, Australia's reputation as a jurisdiction 'serious' about arbitration will surely suffer again.
- In the 2010 amendments there is also no additional clarification about what matters are 'arbitrable' for the purposes of enforcing agreements or awards, or running arbitrations with the seat in Australia,[87] as opposed to being contrary to other mandatory laws such as trade practices legislation.
- The writing requirements for valid arbitration agreements have been liberalized, but not completely (even for arbitrations where the seat is in Australia).
- There is no clarification allowing Australian courts to enforce awards that have been annulled in foreign seat.
- There is no provision for arbitrators to issue (even non-binding) ex parte 'preliminary orders' in support of interim measure of protection, as in almost all other countries that have adopted the 2006 revisions to the ML, and indeed s18C makes it impossible for parties to agree otherwise on this point.

85 See already, for example, the new arbitration ordinance in Hong Kong, entitled 'Arbitration Ordinance (Cap. 609)' has come into effect on 1 June 2011, which unifies the international and domestic arbitration law in Hong Kong. For details see Choong, John and Weeramantry, Romesh, (Eds) (2011): *The Hong Kong Arbitration Ordinance: Commentary and Annotations*, Sweet & Maxwell.

86 See further Garnett, Richard and Nottage, Luke, The 2010 Amendments to the International Arbitration Act: A New Dawn for Australia?, *Asian International Arbitration Journal*, Vol. 7, No. 1, 29–53 (earlier at <http://ssrn.com/abstract=1676604>, accessed 17 March 2011).

87 Continued confusion was recently evident, for example, regarding the arbitrability of disputes involving patent licensing: see *Larkden Pty Limited v. Lloyd Energy Systems Pty Limited* [2011] NSWSC 268 (1 April 2011).

- There is seemingly no possibility of opting out of the ML regime and into a foreign arbitration law, which may be flexible in promoting greater informality in ICA (even though such a choice of curial law is still generally inadvisable).
- There is no reference to international 'soft law' instruments such as the *Rules on the Taking of Evidence in ICA* agreed in 1999 (and amended in 2010) by the International Bar Association (IBA) or the ILA's 2002 *Recommendations* regarding 'public policy' as one of the limited grounds for refusing enforcement of a foreign award.
- There are no provisions on ARB-MED.
- There is no legislative clarification of the extent of reasoning required in awards.
- There is insufficient provision for consolidation of arbitrations.
- New confidentiality provisions are included, but only on an opt-in basis (and it is unclear whether and to what extent the provisions can be further amended by party agreement).

Australia's experience therefore suggests that other countries seeking further reforms to their ICA regimes, especially where ICA caseloads have not yet reached critical mass, may need to work especially hard where big law firms and a billable hours culture are prevalent. Legislative reform arguably needs to extend beyond arbitration legislation, including trade practices law and even regulation on third-party funders of litigation – and potentially of arbitration.[88]

Countries like Australia should also be working hard to develop expertise in the overlapping field of investor–state arbitration. Instead, the Australian Government has blown cold on that field. A report released in December 2010 by its (Treasury-related) Productivity Commission recommended that Australia drastically scale back the scope for including such procedures in its future investment treaties or free trade agreements. The 'Gillard Government Trade Policy Statement', issued in April 2011, went even further – eschewing investor-state arbitration provisions even for future treaties with developing countries. Yet the theory and evidence underpinning even the Commission's recommendation was weak. The Government's remarkable policy shift seems to be an over-reaction particularly to the first ever investment treaty claim brought against Australia,

---

88 Since *Campbells Cash and Carry Pty Limited v. Fostif Pty Ltd* [2006] *HCA* 41, third party funding in exchange for the (non-lawyer) funder taking an agreed percentage of any damages awarded to the claimant (as many law firms do in the US) has become generally acceptable. This makes it unlikely that there will be many challenges, at least within Australia, to funding arrangements in support of arbitration claims (cf. for example Singapore recently: Ng, Jern-Fei (2010): The Role of the Doctrines of Champerty and Maintenance in Arbitration, *Arbitration*, Vol. 76, No. 2, 208). With proper regulatory safeguards, the intervention of a responsible third party may serve as a 'reality check' to claimant lawyers and especially the claimant itself, helping to rein in costs.

by Philip Morris Asia (the Hong Kong-based subsidiary of the global tobacco company) complaining about new plain packaging legislation.[89] This new policy stance reveals Australia's persistent broader ambivalence about resolving disputes through international arbitration, and it further undermines the 2010 reforms in the overlapping field of ICA.

Lessons for Arbitral Institutions

In addition, arbitral institutions will probably need to be bolder in attempts to expand ICA in such jurisdictions. One recommendation is to replace an hourly or per diem remuneration for arbitrators with a fee (or fee range) based on the amount in dispute, including a clear policy on reductions for early settlement of disputes.[90]

In addition, extra care will be needed in the institutions' extremely important role of appointing arbitrators, usually where the parties fail to agree.[91] They should beware of charging high fees to be accepted or maintained on (even now non-mandatory) lists or panel of arbitrators, as this will tend to favour lawyers from large firms who can afford such fees as overheads or publicity. Institutions also need to be cautious about relying heavily on the 2004 *IBA Guidelines on Conflicts of Interest in International Arbitration*. These were drafted by a preponderance of lawyers from large firms and are quite generous in allowing arbitrators to be appointed from such firms even where there may appear to be a conflict of interest.[92]

More generally, institutions should actively seek out arbitrators who do not operate in an environment highly geared to billable hours. In such environments, as in most large law firms, practitioners may well find the role of arbitrator to

89 See Nottage, Luke (2011): The Rise and Possible Fall of Investor-State Arbitration in Asia: A Skeptic's View of Australia's 'Gillard Government Trade Policy Statement', *Transnational Dispute Management*, forthcoming, also at <http://ssrn.com/abstract=1860505>; and Nottage, Luke, Repercussions of Australia's Plain Packaging Act (26 August 2011) at <http://blogs.usyd.edu.au/japaneselaw/2011/08/repercussions_of_australias_to.html>, both accessed 27 August 2011.

90 Cf, for example, ACICA Arbitration Rules 2005, Article 40 (adopting an hourly rate).

91 See ibid, Articles 9 and 10; and ACICA Expedited Arbitration Rules 2008, Article 8. Usually, each party to a three-person tribunal selects one arbitrator each. In such cases, the party generally cannot appoint someone from their own law firm due to conflict of interest, but that firm may recommend a lawyer in another firm partly in the hope of reciprocation. Compared to smaller-scale practitioners, big law firms naturally also encounter more advocates in other arbitral proceedings, who they may come to recommend to their own clients, or at least on platforms for lawyers such as *Who's Who Legal*: see <http://www.whoswholegal.com/practiceareas/20/commercial-arbitration/#lawyers>, accessed 7 July 2010.

92 See Bond, Michael (2005): A Geography of International Arbitration, *Arbitration International* Vol. 21, No. 1, 105–110 (especially the situations involving roles as lawyers included in the 'waivable Red List' and the 'Orange List'). Such conflicts, even after disclosures have been made pursuant to the Guidelines, may be less of a concern where smaller stakes are involved. See, for example, ACICA Expedited Arbitration Rules 2008, Article 8.6.

be more interesting than that of advocate or legal advisor, and get their firms to count time spent arbitrating as equivalent billable hours for promotion and bonus purposes. (That may well be agreed if the hourly rate may be somewhat less than what they could charge as lawyers on other matters, as reputation as an arbitrator should also serve well the lawyer and his or her firm in terms of securing future work as advocate or advisor.) Yet such situations create an incentive for the lawyer serving as arbitrator not to resolve the matter in the quickest and most cost-effective manner, except for the (still very few) who are so well-established as to be virtually guaranteed an equally well-paid and interesting appointment as soon as they complete the pending matter.

Institutions can minimize such problems, even where their rules require hourly fees for arbitrators, by appointing individuals who can credibly claim not to be so driven by such financial imperatives. One category could be retired judges, who often have foregone lucrative careers as advocates – and indeed usually enjoy generous pensions nowadays, making them less likely to needlessly extend arbitration proceedings. On the other hand, precisely because they are now retired, they may still be so disposed because of the interesting role involved in serving as arbitrator. Retired judges may also be too accustomed to practices in litigation, particularly in their home jurisdictions, and hence less open to more flexible and informal practices in ICA (such as ARB-MED).

A second category is professors, not necessarily retired. In fact, many of the leading arbitrators in Europe (and, to a lesser extent, the US) are still professors with full-time appointments, as opposed to part-time adjunct professors and such like.[93] Those from common law jurisdictions, in particular, also often benefit from having already spent several years in full-time legal practice prior to becoming academics and/or involved in ongoing part-time consultancies with law firms. Many often now obtain further experience,[94] building on their comprehensive mastery of ICA law, by assisting in very popular student competitions. Examples including the Vis Moots in Vienna and now Hong Kong or the Intercollegiate Negotiation and Arbitration Competition in Tokyo.[95] These events have become fertile recruiting grounds for law firms seeking able young graduates interested in international commercial law. However, professors will generally have another

93 Examples include Professors Boeckstiegel and Park (already mentioned above) as well as Professors Albert van den Berg, James Crawford, Bernard Hanotiau and Kaufmann-Kohler. An interesting recent development has been for full-time ICA lawyers to obtain appointments as Adjunct Professors or some association with leading law schools with reputations in cross-border dispute resolution.

94 On the (somewhat 'chicken-and-egg') expectation that arbitrators, including professors, demonstrate practical experience in ICA, see Moses, Michael, (2008): *The Principles and Practice of International Commercial Arbitration*, Cambridge, New York, Cambridge University Press, 118–19.

95 See, respectively, <http://www.cisg.law.pace.edu/vis.html>, <http://www.cisg moot.org/> and <http://sydney.edu.au/law/anjel/content/anjel_teaching_comp.html>, accessed 7 July 2010.

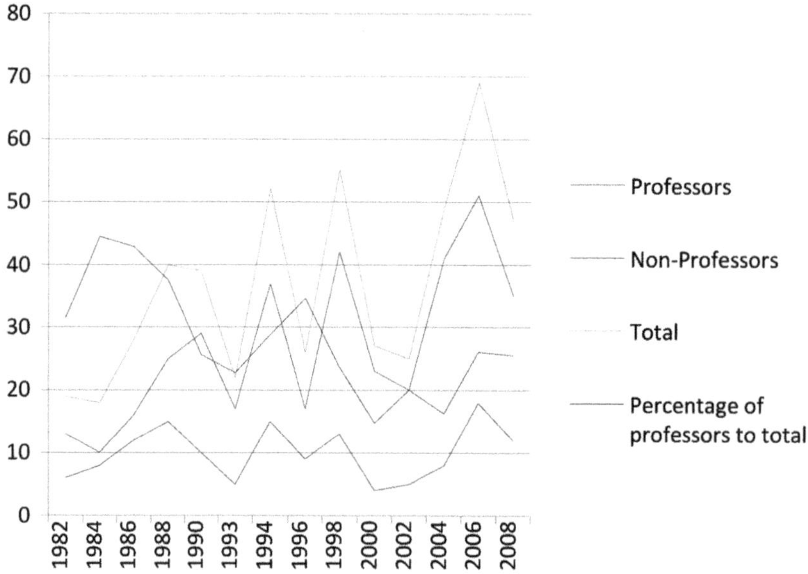

Figure 2.2 Breakdown of ICCA Congress presenters

(hopefully fulfilling) life to go back to, namely in the academic world. This creates another incentive for them to dispose of cases more quickly and cost-effectively when serving as arbitrators.

Having appointed arbitrators from a range of backgrounds, arbitral institutions should then be more proactive in reviewing and disclosing their performance. Confidentiality can and should remain the general principle in ICA – as opposed to investor–state arbitration, where more public interests are at stake – because it allows (but does not guarantee) more informal and flexible practices by parties and arbitrators.[96] But if a well-managed case settles or is disposed of quickly, institutions can and should seek agreement from the parties and arbitrators to publicize redacted information – making the case anonymous regarding the parties, for example, but identifying the arbitrators.[97]

Lastly, arbitral institutions and the associations they are active in (such as APRAG) should promote more diversity in arbitrator appointments by giving a wide range of experts ample opportunities to participate in conferences and other major events. In this respect, it is interesting to track changes in the profiles

96 This is reportedly particularly important in Asia, as evident from Table 2.1 earlier (Part I), derived from the comparative empirical study by Ali (above n. 8).

97 More generally, see Bhatia, Vijay, Candlin, Christopher and Sharma, Rajesh (2009): Confidentiality and Integrity in International Commercial Arbitration Practice, *Arbitration*, Vol. 75, No. 1, 75.

of speakers asked to give presentations at arguably the most prominent ICA conference: the biannual Congresses of the International Council of Commercial Arbitration (ICCA). Analysis of the presentations subsequently published in a Kluwer series, which will include almost all those presented at the Congresses, shows that the proportion provided by professors has declined considerably over the last two decades (see Figure 2.2).[98]

It is true that absolute numbers have remained fairly constant, seemingly related to the growing popularity of topics in investor–state arbitration. The latter is a hybrid field, based primarily in public international law, where professors remain in high demand due to the field's novelty, complexity and legitimacy issues – as they were in ICA's formative era through to 1970s. However, the proportions have changed over the last two decades because Congresses are getting bigger and non-professors are increasingly invited as speakers. It is also worth noting that fees at these Congresses, and many other major conferences run by professional bodies, are often now very high and without any discounts even for full-time academics.

Conclusions

The recommendations in the previous part of this chapter, aimed at addressing more deep-rooted factors behind for renewed complaints about delays and especially costs of international arbitration, also imply changes in attitudes and practices among arbitrators, lawyers and the parties themselves. Many arbitrators will need to change their mindset and improve their skills set. Law firms specializing in cross-border dispute resolution will need to experiment with alternatives to the billable hours system, as indeed a few are doing in the US, the UK and now in Australia.[99] Parties, particularly their in-house counsel, will need to keep pressing for such innovations. If judges, universities, arbitral institutions, professional associations and legislators can also nurture these initiatives, it seems more plausible to expect real 'culture change' along the lines envisaged by the federal Attorney-General when introducing the amended IAA. This also holds true for jurisdictions beyond Australia, especially others in the Asia–Pacific region that still lack critical mass in ICA.

---

98 For source data and broader context, see Nottage (2010), above n. 51. The data comprises published ICCA Congress volumes and some related conference programs.

99 See Martin, above n. 18 (referring to Eversheds in the UK and Wachtel Lipton Rosen and Katz in the US). In Australia, see now <http://www.marquelawyers.com.au>, accessed 9 September 2011.

Chapter 3
Systems of Genres in International Commercial Arbitration

Celina Frade

Introduction

The use of arbitration has dramatically increased worldwide in the last decades, consolidating its nature as the most cost-effective and expeditious way of alternative dispute resolution, particularly in business and commercial international contexts. The relevance of international arbitration has resulted in a series of multidisciplinary investigation on various levels. On the legal level, the benefits of flexibility and 'the security of internationally enforceable award and statutory support' (Jones 2006: 275) have led to the establishment of various arbitral institutions which provide for a set of domestic and international rules and model laws governing the process. On the discourse level, the trend is towards the participants' shared perception of conventions and constraints operating on its construction, interpretation and conditions of use (Frade 2009; Bhatia, Candlin and Engberg 2008a).

If, on the one hand, we can talk about 'genre' associated with the arbitration process, we can also understand it as a series of moves[1] instantiated in subgenres and smaller genres embedded in a stabilized macro-speech act, resulting in what Bazerman (1994) calls a system of genres. From the drafting of the arbitration clause or agreement clearly stating the intention of the parties to solve any controversies which may arise out of a contract by arbitration until the final award issued by the arbitral tribunal, a range of structured and planned oral and written subgenres and smaller genres follows upon another, framing the sequence and consequence of actions shared by the participants.

This chapter discusses international arbitration as a system of genres. Our analysis was based on data drawn from rules set forth by two renowned international arbitration institutions: The International Chamber of Commerce (ICC) and the Arbitration and Mediation Center of the Chamber of Commerce Brazil–Canada (CCBC). The claim is that the identification of the generic system embedded in international arbitration proceedings may guide the participants towards appropriate generic moves open to them at each point of the process so as to fulfill the conditions for a successful arbitration.

1 In this chapter, we will be using the word 'move' as a synonym for 'act' or 'development', and not as Swales's (1990) rhetorical concept.

Systems of Genre

Genre analysis has been valuable in explaining the rationale underlying professional interactions on linguistic, discoursal, rhetorical and socio-cultural levels, among others (Bhatia, Candlin and Engberg 2008a). More particularly, investigators into international arbitration discourse have also relied on genre analysis to 'identify common elements in arbitration legislation as they are constructed and interpreted across multilingual and multicultural contexts' (Bhatia, Candlin and Engberg 2008a: 7).

Nevertheless, most studies have been conducted considering well-defined single moves or interactions or features as part of the arbitration process but which may not be in fact interrelated and/or interconnected to one another. Moreover, very little attention is devoted to providing the participants with the awareness of the potential number of appropriate moves or 'generic utterances [with] identifiable conditions of success' (Bazerman 1994: 96) at each point of the international arbitration process. Therefore, it seems quite reasonable to assume that international arbitration is a genre comprised of a series of 'well defined genres which are closely related to each other', resulting in what Bazerman (1994: 96) calls a system of genres, which will be briefly reviewed below.

The author introduces the notion of systems of genres as part of his classical study on application of patents as 'interrelated genres that interact with each other in specific settings' (Bazerman 1994: 97). He claims that differently from genre recognition which 'usually limits interpretive flexibility' and Devitt's (1991) notion of set of genre, which 'represents one side of a multiple person interaction', the system of genres 'would be the full set of genres that instantiate the participations of all the parties' (Bazerman 1994: 90–99).

The notion is then extended to 'a highly developed set of typified practices' such as the law (Bazerman 1994: 88) wherein every legal activity entails more than a single move or act but rather requires volumes of rules, regulations, proceedings and documents instantiated in appropriate generic forms closely related to each other. Examples of conventionalized and typified legal genres range from contracts, legislation and statutes to oral hearings, cross-examination and lawyer–client interactions. The various small genres under those larger moves contribute to strengthening the 'generic force' of the arbitration agreement itself (Bazerman 1994: 89). On the other hand, any defect in, or misinterpretation of, any of the contributory genres may become the reason for the failure of the genre and, consequently, of the whole arbitration process.

As far as the multiple participants in legal activities are concerned, they can regulate their moves in order to decide for appropriate legal moves with conditions of success and also identify 'unexpected outcomes [...] from opposing moves by the other side and open pathways to more favourable lines of actions' (Bazerman 1994: 97). The moves are therefore instantiated in typified generic forms with the participation of all the parties 'establishing the current act in relation to prior acts' within the system of genres (Bazerman 1994: 99).

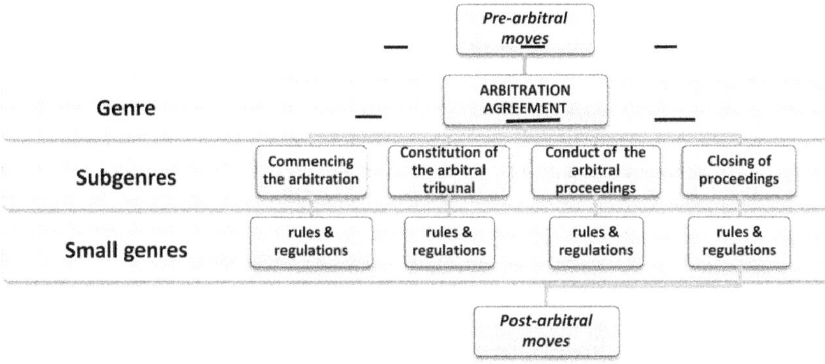

Figure 3.1 International arbitration system of genres
Source: Author.

One of Giddens's (1984: 17) main propositions of structuration theory can be related to the notion of systems of genres insofar as:

> the rules and resources drawn upon in the production and reproduction of social action are at the same time the means and system reproduction (the duality of structure).

By researching some major international arbitration rules and legislation, we were able to identify them as hierarchical systems of genre as illustrated in Figure 3.1.

After some pre-arbitral moves, the arbitration agreement will be instantiated in a type of macro-genre comprised of four broad moves instantiated in subgenres with consequences for the small genres to follow. It is this 'shared sense of genre' (Bazerman 1994: 100) that makes the participants' moves understandable and valid.

Method and Materials

The material comprises two sets of rules and regulations for arbitration proceedings at both domestic and international levels: the International Chamber of Arbitration (ICC)[2] and the Chamber of Commerce Brazil–Canada (CCBC).[3] ICC, according to its institutional website, is the 'world's leading institution for resolving international commerce and business disputes', handling over 15,000 cases since its foundation; and the latter is a pioneer in arbitration in Brazil and

2 <http://www.iccwbo.org/uploadedFiles/Court/Arbitration/other/rules_arb_english.pdf>, accessed 15 June 2011.

3 <http://www.ccbc.org.br/arbitragem.asp?subcategoria=regulamento%20ingles>, accessed 15 June 2011.

Table 3.1 The materials' subgenres

Subgenres	ICC Rules	CCBC Rules
1. Settlement of arbitration agreement	Articles 1 to 6	Sections 1 and 2
2. Composition of arbitral tribunal	Articles 7 to 12	Sections 3and 6
3. Conduct of arbitral proceedings	Articles 13 to 23	Section 9
4. Making of award	Articles 24 to 29	Sections 10 and 11

represents Brazilian and Canadian companies that operate in all major economic sectors, both in Brazil and Canada.

Based on a previous study on generic variation across legislative writing (Frade 2004), an overview of the textual organization of the material is shown in the Appendix. Despite possible variations in layout and information packaging, both materials are relatively uniform and can be organized in four broad moves instantiated in the following subgenres (Articles and/or Sections):

1. Commencing the arbitration;
2. Constitution of the arbitral tribunal;
3. Conduct of arbitral proceedings and
4. Closing of proceedings, not to mention potential pre- and post-arbitral moves.

Under these four subgenres in turn lies a series of interrelated and interconnected moves and intertextual occurrences instantiated in smaller genres (rules and regulations embedded in Articles and/or Sections) (see Table 3.1).

Our analysis will make an attempt to show how smaller genres under each of the subgenres in the materials are sequentially and hierarchically interrelated and interconnected, guiding the participants towards successful and appropriate moves and contributing to the instantiation of the international arbitration system of genres.

International Arbitration System of Genres

International arbitration is a 'highly specialized discourse domain with specific moves and specific rules governing the success of those moves' (Bazerman 1994: 97). Although displaying possible variations, the process is becoming increasingly complex and multi-tiered nowadays as in the cases of multiple-party arbitrations and/or large, complex commercial disputes.[4] Thus it is reasonable to say that parties who wish to have recourse to arbitration will go through 'a thick file' (Bazerman,

4 See American Arbitration Association Commercial Rules and Regulations Including Procedures for Large, Complex Commercial Disputes at <http://www.adr.org/sp.asp?id=22440>, accessed 15 June 2011.

1994: 96) of intentions, negotiations, choices and proceedings. Broadly speaking, an arbitration process will not be initiated unless there is an agreement between the parties; the agreement, in turn, will not be valid unless there is appointment of an arbitration tribunal to conduct arbitral proceedings; arbitral proceedings will not be conducted unless some governing rules are stated and an award is made and, finally, the arbitration will not be completed unless and until the award is enforced. In what follows we display how the process of international arbitration works in terms of a system of genre.

Commencing the Arbitration

Before commencing the arbitration process itself, the parties have to go through some essential pre-arbitral moves or acts, which, without them, the process would not be successful. The parties must be bound by some kind of commercial arbitrable contract wherein they agree on settling any dispute arising out of it by means of arbitration.

Therefore, if and only if a dispute arises, the process of arbitration commences setting up the bases for the follow-up moves or acts (see Figure 3.2).

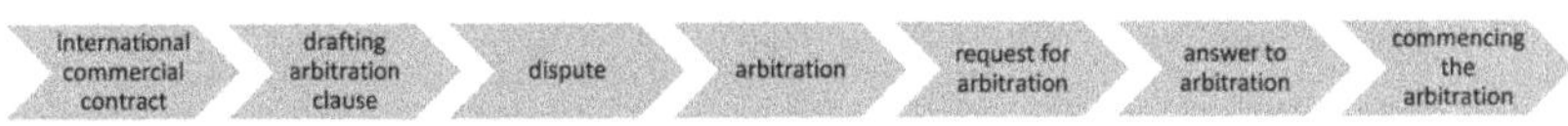

Figure 3.2 Commencing the arbitration

The essence of arbitration lies in the written arbitration clause included in a contract or in an arbitration agreement signed by the parties under the New York Convention. Major arbitration chambers provide for short and simple model clauses which include:

a. all 'requisite elements' and wording required for its validity and enforcement, such as the clearly expressed intention of the parties to arbitrate, the arbitration institute or the rules for *ad hoc* arbitration and the number of arbitrators[5] and/or
b. 'recommended elements' which may or may not be included by the parties, such as the place of arbitration and effects of the arbitral award (Liu 2006).

If not properly drafted, arbitration clauses may lead to unwanted consequences or another dispute and/or litigation:

5 Institutional arbitration is administered by a functional arbitral institution or chamber covering all legal and procedural aspects of the process; whereas *ad hoc* arbitration is administered by the arbitrators themselves who have the burden of scheduling all the moves and provide for the administration of the process.

1. Any dispute arising out of or in connection with the present contract shall be finally settled under the Rules of Arbitration of the International Chamber of Commerce by one or more arbitrators appointed in accordance with the said Rules (ICC).
2. Any litigation resulting from the contract hereunder, including its interpretation or execution, shall be definitely settled by arbitration, in accordance with the Guidelines of the Arbitration Center of the Brazil–Canada Chamber of Commerce by three (03) arbitrators appointed pursuant to said Guidelines (CCBC).

It is worth pointing out that the wordings 'finally settled' in the materials will constrain the following moves of the process insofar as the parties, once having decided to arbitrate, will not be able to have recourse to litigation or to any other means of dispute resolution.

Seen from a linguistic perspective, an arbitration clause is a conventionalized genre which should meet the requirements of syntactic consistency, conventionalized terminology and adequate and/or accurate multilingual versions, in order to avoid linguistically pathological clauses.

After the effectiveness of the arbitration clause, the arbitration process is set in motion with appropriate rhetorical exchanges such as a request for arbitration. In the legal context of international arbitration, a request is 'not only recognizable, but must compulsorily be taken as such by certain people structurally employed to receive requests' (Bazerman 1994: 91). In the ICC Rules, the request for arbitration is related to the prior move of the commencement of arbitration and sets the bases for the follow-up move of answering to the request. Successful moves of both the Claimant and the Respondent can only be met by a limited range of responses: that is, a response to the request or a counterclaim, by filing a response within 30 days containing the information required.

3. Article 4 – Request for Arbitration (ICC)

1. A party wishing to have recourse to arbitration under these Rules shall submit its Request for Arbitration (the 'Request') to the Secretariat, which shall notify the Claimant and Respondent of the receipt of the Request and the date of such receipt.

Article 5 – Answer to the Request; Counterclaims

1. Within 30 days from the receipt of the Request from the Secretariat, the Respondent shall file an Answer ('the 'Answer') which shall, inter alia, contain the following information:

The CCBC Rules provide for follow-up moves to commencing arbitration: there is a prior document granting the Center's competence to conduct the arbitration process which is required to be attached to the contract. The Center then has to send both parties a copy of such document and other information:

4. Section 5 – Institution of Arbitration (CCBC)

5.1. The party, in a separate document containing a compromise clause which establishes the Center's competence to decide on contractual disputes by means of arbitration, shall notify the Center of its intention to arbitrate, declaring forthwith upon, the nature of the dispute, the amount involved and the name and relevant data of the other party, attaching a counterpart of the relevant contract.

5.2. The Center shall send the other party a copy of this notification, as well as the list of names of those who integrate the Panel of Arbitrators and a counterpart of these Rules, inviting said party to appoint one arbitrator and the respective alternate within a 15 day period. Identical communication shall be sent to the other litigant who will have the same period to appoint his arbitrator and the respective alternate.

Although it is beyond the scope of this chapter, it would be interesting to investigate the role of time limits in influencing the smaller genres they are embedded within and which will have consequences for other genres to follow.

Soon after the effect of the arbitration agreement, wherein the parties 'shall be deemed to have submitted *ipso facto* to the Rules in effect of the date of commencement of the arbitration proceedings' (ICC Arbitration Rules, Article 6.1), the composition of the membership of arbitral tribunal starts.

Composition of Arbitral Tribunal

The composition of the arbitral tribunal is said to be one of the most important steps in an arbitration agreement with consequences for the moves or acts to follow. According to Miles (2003: 219):

> The skills and qualifications of the arbitrator(s) and the number of members on the tribunal may have a significant impact on the development of the dispute resolution process and, ultimately, the award itself.

Among the main issues involved in the composition of the arbitral tribunal are the qualifications and skills required of those sitting as arbitrators, the appointment of lawyers *versus* non-lawyers and the number of arbitrators, either sole or panels of three (Miles 2003; Jones 2006). The decisions upon these issues will frame the follow-up genres that instantiate the composition of arbitral tribunal and later on

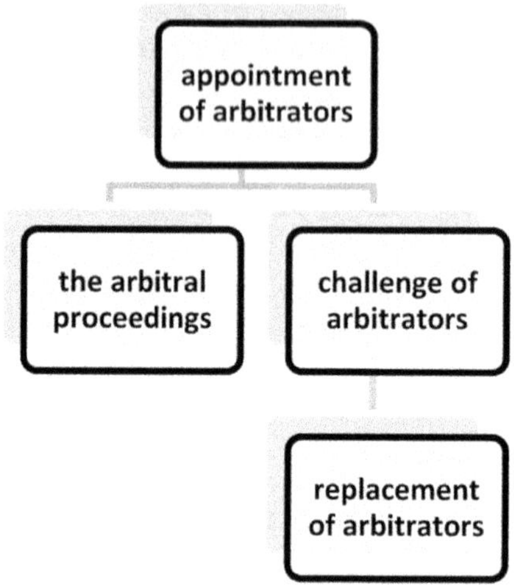

Figure 3.3 Appointment of arbitrators
Source: Author.

the conduct of arbitral proceedings. On the other hand, if unexpected outcomes happen to result from the appointment of arbitrators, such as challenge, death, resignation of arbitrator or others, then new moves concerning the replacing of the arbitrators start, which may result in potential delays and/or costs to the process, before the conduct of arbitral proceedings may even begin (see Figure 3.3).

The ICC Rules are not specific about the arbitrators' qualifications and do not require that an arbitrator be a lawyer. However, as pointed out in Miles (2003: 221):

> in practice the ICC Court's tendency is still to ensure that arbitrators are either trained in or otherwise familiar with the law likely to be applied in the arbitration:

5. The Arbitral Tribunal (ICC)

Article 7

General Provisions

1. Every arbitrator must be and remain independent of the parties involved in arbitration.

Article 8

Number of Arbitrators

1. The dispute shall be decided by a sole arbitrator or by three arbitrators.

Article 9

Appointment and confirmation of arbitrators

1. … the Court shall consider the prospective arbitrator's … ability to conduct the arbitration in accordance with these Rules …

The CCBC Rules are also vague about the arbitrators' qualifications and do not prevent the appointment of non-lawyers as arbitrators as long as they have 'spotless reputation and recognized technical skills' (3.1.).

6. Section 3 – Panel of Arbitrators (CCBC)

3.1. The arbitrators will be chosen among professionals of spotless reputation and recognized technical skill.

Section 5 – Institution of Arbitration

5.6. The parties may agree that arbitration be conducted by a sole arbitrator, appointed by the parties by joint consent, alternate included, within a 15 (fifteen) day period … The institution of arbitration with a sole arbitrator shall follow the same proceedings set forth in these Rules for the arbitration with three arbitrators.

Section 6 – Arbitration Tribunal

6.2. Any person who may be in the following situations cannot be appointed as an arbitrator:

a. is a party of the dispute;
b. has intervened in the settlement of the dispute, as attorney at law of one of the parties, or has acted as witness, expert, or presented any opinion, legal or otherwise;
c. is consort, relative of one of the parties, related by blood or by affinity, in 'linea recta' or collateral, up to the third degree of kindred;
d. is consort, relative of one of the parties, related by blood or affinity, in linea recta or collateral, up to the second degree of kindred, of the lawyer or attorney of one of the parties;
e. takes part in a directorate or administrative body of a corporation that is shareholder or part to the dispute;
f. is a close friend or enemy of one of the parties;

g. is creditor or debtor of one of the parties or its consort, or even relatives, in linea recta or collateral, up to the third degree of kindred;
h. is presumptive heir, donee, employer, employee of one of the parties;
i. receives gifts before or after the beginning of the dispute, advises any of the parties about the object of the dispute or provides resources to meet the arbitration costs;
j. is interested in the settlement of the dispute, on behalf of one of the parties;
k. has acted as a mediator or conciliator, before the institution of the arbitration, except if otherwise agreed by the parties.

Differently however, the CCBC Rules narrow the appointment of potential arbitrators by stipulating the persons who are not qualified for being arbitrators though 'parties ought to be careful not to restrict their options unnecessarily from the outset' (Miles 2003: 22).

Once all the required conditions for a successful constitution of the arbitral tribunal are met, what seems to be the longest and most complex move of the process begins – the conduct of arbitral proceedings – as this may involve third parties and discovery of additional written evidence.

Conduct of Arbitral Proceedings

The conduct of arbitral proceedings comprises a series of constitutive rules[6] whose purpose is to 'assist arbitration practitioners by listing and briefly describing questions on which appropriately timed decisions on organizing arbitral proceedings may be useful'.[7] Also:

> Laws governing the arbitral procedure and arbitration rules that parties may agree upon typically allow the arbitral tribunal broad discretion and flexibility in the conduct of arbitral proceedings. This is useful in that it enables the arbitral tribunal to take decisions on the organization of the proceedings that take into account the circumstances of the case, the expectations of the parties and of the members of the arbitral tribunal, and the need for a just and cost-efficiency resolution of the dispute.

One of the common rules embedded in the arbitral proceedings concerns hearings. A hearing is a move involving the taking of oral evidence of witnesses and may be

6 Constitutive rules are used 'to supply information concerning the application of the [rules] or part of it' (Kurzon 1986: 23).

7 UNCITRAL Notes on Organizing Arbitral Proceedings, <http://www.uncitral.org/pdf/english/texts/arbitration/arb-notes/arb-notes-e.pdf>, accessed 15 June 2011.

conducted by either direct or cross-examination involving parties and witnesses. In the case of experts and expert witnesses, either the arbitral tribunal may appoint the expert or the parties may present expert witnesses on points at issue. The manner of taking oral evidence and the degree of control exercised over the hearings are at the discretion of the arbitral tribunal. One of the various possibilities is that:

> a witness is first questioned by the arbitral tribunal, whereupon questions are asked by the parties, first by the parties who called the witness. Another possibility is for the witness to be questioned by the party presenting the witness and then by the other party or parties, while the arbitral tribunal might pose questions during the questioning or after the parties on points that in the tribunal's view have not been sufficiently clarified.[8]

Hearings may also be preceded by various pre-moves, such as the issuance of a summons, that is, the order to appear in court by the issuance of a written summons, as in the ICC Rules:

7. **Article 21 (ICC)**

    1. When a hearing is to be held, the Arbitral Tribunal, giving reasonable notice, shall summon the parties to appear before it on the day and at the place fixed.
    2. If any of the parties, although duly summoned, fails to appear without valid excuse, the Arbitral Tribunal shall have the power to proceed with the hearing.

On the other hand, the Arbitral Tribunal's discretion in a case where one of the parties 'fails to appear without valid excuse' may generate possible follow-up moves before the hearing: either the hearing proceeds without it or else the Tribunal calls for other moves.

In the CCBC Rules, hearings are preceded by some pre-moves instantiated by smaller oral and written genres such as a preliminary hearing, appointment of secretariat, 'written allegations' for presentation of written documentary evidence and notification date:

8. **Section 9 – Procedure (CCBC)**

    9.1. Once instituted the arbitration, the chairperson of the Arbitration Tribunal may call the parties and the other arbitrators for a

---

8 American Arbitration Association Commercial Rules and Regulations Including Procedures for Large, Complex Commercial Disputes at <http://www.adr.org/sp.asp?id=22440>, accessed 15 June 2011.

preliminary hearing, whereat a secretary *ad hoc* shall be appointed. The parties shall be clarified in connection with the proceedings, and the necessary decisions to regulate the development of arbitration shall be taken.

9.2. The parties shall present their written allegations, indicating the evidences they intend to produce, within a 10 (ten) day period, counted from the hearing date, if any, or from the notification date when sent with such objective.

9.15. In case of expert evidence, the instruction hearing shall be summoned in a period not exceeding 30 (thirty) days from the delivery of the expert's report. In case no expert evidence has been requested, the instruction hearing, if necessary, shall take place within a 30-day period, to be counted from the end of the period mentioned in Article 9.3.

Oral hearings may also be held by hearing witnesses and/or experts appointed by the parties upon request (ICC Rule, Section 9.15 above). A person may be qualified as an expert when he/she 'has specialized knowledge gained by education, training, experience or skill' (Haydock and Sonsteng 1994: 192). Therefore, expert examination is the questioning of an expert of a particular knowledge to assist the parties and arbitrators 'in understanding the evidence or in determining a fact that is in issue' (Haydock and Sonsteng 1994: 192). We assume that the hearing of expert evidence constitutes a specific smaller genre within the small generic structure of hearings as a consequence of its extra-legal intertextual nature. Hearings, as conducted in the materials, are instantiated in generic forms which can also be hierarchically represented (see Figure 3.4).

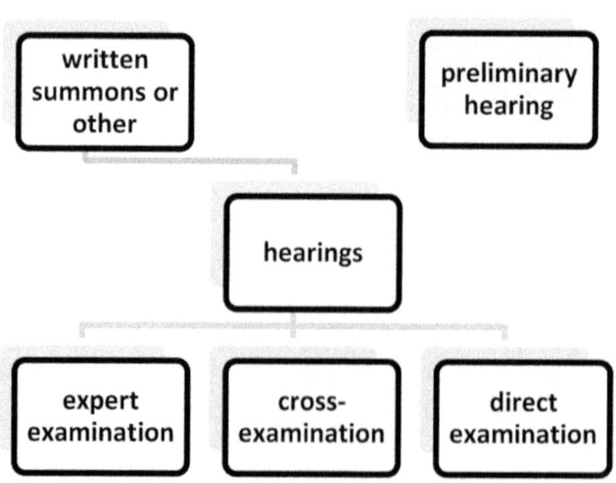

Figure 3.4 Hearings
Source: Author.

In closing the hearings, the arbitral tribunal will normally assume that no further proof is to be offered or submission to be made.[9] However, some follow-up moves can be allowed, such as notes summarizing the oral arguments as long as they do not refer in particular to new evidence or to new arguments.

Closing of the Proceedings

As a rule, arbitral proceedings are closed when 'the hearing is over and the arbitrator[s] is in his/her office with several notebooks full of evidence, the parties' submissions, their pleadings and the advocates' closing submissions' (Tessuto 2008: 181). Although there are no specific or fixed rules guiding the drafting of arbitral awards, awards are conventionalized genres whose tendency is towards relying 'more on content rather than formal features of writing' (Tessuto 2008: 182).

The award shall state the 'reasons' and/or the 'basis' for the decision. For that purpose, it must make clear what the legal authority of the document is, who the parties are, and what they are required to do, what the legal basis for that requirement is and why that legal basis applies to the matter (Hartwell, undated):

> **9. Article 22 – Closing of the Proceedings (ICC)**
>
> 1. When it is satisfied that the parties have had a reasonable opportunity to present their cases, the Arbitral Tribunal shall declare the proceedings closed. Thereafter, no further submission or argument may be made, or evidence produced, unless requested or authorized by the Arbitral Tribunal.
> 2. When the Arbitral Tribunal has declared the proceedings closed, it shall indicate to the Secretariat an approximate date by which the draft Award will be submitted to the court for approval pursuant to Article 27. Any postponement of that date shall be communicated to the Secretariat by the Arbitral Tribunal. (ICC)
>
> **Article 23 Awards**
>
> 2. The award shall state the reasons upon which it is based.

In the CCBC Rules, the closing of the proceedings occurs after the award is made and enforced.

9 American Arbitration Association Commercial Rules and Regulations Including Procedures for Large, Complex Commercial Disputes at <http://www.adr.org/sp.asp?id=22440>, accessed 15 June 2011.

10. **Section 10 Award (CCBC)**

10.5. The award shall necessarily contain:

a. a report with the names of the parties and a summary of the dispute;
b. the basis for the decision, which will settle questions of fact and law, with express statement, when needed, of having been pronounced '*ex aequo et bono*';
c. the decision, with all its specifications and term for the fulfillment of the decision, in case of need; and (d) the day, month, year and place where it was pronounced.

- -

10.7. Upon the award pronunciation, the arbitration will be concluded, and the chairperson of the Arbitration Tribunal shall send a counterpart of the decision to the parties, by mail or by any other means of communication, or, by handing it over personally to the parties against receipt.

The alternative moves for closing of the proceedings are shown in Figure 3.5.

Figure 3.5 Closing of proceedings
Source: Author.

After the rules for the closing of proceedings, both materials provide for some operational rules which in fact consist of pre-arbitral moves since decisions must be taken at the commencing of arbitration such as interpretation, language, waiver and so on. One particularly interesting subgenre is the one related to costs and fees and which deserve further investigation:[10] there is usually an advance to cover the costs of arbitration paid at the commencing of the process, decisions as to the costs of arbitration (including administrative expenses and arbitrator's fees) specified in illustrative tables provided by the institution.

Final Remarks

Multidisciplinary investigations into international arbitration procedures have clearly shed some light on how the whole process is conducted in terms of its communicative purposes, shared legal knowledge and acquisition of generic competence by the parties. If, from a legal perspective, arbitration has been constantly evolving to accommodate standard common-law litigative mechanisms and tools in the current multicultural and multilegal contexts where it is used, on the discourse level, the trend is towards the harmonization of discourse in various genres, subgenres and smaller genres to fulfill the success conditions of the process.

This chapter has addressed international arbitration as a system of genres with the aim of not only identifying the full interaction embedded within the system but also with the aim of guiding the actors towards a limited range of genres to fulfill the conditions for a successful arbitration process. Moreover, as in previous studies, our concern is focused on non-English speaking and civil law experts (such as Brazilians) who face challenges in seeking to act in a more effective manner when taking part in international arbitrations. Our purpose here is to suggest that Bazerman's (1994) notion of system of genres can help in discovering what is partly or completely unknown by such experts and in providing them with 'more favorable lines of actions' (Bazerman 1994: 97) once the current understanding of the generic system is known and mastered.

10 See ICC Rules, articles 30, 31 ('Costs') and Appendix III and CCBC Rules, Section 12 ('Fees, Charges, Compensation and Expenses').

Appendix The Data's Textual Organization

ICC ARBITRATION RULES	CCBC RULES
INTRODUCTORY PROVISIONS	Section 1 – Submission to the Present Rules
Article 1 – International Court of Arbitration	
Article 2 – Definitions	
Article 3 – Written Notifications or Communications; Time Limits	
COMMENCING THE ARBITRATION	Section 2 – Object and Composition of the Center
Article 4 – Request for Arbitration	
Article 5 – Answer to the Request; Counterclaims	
Article 6 – Effect of the Arbitration Agreement	
THE ARBITRAL TRIBUNAL	Section 3 – Panel of Arbitrators
Article 7 – General Provisions	
Article 8 – Number of Arbitrators	
Article 9 – Appointment and Confirmation of the Arbitrators	
Article 10 – Multiple Parties	
Article 11 – Challenge of Arbitrators	
Article 12 – Replacement of Arbitrators	
THE ARBITRAL PROCEEDINGS	Section 4 – Headquarters
Article 13 – Transmission of the File to the Arbitral Tribunal	
Article 14 – Place of Arbitration	
Article 15 – Rules Governing the Proceedings	
Article 16 – Language of the Arbitration	
Article 17 – Applicable Rules of Law	
Article 18 – Terms of Reference; Procedural Timetable	
Article 19 – New Claims	
Article 20 – Establishing the Facts of the Case	
Article 21 – Hearings	
Article 22 – Closing of the Proceedings	
Article 23 – Conservatory and Interim Measures	

Appendix Continued

ICC ARBITRATION RULES	CCBC RULES
AWARDS Article 24 – Time Limits for the Award Article 25 – Making of the Award Article 26 – Award by Consent Article 27 – Scrutiny of the Award by the Court Article 28 – Notification, Deposit and Enforceability of the Award Article 29 – Correction and Interpretation of the Award	Section 6 – Arbitration Tribunal
COSTS Article 30 – Advance to Cover the Costs of the Arbitration Article 31 – Decision as to the Costs of the Arbitration	Section 7 – Parties and Attorneys
MISCELLANEOUS Article 32 – Modified Time Limits Article 33 – Waiver Article 34 – Exclusion of Liability Article 35 – General Rule	Section 8 – Notifications and Terms
	Section 9 – Procedure
	Section 10 – Award
	Section 11 – Fulfillment of Award
	Section 12 – Fees, Charges, Compensation and Expenses
	Section 13 – Interpretation
	Section 14 – Effectiveness
	Section 15 – Mediation

References

Bazerman, Charles (1994): Systems of Genres and the Enactment of Social Intentions. In Freedman, Aviva and Meadway, Peter (Eds) *Genre and the New Rhetoric*, London, Taylor & Francis, 79–104.

Bhatia,Vijay K., Candlin, Christopher N. and Engberg, Jan (Eds) (2008a): *Legal Discourse across Cultures and Systems*, Hong Kong, Hong Kong University Press.

Bhatia,Vijay K., Candlin, Christopher N. and Engberg, Jan (2008b): Concepts, Contexts and Procedures in Arbitration Discourse. In Bhatia,Vijay K., Candlin, Christopher N. and Engberg, Jan (Eds) *Legal Discourse across Cultures and Systems*, Hong Kong, Hong Kong University Press, 3–31.

Devitt, Amy J. (1991): Intertextuality in Tax Accounting: Generic, Referential and Functional. In Bazerman, Charles and Paradis, James (Eds) *Textual Dynamics of the Professions*, Madison, WI, University of Wisconsin Press, 336–57.

Frade, Celina (2004): Generic Variation across Legislative Writing: A Contrastive Analysis of the UNCITRAL Model Law and Brazil's Arbitration Law, *Hermes, Journal of Linguistics*, Vol. 32, 45–75.

Frade, Celina (2009): Generic Variation in Cross-Examination across Legal Systems. In Šarčević, Susan (Ed.) *Legal Language in Action: Translation, Terminology, Drafting and Procedural Issues*, Zagreb, Globus, 377–91.

Giddens, Anthony (1984): *The Constitution of Society: Outline of the Theory of Structuration*, Cambridge, Polity Press.

Hartwell, Geoffrey M.B. (undated): The Reasoned Award in International Arbitration. Online at <http://www.hartwell.demon.co.uk/intaward.htm>, accessed 15 June 2011.

Haydock, Roger and Sonsteg, John (2004): *Examining Witnesses: Direct, Cross, and Expert Examinations*, Eagan, MN, West Publishing Company.

Jones, Doug (2006): Acquisition of Skills and Accreditation in International Arbitration, *Arbitration International*, Vol. 22, No. 2, 275–89.

Kurzon, Dennis (1986): *It is Hereby Performed ... Explorations in Legal Speech Acts*, Amsterdam, John Benjamins.

Liu, Xiaohong (2006): Achieving Effectiveness of Arbitration Clauses – A Practical Survey from a Chinese Legal Perspective, *US-China Law Review*, Vol. 3, No. 6 (Serial Number 19), 33–41.

Miles, Wendy (2003): Practical Issues of Appointment of Arbitrators: Lawyers vs. Non-Lawyer and Sole Arbitrator vs. Panel of Three (or More), *Journal of International Arbitration*, Vol. 20, No. 3, 219–32.

Swales, John M. (1990): *Genre Analysis: English in Academic and Research Settings*, Cambridge, Cambridge University Press.

Tessuto, Girolamo (2008): Discourse Systems in English Arbitration Awards. In Bhatia, Vijay K., Candlin, Christopher N. and Engberg, Jan, (Eds) *Legal Discourse across Cultures and Systems*, Hong Kong, Hong Kong University Press, 181–97.

Chapter 4
Evidence, Oral Testimony, and Cross-interrogatory in International Arbitration

Fabio E. Ziccardi

Evidence in Different Systems of Law

The aim of this chapter is to assess how linguistic issues are presently dealt with in the practice (and rules, if any) of international commercial arbitration (ICA) in the area of evidence. Given the multidisciplinary environment of this volume, it might be proper to recall that evidence, in a legal approach, includes the technical tools through which facts submitted by the parties to a judicial proceeding of any kind, criminal or civil, including those submitted to arbitration, may become the proper basis for any judicial decision. Here we refer to 'evidence', not mere allegations or pleadings, because a legal, and even more a judicial decision has to be based on findings of fact (and of law), not on persuasion, and such findings are legally reached only insofar as they are either admitted by the party other than the one submitting the fact, so that the facts are no longer disputed,[1] or duly evidenced during the proceeding, usually during a specific part of it, well known in English as 'trial'.

As a fundamental part of a legal proceeding, evidence is, or – as we shall see – should be, regulated by provisions of law, either set in codes or part of customary law, as is the case in many common law countries. One of the issues posed by evidence in international arbitration is the frequent absence of a similar body of rules, and an existing trend to avoid recourse to such regulations – in the few cases they are available – governing the taking of evidence in an arbitration 'trial'.

Let us also add that evidence, always in a legal sense, may be divided into two great classes: written evidence, documents, existing evidence,[2] on one side,

1 It may be semantically noteworthy to recall that the Italian judiciary practice, albeit not the law, describes such undisputed facts as *pacifici* [peaceful], in the sense that there is 'peace' between the parties on them; and evidence on such facts is not admitted, because it would not be useful.

2 This class includes also further material evidence, such as goods, the production of which is allegedly in breach of a patent; such 'three-dimensional' evidence is of course of crucial importance in criminal proceedings (for example, a weapon in a murder case), less

and oral evidence – in the English approach – or evidence to be formed within the proceeding, on the other side.[3]

Domestic rules concerning those classes of evidence differ greatly in criminal and civil laws of procedures, being generally more detailed in the former group of laws; and also differ greatly among the many national laws, not necessarily following the 'great divider' between civil law countries and common law countries, however fundamental it may be.[4]

In fact, while common law countries keep a remarkable uniformity in this area of the law,[5] rules on evidence in countries which may be fairly described as pertaining to the civil law group, thus with traceable elements going back to the Roman law experience, have quite different approaches to the development of a civil proceeding, as they have many times changed its forms, sometimes multiplying such forms even beyond logic,[6] and present today sets of rules formally and substantially quite apart from each other, in the sense that a practitioner of Country A (for example, Italy) must be carefully instructed in order to follow, we

---

in civil cases, where often it is brought to the court's attention indirectly, through the action of an expert, as will be detailed later in this work. Even a piece of land may be used as evidence, for example, in a case where pollution or other forms of trespass or nuisance are alleged. All those kinds of evidence, needless to say, do not raise any linguistic problems.

3 In Italian, legal theory, once more not the law, has adopted the creative terms *prove costituite*, or 'evidence already formed', and *prove costituende*, or 'evidence to be formed'. The common law evidence described as 'affidavit', a document issued, and usually sworn by a likely witness, is – from a legal point of view – an anticipation of oral evidence, superseded by the testimony itself, if taken, or becoming written evidence if not challenged by the party other than the one who produces it (cf. also n. 1 above, and observations later in this section).

4 Scholars in comparative law are noting with increasing frequency that the ever growing importance of statutory law (including that of EU origin in the UK and in Eire), on one side, and of case law, on the other side, are making the two systems increasingly converge. Most sincerely, this author is still of the opinion that the two groups of systems remain instead quite apart, especially in daily judiciary practice, which remains the core of a national law system's life, as is proved even by the fact that, within each group, language is usually the only obstacle to the full understanding of a foreign rule of (substantial!) law, of a brief, of a court decision; if coming from the 'other' group, instead, rules, briefs and court decisions often need, albeit not always, the legal cultural mediation of an expert: a Scottish decision may need more than a translation to be understood by an Italian legal practitioner; to the contrary, an Argentinean or Turkish decision (Turkey has codes based on, in fact translated from, the Swiss model), once translated, is 'ready for consumption' by the lawyer educated in the civil law tradition.

5 This uniformity is often unnoticed by practitioners of those countries, who give possibly too much weight to difference in the technicalities of posing questions, opposing them, and to the grounds for such oppositions, or 'objections'; but such differences are far from being structural.

6 As of today, in Italy there is – at least – an ordinary proceeding, a quick proceeding for money orders, and special proceedings for industrial relations and leases litigation, for family litigation, for insolvency litigation.

are not saying to act, the taking of evidence in Country B (for example, Spain), although the substantial laws, the civil codes in the submitted examples, are very similar in their words and in their legal meaning.

This has a specific effect on the issue under exam here: the common law system of evidence is more or less one based on the pre-emption of the oral evidence taken at the trial over the existing evidence, which remains in principle an 'anticipation' of evidence, in the sense that each document may in theory be debated at the trial, and only the fact that a document remains unchallenged makes it a piece of evidence; of course any frivolous challenge of documents is bitterly appraised by courts, and even more by juries.

In the many systems pertaining to the civil law group such similar elements fail, the relationship between documents and oral testimony may be unclear (in Italy, but not only here, the production of a document makes the oral testimony over the same fact no longer useful, and thus not admissible), and the whole procedure certainly does not supply a uniform, alternative model of administering evidence.

In an international environment, and particularly in international arbitration, taking also into account the entirely different nature of any 'domestic' reference given by the practice of ordinary courts of law, each class of evidence may create different linguistic problems, which will be shortly described below.

Issues Concerning Documents in International Commercial Arbitration

Documents in a language other than the one (if one!)[7] of the arbitration proceeding may need translation, and this causes a first important linguistic issue, usually considered a 'technical problem', thus something other than a legal issue. It is maintained here that it is not so even in domestic ordinary litigation. As finely decided, for example, by the Italian Supreme Court of Cassation,[8] the production of the translation of a document into the language of the proceeding is not for the court, but is a burden of that party who has an interest to rely on such a document (and thus – but not necessarily[9] – of the party producing the 'alien' document itself).

7 The language of an arbitration proceeding is frequently designated by the parties in arbitration clauses; otherwise, the language of the agreement (of the whole contract, or of the arbitration agreement only) may be considered, in case of difference between the parties, as the arbitration language; but if the contract or agreement itself is bilingual, which is not so uncommon (with smaller Chinese companies presently, with Soviet State entities in the past – and with Russian companies now – possibly more in view of making some 'superior' review easier, than for real business or contractual reasons), the issue may be a preliminary, uneasy one.

8 Decision of the 1st civil div., 28 December 2006, no. 27593; the recent Spanish Code of Civil Procedure has a detailed, and yet in part unclear set of rules on translations and interpreters; it should be recalled that Spain is a multilingual country.

9 During the year 2008 this author faced twice the apparently ironical situation of having an interest – as defender of parties to Italian ordinary proceedings – in producing

If the other party or parties challenge such a translation, or a part of it, they have the burden to allege the subject matter of such differences, and the difference will be decided by the arbitration tribunal, possibly through an interim order, on the basis of the submissions of the parties, including those of their experts, and if needed – only if needed[10] – the tribunal will appoint an expert of its own: but the issue will be solved through more than a translation, through an order on it, because the litigated meaning of a document in the proceeding language will be the subject of a decision over the content of evidence, and thus it is a part of the decision of the case, and such a decision is a part of the arbitral tribunal's duties.[11]

Issues Concerning Oral Testimony in International Commercial Arbitration

Oral testimonies are usually divided into three classes: parties' testimony, eyewitnesses' testimony and expert testimony, albeit the third one, the expert testimony, cannot be considered as evidence in the strict sense in many procedural laws of the world. The first and second of those classes cause remarkable problems from a linguistic point of view, with direct effects on the legal assessment of such evidence.

The Parties' Testimony

The parties' testimony in civil proceedings, possibly even more in international commercial arbitration, is considered by the best arbitration practice as a powerful tool for reaching the 'truth' on the facts verified during the litigated relationship, and brought to the attention of the arbitration tribunal. Once more, it is maintained here that it is not necessarily so, even, albeit not only, for linguistic reasons. A party, or a party's duly appointed representative (a company's president), with specific experience in such a kind of 'ordeals', perfectly conversant in the arbitration language, be it his own or not, will almost certainly 'do better' than an opponent, speaking either in an oversimplified manner the language of the arbitration as a

---

accurate translations of documents in foreign languages (English and Dutch) produced by the adversary, with an inaccurate, meaningless translation in the former case, and with no translation at all in the latter, Dutch being possibly considered too exotic a language for finding a translator … in Rome (!); but the content of the two documents was in fact much more favourable to the interests of the parties 'against' whom they had been produced, than the opposite.

10 A 'working' knowledge of the many languages involved in an international arbitration may be, possibly should be, a requisite for selecting arbitrators.

11 This submission is fully consistent with one of the few provisions concerning translation which may be found in the world, but it is at the highest level: Art. 17 of the 1976 UNCITRAL Arbitration Rules; the parallel provision on translation of oral evidence (Art. 25.3) is less detailed.

totally 'alien' means of expression for him; or, if answering through an interpreter, with no chance to correct alterations – if any – of his intended meaning.

This might very easily lead to give little or lesser trust, or little or lesser weight to the interrogatory of such 'linguistically non-performing' parties. It should be recalled here that some domestic procedural laws, for example Italian law, attribute quite a limited importance to the parties' testimony, on the basis of a long historical experience, not necessarily to be rejected. Moreover, if the international arbitration practice favours such mere imitations of the common law tradition (which, if no party to the arbitration is a 'common lawyer', has no particular logic or legal foundation whatsoever), let the imitation be at least correct: interrogatories should be held by the parties' defenders (and should be followed by cross-interrogatory), not by the arbitrators as is frequently practiced, but only for few final, 'clarifying' questions. This would allow the arbitration tribunal to perform the fundamental task of reviewing the questions as posed by the parties' defenders (and under the objection of the other defenders), particularly as to their materiality to the litigated matters, fighting against the burdensome and basically unfair practice which the American profession has nicknamed 'fishing expedition', describing long rows of questions posed in the hope to find some favourable elements in the many confused answers of the 'other' party, suffering in the witnesses' box.

In fact, the full application of common law rules on who poses questions and who performs a review over them also fulfils the structural task of creating an adequate protection for the less 'performing' party under interrogatory against any risk of harassment, caused by a flood of non-pertinent questions: because, while it is 'easy'[12] to object to an adversary's question, it is not easy, and anyhow not advisable to challenge the arbitrators', and especially the chairman's questions. Arbitrators should avoid any excess of self-pride – sometimes it is not easy for them to behave this way – but if a defender tries to prevent his client from answering an arbitrator's question, this arbitrator will keep the impression that in that area that party has something to hide, and will be very keen on finding the answer in the many other pieces of evidence gathered during the proceeding.

Now, all this would allow a sometimes fundamental review of the interpreter's work too, in translating both the questions and the answers, as well as, if necessary, a review of the allegedly mistaken use by the party under interrogatory of a language other than his own. The defender who notes[13] that the interpreter has mistaken the translation of a question or of a party's answer is in fact opening a debate over such linguistic issues; and this debate shall be treated – as noted previously for the translation of documents – exactly in the same way as any other litigated issues on evidence, not just as a mere little 'technical' difficulty, because, once more, the issue at stake is a part of the evidence which is formed at the trial,

12 In fact, the task of objecting is not easy at all, and is one of the most appreciated skills of a lawyer.

13 Such oral notes are not even felt as objections, although they are technically such: objections on a linguistic issue.

and failure in such a formation would jeopardize the reliability of the basis for the tribunal's eventual decision: this is, and should be treated as, a legal issue, insofar as material to the case.

Eyewitnesses' Testimony

Most of these remarks also apply to eyewitnesses' testimony, possibly even to a greater scale; assuming – but this is no longer always a correct assumption – that the parties to an international arbitration are companies operating in a global market, the further assumption that its top officers, those representing companies in an arbitration, are conversant in a widely spoken foreign language, may be correct;[14] but witnesses may certainly not be selected because they are 'good fighters', but because they know the facts, they 'were there' (let us think of a litigation on a construction agreement involving decisions and further facts verified on the site, or during the loading on board of a cargo at a sea port), and because they are prepared to come, and render a deposition.[15]

A carpenter or a crane operator may be the best possible witness of what took place on a construction site or along a wharf. Seldom will they know the arbitration language, and often the way they speak their native language will go beyond the professional skills of an interpreter of the place of the arbitration, who knows perfectly, for example, Italian, not necessarily Genoese, or Neapolitan.[16] In those cases, as in those where the strict necessity of an interpreter arises during the same arbitration hearing, members of the same 'staff' of the two parties (junior lawyers, parties' employees, a chairman's aid) may be called to help, to translate.

In all those cases, compliance with well-established rules for taking testimony within a given procedural law is the best and only way for administering this part of the proceeding. If a common law approach is chosen – in our opinion, with the parties' consent, or deciding over disputed submissions, not on the basis of an *ex parte* arbitrators' decision only, even less an implied decision – witnesses will be questioned by the parties, and the other party will have an option to raise objections,

14 In fact, top officers of small medium businesses often do not know any language but their own native one, which is in turn not necessarily entirely similar to the national language, and this applies even more to big nations, with important dialect areas, and to individuals now in their fifties or older. In China, the percentage of company officers speaking only Chinese is still quite high.

15 While compulsory warrants for witnesses in arbitration do exist, but not everywhere, they might not compel witnesses to go abroad to give testimony: such orders are strictly 'national'.

16 In this author's experience, a skilled and brilliant interpreter from Italian into English and vice versa, operating in Köln, was overwhelmed by the purported Italian of a chief carpenter, speaking in fact a fluent dialect of the Bergamo Province; in the same arbitration, the purported English of a Japanese surveyor needed great common efforts in order to become understandable.

including those regarding the inaccurate translation of questions and answers, if any. Then, there will be the cross-interrogatory; at the very end, the arbitrators will pose additional questions. If other approaches are chosen, such as 'free' questions on items previously listed by the parties, which is a usual procedure in Switzerland enjoying some success in international arbitration, but promoting a chairman's investigating function, this might easily cause all the possible problems already noted, even, albeit certainly not only, in case of linguistic difficulties during the taking of testimony.

But if techniques of taking testimony other than the well-known common law one are selected, the arbitrators should be under an even stricter duty to detail which rules they will apply for solving all the disputed elements emerging during the interrogatories: who will question first, whether there will be a cross-interrogatory although not in a common law environment, and again if a redirect and a recross, and how linguistic difficulties will be dealt with.

Taking evidence needs rules, and usually these are not supplied by the Regulations of the Courts of International Arbitration, with – in this author's knowledge – only two exceptions:[17] the 18 March 1965 World Bank (or ICSID) Washington Convention on the Settlement of Investment Disputes, and the 1992 Regulation of CEMARC (*Centro de Mediación y Arbitraje de la Cámara Argentina de Comercio*).

The former, more exactly its *Rules of Procedures*,[18] set some principles on evidence, documents, testimony, experts and visits and inquiries in their Art. 33 through 37: witnesses are examined 'by the parties', not by the Tribunal (Art. 35.1), an element to be kept in mind in assessing the different trend, which is present in Europe, as noted; the parties' consent for altering the line of action set by such rules is constantly needed, a further point worth raising.

The Argentinean rules go further, providing a full set of rules on evidence in their Art. 22 through 30, an excellent example which deserves attention and possibly accurate imitation. It is noteworthy that the principles governing the taking of evidence selected by the Argentinean organization are fully consistent with the civil law tradition; in particular, the questions to be posed have to be submitted beforehand to the arbitration tribunal, which has a duty to cancel those stranger to the issues litigated in the arbitration proceeding (Art. 25). This would greatly help, of course, also the handling of disputes over linguistic issues, if any (although the Argentinean Regulations provide specifically for domestic litigation).

---

17 Art. 24 and 25 of the quoted 1976 UNCITRAL Arbitration Rules do provide for *Evidence and Hearings*, but the rules are so 'wide' in scope, that any technical means for taking evidence can be consistent with them: they are not procedural rules, but just a warning that evidence needs to be taken, during hearings.

18 Such Rules have been adopted by the Administrative Council of the International Centre for Settlement of International Disputes (ICSID), in order to implement the provisions of Art. 43 and 44 of the Convention.

The Expert Testimony

Another area concerning evidence in international arbitration which badly needs rules, and does not have any, is the one of expert testimony, where the sharp difference between the ways of administering such 'technical' evidence in common law and civil law countries is such as to create a real gap of communication between lawyers acting in one or the other system. In common law countries, expert witnesses are produced by the parties, the court or the arbitration tribunal listens to conflicting technical opinions, and makes a choice, whilst in civil law countries the court or the arbitration tribunal appoints its own expert (described as a court aid in some countries), and the latter will administer the technical debate between the parties' experts, will inspect things and places, and will report.[19]

The latter system is by far and large better, because it does not leave the court or the arbitration tribunal with the often rationally impossible task of making a choice between two solutions of problems almost totally unknown to the court or even to the arbitrators, to say the least in their technical nature. The choice between one system or the other by an arbitration tribunal should certainly undergo a formal procedural step, including parties' submissions and a tribunal's order, with an opinion, as short as it may be. It is also true that expert testimony in general seldom raises linguistic issues: expert witnesses in international arbitration are constantly selected taking into account also their linguistic abilities, and in the rare event that a 'unique' expert, having no competitor in his field of expertise, does not know the arbitration language, the selection of an adequate interpreter will be a part of the formation of such a particular way of taking evidence at a trial.

References

Blackaby, Nigel, Lindsey, David M. and Spinillo, Alessandro (Eds) (2003): *International Arbitration in Latin America*, The Hague, Kluwer Law International.

Campbell, Dennis and Meek, Susan (Eds) (2002): *The Arbitration Process*, The Hague, Kluwer Law International.

Caron, David D., Caplan, Lee M. and Pellonpää, Matti (2006): *The UNCITRAL Arbitration Rules: A Commentary*, Oxford, Oxford University Press.

Eijsvoogel, Peter V. (Ed.) (1994): *Evidence in International Arbitration Proceedings*, London, Graham & Trotman – Martinus Nijhoff.

19 Ironically, the alternative to the Court Appointed Expert is expressly provided for by the US Federal Rules on Evidence, but it is almost *never* used: neither lawyers nor judges appear to be prepared to waive their traditional, 'adversary' system, the only one existing in England.

Fouchard, Philippe, Gaillard, Emmanuel, Goldman, Berthold and Savage, John (1999): *Fouchard, Gaillard, Goldman on International Commercial Arbitration*, The Hague, Kluwer Law International.

Frick, Joachim G. (2001): *Arbitration and Complex International Contracts: With Special Emphasis on the Determination of the Applicable Substantive Law and on the Adaptation of Contracts to Changed Circumstances*, The Hague, Kluwer Law International – Schulthess.

Hirsch, Moshe (1993): *The Arbitration Mechanism of the International Centre for the Settlement of Investment Disputes*, Dordrecht, Nijhoff.

Holtzmann, Howard M. and Neuhaus, Joseph E.A. (1989): *Guide to the UNCITRAL Model Law on International Commercial Arbitration: Legislative History and Commentary*, Deventer-Boston, Kluwer-TMC Asser Instituut.

Lew, Julian D.M., Mistelis, Loukas A. and Kroll, Stefan M. (2003): *Comparative International Commercial Arbitration*, The Hague, Kluwer Law International.

Redfern, Alan and Hunter, Martin (2004): *Law and Practice of International Commercial Arbitration* (with Nigel Blackaby and Constantine Partasides), 4th edition, London, Sweet & Maxwell.

Rubino-Sammartano, Mauro (2001): *International Arbitration Law and Practice*, 2nd edition, The Hague, Kluwer Law International.

Sanders, Pieter (1989): *Arbitration in Settlement of International Commercial Disputes Involving the Far East and Arbitration in Combined Transportation*, Deventer, Kluwer.

Smit, Hans and Pechota, Vratislav (1997): *Arbitration Rules Issued by International Institutions*, London, Sweet & Maxwell.

Ziccardi, Fabio (2009): *Il Ruolo dell'ordine Pubblico nel Processo Arbitrale*. In: Rubino-Sammartano, Mauro, *Arbitrato, ADR, Conciliazione*, Torino, Zanichelli, 603–25.

Chapter 5
Enforcement of Arbitral Awards in Hong Kong: Legal and Political Challenges

Rajesh Sharma

Background

Post-1997 era Hong Kong, as a consequence of the unique status of Hong Kong under the policy of 'One Country, Two Systems', has been facing legal and political challenges relating to enforcement of foreign arbitral awards mainly from the mainland of China, Taiwan and Macao. In the context of this policy, the operation of the important legal instrument with regard to the enforcement of awards, that is, the New York Convention on Recognition and Enforcement of Arbitral Awards (NYC), has been affected, which in turn has affected the enforcement of awards in Hong Kong from the mainland of China, Macao and Taiwan. To some extent the enforcement of the mainland awards have been sorted out as a result of a reciprocal agreement to recognize and enforce arbitral awards in Hong Kong and the mainland emanating from each other's territory.[1] However, the enforcement of Macao and Taiwan awards has not been fully settled, at least from the arbitration lawyer's point of view. In addition, Hong Kong is now facing another challenge with regard to the enforcement of awards against a foreign State if that foreign State raises the defence of sovereign immunity in Hong Kong. All these issues need resolution as they are important in order to keep Hong Kong as a leading centre for dispute resolution.

This chapter will first give a short account of the legal regime applicable for the enforcement of awards from the mainland, Taiwan and Macao. Thereafter, it will discuss the issue of application of the sovereign immunity during the enforcement of awards. The discussion, it is hoped, will highlight the different views, interpretations and application of laws adopted by arbitration and litigation lawyers in the context of the application of the 'One Country, Two Systems' principle in Hong Kong.

1 The 'Arrangement Concerning Mutual Enforcement of Arbitral Awards Between the Mainland and the Hong Kong Special Administrative Region' was concluded in June 1999 and came into effect on 1 February 2000. The new Arbitration Ordinance of Hong Kong has included this Arrangement in sections 92–98 of the Ordinance.

Enforcement of the Mainland Awards

Before 1997, the application of the NYC was extended to Hong Kong by Britain. As Hong Kong was a British colony, the awards from the mainland were treated as the Convention awards.[2] Therefore, as per the NYC, mainland awards were enforceable like any other Convention awards from other countries. However, after 1997 the NYC was applicable in Hong Kong through the Peoples Republic of China (PRC), and therefore for other Convention awards the situation remained the same. As the NYC is an international treaty and China is the sovereign of Hong Kong, the application of the NYC for the enforcement of the mainland awards could not be applicable. In other words, the mainland awards were not considered as the Convention awards, and hence this created a legal vacuum for the mainland awards. This uncertainty created a setback for Hong Kong to project itself as the centre for arbitration. During that period an alternative route was adopted by some legal experts by invoking Section 2GG of the Arbitration Ordinance (Cap. 341), according to which an award made or given, whether in or outside of Hong Kong, by an arbitral tribunal is enforceable in the same way as a judgment of the court, but only with the leave of the court.[3] If the leave is granted then the court may enter a judgment in terms of the award. Another route was to bring an action at common law to enforce a mainland award in Hong Kong. The winning party in arbitration may through proceedings by writ apply to court for a summary judgment on the terms of the arbitral awards. In such proceedings the amount in the arbitral award is considered as debt and through summary proceedings the awarded amount could be recovered as debt. Undoubtedly, these two alternative routes were not considered as efficient as the NYC regime.

In order to pave the way for the enforcement of the mainland awards, the Hong Kong Government and the Central Government initiated the discussion pursuant to Article 95 of the Basic Law which provided for the judicial assistance between Hong Kong and the other parts of the mainland of China. In 1999 this negotiation finally culminated in the Arrangement Concerning Mutual Enforcement of Arbitral

---

2 Convention award means an award made in a country or territory which is signatory of the NYC. However, in the context of Hong Kong it means 'an arbitral award made in a State or the territory of a State, other than China or any part of China, which is a party to the New York Convention'. See section 2, New Hong Kong Arbitration Ordinance.

3 Section 2GG States:

> (1) An award, order or direction made or given in or in relation to arbitration proceedings by an arbitral tribunal is enforceable in the same way as a judgment, order or direction of the Court that has the same effect, but only with the leave of the Court or a judge of the Court. If that leave is given, the Court or judge may enter judgment in terms of the award, order or direction.
>
> (2) Notwithstanding anything in this Ordinance, this section applies to an award, order and direction made or given whether in or outside Hong Kong.

awards between the Mainland and the Hong Kong Special Administrative Region (1999 Arrangement), which came into effect in 2000. The 1999 Arrangement is based on the letter and spirit of the NYC. The process of enforcement is simple and the grounds for refusal of enforcement are the same as those in the NYC. Thus, the enforcement of the mainland awards in Hong Kong is now efficiently enforced as it was enforced under the NYC in the pre-1997 era.[4]

Enforcement of Taiwan Awards

The political realities of Taiwan have always been a dilemma for Hong Kong in its pre- as well as post-1997 era. Even the UK did not treat Taiwan as a sovereign country. Moreover, Taiwan is not a signatory to the NYC, therefore any award from Taiwan was never treated as a Convention award. Perhaps, to deal with this situation of Taiwan and many other countries which are not parties to the NYC, the Hong Kong Arbitration Ordinance enacted Section 2GG. This was the same section which came to rescue enforcement of the mainland awards after 1997 until the 1999 Agreement came into operation. According to the Section 2GG, Taiwan awards fall into the category of awards made 'outside' of Hong Kong. When a Taiwan award comes to Hong Kong for enforcement, the winning party may apply for leave to the court and once the court grants leave, a judgment in terms of the award is entered. It is needless to say that any Taiwan award can also be enforced within common law through a summary procedure as the recovery of debt. Although the two alternative routes of enforcement are available for the Taiwan awards, the courts in Hong Kong consider that either means of enforcement should not be radically different. In either case, the court's role should be as 'mechanistic as possible' and unless the award was plainly and obviously incapable of performance, the court should allow the application for its enforcement.[5]

Enforcement of Macao Awards

Hong Kong seemed to have little concern about making any particular arrangements for the enforcement of Macao awards. At the time when Hong Kong was making law to give effect to the 1999 Agreement, it was indicated that a similar arrangement for mutual enforcement of arbitral awards between Hong Kong and Macao should be finalized soon.[6] However, rapid economic development of Macao and a big

4 From 1999 to September 2010, the High Court of Hong Kong has processed nine applications to enforce Mainland awards in Hong Kong and all applications were granted. See LC Paper No. CB (2) 1129/10-11(01).

5 *Xiamen Xinjingdi Group Ltd. v. Eton Properties Ltd* [2008] 4 HKLRD 972 (at para 47 and 63).

6 LC Paper No. CB (2) 1129/10-11(01) also see LC Paper No. CB(2)2016/99-00.

influx of investment from overseas, including that from Hong Kong, coupled with the emphasis being placed on arbitration as the method of dispute resolution by the business community, meant that the Hong Kong Government decided to explore the potential of such arrangements. Any arrangement relating to mutual enforcement of awards between Hong Kong and Macao would be beneficial for Hong Kong because:

1. it would add certainty to the enforceability of Macao arbitral awards in Hong Kong and vice versa;
2. it would establish a simple mechanism in Hong Kong and Macao on reciprocal enforcement of arbitral awards;
3. it would foster legal cooperation between Hong Kong and Macao in civil and commercial matters; and
4. it would enhance Hong Kong's role as a regional arbitration centre for commercial disputes.[7]

With this view in mind, the Department of Justice (DoJ) of Hong Kong and the relevant departments of Macao consulted each other in late 2010 and showed their support for such a proposal. Therefore in January 2011, the Secretary for Justice of Hong Kong made an announcement that in order to foster closer legal cooperation with Macao, the DoJ would actively seek the signing of an arrangement on reciprocal recognition and enforcement of arbitral awards with Macao which would be based in the NYC and the 1999 Agreement.[8] Such agreement would be the first of its kind between two special administrative regions of PRC, that is, Hong Kong and Macao.

Although so far no award from Macao has come for enforcement in Hong Kong, it is possible to enforce any award from Macao either through enforcement by action or application for summary enforcement pursuant to Section 2GG of the Arbitration Ordinance. The Hong Kong Arbitration Ordinance has recently been amended but the provisions of Section 2GG have been incorporated in Section 84 of the New Arbitration Ordinance. In sum, until an arrangement is signed between Hong Kong and Macao, any award from Macao coming up for enforcement in Hong Kong may be enforced in the same manner as an award from Taiwan is enforced in Hong Kong.

Enforcement of Foreign Awards: A New Challenge

Foreign awards were always secured to be enforced in Hong Kong through the NYC route in Hong Kong both before or after 1997. However, due to the unique

7 LC Paper No. CB (2) 1129/10-11(01).

8 See the speech delivered by the Secretary of Justice at the Ceremonial Opening of the Legal Year 2011 on 10 January 2011.

legal situation of Hong Kong, a new challenge has surfaced if an award is enforced against a foreign State. This is a result of the uncertainty in the application of sovereign immunity principles. In the pre-1997 era, Hong Kong was following restrictive sovereign immunity similar to the approach in the UK.[9] However, the PRC follows an absolute immunity principle. The question remains as to what is the current approach in Hong Kong, that is, restrictive or absolute immunity approach. This issue came before the court in Hong Kong when a foreign State raised the issue of sovereign immunity in the case *FGH Hemisphere v. Democratic Republic of Congo ('FGH Case').*[10]

FGH, a New York based company, was the beneficiary of two arbitral awards because the original party to the arbitration, Energoinvest, a Yugoslav company, assigned entire benefits of principal and interest payable by the Democratic Republic of Congo (DRC) under the award rendered in Switzerland and Paris. The arbitration was conducted in accordance with the International Chamber of Commerce (ICC) rules. Knowing the good political and economic relationship between China and the DRC and the Chinese Government's plan to make massive investment in the DRC mainly for mineral exploitation rights in the DRC for which Chinese companies are supposed to pay a fee, FGH took out as originating summons seeking leave to enter judgment to enforce the awards against consortiums of the Chinese enterprises and seeking an injunction to prevent them from making those payments to the DRC. Those consortia are established in Hong Kong as a limited liability company (but are wholly-owned subsidiaries of the Chinese Railway Group Limited, a company incorporated in China with limited liability) and their stocks are listed in the Hong Kong stock market.

In the Court of First Instance, one of the many issues raised was whether the DRC had waived immunity by submitting itself to arbitration. The other related issues were whether after 1997 Hong Kong common law recognized the doctrine of restrictive sovereign immunity or whether immunity from suit was absolute. Although the Court of First Instance did not dwell upon an applicable principle of immunity, it did rule against FGH (and in favour of DRC) on the issue of waiver of immunity.[11] The question before the Court of Appeal was:

> Whether an application for leave to enforce an arbitral award made under the New York Convention against a State impleads that foreign State; whether the law of Hong Kong requires application of the doctrine of absolute State immunity from jurisdiction and execution, as opposed to the restrictive doctrine; and whether by agreeing to refer a dispute to arbitration in a New York Convention country, to be conducted according to the Rules of the ICC, a foreign State which is not

---

9 The UK legislated the State Immunity Act (1978), which set the trend that a State cannot take immunity for its commercial purposes.

10 CACV373/2008 & CACV 43/2009.

11 See FGH case, paras 21–22.

> a party to the Convention waives such State immunity from jurisdiction and execution to which it is otherwise entitled.[12]

In sum, the court was asked to decide on two issues:

1. what is the current practice of Hong Kong in relation to sovereign immunity, that is, it practices absolute immunity or restrictive immunity;
2. whether by agreeing to refer a dispute to arbitration in a the NYC country and as per ICC rules, a State also waives immunity to jurisdiction and execution.

The Court of Appeal is of the view that the doctrine of restrictive immunity currently continues to apply in Hong Kong.[13] The Court of Appeal has explicitly said:

> In my judgment, the application for leave to enforce the foreign arbitral award is an application that seeks to invoke the jurisdiction of the court and which, when directed at an award made against a foreign State, is an application that seeks to implead that State, so that the question of immunity from that jurisdiction is one which at that stage has to be raised and addressed, absent legislation to a broader effect, the submission of a foreign State to arbitration 'operates solely to remove State immunity from the first stage of arbitration in which the national courts exercise supervisory powers', so that in this case, the submission of the DRC to the ICC arbitration did not constitute waiver to the jurisdiction of the Hong Kong courts to consider an application for leave to enforce those awards, or waiver against execution.[14]

In conclusion, the Court of Appeal found that:

1. the DRC has not waived such immunity from jurisdiction and from execution as it enjoys;
2. the application for leave to enforce the foreign arbitral awards is a process that invokes the jurisdiction of the court and that impleads the DRC;
3. the DRC enjoys restrictive but not absolute immunity from the jurisdiction of the courts of Hong Kong;
4. leave should be given to enforce the arbitral awards; and
5. the DRC is not immune from execution in respect of such entry fees as may be due to the DRC and are not intended to be used for sovereign purposes.

---

12 See FGH case, para 2.

13 The FGH case was decided by a 2-1 majority. Justice Stock VP and Justice Yuen formed the majority, but Justice Yeung gave a dissenting opinion. The Court of Final Appeal has yet to give a final ruling on this issue.

14 Justice Stock VP; see FGH case, para 177.

The opinion of Justice Stock VP was supported by Justice Yuen JA (forming the majority view), who also in a separate opinion reached the same conclusion, albeit from a different route. Justice Yuen concluded that restrictive immunity was a customary international law and became part of the common law tradition which is now applicable in Hong Kong after 1997. Therefore, the DRC is subject to restrictive and not absolute immunity. Thus the majority view prevailed and the case went in favour of FGH and against the DRC.[15]

However, Justice Yeung JA, while giving dissenting opinion, respectfully disagreed with Justice Stock and opined that from a 'global perspective, and bearing in mind the constitutional provisions of the Hong Kong SAR as well as the unequivocal foreign policy of the PRC, DRC, in my view, enjoys absolute immunity'.[16] Justice Yeung also said in clear words that, 'The absolute immunity doctrine adopted by the PRC as part of its international legal obligation, applies to the Hong Kong SAR'.[17] Justice Yeung continued to provide a third reason for the decision, that is, 'the restrictive immunity doctrine is not part of the customary international law and therefore the DRC is entitled to absolute immunity, despite its submission to arbitration, had not waived its right to State immunity'.[18]

The majority decision in FGH is mainly based on the common law position in Hong Kong with regards to the application of the restrictive sovereign immunity. This reasoning of the court, therefore, raises an important question as to whether a legal tradition of system is a conclusive indication of the approach taken by a State with regards to the application of absolute or restrictive sovereign immunity.

Legal Traditions, Sovereign Immunity and Enforcement of Award

Legal traditions followed by any country may not be indicative of the practice followed by a State in respect of sovereign immunity. For example, just by knowing that a country follows common law tradition or civil law tradition is not sufficient to conclude as to whether that country will follow an absolute sovereign immunity or a restrictive sovereign immunity principle. It is a different matter that the leaders of common law tradition, that is, the USA and the UK, follow a restrictive sovereign immunity approach.[19] Similarly, there may be a general tendency among civil law countries to practice absolute immunity; nevertheless, legal traditions

15 See FGH case, Justice Yueng, para 246.

16 See FGH case, Justice Yeung, para 182.

17 See FGH case, Justice Yeung, para 224.

18 See FGH case, Justice Yeung, para 231.

19 The USA adopted the *Foreign Sovereign Immunity Act* (1974) and the UK legislated the *State Immunity Act* (1978), which set the trend that a State cannot take immunity for its commercial purposes. This may be said to be the established approach, at least in the common law.

cannot lead to conclude that all common law countries follow restrictive sovereign immunity and all civil law countries follow absolute sovereign immunity.

The majority opinion of the court in FGH is based on the fact that after 1997, the common law continues to apply in Hong Kong due Article 8 of the Basic Law.[20] It is submitted that in the FGH case, the court has taken a wrong approach in reaching the conclusion that Hong Kong SAR is currently practicing restrictive immunity simply because that was the position in the common law which continued to apply in Hong Kong after 1997. It is also true that before 1997, the *UK State Immunity Act*, 1978 ('the UK Act') was applicable in Hong Kong, and hence Hong Kong was practicing restrictive sovereign immunity. However, after 1997, this UK Act is no longer applicable and also no law of China equivalent to the UK Act was extended to or introduced in Hong Kong, which has created a statutory vacuum. In the absence of any statutory law and as a result of the operation of common law, the court applied common law position relating to sovereign immunity as applicable to Hong Kong before the UK Act was introduced. By tracing backwards the court found that the case law of *Mighelle*,[21] *Duff Development*[22] and other cases is binding on Hong Kong (and hence requires 'express' waiver), on which Justice Stock VP concluded, 'I would hold therefore that the common law of Hong Kong as at 30 June 1997 recognized the doctrine of restrictive immunity'.[23] The court further said:

> It must logically follow that the rule to be applied by the courts in Hong Kong remains that reflected by the restrictive doctrine unless the common law itself has changed. Since it cannot have changed by reason of any alteration in customary international law, it can only have changed if a change has been demanded by its constitutional and societal setting. The demand would, I suggest, have to be clear since there can be little doubt that the change would be regressive. By this, I do not refer to the obvious fact that it would return the common law to a position long abandoned but I refer rather to the assault which would be occasioned to the equal justice principle for which commercial litigants look to our courts. The equal justice principle is assailed when it permits State to utilize this jurisdiction as a forum when it suits them but to reject the forum when it does not, thus shutting out those who may have valid claims which have nothing to do with acts of a State in a sovereign, as opposed to a commercial, capacity.[24]

20 Article 8 of the Basic Law states 'The laws previously in force in Hong Kong, that is, the common law, rules of equity, ordinances, subordinate legislation and customary law shall be maintained, except for any that contravene this Law, and subject to any amendment by the legislature of the Hong Kong Special Administrative Region'.

21 *Mighelle v. Sultan of Johore* [1894] 1 Q.B. 149.

22 *Duff Development Company Limited v. Government of Kelantan* [1924] A.C. 797.

23 FGH case, para 122.

24 FGH case, para 81.

Though the court is speaking in a voice that brings cheer to the commercial world and to the supporters of Hong Kong as international arbitration centre, the reasoning of the court shows two fallacies. First, in the absence of a codified law (that is, the UK Act) and due to continuation of common law, the Hong Kong courts are required to follow the common law position before the UK Act came in force, that is, the common law position before 1978. Just prior to the UK Act, the UK was following absolute immunity. Therefore, before 1978 the rule of absolute immunity was applicable as part of common law which should continue to be applicable in Hong Kong after 1997. This is also supported by the fact that the UK Act being a statutory law replaces or displaces the existing common law, that is, absolute immunity when it came in effect in 1978. In other words, the common law position before 1978 remains under eclipse as a result of operation of the UK Act in the UK as well as Hong Kong. After 1997 the UK Act was withdrawn; that means the common law which was under eclipse became operative again and hence could be applied in Hong Kong. It is to be noted that Justice Stock accepted that this may happen when he said that, 'The obvious fact that it would return the common law to a position long abandoned'. At the same time he also stated that if that happens then it would cause an assault to the 'equal justice principle'. It was wrong for the judge not to reach the logical end of his own reasoning but to deviate from the logic as a result of other reasons, that is, 'equal justice principle'. It may be hard to accept but logically the common law position should revert back to the situation of absolute immunity in Hong Kong after 1997 as argued by Justice Stock VP, which would have been the correct approach.

Another fallacy in the logic of Justice Stock is that while discussing the situation of common law one important aspect of sovereign immunity was ignored, that is, only a sovereign can enjoy sovereign immunity. Sovereign immunity cannot exist in the absence of a sovereign itself. In the case of Hong Kong it is an undeniable fact which was also accepted by the court, that China is the sovereign of Hong Kong. In that situation, by applying common law principle to reach the conclusion of restrictive immunity approach for Hong Kong whilst the real sovereign of Hong Kong follows absolute immunity is wrong. Whether a country follows a common law or a civil law tradition, or follows absolute or restrictive principles of sovereignty, one fact is always common: that in a country there could be only one sovereign.[25] Under one sovereign, two sovereign immunity practices were never thought of or envisaged under the principle of 'One Country, Two Systems'.

In his judgment, Justice Stock, with regards to common law position on sovereign immunity, also mentioned, 'It can only have changed if a change has been demanded by its constitutional and societal setting'.[26] In this respect, Mr Justice Stock did accept that for Hong Kong, societal setting has changed:

---

25 In Canada, as a result of specific provisions in the Constitution, constituent provinces of Canada consider themselves separate from each other and may invoke immunity. However, this situation is widely accepted to form a customary norm.

26 FGH case, para 81.

> The setting has changed because Hong Kong is no longer a dependent territory of the sovereign power that had abandoned the doctrine of absolute immunity but is rather 'an inalienable part of the People's Republic of China' which, has not [abandoned the doctrine of absolute immunity].[27]

In this situation, it is important to make it clear for arbitration lawyers as well as for international lawyers as to which immunity approach will be followed in Hong Kong. If such situation arises for the first time in a State, then it is a generally the executive branch of the government which gives its intention to courts so that the courts and the executive should speak with one voice. In the FGH case, the Chinese Government representative in Hong Kong, that is, the Office of the Commissioner of the Ministry of Foreign Affairs of the PRC in the Hong Kong Special Administrative Region issued two letters for the courts to consider. The first letter was written to the Court of First Instance and then a second letter was written to the Court of Appeal. In the first letter, it was stated that the Commissioner is 'duly authorized' to make a statement about the principled position of PRC (with regards to sovereign immunity) which is an issue in the FGH case.[28] Further, the first letter states:

> The consistent and principled position of China is that a State and its property shall, in foreign courts, enjoy absolute immunity, including absolute immunity from jurisdiction and from execution, and has never applied the so-called principle and theory of 'restrictive immunity'.

The letter further clarified that the Chinese courts have also applied absolute sovereign immunity on foreign State and government and also on their property whenever they are made defendant. The letter puts it very emphatically that, 'China has never accepted any foreign courts having jurisdiction over cases in which the State or Government of China is sued as a defendant, or over cases involving the property of the State or Government of China'. Through that letter it made clear to the court that, 'This principled position held by the Government of China is unequivocal and consistent'.[29]

Despite this clear statement by the executive branch, the Court of First Instance did not give weight to this letter and instead of speaking with the executive in one voice decided to speak differently. Justice Reyes was not convinced with the position of the executive reflecting the Chinese Government's position because, according to him, the Chinese position is not consistent in this regard. He relied on the fact that China has signed the UN Convention on Jurisdictional Immunity of State and its Properties 2004 (the 2004 Convention) which acknowledges the

---

27 FGH case, para 82.

28 The first letter was issued on 20 November 2008, part of the letter is reproduced in the FGH case, para 90.

29 FGH case, para 90.

doctrine of restrictive immunity, and therefore the first letter did not show the consistent position of China.

Since the Court of First Instance showed reservation on putting any weight on the first letter, the Commissioner wrote the second letter to the Court of Appeal which explained the Chinese position in the light of signing of the 2004 Convention.[30] The second letter made it abundantly clear that:

> After signature of the Convention, the position of China in maintaining absolute immunity has not been changed, and has never applied or recognized the so-called principle or theory of 'restrictive immunity'.

The reason China signed the 2004 Convention is to 'express China's support of the above coordination effort made by the international community'. China participated in the Convention 'in the spirit of consultations, compromise and co-operation. Although the final text of the Convention was not as satisfactory as China expected, as a product of compromise by all sides, China supported the adoption of the Convention by the United Nations General Assembly'. According to the second letter, signing of the 2004 Convention by China 'cannot be the basis of assessing China's principled position on relevant issues'.[31]

Although the 2004 Convention has not been ratified by China and the 2004 Convention itself has not yet become binding, it is important to note a few points. According to the Vienna Convention on Law of Treaty, a State, after signing of a treaty, is duty bound in good faith to conduct its act which should not be inconsistent with the treaty and this good faith obligation exists even when the treaty is not adopted and/or ratified in the signatory State or the treaty itself has not yet become binding.[32] In other words, China, after signing the 2004 Convention, which acknowledges restrictive immunity, cannot conduct herself in a way which contradicts the restrictive immunity principle. The Court of Appeal found the Chinese assertion inconsistent in that signing of the 2004 Convention (which accepts restrictive immunity) cannot reflect the Chinese position on sovereign immunity. Therefore, by extending this logic one step further, one could say that a State which has signed the 2004 Convention which propagates restrictive immunity, even after its ratification in that State and after coming into operation of that Convention, that State may also argue that it still follows a position which was not accepted by the Convention. Would that not be considered as breach of treaty obligation? Therefore, after considering the effect of signing of the 2004 Convention, the court did not take the statement of the Commissioner as conclusive to apply absolute immunity in Hong Kong.

---

30 The second letter was written on 21 May 2009. Part of the content of the second letter is reproduced in FGH case, para 91.

31 FGH case, para 91.

32 Vienna Convention on Law of Treaty, Article 18.

One further issue arises from the different positions taken by the judiciary and the executive, that is, if it is to be decided that whether a State practices absolute or restrictive immunity, who is the authorized institution to give a conclusive word, the judiciary or the executive? If it is the practice that the judiciary and the executive must speak in one voice, then who should speak whose voice? It is submitted that it is the executive which is able and authorized to give a statement about its practices, and the judiciary should follow or adopt the position of the State in deciding the cases. That is how both the executive and the judiciary would be able to speak in the same voice. If judiciary were able to decide on the executive view then it might create an awkward situation. Therefore, in the context of Hong Kong, when there is a legal vacuum in this area, the judiciary, while facing the issue for the first time, should have followed the clear and unequivocal position of China and ruled that the principle of absolute immunity is applicable in Hong Kong. After all China is the sovereign for Hong Kong. Also it is not for the Hong Kong courts to make a second guess as to what could be inferred from the fact of the signing of the 2004 Convention when a clear statement from the executive was before the court. If PRC breaches its treaty obligations under the 2004 Convention, then it is for the international community or other signatories to give their comments or views and take any action, if at all possible, against the PRC. The courts of Hong Kong cannot dictate or conclude or infer (in presence of clear and equivocal statement) about the approach of China on sovereign immunity.

Even under the 'One Country, Two Systems' principle, if common law is continued to be applied in Hong Kong, the position on sovereign immunity cannot be decided by the courts of Hong Kong. It is for the sovereign to decide, and if the sovereign says that it follows absolute immunity, then Hong Kong courts should follow the same after 1997. That should also become part of the Hong Kong common law from 1997, because from then a societal change triggers which demands change in the common law position from restrictive to absolute immunity. In the context of Hong Kong, the court put a wrong emphasis on the fact of China's signing of the 2004 Convention. What if China later decides to withdraw from the 2004 Convention, would that not mean that China has again changed its position? And if so, would it then be possible to follow restrictive immunity in Hong Kong and absolute immunity in China? Such a situation would certainly be absurd. Moreover, a treaty which China has signed does not bind Hong Kong automatically, unless it is extended to Hong Kong. So far, China has not indicated that the 2004 Convention also binds Hong Kong. Therefore, it is submitted that the Hong Kong courts should follow the same practice as followed by the PRC, that is, absolute immunity, and this principle cannot be changed or deviated from as a result of the operation of the common law in Hong Kong. For any practice of sovereign immunity, there has to be one sovereign and for Hong Kong there is one sovereign so the practice of that sovereign must be binding on Hong Kong.

While practicing the principle of absolute immunity, the case of waiver of sovereign immunity should be used when it comes to the enforcement of arbitral awards, and the arbitration agreement should serve as the evidence of such waiver, either 'expressly' or 'by implication'. This waiver of immunity should continue to apply until the execution is fully done, save in those cases when the execution is exercised against the property of the State which is used for pure State function. Otherwise, the waiver of sovereign immunity should continue to apply where the property of the State is for commercial use.

Waiver of Immunity and Enforcement of Awards

In arbitration between a private party and a State, waiver of immunity on behalf of a State may be demonstrated in three ways:

a. if State has agreed to arbitrate;
b. if that State is a party to the NYC or agreed for the seat of arbitration in a NYC country; and
c. if that State has agreed to arbitration rules which contain waiver of immunity.

Once a State agrees for commercial arbitration with a private party, it waives its immunity from the arbitration as well as execution of award. In the views of arbitration lawyers, if a State is allowed to raise the defence of immunity at execution stage, then it will frustrate the agreement to arbitrate. The contentious question in this regard is that by submitting to arbitration, does a State also waive its sovereign immunity defence at the enforcement stage? Scholars have analyzed this issue by proposing two stage approaches.[33] This means consent to arbitration by a State is different from consent or waiver of the sovereign immunity at the enforcement stage by the State. The enforcement stage is further subdivided into:

a. recognition stage; and
b. actual enforcement stage.

Recognition stage simply means when the winning party in the award submits the award in the enforcement court and the court gives full recognition to the award. The actual enforcement stage refers to the situation where the enforcement court has already recognized the award as enforceable (after ruling on the objections made by the other party) and hence orders for enforcement. However, some scholars argue that once a State has given consent for arbitration, the waiver of sovereign immunity at the enforcement stage is deemed to have been given so that the arbitration could lead to its logical and practical

33 See in general, Fox (2008): *The Law of State Immunity*, 2nd edition, Oxford, Oxford University Press.

conclusion through enforcement.[34] Therefore, the agreement to arbitrate should include the enforcement and execution of award stage and 'unless commitment to arbitration is firm and enforceable, arbitration agreements with States are rendered pointless' and in violation of equal justice.[35] In countries like the Netherlands, the USA and France, it is a general understanding that, 'When a State has waived its immunity by submitting to arbitration, the scope of the waiver extends to proceedings for confirmation or recognition and enforcement of resulting award'.[36]

In the FGH case, a point was raised that the DRC is not a signatory to the NYC; therefore, it cannot be assumed that the DRC, like other signatories of the NYC, has impliedly consented not to raise sovereign immunity at the time of enforcement, that is, signatories State will follow restrictive immunity when it comes to enforcement of award.[37] This farfetched assumption is based on the fact that signatories to the NYC know well that in the NYC sovereign immunity is not a ground of refusal of enforcement of arbitral awards. However, it is to note that for the purpose of enforcement of award, even a non-signatory may take the benefit by agreeing to select the seat of arbitration in a signatory State so that the resulting award will be considered as the Convention award and therefore it could be enforced in any Convention State. That was perhaps one of the reasons for the commercial partner of the DRC and the DRC to agree for the place of arbitration to be in Switzerland and France so that the award could be enforced in any Convention country by using the easy process of the NYC with regards to recognition and enforcement of arbitral awards. Therefore, in cases where a non-signatory to the NYC selects the seat of arbitration in a country which is a signatory State, then it should be interpreted that the non-signatory knows and accepts the consequence that the resulting award will be enforced like a Convention award in any other Convention countries.

Some rules of arbitration may also be indicative of the waiver from execution of awards. For example Article 28(6) of ICC Rules states:

> Every award shall be binding on the parties. By submitting the dispute to arbitration under these Rules, the parties undertake to carry out any Award without delay and shall be deemed to have waived their right to any form of recourse insofar as such waiver can validly be made.

34 Toope, Stephen J. (1990): *Mixed International Arbitration: Studies in Arbitration between States and Private Persons*, Cambridge, Cambridge University Press, 146–50, as cited in FGH case, para 140.

35 FGH case, para 138 as per the counsel for the Appellant which was based on the article written by Professor Bachand (2009): Overcoming Immunity-Based Objections to the Recognition and Enforcement in Canada of Investor-State Awards, *Journal of International Arbitration*, Vol. 26, No. 1, 59–87.

36 FGH case, para 138.

37 FGH case, para 171.

The old ICC Rules, Article 24, which was equivalent to Article 28(6), contained the words 'final' and 'appeal' which are now changed from 'final' to 'binding' and 'appeal' to 'recourse'. It is not clear whether ICC considered the inclusion of sovereign immunity within the ambit of Article 28(6) or not.[38] However, a French court has held that agreeing to ICC Rules, Article 28 amounts to an undertaking of parties to carry out an award without delay and thereby grant a waiver of immunity from execution.[39] Similarly, the US court has also indicated that agreeing to ICC Rules, Article 28(6) constitutes 'explicit' waiver of immunity.[40]

In the FGH case, the parties agreed to apply ICC Rules, however, the Hong Kong court did not concur that agreeing to ICC Rules constituted explicit or implicit waiver. The court said:

> It cannot in my judgment be said that by entering upon an ICC arbitration agreement with a private party, a foreign State that is not a party to the NYC is going beyond the making of a representation to each Convention State that it consents to the enforcement against it in the Convention State of such arbitral awards as may be made. It seems to me that jurisdiction in the forum State can, in such circumstances, only be conferred by legislation or by express representation by the foreign State to the forum State.[41]

The court also relied on Diecy who says:

> In common law, sovereign immunity could be waived by or on behalf of the foreign State, but waiver had to have taken place at the time the court was asked to exercise jurisdiction and could not be constituted by, or inferred from, a prior contract to submit to the jurisdiction of the court or to arbitration.[42]

Therefore, the public international lawyers argue that at the time of enforcement by recognizing arbitral awards, the foreign courts exercise jurisdiction, and accordingly at that time a State may ask for waiver from jurisdiction. And since

---

38 Deraines, Yves and Schwartz, Eric A. (2005): *Guide to the ICC Rules of Arbitration*, 2nd edition, London, Kluwer Law International, 303–28.

39 *Creighton Ltd v. Government of the State of Qatar* (French Ct of Cassation, ch.civ,1; 6 July 2006).

40 W*alker International Holdings ltd v. the Republic of Congo* (395 F.3d 229 (5th Cir) (2004). in which the US Appellate Court ruled that 'in addition, the ROC agreed to abide by the rules of the ICC (*Article 28(6)*) which precludes the ROC from asserting a sovereign immunity defense' and concluded that 'Therefore, we hold that the ROC explicitly waived its sovereign immunity. Accordingly, we need not address a potential implicit waiver'. See FGH case, at p. 234.

41 FGH case, para 171.

42 Collins, Lawrence, Morse, C.G.J, McClean, David, Briggs, Adrian, Harris, Jonathan, McLachlan, Campbell and Hill, Jonathan, *Dicey, Morris & Collins on the Conflict of Laws*, 14th edition, Vol. I, London, Sweet & Maxwell, para 10-028, 285.

'prior contract to submit to the jurisdiction of the court or arbitration' is not sufficient to waive sovereign immunity, therefore the arbitration agreement or agreement to use ICC Rules (containing implied waiver) cannot be construed as implied waiver by the DRC.

Such a view of public international lawyers is difficult to accept by the arbitration lawyers for the main reason that arbitration process, including rendering of award and its execution, is inherently different from a court proceedings including enforcement of judgments. In the field of arbitration, as agreement to arbitrate sets the arbitration into motion, and parties, right from the time of agreeing to arbitrate know and could imagine the consequence, that is, if dispute will arise then it will be resolved through arbitration, agreed rules of arbitration will be applicable, at the agreed place the arbitration will be conducted, and award will be enforced by using the NYC, and at the enforcement stage the party will have only limited grounds to challenge the award. If arbitration lawyers and private parties have to deal with the issue of sovereign immunity at every stage of arbitration, then they will be reluctant to enter into any commercial deals with a State. Moreover, even if arbitration lawyers will take steps to deal with the sovereignty issue at the enforcement stage, such as to put a clause in the contract preventing a State from exercising its right of sovereign immunity, then also it is not clear whether a foreign court will give weight to such agreements because prior 'agreements' may not be construed as the waiver of sovereignty. Therefore, the use of public international law principles in a private international law situation will not help the commercial world and arbitration process particularly while dealing with State and the issue of sovereign immunity.

The very reason that the DRC agreed for arbitration, used ICC rules for arbitration (knowing that it requires parties to waive their rights) and agreed for a Convention country as a seat of arbitration, together show that the DRC has impliedly (if not explicitly) waived its right of sovereign immunity at the time of execution of award.

Execution of Awards Against State Properties

At the time of enforcement of arbitral awards, after dealing with the issue of jurisdiction of the court over a State, the enforcing court is required to deal with the issue of execution of award against the State's properties. However, caution must be raised that those State properties or accounts which are used for the pure State function or for diplomatic use cannot be subject to execution. Only those properties which are for commercial purpose of the State could be subject to execution to satisfy the awards. All States which have accepted the theory of restrictive immunity have invariably adhered to the absolute immunity principle, when it comes to State properties, meant for military, diplomatic and non-commercial use.[43] Therefore, the courts need to ascertain whether a property or an account which is attached for execution belongs in the category of pure State use or for commercial use. The test for the determination of the nature of the property or account is the functionality test, that is, what is the use or function of that property rather than how that property or account was acquired.[44] For example, if a ship is bought by the State but it is used for a commercial purpose, then it is subject to execution; but if a warship is bought by the money earned from the commercial activity, then it is immune from execution. The only problem comes when a State property or account is used for both pure State purpose and also for commercial purpose. In that situation, whether that State property should enjoy immunity or become subject of execution is an undecided matter.[45]

The 2004 Convention, Article 19, makes it clear that State properties are no post-judgment of constraints such as attachment, arrest or execution, unless a State has expressly consented to it through arbitration agreement. It does not say that mere signing of arbitration agreement does not by itself make that State's property subject to post-judgment constraints. That means a separate specific waiver of immunity is required. Therefore, if an arbitration agreement also includes an express waiver of immunity on State's property, then that arbitration agreement may constitute a waiver of immunity from jurisdiction as well as from execution. If a State has earmarked a property for the satisfaction of a claim, then during the execution of such claim, the earmarked property will not enjoy sovereign immunity. Also a State property which is intended to be for the use of governmental non-commercial purpose (that is, for commercial purpose), and if that property is within the territory of the State of the forum and the said property is connected to the entity against which the execution is sought, then it is beyond immunity ambit. The express waiver of immunity against the State property may also be inferred from international agreements to which the State is a party, that is, the New York Convention.

In the FGH case, FGH requested for injunction against payment of certain 'entry fee' to the DRC by Chinese Railway Consortiums. The FGH will have no case of enforcement if no payment is due to DRC by Chinese Railway Consortiums which have offices in Hong Kong and their stocks are listed on the Hong Kong stock market. The 'entry fee' amounts to US$350 million which is payable to DRC and Gecamines (a DRC State mining company).[46] There were few changes made in the composition of the investment vehicle which ultimately resulted in the possibility that the entry fee of US$144 million become payable to Gecamines and Congo Simco, rather than to the DRC and Gecamines as before. On the face of it,

43 Diplomatic immunity has a different regime due to the 1861 Vienna Convention on Diplomatic Relations, which accords special immunity.

44 FGH case, para 179.

45 Redfren, Alan, Hunter, Martin et al. (2004): *Law and Practice of International Commercial Arbitration*, 4th edition, London, Sweet & Maxwell, 467.

46 FGH case, para 10.

it may be possible that the DRC is no longer the recipient of that entry fee; it is the case of FGH that Gecamines and Congo Simco are merely agents or fronts acting for the DRC. Even if that is true, the fact that if the entry fee once collected will be put to use for public good, then it will become governmental non-commercial fund which will enjoy sovereign immunity. However, if that entry fee will be used for commercial purposes, then it will not be immune from execution as per the decision of the court. Justice Yeung in the FGH case said: 'It must be recognized that the seizure and sale of a State's assets in order to satisfy a judgment against it constitutes a particularly dramatic interference with its interests and could damage its ability to function properly'.[47] From the materials available before the court, it was concluded that US$200 to US$250 million will go to the budget of the DRC, which will be used for public purposes. Therefore, that part of entry fee will be immune from execution. The remaining US$100 to US$150 million which the DRC Government will pass on to Gecamines may become subject to execution and no immunity will be given to that money.[48] Whether the money given to Gecamines would qualify as the money for public use or not is different question. However, the court has concluded that money given to Gecamine, which is a Government arm with its own commercial interests, may not use money for public use, and therefore that money will be subject to execution of award. Ultimately, if the entire entry fee is used for the public purposes, then even if Hong Kong follows restrictive immunity, the FGH cannot obtain the money against the award. This is the situation where enforcement of award may come to a halt, which may cause hardship to the private party, but it will be in line with the practice which the arbitration community will accept and such rare circumstances will not make arbitration as a process of dispute resolution redundant.

Conclusion

Enforcement of arbitral awards in Hong Kong faces some unique challenges. Awards from different places are enforced differently. As an inalienable part of China and China being sovereign, the main legal instrument for enforcement, that is, the NYC does not apply. Therefore, the mainland awards are enforced through a particular arrangement agreed between Hong Kong and China which is based on the NYC spirit. However, specific arrangement has been made for the enforcement of Taiwan awards, which are enforced according to Section 2GG (Section 84 of the New Arbitration Ordinance) or under common law. The situation is the same for the Macao awards. It is expected that very soon the Hong Kong Government and the Macao Government will reach an arrangement for reciprocal enforcement of awards based on the NYC.

47 FGH case, para 234.

48 FGH case, paras 277–8.

Awards from other places which are signatory to the NYC have always been enforced in Hong Kong as per the NYC. However, Hong Kong has recently faced a new challenge with regards to enforcement of awards against a foreign State in Hong Kong which is not a party to the NYC. This situation has raised an important legal issue, that is, whether restrictive or absolute immunity principle is applicable in Hong Kong. This issue is also very significant for the purpose of enforcement of awards against foreign States or their properties. This issue is not settled yet as the highest court in Hong Kong is in process of delivering its judgment. The decisions of the Court of First Instance and the Court of Appeal have highlighted the tensions and different understandings of arbitration lawyers and public international lawyers on this issue. At a very fundamental level, the Court of Appeal has engaged in judicially deciding the type of sovereign immunity principle applicable in Hong Kong, which should be, it is submitted, decided by the executive branch of the government. For the purpose of enforcement of award, the unique legal situation of Hong Kong and different approaches of internal and arbitration lawyers with regards to sovereign immunity has made the enforcement of awards against a foreign State uncertain and unpredictable.

The situation becomes even more difficult 'because national courts (dealing with enforcement of awards) refuse to develop special rules for the enforcement of arbitral awards' and they are guided by the principles applicable in judicial proceedings.[49] Arbitration has not been allowed to develop its own substantive law as a freestanding system of dispute resolution, which, in itself, makes arbitration not an alternative but a dependent system of dispute resolution. [50] As long as arbitration is treated like a court process the problems of sovereign immunity and many other problems will create hurdles in the path of the smooth operation of arbitration.

References

Bachand, Frederic (2009): Overcoming Immunity-Based Objections to the Recognition and Enforcement in Canada of Investor-State Awards, *Journal of International Arbitration*, Vol. 26, No. 1, 59–87.

Convention on Diplomatic Relations (1861).

Convention on the Jurisdictional Immunities of States and their Property (2004).

Convention on the Recognition and Enforcement of Foreign Arbitral Awards (10 June 1958).

49 Fox, Hazel, State Immunity and the New York Convention. In: Gaillard Emmanuel and Di Pietro, Domenico, (Eds) *Enforcement of Arbitration Agreements and International Arbitral Awards: the New York Convention in practice*, 829–64, at 860.

50 Lord Wilberforce during the second reading of the English Arbitration Act, 1995 in the House of Lords. See Hansard, col 778, 18 January 1996.

Creighton Ltd v. Government of the State of Qatar, French Court of Cassation, ch.civ,1; 6 July 2006.

Deraines, Yves and Schwartz, Eric A. (2005): *Guide to the ICC Rules of Arbitration*, 2nd edition, London, Kluwer Law International, 303–28.

Collins, Lawrence, Morse, C.G.J., McClean, David, Briggs, Adrian, Harris, Jonathan, McLachlan, Campbell and Hill, Jonathan (2010): *Dicey, Morris & Collins on the Conflict of Laws*, 14th edition, Vol. I, London, Sweet & Maxwell, para 10–028, 285.

Duff Development Company Limited v. Government of Kelantan [1924] A.C. 797.

FG Hemisphere Associates LLC and Democratic Republic of Congo and ors, CACV373/2008 & CACV 43/2009.

Foreign Sovereign Immunity Act (1974).

Fox, Hazel (2008): *The Law of State Immunity*, 2nd edition, Oxford, Oxford University Press.

Fox, Hazel (2008): State Immunity and the New York Convention. In Gaillard Emmanuel and Di Pietro, Domenico (Eds) *Enforcement of Arbitration Agreements and International Arbitral Awards: The New York Convention in Practice*, Cameroon, May, 829–64.

Lord Wilberforce, The Second Reading of the *English Arbitration Act*, 1995 in the House of Lords, Hansard, col 778, 18 January 1996.

Mighell v. Sultan of Johore [1894] 1 Q.B. 149.

Redfren, Alan and Hunter, Martin (2004): *Law and Practice of International Commercial Arbitration*, 4th edition, London, Sweet & Maxwell, Thompson, 467.

State Immunity Act (1978).

Toope, Stephen J. (1990): *Mixed International Arbitration: studies in Arbitration Between States and Private Persons*, Cambridge, Cambridge University Press, 146–50.

Walker International Holdings Ltd v. the Republic of Congo 395 F.3d 229 (5th Cir.) (2004).

Chapter 6
Language and Power in Arbitration Proceedings: Insights into Theory and Practice

Patrizia Anesa

> Most of us learn at an early stage that, in general, we don't get what we want by lying down, screaming hysterically and drumming our heels on the floor. The art of persuasion involves a more subtle process in which we consciously or unconsciously seek to establish rapport with the person or persons we are trying to persuade. (Hunter 1995: 275)

Introduction

This chapter aims to describe the main linguistic and discursive features that characterize arbitration proceedings within the current Italian context. The main objective is therefore to offer insights into some instances of arbitration proceedings and their development, as well as the power dynamics that come into play in this specific professional context. This analysis is based on the recording of recent authentic arbitral proceedings and also draws on the information acquired from professionals in the field (especially Italian arbitrators). More specifically, the study takes into consideration how power dynamics and social and professional roles may determine the development of the spoken interaction. Furthermore, the investigation focuses on the use of some of the features of courtroom language in arbitration, with particular reference to their use in oral communication, and it considers how the concept of colonization of arbitration by litigation (Flood and Caiger 1993) emerges in this context.

It is generally agreed that one of the main aspects that distinguishes arbitration from litigation is that the former should represent a quicker and simpler system. However, arbitration is still a legal procedure and the language is inevitably used accordingly. In particular, awards, the final decisions taken by the arbitrator, are legally binding and can be enforced with the same validity as a court judgment. This aspect is particularly significant as it is a distinctive feature that arbitration does not share with other forms of alternative dispute resolution, such as mediation or conciliation, whose aim is the attainment of a negotiated settlement (Redfern and Hunter 2004: 12). In arbitration the principle of *res judicata* is applied, which means that the final decision of a court of a competent jurisdiction cannot generally be challenged. Consequently, awards tend to assume all the characteristics of a legal decision and the language reflects the conventions used in litigation proceedings.

It is not the aim of this chapter to justify or condemn the complexity of this type of language in this context, but to observe if, and to what extent, arbitration proceedings are influenced by courtroom language and legalistic style. The influence of litigation language on arbitration texts is often displayed in written arbitration texts such as awards (Gotti and Anesa forthcoming). The peculiarity of this analysis is that it attempts to explore the spoken level of interaction between the participants and show how courtroom practices and language may influence the conduction of arbitration proceedings.

Moreover, this investigation may suggest a reflection upon the structure and role of arbitral hearings and upon the changes this communicative event may undergo. As early as 1950 Warren and Bernstein posed a fundamental question: 'Should the mechanics of the hearing encourage informality or the atmosphere of a court?' (Warren and Bernstein 1950: 21). This sort of tension between the search for a simpler procedure and the need for a legalistic style is clearly present in arbitration proceedings. Indeed, legal experts use a highly formal and technical style, which is inevitably part of their *forma mentis* and their professional background.

Background

The Use of Arbitration in Italy

In Italy the use of arbitration has increased significantly in recent years and it is now considered to be a well-established method for settling disputes. This development is the consequence of a growing need for alternative means of resolving disputes, resulting from the fact that litigative proceedings are often associated with high costs and very long and time-consuming procedures, as well as with the risk of unfair and unjust judgments (Stesuri 2001: XIII). This sort of widespread diffidence towards ordinary means of dispute resolution has often urged private clients and companies to consider arbitration as an efficient alternative tool. In recent years the number of disputes dealt with through the use of arbitration has grown significantly in Italy. The Arbitral Chamber of Milan confirms that the number of requests for arbitration has constantly grown in recent years; for instance, 35 requests were filed in 1997, whereas in 2010 the number of requests was 129.[1]

Even though these data cannot offer a comprehensive picture of the development of arbitration in Italy, they seem to confirm a general growth in the use of arbitration. This trend is related to the advantages that are traditionally associated with this procedure, such as flexibility, technical expertise, privacy, confidentiality, speed and limited costs.

1 For further details see <http://www.camera-arbitrale.it/consulta.php?sez_id=4&lng_id=14>, accessed 15 June 2011.

Before analyzing some instances of Italian arbitration proceedings, it is important to highlight that in Italy some new arbitration rules came into force in 2006 (Legislative Decree no. 40 of 2 February 2006) which introduced some important modifications to the Code of Civil Procedure (CCP) regarding arbitral proceedings under the Italian jurisdiction (see *inter alia* Barbieri 2007). All references to CCP in this chapter are in accordance with the 2006 text.

Choosing the Arbitrator(s)

The importance of the choice of the arbitrator(s) (sole arbitrator or arbitral tribunal) cannot be overemphasized, as the selection of the arbitrator is one of the most critical decisions parties have to make, especially in *ad hoc* arbitration,[2] where the parties are entitled to a certain freedom in the selection of the arbitrators. However, it is clear that the parties' right of choice is limited by a series of factors, such as the provisions of the relevant law and the elements included in the arbitration clause. For instance, the number of arbitrators is generally either one or three, and Section 809 of the Italian Code of Civil Procedure[3] clearly defines what the number of arbitrators should be:

> There may be one or more arbitrators, provided their number is uneven.
>
> The arbitration agreement must contain the appointment of the arbitrators or establish their number and the manner by which they are to be appointed.
>
> Where an even number of arbitrators is indicated, an additional arbitrator shall be appointed by the president of the tribunal in the manner specified by Article 810, unless the parties have agreed otherwise. Where the number of arbitrators is not indicated and the parties do not agree in that regard, there shall be three arbitrators; failing their appointment, the president of the tribunal shall proceed to such appointment in the manner specified in Article 810, unless the parties have agreed otherwise.

In the cases examined in this chapter the number of arbitrators had been stated in the arbitration clause included in the contract between the parties, as in the following example:

---

2 *Ad hoc* arbitration is conducted, in broad terms, according to rules agreed by the parties or established by the arbitral tribunal. Conversely, institutional arbitration is administered by a named arbitral institution, such as an Arbitral Chamber, and it is conducted pursuant to its rules of arbitration.

3 The English version of the Italian Code of Civil Procedure is by Professor Piero Bernardini and can be found in *Yearbook Commercial Arbitration*, Vol. 31 (2006). This text is available at <http://www.camera-arbitrale.com/upload/file/1241/620822/FILENAME/synoptic_chart.pdf>, accessed 15 June 2011.

(1) Qualunque controversia [...] sarà decisa in via esclusiva da un Collegio Arbitrale [...]. In caso di controversie che coinvolgano *[4] e una o più delle altre parti, il Collegio Arbitrale sarà composto di tre arbitri. Un arbitro verrà nominato di comune accordo da *. Un arbitro verrà nominato dall'altra parte in lite. I due arbitri di potere designeranno di comune accordo il terzo arbitro, che assumerà le funzioni di presidente del Collegio Arbitrale.
[All disputes [...] shall be settled by an Arbitral Tribunal. [...] In case of disputes involving * and one or more of the other parties, the Arbitral tribunal shall consist of three arbitrators * shall commonly agree on the appointment of one arbitrator. One arbitrator shall be appointed by the other party involved in the dispute. The two arbitrators so appointed shall agree on a third arbitrator, who shall fulfil the function of Chairman of the Arbitral Tribunal.]

The CCP also clearly describes the procedure to be followed for the appointment of arbitrators:

> Where in accordance with the arbitration agreement the arbitrators are to be appointed by the parties, each party, by written notice, shall inform the other party of its appointment of an arbitrator or arbitrators and request said other party to name its own arbitrators. The party so requested shall, within the following twenty days, serve written notice of the personal data of the arbitrator or arbitrators appointed by it (Article 810, CCP).

Arbitrators must be impartial, and they must fulfil their role despite their relationship with the party which appointed them. More specifically, the concepts of 'independence' and 'impartiality' are fundamental in an arbitration context and Rhoades, Kolkey and Chernick (2007: 355) describe them as follows:

> 'Independence' means that the arbitrator is not connected with any of the parties or someone closely connected with a party; 'impartiality' means that the arbitrator does not have a bias in favor or against one of the parties.

This distinction is further explained by Tampieri (2001: 562):

> Impartiality pertains to the actual conduct of the arbitrator in the arbitral procedure, whereas independence pertains to the relationship – personal, social or financial – between the arbitrator and the party, or its counsel.

According to some commentators a further distinction between impartiality and neutrality could be made as regards international arbitration. Lalive (1984: 24) suggests that national neutrality is to be intended as the fact that the nationality

4 For privacy reasons, names and other sensitive data have been replaced with an asterisk.

of the third arbitrator (or in general the president of the panel) should be different from the nationalities of the parties. However, for the purpose of this chapter, following Murray (1990: 323), the two terms will be used synonymously.

The question regarding the impartiality and the independence of party-appointed arbitrators is particularly complex, as a conflict of interests may emerge. If we consider different countries and different legal systems there may be substantial differences with regard to the role played by party-appointed arbitrators, but a widely shared opinion is that, '[T]he general custom in Europe is for the party-appointed arbitrator to remain independent and impartial and not to act as a representative' (Murray 1990: 323). In this respect, Murray also remarks:

> If what the parties want is a compromise result based on negotiations in deliberations, then why not just agree to a negotiation? There can be little justification for the expense of two extra arbitrators to duplicate the function of counsel (Murray 1990: 342).

Indeed, even when the arbitrators are appointed by the parties, the principles of independence, impartiality and neutrality must always be applied. Craig, Park and Paulsson (2000: 196) state that, '[A] party-appointed arbitrator staunchly adhering to the positions of the party which nominated him or her will not have much influence on the decision-making process'. Partasides (2001: 217) affirms that the parties should be able to identify the characteristics of an arbitrator that may lead him/her to be 'favourably predisposed to their case' and adds:

> The parties are, of course, far from spectators [...]. Their ability to influence the composition of the arbitral tribunal is one of the defining aspects of the arbitral process. Their power to appoint, and the power to challenge, arbitrators are two of their most powerful tools. (Lawyers may be loath to admit it, but the selection or de-selection of arbitrators might even be more important than their choice of counsel – although perhaps only just) (Partasides 2001: 217).

However, such a predisposition should not prevent the arbitrator from acting independently and impartially, as it is in the interest of any arbitrator to act neutrally in order not to undermine his/her credibility. Impartiality and independence are generally considered to be a precondition of acting as an arbitrator. Indeed, the arbitral due process essentially requires a fair treatment of the parties in all the parts of the proceedings, and the violation of this basic principle could have serious consequences with regard to the enforcement of the award.

Analysis: Roles and Power Relations

The arbitration process obviously comprises different communicative situations, modes and means of production. Considering the vast spate of micro-contexts of production that constitutes an entire arbitration procedure, this analysis will focus only on one specific phase, that is, the *interrogatorio libero delle parti*. Although the expression 'free party examination' is sometimes used, the definition 'informal party examination' is the most widely used and this is the translation that will be used here. The importance of this phase of the procedure is fundamental as the arbitrators can acquire information from the parties about the dispute.

Our analysis is based on data concerning three arbitration proceedings held in Italy between 2004 and 2007 referring to business-related disputes. In the three cases the participants involved are always the respondent and his lawyer, the claimant and his lawyer, a secretary, and the arbitrator(s). The number of arbitrators is either one (dispute 1) or three (disputes 2 and 3). Inevitably, the different interactants assume clearly distinctive roles and the relations between them are determined by complex dynamics of power and authority.

The Arbitrator(s)

In this specific context the role of the arbitrator is fundamental, and therefore he/she has to maintain a high level of credibility, as this is vital for the success of the current proceedings and for future proceedings too. This role is particularly complex because, on the one hand, the arbitrator needs to seek approval and alignment but, on the other hand, he/she must make clear that certain procedures have to be followed strictly.

According to the interviews carried out with some professionals in the field, even though the arbitrator *may* introduce mediation techniques in arbitration, their use is quite restricted in practice, because the room for mediation, once the arbitration proceeding has started, is usually limited. Whereas mediation is generally considered potentially a win/win situation, arbitration is often perceived as a win/lose situation, which means that one of the parties necessarily wins at the expense of the other (Berger 2006: 537–8) and this fundamental aspect clearly contributes to the limited use of mediational strategies in this context. Moreover, Berger (2006: 433) points out that 'unlike the mediator, the arbitral tribunal remains bound by the mandatory procedural principles of the applicable arbitration law'.

The dominant role of the arbitrator Arbitration proceedings have to be conducted according to specific rules and principles. For instance, following a clear procedural order is fundamental for a correct, clear and logical development of an examination. In example 2 the arbitrator emphasizes how important it is to follow a specific order:

(2) A1:[5] Un momento. Adesso noi dobbiamo procedere con ordine.
[A1: One moment. Now we must proceed in an orderly way.]

---

5 In order to identify the speakers, the following codes have been assigned:

A1, A2, A3: arbitrator (sole arbitrator or president of the panel) (dispute 1, 2, 3).
AB2: arbitrator (member of the panel) (dispute 2).

Moreover, references to the beginning and the end of a certain phase of the proceeding are explicitly signalled, as generally happens in litigative procedures. This approach contributes to conveying clarity in identifying the different phases and belongs to a set of procedural conventions.

(3a) A2: Do corso all'interrogatorio delle parti.
[A2: I hereby open the party examination.]

(3b) A2: Bene, allora io direi che l'interrogatorio libero pertanto lo possiamo ritenere terminato.
[A2: Well, I would say that the informal examination can be considered concluded.]

During party examinations arbitrators often have to remind the other parties about the function of this specific phase of the proceedings:

(4) RL1: Ritengo che la domanda sia ininfluente [...]
A1: Però siccome qui siamo in un interrogatorio libero che serve per chiarire i fatti, io piuttosto pregherei l'avv. CL1 di chiarire più esattamente qual è il punto che vuol fare evidenziare.
[RL1: I think the question is irrelevant [...].
A1: But, as this is an informal examination whose aim is to clarify the facts, I'd ask Ms. CL1 to clarify more precisely what the point she would like to underline is.]

In this case one of the lawyers labels one of the questions asked by the other party as irrelevant, but the arbitrator reminds the parties that the main aim of that phase is to understand the situation and the facts and, therefore, asks the

---

AB3: arbitrator (member of the panel) (dispute 3).
AC3: arbitrator (member of the panel) (dispute 3).
C1: claimant (dispute 1).
CL1: claimant's lawyer (dispute 1).
R1: respondent (dispute 1).
RL1: respondent's lawyer (dispute 1).
C2: claimant (dispute 2).
CL2: claimant's lawyer (dispute 2).
R2: respondent (dispute 2).
RL2: respondent's lawyer (dispute 2).
C3: claimant (dispute 3).
CL3: claimant's lawyer (dispute 3).
R3: respondent (dispute 3).
RL3: respondent's lawyer (dispute 3).

References to male and female participants have been excluded and masculine forms have been used in all cases.

speaker to continue. In particular, what emerges is that certain specific aspects, such as the level of legal relevance or appropriateness of a question from a more technical point of view, do not seem to be the overriding priority of the informal examination, which is based on the need to better understand the events and the issues. The arbitrator stresses the objective of this phase in different situations and also reminds the parties about the practice that has to be followed:

(5a) A2: Ecco, allora ribadisco: questo è esclusivamente un interrogatorio libero che il Collegio esperisce a chiarimento. Le chiarificazioni sono ammesse esclusivamente sul fatto principale, quindi tutte le altre considerazioni in questa sede non hanno in questo momento alcun rilievo.
[A2: Right, then I'll repeat: this is only an informal examination that the Panel carries out for clarification. Clarifications are admitted solely as regards the main fact, therefore all other considerations are of no relevance in this context.]

(5b) A1: Però siccome qui siamo in un interrogatorio libero che serve per chiarire i fatti, io piuttosto pregherei * di chiarire più esattamente qual è il punto in fatto che vuole evidenziare.
[A1: But as this is an informal examination, whose aim is to explain the facts, I'd rather ask * to state more precisely what point he would like to underline.]

Moreover, the arbitrator repeatedly has to make sure that questions are answered precisely and that they are relevant, as clearly emerges in the following examples:

(6a) AB3: Mi scusi ma la domanda non è tanto se [.], ma se [...]
[AB3: Sorry, but the question is not whether [.], but whether [...]]

(6b) AC3: La domanda non è se lei [...] o [...] fossero la stessa cosa, la domanda era [...] La domanda è [...]
[AC3: The question is not whether you * or * were the same thing, the question was [...]. The question is [...]]

(6c) AC3: Non vorrei che la mia domanda fosse stata male intesa. [...] La mia domanda era relativa specificamente a [...] Questa è la domanda perché di questo noi stiamo parlando.
[AC3: Maybe my question has been misunderstood [...] My question referred specifically to [...] This is the question, because this is what we are talking about.]

In order to guarantee clarity and precision and to facilitate understanding, arbitrators may also ask their interlocutors to repeat or reformulate certain concepts:

(7a) AB3: Ritorno su una domanda che le ho fatto prima e desidero se possibile una più precisa risposta.
[AB3: I'll refer again to a question I asked earlier and I'd like a more precise answer.]

(7b) A3: Le chiedo di ripetere con molta calma le ultime affermazioni.
[A3: Please repeat the last statements calmly.]

The interaction is mainly guided by the arbitrator and on some occasions he/she interrupts other speakers in order to guarantee that a certain procedure and a certain order are followed and that the points that have a certain relevance to the dispute are analyzed in further detail:

(8) A1: [...] concorda con quanto ha detto ora il signor C1, che aveva questo ruolo di *?
R1: Penso di sì io |
A1: | le chiedo se a lei risulta [...]
[A1: [...] do you agree with what Mr C1 said, that he had the role of *?
R1: I think so |
A1: | I'm asking you if you know [...]]

In this case the arbitrator interrupts the speaker in order to clarify the question and, above all, to make sure the answer is relevant.

The arbitration panel As already mentioned, the role played by the arbitrator in the communicative interaction in an informal party examination and in the entire procedure, is fundamental. In particular he/she tends to assign the speaking turns to the participants and fulfills the function of regulator of the right to speak (Anesa 2010).

In cases where an arbitration panel is present, the role of the president of the panel is crucial because 'the chairman dominates the conduct of the procedure and is a decisive factor for the success of the arbitration as a whole' (Berger 2006: 377). The dynamics that may develop within the panel are particularly complex, especially considering that two arbitrators are generally appointed by the parties (see above). The president of the panel usually leads the interaction throughout the hearings and it is interesting to note that in one of the cases analyzed, when another arbitrator wants to ask a question, he clearly asks the president for permission:

(9) AB3: Scusi posso fare una domanda io?
[AB3: Sorry, may I ask a question?]

Even though this is not the general situation, it is interesting to note that a sort of hierarchical power inside the panel may be displayed, as in the following example:

(10) AB2: Mi scusi presidente io su questo avrei un attimo la mia idea [...] quindi io francamente |
A2: | allora ci riserviamo.
AB2: Sarebbe stata comunque una domanda [...] che io avrei rivolto comunque poi alle parti.
A2: Allora se vuoi gliela rivolgi tu dopo, però non è a chiarimento su questo.
[AB2: Sorry, President, but I would have my own idea about this [...] so, frankly, I |
A2: | so we'll reserve [the right to deal with it later].
AB2: That would have been a question [...] that I wanted to ask the parties later.
A2: So if you want you'll have it later, but it is not a clarifying question about this point.]

In this case one of the members of the panel would like to pose a question regarding one of the issues, but the president immediately interrupts him and reminds him that it is not immediately relevant, whereas the president is generally not interrupted. Moreover, the power relations developing are shown also by an asymmetry in the way the speakers address each other. AB2 uses the third person subject pronoun (*lei*) which corresponds to the Italian courtesy form, whereas the president uses the more informal subject pronoun *tu* while addressing the other arbitrator.

Addressing the arbitrator The way of addressing the president of the panel is, predictably, characterised by a very high level of courtesy and formality, referring to him/her using titles such as *Presidente* (President) or *Professore* (Professor). This happens both on the part of the lawyers (11a) and of the parties themselves (11b):

(11a) RL2: Sì *presidente*. Intanto mi permetto sommessamente di ribadire come [...]
[RL2: Yes *president*. But I would like to humbly reaffirm that [...]]

(11b) RL2: Grazie *presidente.*
[RL2: Thank you *president.*]

(11c) C3: No, *professore* è il contrario.
[C3: No, *professor*, it's the opposite.]

Such an approach appears rather obsequious, but it may derive from a (more or less conscious) submissiveness towards the people who hold the decisional power.

The Lawyers

The importance of the role played by the lawyers in the context of an informal party examination is quite evident. Lawyers, as in court trials, ask the party they represent questions in order to stress certain favourable points, and also ask the other party questions with the aim to show fallacies in their case theory. Counsels may also guide their clients' answers or reformulate certain concepts that have been expressed by their clients in order to rephrase certain points in the most appropriate legal terms.

As has been mentioned, professional expertise is one of the key features on which arbitration is based and is a crucial quality arbitrators should display. It is therefore not unexpected that whenever lawyers possess specific technical competence regarding the object of the dispute, they are generally keen on displaying their level of knowledge in the field. In one case, one of the lawyers admits not being an expert in the area being discussed:

(12) CL1: Io, che non son un esperto di *, mi chiedo [...]
[CL1: I, who am not an expert of *, am wondering [...]]

This sort of 'confession' is immediately exploited by the other lawyer, who remarks:

(13) RL1: Contesto quanto detto da *, che per sua stessa ammissione non ha esperienza di *. Io ho praticato * [...]
[RL1: I contest what has been said by *, who, as he has admitted, does not have any experience in *. I have practised * [...]]

The respondent's lawyer does not miss the opportunity to point out that he displays some professional experience and, indirectly, seems to express the idea that he is more competent in the field and, consequently, should be able to deal with the issues in a more professional and competent way.

The Parties

As has been mentioned, the speech of arbitrators tends to be markedly formal, as is conventionally expected within their professional culture. It is not surprising that the parties that are being examined display a type of language that is characterized by a minor level of formality and legal technicality in comparison with members of the legal profession. For example, on one occasion, one of the parties even recurs to expressions in non-standard Italian:

(14) C3: O te magni 'sta minestra o te butti dalla finestra.[6]

6 Regional variation of the saying '*o mangi questa minestra o ti butti dalla finestra*' used to refer to a situation where no alternative solutions are possible.

Conversely, regional variations, colloquialisms or other features diverging from a highly formal and standardized type of language are generally used neither by arbitrators nor by lawyers. Indeed, this kind of style is simply not in-line with their professional culture, does not comply with the common practices of arbitration, and would also be detrimental to the status building legal professionals constantly seek.

Moreover, as effective communication is at the basis of their profession, the speech of members of the legal profession does not generally present false starts or hesitations, whereas this happens very often when the parties are speaking and their words sound more hesitant, uncertain and insecure:

(15) C3: Assolutamente sì ehm credo di sì. non so che risponderle professore. credo cioè ehm credo ehm capisco il suo punto ma non so come risponderle professore.
[C3: Absolutely, urm, I think so. I don't know what to answer, professor. I think I mean, urm, I think, urm, I see your point but I don't know what to answer, professor.]

In this phase of the proceedings, it is not surprising that, more or less intentionally, parties may tend to generate sympathy in their listeners referring to their own personal situation:

(16a) C3: […] il mio stato d'animo attuale lo può immaginare, quello di quel momento era forse peggio.
[C3: […] you can imagine my current state of mind; it was even worse at that time.]

(16b) C3: Cerco di tirare avanti. Io ho perso tutto, professore. Non sono un uomo che ha ancora delle riserve, non ho più niente. Quindi cammino e campo grazie a qualche amico e alla famiglia.
A3: Se vuole concentrarsi sulla domanda, cioè per quali ragioni […]
C3: […]
A3: No dopo nel *
C3: Scusi mi ero perso. Questo è precedente ha ragione.
[C3: I'm trying to carry on. I've lost everything, professor. I'm a man who does not have anything left, I don't have anything anymore. So I go on and I survive thanks to some friends and my family.
A3: Please focus on the question, that is why […]
C3: […]
A3: No, later, in *
C3: Sorry, I was lost. This was before, you are right.]

It is clear that whereas members of the legal community use technical and objective language, laymen tend to employ a more emotional and personal style.

The arbitrator, however, tries to constantly focus on the procedure to be followed ('*please focus on the question*') and the facts to be described.

The Tension between Formality and Informality

The tension between the need for simplicity, flexibility and speed on the one hand, and for procedural correctness, compliance with legal requirements and formality on the other, is at the core of arbitration procedures. This tension and the intrinsic nature of the process place arbitration in a particular position, to the extent that it may be argued that, '[A]rbitration is neither fully informal as, say, mediation, nor as fully formal as court litigation' (Flood and Craiger 1993: 415). Some of the differences and the similarities between litigation and arbitration will now briefly be discussed.

The Setting

The setting of this event is remarkably different from the one that characterizes a courtroom examination. Indeed, the courtroom represents for most people 'a strange and alien setting' (Gibbons 1994: 32) and this seems to have a significant semiotic implication, that is, that 'the strongest meanings communicated by the physical setting of the room and behaviour of those in it are those of hierarchical power' (Gibbons 1994: 32). Instead, in the cases analyzed the setting is always an office and it certainly does not convey the idea of a 'strange and alien' context. This approach is shared by arbitration proceedings in different countries and in different legal systems. Aron, Fast and Klein affirm that, 'The forum for most ADR procedures is private offices rather than majestic court buildings' (1996: 22) and confirms that:

> in ADR procedures there is an atmosphere of respect and courtesy in all stages of the process, but there is also a certain unceremoniousness that makes lawyers' and parties' performances more casual and unconventional (1996: 25).

Describing arbitration proceedings, Redfern and Hunter talk of a 'striking lack of formality' and remark:

> There are no ushers, wigs or gowns – simply a group of people seated around a row of tables, in a room hired for the occasion. To an outsider, it would look as if a conference or business meeting was in progress. It does not look like a legal proceeding at all (Redfern and Hunter 2004: 1).

Physical aspects such as the setting and the position of the participants play a crucial role for the communicative process: the arbitrators are sitting around the same table as the parties and not behind a podium, as generally happens with judges in a courtroom. This situation may convey the idea that roles (and the attribution of power that goes with them) are less immediately identifiable. However, as has been shown above, the distinction of roles and levels of power inevitably emerge through different dynamics. Moreover, the physical space in which arbitration takes place is generally smaller than a courtroom, and so is the number of people involved; consequently, a series of paralinguistic elements vary, such as the tone of voice employed. Similarly, it is easy to intuit that kinesis, proxemis, haptics and other non-verbal aspects assume different contours in arbitration compared to litigation, but these features go beyond the scope of this chapter.

According to formal and informal interviews carried out with arbitrators and other professionals working in the field, the physical setting of the procedure is less distinctive than in other legal contexts. In particular, fewer physical elements characterize the different phases of the procedure. For example, standing-up and sitting-down are crucial in courtroom interaction as they also identify a sequence of events and communicative acts; in arbitration hearings, on the other hand, the participants usually remain seated for the entire examination. Moreover, in courtroom examination certain conversational conventions, such as greetings or enquiries about well-being, are omitted (Jackson 1995: 413). Conversely, in an arbitration hearing, when the parties are welcomed into the arbitrator's office, these kinds of conventions are always used, even though they are kept very brief.

The arbitrator generally tends to assume a more welcoming and sociable approach; for example, the parties can be asked if they need a break:

> (17) A1: Poi chiedo, siccome io ho ancora qualche serie di domande, volete fare una pausa o preferite proseguire?
> [A1: I'd like to ask you, as I still have some sets of questions, would you like to have a break or would you like to continue?]

Although such an offer is not excluded *a priori* even in courtroom examination, it is certainly less common. Conversely, on certain occasions, using a friendlier (or 'less hostile') approach represents a well-established practice in arbitration proceedings. It is generally agreed that a higher level of intimacy and informality may emerge, but not everybody would share Aron, Fast and Klein's view that in the ADR process 'strict formalities are replaced by amicable conversations' (Aron, Fast and Klein 1996: 25). Arbitration takes place because a dispute exists and therefore the tone of the conversation cannot always be amicable. Furthermore, formalities are to some extent essential, as they are often associated with procedural correctness, as will be seen in the following section.

Legal References and Practices

As has been shown, the general context within which arbitration takes place can be considered, to a certain extent, less ceremonious and formal than the practices that characterize litigation. However, the conventions of a legal procedure inevitably require a certain level of formality. Indeed, the language of arbitration also presents elements that are typical of litigation. There is, for example, constant reference to legal principles or to a series of legal documents and texts that are relevant to the case. The *principio del contradditorio ('audi alteram partem' principle)*, according to which all parties should have an equal and reasonable opportunity to present their case, is one of the principles on which the examination is based and is clearly described in the CCP (Article 816-bis):

> The parties may establish in the arbitration agreement or in a separate document, prior in any case to the commencement of the arbitral proceedings, the rules that the arbitrators must apply in the proceedings and the language of the arbitration. In the absence of such rules, the arbitrators are free to regulate the course of the proceedings and to determine the language of the arbitration in the manner they deem most convenient. They must respect in any case the principle of contradictory proceedings[7] (*'principio del contraddittorio'*) by granting both parties reasonable and equivalent opportunities to present their case. The parties may take part in the proceedings through counsel. Failing an express limitation, the power of attorney granted to counsel shall extend to any procedural activities, including the waiver of the proceedings and the determination and extension of the time limit for rendering the award. In any case, counsel may receive communication of the notification of the award and of the notification of the recourse against it.

This legal principle is clearly mentioned by the arbitrator in the following example:

(18) A1: Allora adesso, per diritto di contradditorio, chiederei a * di riproporre la domanda di prima.
[A1: Now, as for *diritto di contraddittorio* (*'Audi alteram partem'* principle), I would ask * to ask the previous question again.]

Reference to legal texts, in particular written documents which are strictly related to the examination that is being carried out, is quite common in arbitration proceedings. It is by no means surprising that the legal experts assisting their parties constantly quote other legal documents, as such an approach is typical of legal proceedings and is also part of the wider Italian legal tradition. In certain cases, the texts cited are operative legal documents with general applicability, such as the Code of Civil Procedure:

(19) RL2: [...] se ciò è da porre in relazione con la domanda di condanna al risarcimento dei danni ex art. 2497 Codice Civile [...]

7 This is the term used by Professor Bernardini in his translation of the CCP. However, a widely accepted translation for the concept of *principio del contraddittorio* is the Latin expression *audi alteram partem*.

[RL2: […] if this is to be related to the claim for damages (*ex article 2497 Code of Civil Procedure*) […]]

In other cases intertextual references are made to documents related to the current procedure, especially briefs:

(20a) RL2: Intanto mi permetto sommessamente di ribadire come alla Parte Convenuta, siccome ad oggi non è stata data la possibilità di depositare una memoria, […] in replica alla memoria del * depositata da Parte Attrice, l'oggetto di questo giudizio è solo parzialmente conosciuto dal Collegio in relazione a quella che è la memoria depositata soltanto dall'una Parte.
[RL2: But I would like to humbly reaffirm that the respondent party has not been given yet the possibility to file a brief, […] in reply to the brief of * filed by the claimant, the subject-matter of this case is only partially known to the Panel in relation to the brief that has been filed by only one of the parties.]

(20b) C1: A pagina * della nostra *memoria* si parla di questo
[C1: This is mentioned on page * of our *brief*.]

Even though arbitration should represent a simpler procedure, the complexity of the legal principles being applied, and the linguistic tools used have often been confirmed. In this respect, it is interesting to note that Section 816-bis of the Italian Code of Civil Procedure states that the parties *may* be represented by a lawyer, but in most cases parties appoint a lawyer, as they generally believe that such a complex procedure must necessarily be dealt with by legal experts. Attorney representation in arbitration is widespread across different systems and it has often been remarked that the parties believe that being represented by a lawyer increases their chances of a favourable award, even though it adds markedly to the cost of the proceedings (Block and Stieber 1987: 543).

Towards a Juridification of Arbitration?

Mattli (2001: 920) states that, '[U]nlike judges in public courts, who must follow fixed rules of procedure, and apply the laws of the land, arbitrators can dispense with legal formalities and may apply whatever procedural rules and substantive law best fit the case'. Even though it is undeniable that the choices made by the arbitrators are of fundamental importance, Mattli's interpretation does not seem to take into consideration the influence that litigation has on arbitration procedures and the fact that arbitrators tend to follow a set of standardized practices, in order to avoid, for instance, potential challenges of arbitrators or awards.

The complexity of the arbitrator's role has often been stressed and a controversial issue has always been 'whether the arbitrator should attempt to reconcile differences rather than render an award based on a strict interpretation of the contract' (Warren and Bernstein 1950: 21). Some people have been led to think that arbitration corresponds to a form of 'friendly justice', but it cannot be forgotten that, '[A]n arbitrator is faced with the same tasks as the judge. He must find the law, identify relevant facts, and apply the law' (Tobias 1960: 597).

Many commentators have observed that arbitration is being contaminated, or simply influenced, by litigative procedures. The high use of arbitrators coming from the legal field may be seen as one of the causes or the consequences of a sort of 'colonization' of arbitration by litigation. As Flood and Caiger (1993: 440) remark, 'Lawyers are in a strong position to effect colonisation because of their power over the discourse of legalism'. This process of juridification is not a new phenomenon. As early as 1960, Tobias wrote, '[R]ecent criticism of the arbitration process protests that it is becoming too "legalistic" and mourns the loss of the informal approach' (Tobias 1960: 596) and the author highlights the concept that legalism may be perceived in very different ways: 'If you believe that law is evil, *per se*, legalism is also evil. If you believe that law can be useful and bring justice, legalism is a positive good' (Tobias 1960: 596). From this perspective, therefore, the juridification of the process should be acknowledged as an inevitable phenomenon and should not be the object of a priori justification or condemnation.

Conclusions

This chapter has focused on some of the linguistic and communicative dynamics that are reflected in informal party examinations within arbitration proceedings. The aim was not to offer a generalized theory about how arbitration proceedings are conducted, especially considering the uniqueness of different proceedings. Indeed, '[E]ach arbitration is different, and each arbitral tribunal is different too' (Redfern and Hunter 2004: 437). The objective was instead to provide a contribution to the understanding of social practices in a specific institutional context, and, more specifically, to offer insights into the linguistic and discursive peculiarities of this procedure by means of some authentic instances. The construction of this communicative event is necessarily embedded in specific discourse practices and power relationships and I attempted to show how these dynamics may develop, by analyzing the data, and also by acquiring information from professionals in the field, whose collaboration has been extremely precious.

Making claims about intricate issues such as authority and power means walking a delicate line and this chapter by no means purports to be an exhaustive analysis of the multifaceted patterns on which the theory and practice of arbitration are based. As emerged from the analysis carried out, the allocation of power and decision-making authority over the proceedings and their different phases constitutes a complex issue. The oft-repeated presumption that arbitrators are granted the power to determine most aspects of an examination holds true to some extent, especially in comparison with litigative procedures; however, the scope for procedural practices that are not widely accepted and commonly used is considerably limited by the need to comply with standardized practices and routines.

The chapter has described the use of some of the features of courtroom language in arbitration, focusing on their use in oral communication. It has also attempted to present some of the dynamics which underlie the situated exercise of power by analyzing the communicative role assumed by different participants involved in the event, with particular attention being devoted to the role of arbitrators. This analysis also calls for a deeper investigation in this direction, as professional and communicative roles play a fundamental function in the development of arbitration discourse.

References

Anesa, Patrizia (2010): Spoken Interaction in Arbitration: An Analysis of Italian Arbitration Proceedings. In Bhatia, Vijay K., Candlin, Christopher N. and Gotti, Maurizio (Eds) *The Discourses of Dispute Resolution*, Bern, Peter Lang, 207–30.

Aron, Roberto, Fast, Julius and Klein, Richard B. (1996): *Trial Communication Skills*, Deerfield, IL, Clark Boardman Callaghan.

Barbieri, Giorgio (2007): *Il Nuovo Diritto dell'Arbitrato* [*The New Law on Arbitration*], Padova, Cedam.

Berger, Klaus Peter (2006): *Private Dispute Resolution in International Business: Negotiation, Mediation, Arbitration*, The Hague, Kluwer Law International.

Block, Richard N. and Stieber, Jack (1987): The Impact of Attorneys and Arbitrators on Arbitration Awards, *Industrial and Labor Relations Review*, Vol. 40, No. 4, 543–55.

Craig, William L., Park, William W. and Paulsson, Jan (2000): *International Chamber of Commercial Arbitration*, 3rd edition, New York, Oceana.

Flood, John and Caiger, Andrew (1993): Lawyers and Arbitration: The Juridification of Construction Disputes, *The Modern Law Review*, Vol. 56, No. 3, 412–40.

Gibbons, John (1994): *Language and the Law*, Harlow, Longman.

Gotti, Maurizio and Anesa, Patrizia (forthcoming): Professional Identities in Italian Arbitral Awards: The Spread of Lawyers' Language. Proceedings of the International Conference, *Issues of Identity in and Across Cultures and Professional Worlds*, Rome, 25–27 October 2007.

Hunter, Martin (1995): Reflections on Advocacy and the Art of Persuasion. *The Litigator*, 275–8. Online at <http://www.arbitration-icca.org/media/0/12232938101410/art_of_persuasion.pdf>, accessed 15 June 2011.

Jackson, Bernard S. (1995): *Making Sense in Law*, Liverpool, Deborah Charles Publications.

Lalive, Pierre (1984): On the Neutrality of the Arbitrator and of the Place of Arbitration. In Reymond, Claude and Bucher, Eugène (eds) *Swiss Essays on International Arbitration*, Zürich, Schulthess, 23–33.

Mattli, Walter (2001): Private Justice in a Global Economy: From Litigation to Arbitration, *International Organisation*, Vol. 55, No. 4, 919–47.

Murray, L. Smith (1990): Impartiality of the Party – Appointed Arbitrator, *Arbitration International*, Vol. 6, 320–42.

Partasides, Constantine (2001): The Selection, Appointment and Challenge of Arbitrators, *Vindobona Journal of International Commercial Law and Arbitration*, Vol. 5, No. 2, 217–28.

Redfern, Alan and Hunter, Martin (2004): *Law and Practice of International Commercial Arbitration*, 4th edition, London, Sweet & Maxwell.

Rhoades, Rufus, Kolkey, Daniel and Chernick, Richard (2007): *Practitioner's Handbook on International Arbitration and Mediation*, 2nd edition, Huntington, NY, JurisNet.

Stesuri, Aldo (2001): *Gli Arbitri: Mandato, Responsabilità e Funzioni* [*Arbitrators: Tasks, Responsibilities, and Functions*], Milano, Giuffrè.

Tampieri, Tiziana (2001): International Arbitration and Impartiality of Arbitrators, *Journal of International Arbitration*, Vol. 18, No. 5, 549–71.

Tobias, Paul H. (1960): In Defense of Creeping Legalism in Arbitration, *Industrial and Labor Relations Review*, Vol. 13, No. 4, 596–607.

Warren, Edgar L. and Bernstein, Irving (1950): The Arbitration Process, *Southern Economic Journal*, Vol. 17, No. 1, 16–32.

Chapter 7
Appraisal Analysis of Dissenting and Concurring Opinions[1]

Ruth Breeze

Introduction

International arbitration disputes are generally conducted under strict confidentiality, and often the only public evidence of what happened during the proceedings is the award itself (To 2008). However, most published arbitration rules permit arbitrators who are unwilling to sign the final award to issue dissenting opinions. Arbitrators who sign the award yet feel that it has not dealt adequately with a particular aspect of the case may also publish a separate reasoned statement, known as a concurring opinion. This practice, which originated in common law systems, is thought to be extending throughout the world, perhaps because of its use in influential arbitral proceedings such as those of the Iran–US Claims Tribunal and those conducted under the auspices of the International Centre for Settlement of Investment Disputes (ICSID) (Hussain 1984).

So far, linguists have shown little interest in the dissenting or concurring opinion. However, it is arguably of crucial importance, in that it provides a fascinating insight into what may go on behind closed doors in arbitral proceedings. For this reason, the practice of issuing separate opinions has been criticized by some experts, who feel that the confidentiality of the proceedings and the finality of the award are threatened by the publication of dissenting and concurring opinions, which reveal the major areas of dispute and, in some cases, throw the shortcomings of the award into relief (Lévy 1989; Gaillard and Savage 1999; Sanders 1999; Wangelin 2004). Quite aside from the controversy surrounding their use, these documents constitute an important source of information for linguists interested in arbitration, because they are highly likely to shed light on the way arguments are conducted during arbitration procedures. Arbitrators who draft separate opinions presumably draw on the arguments and objections that they raised during the sessions, as well as on the written documentation submitted during the proceedings. Although the published opinion belongs to a formal written genre, and has been prepared

1 The research on which this chapter is based is part of an international research project funded by the Research Grants Council of the Government of HKSAR [Project No. 9041191 (CityU 1501/06H)] entitled *International Commercial Arbitration Practices: A Discourse Analytical Study.* See <http://www.english.cityu.edu.hk/arbitration/>.

carefully and revised several times, it probably still bears the traces of the spoken discussions that preceded it in time. For this reason, close examination of the language of the divergent opinion may bring us as close as we can reasonably get to the linguistic realities of international commercial arbitration.

In linguistic terms, a dissenting or individual concurring opinion is essentially dialogic, addressing readers of various kinds (including the other arbitrators on the tribunal, the claimant or respondent, the wider professional community of arbitrators and those interested in the ongoing development of international law) and seeking to persuade them of the truth, legitimacy or logicality of certain views or arguments, and of the untruth, illegitimacy or illogicality of others. It is thus dialogic in that it is written in reaction to other (previous) texts and with the reader's (future) reaction in mind. Moreover, the text itself is also dialogic in that it contains accounts of different arguments or assertions and the corresponding counter-arguments, so that a great deal of the text is concerned with resolving a conflict between opposing or contradictory moves in a cogent and coherent manner. In all of this, both text-externally, looking to readers, and text-internally, resolving the conflicts presented, the arbitrator uses language to sharpen, emphasize, undermine or attack particular assertions. Adjective and adverbs, which are usually non-essential and contribute more to the tenor than the ideational content of the text, are a particularly interesting phenomenon in this sense, and may provide a key to underlying attitudes and values which help to shape the discourses of arbitration (Tessuto 2008).

In the present chapter, the tools of appraisal analysis (Martin 2000; Martin and Rose 2003) are used to explore the way adjectives and adverbs are used to evaluate, to adopt stances and to construct textual personae. The study focuses on six dissenting and two individual concurring opinions published on the website of the ICSID over the last 20 years. English was stated to be the official original language of the published opinion in all cases. The appraisal analysis of the adjectives and adverbs in these texts brings to light the distinctive features of the value system operating in arbitration practice, and affords insights into the way arbitrators project their professional persona and manage relationships within the process.

Background: Appraisal Analysis

Appraisal analysis is the name given to a set of tools that has been developed to examine the linguistic basis for differences in a writer's or speaker's style (Martin 2000; Martin and Rose 2003). It has chiefly been used with media texts, since it lends itself to the detection of bias or discrimination, but may be applied to texts of almost any kind in order to discern the underlying, even covert value systems which shape the language that is used and influence the effects that it may have on the reader. Appraisal analysis constitutes a rigorous framework for qualitative language study, allowing the researcher to explore the tenor of a particular text or text type by close examination of a multiplicity of factors. This system distinguishes between attitudes, judgements and emotive responses that are presented in texts, and looks at how the expression of such attitudes and judgements is often carefully managed to take into account the possibility of challenge or contradiction. This method in linguistic research has some similarities to that used in corpus studies by Hyland (1999), but is more suited to studies involving close analysis of a small number of texts.

Martin's framework for appraisal analysis was developed within the framework of systemic functional linguistics as a toolkit for discourse analysis. It offers a scheme for classifying particular lexical items in terms of the interpersonal tenor of the text. Of particular interest in this are non-essential lexical items, such as adjectives and adverbs, which are used, consciously or subconsciously, to communicate a degree of emotion, an ethical judgement, or some aspect of aesthetic appreciation. These come under the heading of appraisal, an aspect which belongs to the interpersonal metafunction of language, since it involves negotiating attitudes with readers or listeners. Appraisal analysis offers a way of gauging the strength of feeling conveyed through a text, and testing how values are sourced and readers aligned (Martin and Rose 2003: 22).

Appraisal encompasses three main aspects of attitude: affect, judgement and appreciation (Martin and Rose 2003: 62). These in turn may each be subdivided into various categories, so that, for example, judgement may relate to social esteem, in the form of normality, capacity or tenacity, or to social sanction, expressed as veracity and propriety. In each of these sub-categories, there is a positive and a negative dimension, so that the category of normality includes positive qualities that make someone or something special, in the positive dimension, and negative qualities that make someone or something the object of criticism, on the minus side. Similarly, the area of appreciation subdivides into reaction, composition and valuation, all of which have a positive and a negative dimension. Appraisal analysis also covers the slightly different issue of amplification (intensifiers), which may operate in tandem with one of the other aspects.

This would seem to be clear enough, but in some cases it is not particularly easy to distinguish between the different categories. Indeed, one lexical item may, in different contexts, convey either judgement (approval of a human action, for example) or appreciation (of a product of human action). Thus utterances like, 'That's a brilliant plan' are, Martin argues, positioned somewhere in the overlap between judgement and appreciation. This alerts us to the existence of borderline or fuzzy categories in appraisal, which represent a special sub-grouping of evaluations which are ambiguous in terms of attitudinal positioning. In such cases, only the context can reveal whether the appraisal is essentially judgemental or appreciative. The context may guide us towards seeing a particular utterance as more about human behaviour (judgement) than about the internal qualities of some entity (appreciation). Examples of this kind stand apart from the majority of evaluations, which are not ambiguous in this way.

In the present case, it is assumed that appraisal analysis may bring to light aspects of the way arbitrators construct their authorial voice or textual persona. It will also shed light on the relational issue of how they position themselves with regard to their debating partners, in both a positive and a negative sense. Appraisal analysis will thus provide insights into the tenor of the discussions in international arbitration disputes, and might pave the way for more detailed future comparisons with the language of the courtroom.

In the first stage of the study, the texts were studied in depth in order to obtain all the adjectives and adverbs used in an evaluative sense in the opinions. These adjectives and adverbs were divided into two categories: those used in reference to the writer's own actions and his or her own arguments and ideas, or to denote approval of other people's actions, arguments or ideas, principally those of the tribunal or those expressed in the award itself (positive dimension); and those used in the context of disagreement with or disapproval of the arguments, actions or ideas expressed by the majority on the tribunal or in the award itself (negative dimension). These adjectives and adverbs were then classified using Martin's principles of appraisal analysis, for both the positive and the negative dimensions. Quantitative results were obtained for the different categories of adjective and adverb. Specific examples of adjective and adverb use were analyzed in greater depth in order to build a more detailed picture of the way appraisal functions in this genre. Finally, the results of the study were analyzed in terms of the value system that underpins the discourses of arbitration.

Results: Overall Frequency of Adjectives and Adverbs

Adjectives and adverbs were relatively sparse in these texts, yet appeared to play a significant role in colouring the discourse, sharpening the arbitrator's own arguments and undermining those which he or she rejected. Table 7.1 shows

Table 7.1 Number of evaluative adjectives and adverbs used by each arbitrator to signal agreement/endorsement or disagreement

Case	Word length	Adj. agree	Adv. agree	Total agree 1,000 words	Adj. disagree	Adv. disagree	Total disagree 1,000 words
1. Asante	10,759	18	12	2.7	23	5	2.6
2. Berman	3,885	24	15	10	11	13	6.2
3. Covarrubias	5,422	4	4	1.5	23	8	5.7
4. Highet	11,821	25	10	3	14	2	1.4
5. Lalonde	503	5	2	13.9	1	1	4
6. Rovine	12,212	31	16	3.8	11	10	1.7
7. Suratgar	1,654	4	6	6	0	1	0.6
8. Weil	5,809	23	10	5.7	4	2	1

the total number of adjectives and adverbs used in an evaluative sense in the ten opinions. The numbers in the two columns of data headed 'Adj. agree' and 'Adv. agree' account for those adjectives or adverbs used when indicating the writer's endorsement or approval (that is, when expressing his/her own ideas or when setting out ideas or principles with which he/she agreed). The two columns headed 'Adj. disagree' and 'Adv. disagree' give the figures for the total numbers of adjectives and adverbs used when expressing disagreement, normalized to the number per 1,000 words, in order to facilitate comparison of data.

As can be seen in Table 7.1, the frequency of adjectives and adverbs varies among the opinions. Most writers use more positive than negative elements, the exception being Covarrubias. Some texts had a relatively high frequency of adjectives (Lalonde, Berman), while others had very few. We could speculate that some of these differences may be accounted for by personal style, by the type of argument used, or by the length of the texts. The first language of the author of the opinion may also be influential: in the case of Covarrubias, official original versions of his opinion were published side by side in English and Spanish on the ICSID website, but no indication is given as to which was written first. Covarrubias appears to have a rather austere style with a noticeably low frequency of adjectives and adverbs, which may well reflect approaches to legal drafting and forensic discourse in Roman law traditions. Šarčević (2008) has pointed out that the non-native user of English is at a certain disadvantage in international arbitration, and we might surmise that language problems may extend beyond major issues of error and ambiguity to subtler features of discourse such as the use of adjectives and adverbs. However, it is not prudent to draw strong conclusions on this point in the absence of further information about how the opinion was drafted. It should be noted that there is considerable variation among the figures for the other arbitrators, who all published a single original opinion in English, and there is insufficient evidence to permit us to assert that language background is a significant factor in the frequency of adjective and adverb use.

Detailed Analysis: Affect, Judgement, Appreciation

A more systematic examination of the patterns that emerge in dissenting and concurring opinions is necessary so that the professional values which help to shape the discourses of arbitration can emerge more clearly.

In the present sample of texts, the adjectives and adverbs used to project oneself positively or endorse others' propositions tend mainly to belong to the categories of judgement and appreciation. Affective adjectives/adverbs, augmentatives and hedges are relatively scarce.

The overall prevalence of adjectives and adverbs belonging to different categories of appraisal is shown in Table 7.2.

Table 7.2 Prevalence of different categories of appraisal

Category	Positive dimension	Negative dimension
Affect	13	8
Judgment		
Normality	19	4
Capacity	1	1
Tenacity	12	4
Veracity	19	19
Propriety	12	14
Appreciation		
Reaction	11	15
Composition	50	42
Valuation	62	11
Augmentatives	12	5
Hedges	0	5

As can be seen from the high frequency of adjectives and adverbs referring to composition, these arbitrators are particularly concerned with the balance and complexity of argument, both in the positive and negative sense. Thus their own views, or those they support, are portrayed as clear or reasonable, while those of their opposite numbers are inconsistent or unclear. These arbitrators also make ample use of positive valuations (*significant*, *important*, *considerable*), but are less likely to use the negative counterparts to these. Other categories of appraisal that stand out in quantitative terms are judgements of normality, mainly in the positive dimension (*normal*, *general*, *ordinary*), judgements of veracity, both positive (*true*, *genuine*) and negative (*alleged*, *apparent*), and judgements of propriety, both positive (*rightly*, *properly*, *acceptable*) and negative (*unacceptable*, *reproachable*, *inadmissible*). On the other hand, adverbs used as standard intensifiers (*highly*, *wholly*, *absolutely*) and hedges (*virtually*, *hardly*) are also occasionally encountered, but seem not to enjoy great prominence in these opinions.

In all this, it should be noted that the adjectives and adverbs were not evenly distributed through the text, but rather tended to appear at the beginning, where the arbitrator is introducing his/her public statement of dissent, or near the end, where he/she is summarizing his/her position. It can be assumed that these parts of the text tend to be more interpersonal in the way they are formulated, whereas the middle section of the opinion is often a detailed discussion of points of law, precedents or details of the case, which is expressed in a style that is concise, objective and somewhat dry.

In what follows, the texts will be analyzed in terms of each of Martin's appraisal categories in turn.

Table 7.3 Types of affect in arbitration

	Positive dimension	Negative dimension
Affect: Quality	respectful, advisable, instructive	harsh, repugnant
Affect: Process	wholeheartedly	

Appraisal: Affect

Table 7.3 illustrates the types of adjective or adverb found in these texts belonging to the area of affect. As was noted above, there are relatively few instances of negative affect, while there are rather more belonging to the positive dimension.

The relative frequency of positive indices of affect is interesting, in that the evidence suggests a formal culture of respect in which participants may construct themselves in an advisory or even educational role. In fact, many of the instances of positive affect in this sample can be accounted for by conventions of courtroom language (*respectful*, *humble*). Even though arbitrators are, strictly speaking, not working in a courtroom setting and not bound by conventional court etiquette, it would seem that their language, at least in this aspect, is coloured by their previous experience as counsel. These words have a relational function, and it might be supposed that the relationships created in arbitration proceedings reflect the type of relationships and professional self-projections generated by the courtroom.

Finally, some of the arbitrators in this sample also used affective elements in what seems to be a more personal way. Thus one arbitrator declares himself to take 'a *sterner* view', conveying some degree of emotion: it might be speculated that in context, this represents a form of self-deprecating humour which is rare in written legal documents. Other arbitrators make use of the term *wholeheartedly*, in order to stress their endorsement of some argument, adding a degree of warmth to the rather dry nature of their legal argumentation.

Negative affect is rarely expressed, but when it is, it is used to strong effect. Arbitrators in the present sample occasionally attack their opponents' arguments or judgements as cruel or even repulsive. However, it should be noted that the use of these words is depersonalized, applied to the argument or decision rather than the person or people responsible.

Appraisal: Judgement

As Table 7.2 shows, types of judgement are fully represented in these texts, and so it is worth examining this phenomenon in more detail. Table 7.4 shows examples of the adjectives and adverbs used in the opinions, classified according to the categories of appraisal analysis.

Table 7.4 Types of judgement in arbitration

	Positive dimension	Negative dimension
Social esteem		
Normality	exclusive, invariably, normal, general, plain, natural, ordinary	Anomalous
Capacity		
Tenacity	reliable, stable, wise, strong	unreliable, risky, delicate
Social sanction		
Veracity	genuine, credible, undisputed, indisputable, true, authoritative	controversial, alleged/ly apparent/ly, artificial
Propriety	rightly, correct, acceptable, properly, proper	unacceptable, reproachable, erroneous, regrettable, inadmissible, self-serving

In order to understand the categories that belong under the heading of judgement, it is worth considering how they are generally defined. According to Martin and Rose (2003: 62), judgements are the institutionalization of feeling about how people should and should not behave. As they are socially constructed, they will be shaped by the system of values that is current in a particular discipline. Judgements generally fall into two major categories, social esteem, involving admiration and criticism, and social sanction, involving praise and condemnation. For the former, the analyst must ask, 'Is it special?' (normality), 'Is it capable?' (capacity) and 'Is it dependable?' (tenacity). Social sanction, on the other hand, requires us to ask, 'Is it honest?' (veracity) and 'Is it beyond reproach?' (propriety). It is noticeable that normality, veracity and propriety are particularly salient values in these texts, while the negatives of veracity and propriety are also important. Tenacity also figures as a value, but capacity is completely absent. In general, social sanction is the main focus of criticism, with propriety being the single category with the greatest number of word types.

On the positive side, the arbitrators in this sample frequently bolster their own arguments or those to which they subscribe with references to their normality, veracity or propriety. In legal contexts, concepts like *general*, *ordinary* and *natural* are applied to reinforce the notion that something is the usual practice or the normal way of seeing things. Law – and by extension, arbitration practice – revolves around normativity, and what is *normal* is generally acceptable. Veracity is also extremely important in legal discourses, since it is essential to have access to the truth about a given matter in order to make decisions about it. Thus arbitrators reinforce their own arguments by emphasizing their truth or authenticity. Propriety, which belongs to the realm of what is proper, is also an important value, and the frequent use of words like *rightly*, *properly*, *correct* and *acceptable* suggests that arbitrators are very concerned to show that their own arguments or actions are appropriate on a professional level.

Adjectives and adverbs belonging to the area of judgement are also frequent in the arbitrators' accounts of views to which they do not subscribe. These include:

negative uses or opposites of normality (*anomalous*), veracity (*alleged, apparent*) and propriety (*unacceptable, reproachable, not proper*). In this, the term *alleged* is particularly frequent, playing a specific role of its own in casting doubt on the veracity of propositions that are being reported.

Regarding the adverbs used when expressing disagreement, they again followed a similar pattern to the adjectives. Adverbs are mainly used to intensify the attack on others' arguments, accounts or handling of the case in judgemental terms (*fundamentally, essentially, strikingly, not adequately, not diligently and systematically, not explicitly, not properly, too perfunctorily, precipitously*, and so on). Moreover, adverbs would seem to have a special role in undermining reports of propositions that other parties have put forward: some of the arbitrators in this study made frequent use of this device (*superficially attractive, apparently, allegedly*) in order to distance themselves from claims that have been made by one of the parties, or even by members of the tribunal, as in the following excerpt:

> The evidence produced by the Claimant is insufficient. What is more noticeable is how little emphasis he has placed on proving the *allegedly* more favorable treatment of the Poblano Group. (Covarrubias)

The area of judgement thus represents a crucial value in the discourses of arbitration, and the categories of normality, veracity and propriety are particularly salient, with the latter two also occupying a prominent position when negative judgements are formulated.

Appraisal: Appreciation

Appreciation can be thought of as the institutionalization of feeling in the context of propositions. Like affect and judgement, it has both a positive and a negative dimension corresponding to positive and negative evaluations of texts and other phenomena. The system is organized around three axes: reaction, composition and valuation. Reaction is to do with the emotional impact something has on us. Composition concerns our sense of proportionality (balance) and detail (complexity). Valuation reflects our assessment of social significance. According to Martin and Rose (2003: 64), valuation is particularly field-specific, since the criteria for valuing an argument, person or text are mostly specific to particular disciplines.

As can be seen from Table 7.5, in the present case, the adjectives and adverbs used for positive and negative valuation have a particularly legal flavour, contrasting neatly with the set of adjectives for valuation listed by Martin and Rose (2003: 64) for linguistics (useful, penetrating, illuminating, challenging, and so on).

However, the most striking aspect to emerge from Table 7.5 is the preponderance of adjectives and adverbs denoting composition (balance and complexity are here

Table 7.5 Types of appreciation in arbitration

	Positive dimension	**Negative dimension**
Reaction (impact)	inescapable, convincing, compelling, striking, promising	unfortunate, absurd,
Reaction (quality)	brilliant	poor
Composition (balance and complexity)	reasonable, rational, logical, tenable, evident, basic, clear/ly, precise, lucid	mystifying, defective, misleading, inconsistent
Valuation	relevant, important, significant, crucial, sufficient, essential, considerable	insufficient, incomplete, perfunctorily

grouped together). In this, the words *clear* and *clearly* have a special position. They appear to represent a special value in legal practice, as a value which must be invoked frequently, even though analysis of their actual use reveals that the clarity to which they allude is frequently only rhetorical.

In the area of appreciation, adjectives and adverbs fitted the categories of: reaction (*compelling*, *indisputable*, *inescapable*); composition in terms of degrees of simplicity or complexity (*obvious*, *evident*, *basic*, *complex*, *precise*, *straightforward*); composition in terms of clarity of argument or thought (*clear*, *lucid*, *logical*, *cogent*, *consistent*, *tenable*, *sound*, *reasonable*, *rational*); and valuation (*adequate*, *sufficient*, *important*, *relevant*, *crucial*, *essential*, *considerable*, *decisive*). Some arbitrators also made use of these adjectives in double negative constructions (*not insignificant*, *not untenable*), which has long been recognized as a feature of legal language in other contexts.

The preponderance of adjectives and adverbs denoting clarity and importance is not unexpected, because logical reasoning and salience are key issues in legal discourse. However, from the point of view of appraisal analysis these categories are interesting, in that they would appear to be closer to Martin's fuzzy categories straddling judgement and aesthetics. Like *brilliant*, in the example provided above, *clear* in these contexts seems to be appraising a product, something that can be contemplated as a pleasing image (one arbitrator even uses the phrase *crystal clear*), yet also evaluating an action (an argument or idea which is not clear is not dependable). In the context of the dissenting opinion, *clear* and its synonyms are particularly interesting, since the propositions reinforced by the use of *clear* must often have been anything but clear in the context of the case. There is no doubt that being clear is a powerful value in the discourses of law (Bhatia 1993), as is emphasized by the repeated prescriptive use of *clear* by some arbitrators such as Berman:

> The grounds for doing so must be *clear* and strong [...] they must be *clearly* explained and justified [...].Where, on the other hand, the case is not sufficiently

> *clear* as to enable the issue to be convincingly determined *in limine*, the proper course is *plainly* that provided for in Article 41(2) of the Convention.

Clear is thus often used to consolidate points on which there is consensus among the tribunal, as in the following example where Highet is establishing a firm point of agreement in order to go on to distinguish between this situation and the actual case under discussion:

> If the Article 1121 waiver had been intended to cover any and all concurrent legal activity, then clearly Claimant's course of conduct in Mexico would be inconsistent with it and would vitiate the waiver.

It would thus seem that *clear* is often used not as a purely objective appraisal of the clarity or logic of an assertion or fact or argument, but as a rhetorical device to bolster the consensus on a particular point, often before showing how this point does not apply in the case at hand.

On other occasions, the use of *clear* serves to reinforce the dissenting arbitrator's view that a particular fact or argument is clear in the face of the majority who have taken a different view, as in the following example, where Covarrubias makes an assertion that stands out as being rather shocking, in the context of an arbitral decision in favour of CEMSA against Mexico:

> Thus, CEMSA's cigarette export business, being a legal activity, was based on premises that clearly violated Mexican laws.

Thus although *clear* is ostensibly about establishing a consensus about facts or arguments, it may be used where there is no consensus, as an element of reinforcement or persuasion. In the example that follows, Weil is making a very strong assertion that flies in the face of the majority decision:

> The situation in the instant case is crystal clear and in effect undisputed: it is a situation where there is simply no question of any foreign – whether Lithuanian or other – investment in Ukraine, and where there is a question only, and indisputably, of an Ukrainian investment in Ukraine. And to such a situation the ICSID Convention and the ICSID procedures are not meant to apply.

He thus appeals to clarity as a principal value for deciding the case, reinforcing his judgement of the situation by using the appreciative term *crystal clear*, with evident aesthetic connotations.

The range of adjectives drawn upon to characterize arguments and opinions with which the writer did not agree is similar to that outlined above, but most examples are used in a negative sense. Thus in the area of appreciation, we find the absence of logic and clarity, which is most commonly expressed with *not* (*not rational*, *not logically valid*, *not reasonable*), but which is also conveyed using antonyms (*illogical, flawed, inconsistent, defective, mystifying*). There are also references to valuation, which are usually employed in the affirmative form (*crucial, considerable*), but which are also encountered as negatives or antonyms (*insufficient, inadmissible, unacceptable, incomplete, perfunctorily, void*).

The broader picture emerging from this survey of adjectives and adverbs connoting appreciation is that composition (balance and complexity) is an area of key importance for arbitrators, with logic and clarity figuring as outstanding values, while their opposites are major flaws. Reaction is also important, and is generally expressed in terms of conviction, that is, whether or not an idea is felt to be compelling. Valuation tends to centre on importance, in the positive dimension, and insufficiency, in the negative.

Conclusions

All professional communities engage in discursive practices that draw on knowledge of what forms of communication are suitable in particular kinds of professional action (Bhatia 2004). An accomplished professional is able to operate skilfully, managing a range of linguistic resources to achieve a particular communicative end. The language options available in a given situation are constrained by what is socially recognized as appropriate, on the level of register and relational discourse, and by the professional consensus as to what is acceptable, on the level of attitudes and values.

In the case of international dispute resolution, discourse analysts have focused on material that is in the public domain such as awards (Giner 2009; Martinez 2009), but little published research is available on the language used behind the closed doors of the arbitration court. Dissenting and concurring opinions are texts that have emerged from the conflict between one arbitrator and the majority, and are therefore likely to bear traces of the discourses of arbitration proceedings. In them, arbitrators refer to the award and to the memorial or reply, and even reproduce verbatim excerpts from cross-examinations held *in camera*. It is reasonable to suppose that the voice of the arbitrator which emerges from these divergent opinions has much in common with the voice of the same arbitrator during the proceedings. The evidence presented here is thus more than a mere textual analysis of a published document; it opens a window on to the closed rooms where international arbitration disputes are held.

The appraisal analysis conducted here might therefore serve as a pilot study for linguists interested in investigating arbitration disputes on a larger scale. It also provides evidence that could be useful in contrastive studies designed to gauge commonality and contrast between the language of arbitration and that of litigation.

To summarize the main findings of the present study, the appraisal analysis carried out here brought to light a series of values which shape the arbitrator's discursive possibilities. Expression of affect is rare, and often conventionalized, but may occasionally be used for particular rhetorical effect. Judgement tends to centre on the key values of normality, veracity and propriety, the latter two frequently being indexed in negative as well as positive senses. Appreciation focuses on valuation of importance or significance, but also centres on aspects of composition, namely clarity and logic of argument, which appear to be key values in the discourses of arbitration. The persuasiveness of arguments or evidence is also the main focus of positive reaction on the part of the writer.

Extrapolating from the study of these adjectives and adverbs, it is possible to assert that the underlying value system of arbitration is one in which argument is valued for its own qualities of clarity and consistency, and for its ability to persuade. Normality or ordinariness is also a value, insofar as it means adhering to standard ways of understanding legislation or carrying out procedures. Propriety is important, in the sense of doing things properly, following the proper proceedings, acting or arguing in a way that is regarded as correct within the profession. Finally, veracity must also be mentioned as a key value, because, as in most legal proceedings, it is essential to establish the truth, and doubt about issues of fact will undermine the entire case.

In terms of authorial stance, it is clear that these arbitrators wish to position themselves as representing truth, correctness and normality, as against uncertainty or deceitfulness, and improper or anomalous practices. Their textual persona also lays strong claims to clarity and logic, setting itself up firmly against defective, misleading or inconsistent arguments. Moreover, the arbitrators also occupy a powerful discourse position as arbiters of importance, ranking issues in terms of their significance or lack of it. The discursive self-construction of the arbitrator projected in these texts can thus be characterized above all as authoritative. They speak as masters of clarity and logic, who seek truth and propriety in a way that is natural and appropriate for members of their profession.

References

Bhatia, Vijay K. (1993): *Analysing Genre: Language Use in Professional Settings*, London, Longman.

Bhatia, Vijay K. (2004): *Worlds of Written Discourse*, London, Continuum.

Gaillard, Emmanuel and Savage, John (Eds.) (1999): *Fouchard Gaillard Goldman on International Commercial Arbitration*, The Hague, Kluwer Law International.

Giner, Diana (2009): *A Contribution to the Contrastive Analysis of Persuasion through Interactional Elements in International Commercial Awards and Judgements*. Paper presented at First International Seminar on Languages for Business, Avila, June 5–6, 2009.

Hussain, Ijaz (1984): *Dissenting and Separate Opinions at the World Court*, Dordrecht, Martinus Nijhoff Publishing.

Hyland, Ken (1999): Disciplinary Discourses: Writer Stance in Research Articles. In Candlin, Christopher N. and Hyland, Ken (Eds) *Writing: Texts, Processes and Practices*, London, Longman, 99–121.

Lévy, Laurent (1989): Dissenting Opinions in International Arbitration in Switzerland, *International Arbitration*, Vol. 5, 34–41.

Martin, Jim (2000): Beyond Exchange: Appraisal Systems in English. In Hunston, Susan and Thompson, Geoff (Eds) *Evaluation in Text: Authorial Stance and the Construction of Discourse*, Oxford, Oxford University Press, 142–75.

Martin, Jim and Rose, David (2003): *Working with Discourse: Meaning Beyond the Clause*, London, Continuum.

Martinez, Laura (2009): Analysing Generic Integrity in Professional Discourses: The Case of Intellectual Property Arbitration. In Pérez-Llantada, Carmen and Watson, Martha (Eds) *Language for Business: A Global Approach*, Zaragoza, Prensas Universitarias de Zaragoza, 217–32.

Sanders, Peter (1999): *Quo Vadis Arbitration? Sixty Years of Arbitration Practice: A Comparative Study*, The Hague and Boston, Kluwer Law International.

Sarčevič, Susan (2008): Translation in International Arbitration. In Bhatia, Vijay K., Candlin, Christopher. N. and Engberg, Jan (Eds) *Legal Discourse across Cultures and Systems*, Hong Kong, Hong Kong University Press, 291–307.

Tessuto, Girolamo (2008): Discourse Systems in English Arbitration Awards. In Bhatia, Vijay K., Candlin, Christopher N. and Engberg, Jan (Eds) *Legal Discourse across Cultures and Systems*, Hong Kong, Hong Kong University Press, 181–98.

To, Christopher (2008): Confidentiality in Arbitration. In Bhatia, Vijay K., Candlin, Christopher N. and Engberg, Jan (Eds) *Legal Discourse across Cultures and Systems*, Hong Kong, Hong Kong University Press, 75–107.

Wangelin, James D. (2004): *Buttressing the Pillars of Arbitration*, Mealey's International Arbitration Reports, January. Online at <http://www.cidra.org/articles/pillarb.htm>, accessed 15 June 2011.

Cases

Asante. *Asian Agricultural Products Limited v. Democratic Socialist Republic of Sri Lanka* (ICSID Case No. ARB/87/3) Dissenting opinion of Samuel K.B. Asante.

Berman. *Industria Nacional de Alimentos, S.A. and Indalsa Perú, S.A. (formerly Empresas Lucchetti, S.A. and Lucchetti Perú, S.A.) v. Republic of Peru* (ICSID Case No. ARB/03/4) Dissenting opinion of Franklin Berman.

Covarrubias. *Marvin Roy Feldman Karpa v. United Mexican States* (ICSID Case No. ARB(AF)/99/1) Dissenting opinion of Jorge Covarrubias Bravo.

Highet. *Waste Management, Inc. v. United Mexican States* (ICSID Case No. ARB(AF)/98/2) Dissenting opinion of Keith Highet.

Lalonde. *Sempra Energy International v. Argentine Republic* (ICSID Case No. ARB/02/16) Partial dissenting opinion of Marc Lalonde.

Rovine. *Archer Daniels Midland Company and Tate & Lyle Ingredients Americas, Inc. v. United Mexican States* (ICSID Case No. ARB(AF)/04/5) Concurring opinion of Arthur W. Rovine.

Suratgar. *Mihaly International Corporation v. Democratic Socialist Republic of Sri Lanka* (ICSID Case No. ARB/00/2) Concurring opinion of David Suratgar.

Weil. *Tokios Tokelės v. Ukraine* (ICSID Case No. ARB/02/18) Dissenting opinion of Prosper Weil.

Chapter 8
The Judicialization of Arbitration Discourse in the Italian Context[1]

Maurizio Gotti

Arbitration, one of the main procedures for alternative dispute resolution (ADR), is living in a troublesome period. On the one hand, the spread of globalization is causing a great enlargement of international trade with the consequent increase in contractual conflicts, which are not always resolved through litigation but also through ADR procedures, among which arbitration has for many decades represented the principal way. For these reasons, in certain areas arbitration seems to be expanding, particularly in the Far East (Browker 2008). On the other hand, the last few years have witnessed greater and greater dissatisfaction with the process of arbitration, which was once considered to be quicker, cheaper and more confidential than litigation. This dissatisfaction is well summed up in a recent survey of corporate attitudes and practices in international arbitration (Mistelis 2004), which has highlighted the following main concerns on the part of the corporations involved:

- expense: 49 per cent;
- time: 18 per cent;
- no third-party mechanism: 11 per cent;
- lack of appeal structure: 9 per cent;
- national court intervention: 5 per cent;
- other: 8 per cent.

Indeed, it is often alleged that arbitration is becoming increasingly expensive and this is the single main concern of the users of arbitration. As Okekeifere (1998: 87) asserts 'In earlier times, arbitration was much cheaper than court litigation in practically all ways. Today, it may still be so in several particular cases, but hardly

1 The research on which this chapter is based is part of an international research project funded by the Research Grants Council of the Government of HKSAR [Project No. 9041191 (CityU 1501/06H)] entitled *International Commercial Arbitration Practices: A Discourse Analytical Study* <http://www.english.cityu.edu.hk/arbitration/>. It also contributes to the National Research Programme *Tension and Change in Domain-specific Genres* directed by Professor Maurizio Gotti of the University of Bergamo, funded by the Italian Ministry of University (COFIN Grant No. 2007JCY9Y9).

so as a general rule'. Arbitration proceedings are also deemed to take longer than the parties anticipated, particularly due to the fact that proceedings increasingly try to simulate court cases. Another problematic issue is the fact that arbitration is bi-polar, designed for and typically operating between two parties, which may present difficulties in international trade where many parties are frequently involved. It is also a prevalent perception that the finality of arbitral award (that is, the fact that there is no possibility of appeal within the arbitration system) has led to an increase in the number of applications to national courts for the challenge of arbitration awards. And this also explains the concern about national court intervention in the arbitration system.

The opinion that arbitration is losing ground has been expressed by several experts in the field (cf. Okekeifere 1998; Rubino-Sammartano 2003). This loss of favour in certain countries is also due to the change in nature that arbitration is undergoing. According to several practitioners, there has recently been a process of 'judicialization' of international commercial arbitration (ICA), meaning:

> both that arbitrations tend to be conducted more frequently with the procedural intricacy and formality more native to litigation in national courts and that they are more often subjected to judicial intervention and control (Browker 2008: 183).

Already at the turn of the century, one of the main experts in ICA pointed out the seriousness of this change:

> ICA [International Commercial Arbitration] has become almost indistinguishable from litigation, which it was at one time intended to supplant – with law, more law, legalese and more legalese: [...] motivated or reasoned decisions [...] are now increasingly long and turgid, and too full of legal learning (Nariman 2000: 262).

As can be seen, the main reasons for this 'judicialization' of ICA are identified in the greater space taken up by legal practice on the one hand, and, in the use of legal discourse, on the other. Another instance of the influence of litigation on this ADR procedure has been found in the fact that '[I]t [ICA] has become increasingly precedent-bound, and arbitral awards frequently contain citations from other arbitral awards, building up the *lex mercatoria*' (Nariman 2000: 263). These changes have been harshly criticized by practitioners, who now often refer to the whole process with 'the pejorative sobriquet: *arbitigation*' (Nariman 2000: 264).

This negative attitude on the part of practitioners is mainly due to the fact that the importation of litigation practices into the arbitration process has greatly slowed down the entire process and procedure, with the consequent increase in its cost. This opinion is clearly expressed by Okekeifere:

> Multiple legal rules have also been introduced, presumably for the attainment of more justice in arbitral proceedings and awards. These factors have introduced delay – monumental delay – but a device for the eradication or containment of the delay has hardly been found. The result is that, as the years pass, the problem of delay becomes more serious. [...] By their very nature of formality and elaborate administrative steps (bureaucracy), many institutional arbitrations are as time consuming as court proceedings. The ironical reality is therefore that delay – much delay – is now often a feature of arbitration. Several arbitral proceedings now take as much time as (and sometimes even more than) court adjudication of the same dispute(s) would (Okekeifere 1998: 85–6).

A further complaint is towards the passive attitude of modern arbitrators, who tend to limit their role to merely listening to the parties and then expressing their opinion, and not taking advantage of the greater possibilities of autonomous decision and independent action that are possible in this ADR procedure. As Rubino-Sammartano (2003: 342) states:

> A frequent reference is made in England to arbitrators who sit totally passively while the parties argue the case. Such arbitrators tend to imitate judges and miss the point that the parties refer the dispute to arbitration because they want something different and better than court proceedings.

The Judicialization of International Commercial Arbitration in Italy

The changes in arbitration procedures pointed out above denoting greater and greater influence of litigation practice and discourse have also taken place in the Italian context. Indeed, the recent reform of the Italian Arbitration Law (2006) has increased the risk of making arbitration too similar to civil proceedings as they treat arbitrators in a manner comparable to State judges. Moreover, the excessively formal and legalistic character of the new legislation has influenced negatively the effectiveness and speed of the proceedings with the consequence that arbitration in Italy has continued to represent a system of dispute resolution too troublesome to appeal to the interests of industry and commerce. Indeed, in Italy arbitration has always been a more costly option than recourse to ordinary justice. The main problems with the new system are summed up by Cutolo and Esposito (2007) as follows: too strict legal regulations, too high fees and excessive time limits which are virtually the same as those of ordinary civil proceedings. This opinion is confirmed by the interviews with Italian arbitration practitioners carried out by Ulisse Belotti (cf. his chapter in this volume) who has found that the main areas of concern are arbitration costs, interference from national laws and courts in challenging arbitration awards, and the relative speed of completion of arbitration proceedings. The high costs and long time of arbitration proceedings are due to the fact that parties often agree to extend the time limits set by institutional rules, while in some cases parties who find themselves in a weaker position tend to produce complex documentation in order to prolong procedures.

The recent reform clearly specifies that in case issues are not deemed arbitrable by the arbitrators, the arbitration proceedings are terminated and, consequently, parties have to involve the courts during arbitration proceedings in order to have a final decision. As a consequence, although Italian law does not require specific qualifications to become an arbitrator except for the requirement of impartiality and independence, local Chambers of Commerce strongly invite the parties to appoint legal experts as arbitrators. Indeed, although theoretically any professional can be enrolled at the Board of Arbitrators of the local Chamber of Commerce, in practice legal experts are generally appointed as arbitrators in an arbitration procedure, whereas all the other experts are appointed as consultants. This practice seems to have become entrenched, and the tacit convention of appointing lawyers appears to be well-established. On their part, the legal community have found that arbitration may be a significant means of extending their professional calling and augmenting their business income. Therefore, if the parties are strongly recommended to have recourse to legal experts as arbitrators, arbitration practices are very likely to adopt litigation procedures, which in turn will encourage the exploitation of litigation features in arbitration discourse. The influence of litigation on the process of arbitration is also favoured by the fact that, in order to better protect their interests and prevent the risk of challenge to final awards, the parties often have recourse to legal experts as arbitrators. The Code of Civil Procedure (CCP) (Section 829) indicates a list of circumstances in which an arbitral award can be challenged. Among other cases this happens when:

- the award contradicts either another award or a court decision;
- relevant legal rules have not been applied in the correct way.

It is clearly important, therefore, that arbitrators should have a solid legal background in order to ensure their familiarity with legal procedures and avoid incorrect practices that may make the award challengeable or annullable. Indeed, the majority of awards delivered up to 2006 had been challenged in front of the Court of Appeal mainly on legal grounds. This is one of the main reasons why, in the vast majority of cases, the arbitrator is also a lawyer. This appointment of a legal professional encourages the importation of typical litigation processes and procedures into arbitration practices and leads to an increasing mixture of discourses, thus threatening the integrity of arbitration practice.

Against this background, it is the purpose of this chapter to analyze arbitration awards written in Italian to point out the presence of instances of typical features of Italian legal discourse, which could thus furnish evidence for the process of judicialization of Italian arbitration discourse. The corpus analyzed consists of 20 commercial arbitration awards written in Italian in the last ten years, available in the archives of the Chambers of Arbitration of Bergamo, Milan and Reggio Emilia, totalling over 900,000 words. The results of a previous analysis carried out by the present author and Patrizia Anesa (Gotti and Anesa forthcoming) aiming to analyze whether the different professional backgrounds might influence the way in which awards are written, and whether the arbitrator's professional identity has any effect on the syntactic, lexical and stylistic choices made, have shown that the recourse to a lawyer as arbitrator is typical and that even in those rare cases in which non-legal practitioners are appointed as arbitrators, the structure and form of their awards are very similar to those of the awards written by legal professionals.

Features of Italian Arbitration Awards

Textual Features

From a macrostructural point of view, there are several similarities between an arbitration award and a court judgment.[2] The latter, in the Italian tradition, usually has the following typical structure (Santulli 2006):

- establishing the facts of the case;
- presenting arguments;
- pronouncing judgment.

A preliminary part of both awards and judgments is devoted to the identification of the case. In the case of the award, this part mentions the composition of the arbitral panel, the two parties and their representatives, and the identification number and the date of the award. The different roles of the two parties are well specified: the claimant is usually introduced by the title *attore/attrice*, while the respondent by the word *convenuto*. The main difference between the two documents is that the court judgment usually begins with the formulaic expression *Repubblica Italiana. In nome del Popolo Italiano* [Republic of Italy. In the name of the Italian People],[3] which underlines the legal authoritativeness of the document and of the institution that issues it.

Establishing the facts of the case The first main section of the award is devoted to the reconstruction of the facts of the dispute. This part too is similar to the first main section of a court judgment, which has the same function. The section is headed *Svolgimento del procedimento* [Development of the proceedings] or *Fatto e svolgimento della procedura* [Facts and development of the proceedings] or *Svolgimento della procedura arbitrale* [Development of the arbitral proceedings]. In this section – both in the award and in the court judgment – the relevant facts

2 Maci (forthcoming) has also shown great similarities between the structure of the award and that of the legal case.

3 Unless otherwise specified, all translations in this chapter are my own.

are reported in strict chronological order, mentioning in a detailed way all the documentation presented and examined. It is interesting to note that in both documents the facts are reported by means of the Italian *imperfetto* verb form, which is the typical tense used for narrative purposes:

(1) Con atto depositato il giorno [...] l'attore *chiedeva* l'attivazione di un procedimento arbitrale
[With the request presented on [...] the claimant asked for arbitration proceedings to be started (Award 14).

(2) Con ordinanza in data [...] il Tribunale *rigettava*
[With decree dated [...] the Court rejected] (Court judgment quoted in Mortara Garavelli 2001: 171)

Presenting arguments In both documents, this section is devoted to the illustration of the claims put forth by the parties, and has a clear argumentative function. In the award this section is often concluded by the presentation of the specific requests of the parties, clearly introduced by appropriate headings: *Quesiti per l'attore* [Claimant's requests] and *Quesiti per la parte convenuta* [Respondent's requests]. These requests are frequently summed up in numbered lists detailing the actions to be undertaken with the use of infinitival forms:

(3) 1. *Accertare e dichiarare* la nullità della domanda [...]
2. *Accertare e dichiarare* la decadenza e/o prescrizione [...]
3. *Accertare e dichiarare* la infondatezza della domanda [...]
[1. Ascertain and state the nullity of the request [...]
2. Ascertain and state the limitation and/or lapse [...]
3. Ascertain and state the groundlessness of the request [...]] (Award 15)

This section also contains the arbitrators'/judge's argumentations for and negotiation of their final decision. In the award, this part is often indicated by the headline *Motivazioni* [Reasons] or *Motivi della decisione* [Reasons for the decision] which are meant to highlight the *ratio decidendi* [criteria for the decision] that will be adopted in the formulation of the final decision. In the court judgment this part is usually devoted to a detailed examination of the current legislation concerning the case in question. It is interesting to note that while in the past, awards made reference mainly to the clauses of the contract or to previous agreements between the parties; nowadays, they often make reference to laws and regulations, thus resembling judgments in this respect. The most frequently cited legal text in Italian awards is the CCP, which is the most important compendium of laws relating to commercial transactions in the Italian context:

(4) Occorre chiarire che [...] l'attrice ha eccepito la decadenza e/o la prescrizione dall'azione che spetta alla società convenuta quale compratore

delle 'cose' oggetto del contratto, azione regolata *dagli Art. 1490 e segg.ti del Codice Civile*.
[It should be clarified that [...] the claimant has contested the limitation and/or lapse of the action that pertains to the respondent as buyer of the 'things' which constitute the object of the contract, an action ruled by Art. 1490 and foll. of the Civil Code.] (Award 15)

Another important legal text quoted in the award is the set of rules of the Arbitration Chamber which oversees the proceedings, and which in the end will verify the correctness of the award itself.

(5) Qualunque dubbio o divergenza possa sorgere tra le parti [...] saranno risolte [...] da un Collegio di tre arbitri, uno dei quali con funzioni di Presidente, nominati direttamente dalla Camera Arbitrale Nazionale e Internazionale di Milano, il cui *Regolamento Arbitrale Nazionale* le parti dichiarano di conoscere ed accettare interamente.
[Any doubt or disagreement that may arise between the parties [...] will be settled [...] by a Panel of three arbitrators, one of whom will function as President, appointed directly by the National and International Arbitral Chamber of Milan, whose National Arbitration Rules the parties declare to know and accept entirely.] (Award 18)

In some cases references are made also to court judgments, as can be seen in the following example where long quotations from verdicts of the *Corte di Cassazione* [Supreme Court of Appeal] are reported:

(6) [...] richiamate dalla stessa Convenuta, riconoscono 'la possibilità di ratifica da parte dell'interessato della nomina compiuta dal difensore senza potere' costituendo la ratifica 'un atto unilaterale recettizio, con il quale il soggetto falsamente rappresentato manifesta all'altro contraente, in modo univoco, e nella forma richiesta per il contratto da ratificare, la volontà di fare propri gli effetti del negozio concluso dal *falsus procurator*' (così *Cass. 23 novembre 2000, n. 15134*). Più in particolare la *Corte di Cassazione*, nella sentenza 4 giugno 1992, n. 6866 ha riconosciuto espressamente la legittimità, in un caso simile, della 'ratifica, con conseguente sanatoria del vizio di designazione dell'arbitro, attraverso una scrittura giudiziale o stragiudiziale che manifesti comunque la volontà della parte di investire l'arbitro del potere di decidere la controversia' (così *Cass. 4 giugno 1992, n. 6866*). (Award 18)

Pronouncing judgment The last main section of the document is the one expressing the final decision of the arbitral tribunal/judge. As is typical of court judgments, many awards also head this section with the acronym PQM (*Per questi motivi* [For these reasons]). This acronym is very common among legal practitioners and is never written in full; its frequent use by arbitrators means that they too are fully aware of its meaning. The verbs indicating the arbitrators' final decision are all in the present tense, which is the standard verb form used in legal texts to express performative acts (Garzone 2003):

(7) Il Collegio Arbitrale [...]
 1) *dichiara* infondata e respinge la domanda di illegittimità [...];
 2) quanto alle spese del Collegio Arbitrale, di Segreteria e di assistenza delle parti, così *decide*:
  a. *determina* le spese del Collegio Arbitrale [...] nel complessivo importo di € [...];
  b. *determina* le spese amministrative della Camera Arbitrale nell' importo di €[...].
 [The Arbitral Tribunal [...]
 1) declares the request of illegitimacy unfounded and rejects it [...];
 2) as regards the Arbitral Tribunal's fees, the secretarial expenses and those for the assistance to the parties, [the Tribunal] decides as follows:
  a. [the Tribunal] determines that the Arbitral Tribunal's fees [...] should correspond to the total amount of €[...];
  b. [the Tribunal] determines that the administrative expenses of the Arbitral Chamber should correspond to the total amount of €[...].] (Award 17)

The award then closes with the signatures of the members of the arbitral panel and the indication of the date and place where the document has been signed.

Lexical Features

As arbitration was conceived as an alternative way to solve disputes avoiding the recourse to lawyers and courts, one would expect the texts of the awards to be written in a language which is more ordinary discourse than legal discourse. Instead, from a lexical point of view, there are remarkable similarities between the language of awards and that of legal documents. One of the typical features of legal style is the use of doublets or longer synonymic strings of words often referred to as 'binomials or multinomials' (Bhatia 1993). In legal discourse multinomials are much more common than in general discourse, and this statistical significance makes them a definite style marker of the language of the law. Binomial expressions have a long tradition in legal texts and their main function is to guarantee technical accuracy and greater precision, unambiguity, as well as all-inclusiveness. These are very frequent also in awards, as the following quotations show:

(8) L'attore chiedeva che il Collegio Arbitrale *accertasse e dichiarasse* la società convenuta tenuta a versare il compenso pattuito.

[The claimant requested that the Arbitral Tribunal should *ascertain and state* that the respondent was liable to pay the compensation agreed upon.] (Award 14]

(9) Stante la *decadenza e prescrizione* dell'azione, la domanda svolta da parte convenuta non può essere accolta.
[In view of the *limitation and lapse* of the action, the request filed by the respondent cannot be granted.] (Award 15)

Another characteristic of legal documents is its intense conservatism. Indeed, in the field of jurisprudence, fear that new terms may lead to ambiguity favours the permanence of traditional linguistic traits, which are preserved even when they disappear from general language. Old terms are preferred to newly-coined words because of their century-old history and highly codified, universally accepted interpretations. The reverence for tradition observed in legal language leads to the use of archaic spellings or obsolete forms. As regards the former, there are instances of archaic spellings also in the corpus of awards analyzed here, such as *denunzia* instead of the usual *denuncia* [denouncement] and *denunziare* instead of the more common *denunciare* [denounce]. As regards the use of obsolete forms, the reading of the Italian awards has confirmed the presence of terms such as *erroneo* [wrong] instead of the common adjective *sbagliato*, or *sito* [located] preferred to the usual past particle used in an adjectival position *situato*. Most of the typical obsolete forms commonly used in legal texts and avoided in general language have been found in awards, as is the case of *addì* [on the [day] of], *all'uopo* [to the purpose], *altresì* [moreover], *ancorché* [although], *atteso che* [inasmuch as], *d'altronde* [on the other hand], *nel caso di specie* [in this specific case], *nella specie* [in particular], *onde* [whence], *orbene* [hence], *posto che* [given that], *siffatto* [such], *talché* [thus], *testé* [just].

Very frequent also is the use of technical phrases typical of legal discourse, in which words occurring in general speech collocate with other common words to make expressions that are used only in legal contexts (Dardano 1994), such as *espletare un incarico* [perform a task], *prestare il proprio consenso* [to give one's consent], *produrre un documento* [produce a document], *rigettare la domanda* [to deny a request], *stipulare un contratto* [to enter into a contract]. Similarly, awards contain verbs with meanings that are different from the usual ones and that instead are only found in legal contexts, such as *dedurre* ['argue', instead of the common meaning 'deduce'] or *lamentare* ['denounce', instead of 'complain'].

The influence of the discourse of litigation on that of arbitration is also clearly visible in the many legal expressions that occur in the awards taken into consideration. Here are a few examples: *adire il giudizio arbitrale* [resort to arbitral proceedings], *caducazione di un contratto* [annulment of a contract], *escussione di testi* [witness examination], *impugnare una sentenza* [appeal against a sentence]. Very frequent in awards is also the use of prepositional phrases typical of legal language (Cortelazzo 2006), such as: *a carico di* (for example, *a carico del datore di lavoro* [to be borne by the employer]), *a norma di* (for example, *a norma di legge* [according to law]), *a seguito di* (for example, *a seguito della risoluzione del contratto* [as a consequence of the cancellation of the contract], *a titolo di* (for example, *a titolo di ravvedimento oneroso* [by way of compensation against payment], *ai sensi di* (for example, *ai sensi dell'Art. 12 dello Statuto della Camera Arbitrale* [according to Art.12 of the Statutes of the Arbitral Chamber), *in sede* (for example, *in sede giurisdizionale od arbitrale* [during judicial or arbitral proceedings]).

Yet another typical characteristic of Italian legal lexis is zero derivation, which allows specialists to omit affixes when deriving a noun from a verb (Gotti 2011). Examples of this word-formation structure have also been found in arbitration awards as in the case of *convalida* [validation] from *convalidare, notifica* [notification] from *notificare, proroga* [extension] from *prorogare, ratifica* [ratification] from *ratificare, rimborso* [reimbursement] from *rimborsare, saldo* [settlement] from *saldare*, and *utilizzo* [utilization] from *utilizzare*.

One of the most evident features of Italian legal discourse is the use of Latinisms, which are derived from the long tradition of jurisprudence dating back to Roman times (Fiorelli 1998). Several Latinisms are also found in awards, which strengthens the impression of 'colonization' of arbitration from the legal field. Here are a few Latinate forms found in our corpus: *ab origine* [from the beginning], *causa petendi* [the grounds of the claim], *contra legem* [against the law], *de facto* [according to facts], *dominus* [the owner of a right], *ex ante* [since then], *ex nunc* [since now], *in toto* [as a whole], *inter alia* [amongst others], *ope legis* [by law], *par condicio* [the same condition], *petitum* [the claim], *potestas judicandi* [judicial power], *ratio legis* [the spirit of the law], *una tantum* [once and for all].

Syntactic Features

A comparison between court judgments and arbitration awards also shows great similarities from a syntactic point of view. One of the main features of legal documents is the great length of their sentences which is much higher not only than those found in general texts but also of those used in other specialized domains (Cavagnoli and Ioriatti Ferrari 2009). Even the recent reform of legal drafting promoted by the Italian branch of the Plain Language Movement (*Italiano Chiaro*) recommending that sentences in legal and administrative texts should contain no more than 25 words has not attained its goal, as sentences in legal texts commonly contain an average of twice as many words. The considerable sentence length of legal texts is due to the heavy information load required not only to minimize ambiguity and misunderstandings, but also to bring in all-inclusiveness (Bhatia 1993). Each mention is supported by specifications that clarify its status and identity. The awards contained in our corpus contain long sentences with an average sentence length of 43 words per sentence. Moreover, each sentence is subdivided into a number of embedded clauses. The following quotation exemplifies the typical structure of a sentence in the awards analyzed:

(10) Con tale domanda, come del resto ha esposto nella propria memoria conclusiva, la convenuta ha fatto valere la garanzia per i vizi della cosa che l'Art. 1490 c.c. le accorda nella sua qualità di compratore e, lamentando l'inesatto adempimento nel quale a suo avviso sarebbe incorsa l'attrice consegnando cose affette da vizi, ha reclamato il suo diritto di non adempiere richiamando il precetto *inademplenti non est ademplendum* di cui all'Art. 1460 c.c.
[With that request, as she also expressed in her conclusive memorial, the respondent has asserted her right to a guarantee for the faults of the thing that Art. 1490 c.c grants her in her role of buyer and, bemoaning the inaccurate fulfilment of her task that according to her the claimant would have incurred delivering faulty things, she has claimed her right not to comply, referring to the principle *inadimplenti non est adimplendum* formulated in Art. 1460 c.c.] (Award 15)

This sentence, comprising 72 words, contains two main clauses coordinated by *e* [and] to express two legal actions carried out by the claimant (*ha fatto valere la garanzia* [has asserted her right to a guarantee] / *ha reclamato il suo diritto di non adempiere* [has claimed her right not to comply]. These two main clauses are then integrated by a series of specifications concerning the modalities of the request (*Con tale domanda, come del resto ha esposto nella propria memoria conclusiva* [With that request, as she also expressed in her conclusive memorial], the legal grounds of her claim with appropriate reference to specific articles of the Civil Code (*l'Art. 1490 c.c.* [Art. 1490 c.c.] / *di cui all'Art. 1460 c.c* [formulated in Art. 1460 c.c.] and the quotation of a principle in Latin reported in one of them (*inadimplenti non est adimplendum* [he who fails to fulfil his part of an agreement cannot enforce that task against the other party, that is, there is no duty to perform for the other side when it is in breach)]). From a cognitive point of view, all these specifications and justifications lead to an increase in terms of information density; from a syntactic point of view instead, they give rise to the insertion of a series of embedded secondary and prepositional clauses, which makes the syntactic level of the whole sentence highly elaborate, relying on very complex coordination and subordination structures.

Another syntactic feature which characterizes Italian legal language is that it is highly formal and impersonal in style. Indeed, the legal text aims to present facts and opinions in an objective and depersonalized way. A typical device used to obtain this style is the use of the impersonal particle *si*:

(11) In merito a quest'ultimo punto, *si* sottolineava che il parere vincolante, negativo e limitativo della Soprintendenza era volto a limitare il numero di stanze della futura struttura alberghiera.

[As regards this last point, it was underlined [that is, the document underlined the fact] that the binding, negative and restrictive opinion of the Superintendence was meant to limit the number of rooms of the future hotel.] (Award 14)

(12) *Si* ritiene opportuno decidere.
[It is considered appropriate to decide.] (Award 15)

A peculiar legal usage of this particle is found in those periphrastic forms where the *si*-particle is attached to the infinitive of the main verb rather than being put before the modal expression (such as *può procedersi* [one may proceed], *è da ritenersi* [it is to be believed], *deve trascriversi* [it must be transcribed]). This postposition is very frequent also with the verb *trattarsi* [be about, concern]).

(13) *Trattasi* di una prospettazione a tal punto generica da non consentire neppure l'instaurazione di un seno ed effettivo contraddittorio.
[This is such a vague hypothesis that it is not to be held sufficient to start a serious and effective investigation.] (Award 6)

Several other expressions are used to make the style impersonal, such as the verb *essere* [to be] + adjective (for example, *è chiaro* [it is clear], *è evidente* [it is evident], *è noto* [it is well-known], *è possibile* [it is possible]) or impersonal expressions such as *appare* [it appears], *occorre* [it is necessary], *sembra* [it seems]. Here are two examples found in the corpus analyzed:

(14) *Occorre* verificare se sono state eseguite le prestazioni contenute nel contratto.
[It is necessary to verify whether the services mentioned in the contract have been performed.] (Award 14)

(15) *Sembra* a questo Collegio che
[It seems to this Board that] (Award 3)

Depersonal style is also characterized by its above-average use of passive forms, and legal texts, whenever there is a need to emphasize the effect or outcome of an action rather than its cause or originator, often make use of this form. Significantly, the agent is normally omitted in passive clauses in order to strengthen this depersonalizing effect. Here is an example:

(16) La domanda della società attrice di pagamento, in proprio favore, del compenso nella misura del 20 per cent dell'importo del finanziamento approvato e, dunque, di €20,000.00 *può essere solo parzialmente accolta.*

[The claimant's request of the payment in its favour of a compensation corresponding to 20 per cent of the amount of the approved funds and therefore of €20,000.00 can only partially be granted.] (Award 14)

Yet another typical linguistic device used in awards to make the style less personal and more objective is the use of third-person pronouns or noun phrases even when the author refers to himself such as *l'arbitro* [the arbitrator], *il Collegio arbitrale* [the arbitral tribunal] or *il Collegio* [the Panel] in expressions like the following: *l'arbitro ritiene* [the arbitrator believes], *il Collegio arbitrale così provvede* [the arbitral tribunal decides as follows], *il Collegio ha così deciso* [the Panel has decided as follows]. A high degree of objectivity is also attained by the suppression of the human element and the depersonalization of the arbitrators' activities. In expressive terms, this phenomenon is realized by the adoption of inanimate subjects denoting documents or facts for typical argumentation-process verbs such as *confermare* [confirm], *dimostrare* [demonstrate], *indicare* [indicate], *ritenere* [believe], *suggerire* [suggest], as if to indicate that the validity of such conclusions was self-evident and unquestionable, resulting from the analysis of the facts and documents analyzed in the arbitral proceedings. In this way conclusions are presented as a state of affairs which is analyzed by the arbitrators in an impartial way and reported objectively as matters of fact. Here are two examples found in the awards corpus:

(17) *Le motivazioni* già indicate nell'ordinanza [...] *hanno portato il Collegio Arbitrale* a respingere l'eccezione.
[The motivations already reported in the decree [...] have led the Arbitral Tribunal to reject the objection.] (Award 17)

(18) *Tale documento dimostra* che alla data del 10 febbraio il rapporto commerciale con il cliente X proseguiva normalmente ed era, quindi, lungi dall'essere cessato.
[This document demonstrates that on February 10 the business relationship with customer X was progressing normally and was, therefore, far from having ceased.] (Award 3)

Another area in which the adoption of a legal style can be detected in awards is that of word order. Indeed, in arbitration documents one can find phrasal structures that are common in court documents such as the positioning of qualifying adjectives before their respective nouns rather than after them (as would be more common in general usage) in such cases as *contestuale esercizio* [simultaneous exercise], *espressa richiesta* [express request], *legale rappresentante* [legal representative]. A much more evident modification of the standard word order at sentence level is the positioning of the verb in the initial position (VS(O)) rather than after its subject as is common in general speech (SV(O)): *Ritiene [V] il Collegio [S]* [The

Panel believes]; *Rileva [V] la resistente [S] che [O]* [the defendant claims that], *Sono stati ultimati [V] i lavori [S]* [Work has been completed].

A typical characteristic of Italian legal discourse is the omission of the article before a noun in specific technical sentences (Rovere 2002). A few instances have also been found in the awards in the corpus, as in the expressions *avere diritto* [to have the right], *depositare denuncia* [to lodge a complaint], *far pervenire memoria* [to present a memorial], *presentare ricorso* [to file an appeal], *rigettare istanza* [to reject a request]. Similarly to what occurs in legal discourse, the article is frequently omitted before a noun phrase introduced by *a mezzo di* [by means of], *a seguito di* [following up], *con* [with], *mediante* [by means of], like in the following examples:

(19) *Con atto* introduttivo depositato alla Camera Internazionale di Arbitrato di Parigi il [...] R.G., società di diritto francese conveniva in procedura arbitrale la società di diritto italiano [....] S.p.A.
[With a preliminary deed filed with the International Arbitration Chamber in Paris on [...] R.G. a French company started arbitral proceedings against the Italian company [...]S.p.A. (Award 6)

(20) Tale attività veniva regolarmente prestata per un anno, fino a che il legale rappresentante della società revocava l'incarico *mediante comunicazione* a mezzo e-mail.
[This activity was regularly carried out for a year, until the legal representative of the company revoked the task by means of a message sent by e-mail.] (Award 18)

Very common in legal documents are also elliptical forms used to make sentences more compact. In the awards corpus these elliptical forms often correspond to past or present participles used to avoid complex active or passive verbal clauses:

(21) *Sentito il teste*, si deve concludere che la società attrice fosse a conoscenza dell'esistenza dei vizi dei beni acquistati.
[After hearing the witness, it must be concluded that the claimant was aware of the faults in the goods that had been bought.] (Award 15)

(22) La convenuta chiedeva di accertare e determinare ai sensi dell'art. 8) del contratto un compenso *corrispondente* all'attività effettivamente espletata dall'attore.
[The respondent requested that the arbitration Panel should ascertain and determine the remuneration corresponding to the activity actually performed by the claimant according to art 8 of the contract.] (Award 14)

Typical of legal discourse is also the frequent use of present participles as nouns. The examples found in the awards examined are several, such as *l'accettante* [the acceptor], *l'alienante* [the alienating person], *il delegante* [the delegant], *il dichiarante* [the declarant], *l'istante* [the petitioner], *il mandante* [the mandator], *la somministrante* [the supplier], *il rivendicante* [the claimant], *lo stipulante* [the stipulator]. Nominalization too is a characterizing feature of legal discourse, which is particularly evident in deverbalized abstract nouns commonly based on suffixes such as *-anza* (*istanza* [petition], *ordinanza* [injunction]), *-enza* (*decadenza* [lapse], *soccombenza* [loss]), *-ità* (*configurabilità* [configurability], *inammissibilità* [inadmissibility]), *-mento* (*accoglimento* [acceptance], *procedimento* [proceedings]), *-sione* (*escussione* [examination], *estensione* [extension]) and *-zione* (*risoluzione* [resolution], *stipulazione* [stipulation]).

Conclusion

As the analysis has shown, the awards examined in this chapter clearly demonstrate a marked influence of legal discourse on these texts. All the main features of legalese (both lexical and syntactic) have been traced in abundance in the arbitration documents taken into consideration. Also the main textual structure of legal judgments has been found to be at the basis of the layout of arbitration awards. In spite of the fact that arbitration is a procedure that is meant to be simpler and quicker than its much more complex and slow counterpart litigation, the language used in awards still presents the complexity that is typical of legal language. This situation is mainly due to the fact that more and more legal professionals are chosen as arbitrators, thus favouring the exportation of legal practices and legalese into the arbitration field. As was pointed out in the Introduction to this chapter, this is a general phenomenon taking place on a global level. In Italy this 'colonization' trend has been strengthened by the 2006 Reform of Italian Arbitration Law, which has induced the local Chambers of Commerce managing arbitral proceedings to strongly invite the parties to follow a standard relatively more judicialized arbitration procedure under the control of an institutional body and to appoint arbitrators who are legal experts in order to limit the risk of award challenges. As a consequence, arbitration practices in Italy are getting strongly influenced by litigation features.

The presence in awards of the main lexical, syntactic and textual patterns typical of legal language can be further explained by a process of standardization which seems to be conditioning also the non-legal experts working in this field. Indeed, the linguistic differences between awards written by lawyers and non-lawyers are extremely subtle, as the few non-legal professionals generally choose to adopt the same style in order to ensure the homogeneity of the genre, or maybe, to establish a more legalized self-identity by adopting the discursive conventions commonly adopted in the field. Consequently, all awards present a style typical of the legal tradition, which uses a highly complex type of language. The lexical and stylistic differences between various arbitrators are nearly imperceptible; in these kinds of texts a personal style is overcome by the need to respect the textual conventions that belong to the tradition of arbitration. The general frame of the award is often identical, and standard clauses are used throughout. It is not possible to explore new writing styles; it is important to adopt the conventional and accredited style. Indeed, Chambers of Commerce organize training courses for both new and experienced arbitrators in order to guarantee uniformity and homogeneity in the procedure. The analysis of our corpus has shown a standardized layout and a set of linguistic expressions commonly adopted. This not only allows the arbitrator to make some savings in drafting time and costs, but also ensures that the clauses used are interpreted in the correct way. The advantages of using the tried-and-tested format and style, almost like templates, are clearly perceived by all members of the arbitrators' community as this guarantees greater legal validity and wider enforceability of the awards. In fact, it is now considered preferable to keep awards within a standardized and generally agreed upon framework, in order to reduce the possibility of the award getting challenged by a dissatisfied party, a point that emerged in informal interviews with experts in the field. A different and less standardized approach would lose the advantage of consolidated meaning, and, consequently, would be more likely to be controversial.

The results of our analysis may thus lead us to conclude that in the present context this process of 'judicialization' of arbitration discourse may well favour a redefinition of the dialogistic positioning (Martin and Rose 2003) of the status of the award within the domain of legal textualization, by making it more strictly linked with the typical genres of litigation practices and in particular with the court judgment. The analysis carried out in this chapter indeed evidences the fact that the discourse of arbitration awards constitutes an intimate and reflexive network of discourses within the legal field, within which there is considerable influence and mutual exchange. This interdiscursivity is not only indicative of a process of 'colonization' of arbitration discourse by the practices of litigation, but also provides evidence for a more overarching phenomenon of textual dynamism taking place in the wider domain of the discourse of dispute resolution (Candlin and Maley 1997; Bhatia, Candlin and Gotti 2010).

References

Bhatia, Vijay K. (1993): *Analysing Genre: Language Use in Professional Settings*, London, Longman.

Bhatia, Vijay K., Candlin, Christopher N. and Gotti, Maurizio (Eds) (2003): *Legal Discourse in Multilingual and Multicultural Contexts: Arbitration Texts in Europe*, Bern, Peter Lang.

Bhatia, Vijay K., Candlin, Christopher N. and Gotti, Maurizio (Eds) (2010): *The Discourses of Dispute Resolution*, Bern, Peter Lang.

Bhatia, Vijay K. and Evangelisti Allori, Paola (Eds) (Forthcoming): *Issues of Identity In and Across Cultures and Professional Worlds*, Bern, Peter Lang.

Browker, Charles N. (2008): W(h)ither International Commercial Arbitration?, *Arbitration International*, Vol. 24, No. 2, 181–97.

Candlin, Christopher N. and Maley, Yon (1997): Intertextuality and Interdiscursivity in the Discourse of Alternative Dispute Resolution. In Gunnarsson, Britt-Louise, Linell, Per and Nordberg, Bengt (Eds) *The Construction of Professional Discourse*, London, Longman, 201–22.

Cavagnoli, Stefania and Ioriatti Ferrari, Elena (2009): *Tradurre il Diritto. Nozioni di Diritto e di Linguistica Giuridica*, Milano, CEDAM.

Cortelazzo, Michele A. (2006): Fenomenologia dei Tecnicismi Collaterali. Il Settore Giuridico. In Cresti, Emanuela (Ed.) *Prospettive Nello Studio del Lessico Italiano*, Firenze, FUP, I: 137–40.

Cutolo, Daniele and Esposito, Antonio (2007): The Reform of the Italian Arbitration Law: The Challenging of Arbitrators and the Setting of Time Limits, *Journal of International Arbitration*, Vol. 24, No. 1, 49–62.

Dardano, Maurizio (1994): Profilo dell'Italiano Contemporaneo. In Serianni, Luca and Trifone, Pietro (Eds) *Storia della Lingua Italiana*, Torino, Einaudi, II, 343–430.

Fiorelli, Piero (1998): L'Italiano Giuridico dal Latinismo al Tecnicismo. In Domenighetti, Ilario (Ed.) *Con Felice Esattezza. Economia e Diritto fra Lingua e Letteratura*, Bellinzona, Casagrande, 139–83.

Garzone, Giuliana (2003): Arbitration Rules across Legal Cultures: An Intercultural Approach. In Bhatia, Vijay K., Candlin, Christopher N. and Gotti, Maurizio (Eds), *Legal Discourse in Multilingual and Multicultural Contexts: Arbitration Texts in Europe*, Bern, Peter Lang, 177–220.

Gotti, Maurizio (2011): *Investigating Specialized Discourse*, 3rd edition, Bern, Peter Lang.

Gotti, Maurizio and Anesa, Patrizia (Forthcoming): Professional Identities in Italian Arbitral Awards: The Spread of Lawyers' Language. In Bhatia, Vijay K. and Evangelisti Allori, Paola, (Eds) *Issues of Identity In and Across Cultures and Professional Worlds*, Bern, Peter Lang.

Maci, Stefania M. (Forthcoming): Arbitration in Italy: Litigation Procedures in Arbitral Practice. In Bhatia, Vijay K. and Evangelisti Allori, Paola (Eds) *Issues of Identity In and Across Cultures and Professional Worlds*, Bern, Peter Lang.

Martin, James R. and Rose, David (2003): *Working with Discourse: Meaning Beyond the Clause*, London, Continuum.

Mistelis, Loukas (2004): International Arbitration – Corporate Attitudes and Practices – 12 Perceptions Tested: Myths, Data and Analysis: Research Report, *The American Review of International Arbitration*, Vol. 15, 525–91.

Mortara Garavelli, Bice (2001): *Le Parole e la Giustizia. Divagazioni Grammaticali e Retoriche su Testi Giuridici Italiani*, Torino, Einaudi.

Nariman, Fali S. (2000): The Spirit of Arbitration: The Tenth Annual Goff Lecture, *Arbitration International*, Vol. 16, No. 3, 261–78.

Okekeifere, Andrew I. (1998): Commercial Arbitration as the Most Effective Dispute Resolution Method: Still a Fact or Now a Myth?, *Journal of International Arbitration*, Vol. 4, No.1, 81–105.

Rovere, Giovanni (2002): L'Articolo Zero nel Linguaggio Giuridico. In Beccaria, Gian Luigi and Marello, Carla (Eds) *La Parola al Testo*, Alessandria, Edizioni dell'Orso, I, 387–404.

Rubino-Sammartano, Mauro (2003): Is Arbitration Losing Ground?, *The American Review of International Arbitration*, Vol. 14, 341–4.

Santulli, Francesca (2006): Strutture Argomentative e Scelte Lessicali nel Linguaggio della Giurisprudenza. In Cresti, Emanuela (Ed.) *Prospettive nello Studio del Lessico Italiano*, Firenze, FUP, I, 461–9.

Chapter 9
Arbitration Awards as Accounts

Vijay K. Bhatia, Christopher N. Candlin and Christoph A. Hafner

Accountability and Legal Reasoning

Accounts are rhetorical constructs that are often used to justify, explain or clarify one's views, arguments and/or communicative actions in a specific social or professional context. The concept goes back to the works of Garfinkel (1956, 1967) and Goffman (1959), who proposed accounts as social explanations of events and verbal actions to justify unexpected or disputed social behaviour. Garfinkel (1956, 1967) argues that accounts are an inevitable aspect of social life when he points out that individuals organize and manage their everyday affairs so as 'to be accountable' to others for their social actions. He goes on to argue that the importance of institutional texts lies not in the text itself, but in the ties between records and social systems that service, and are serviced by, these textual records; this is what he refers to as the 'indexical nature' of accounts (Garfinkel, 1967; Hartland, 1989: 403). He also points out that there is a 'tie between such records and the system they serve' and that such accounts are 'not readily noticeable to the researcher, but routinized by institutional members carrying out the practice' (Garfinkel, 1967: 192). This is particularly so when accounts in the form of explanations or interpretations are used as an important rhetorical strategy when the circumstances unfortunately become difficult and problematic.

Thus, according to Garfinkel, 'accounts are not independent of the socially organized occasions of their use' (Garfinkel 1967: 3) but rather are 'the activities whereby members produce and manage settings of organised everyday affairs' (Garfinkel 1967: 3). As Heritage points out (1987: 141), what is important for Garfinkel in these institutional accounts and descriptions is to show how they are evaluated, accepted or contested by institutional members. Accordingly, as Firkins and Candlin (submitted) emphasize, we should not fall into the trap of suggesting that these descriptive accounts in themselves provide unproblematic access to the nature of the activities they describe (Heritage 1987: 248; Hartland 1989: 403). On the contrary, as Garfinkel emphasizes, such accounts have a 'loose fit' with the circumstances they depict, and the nature of the fit between accounts and their circumstance is to be established through an active course of analysis; in the case of this chapter, through genre and discourse analyses.

Accordingly, the 'sense' of an account is indexically linked to the context of its production (Heritage 1987: 141) and as such we can say that litigation judgments and arbitration awards are indexically linked to the litigation and arbitration process. Goffman (1959), in his seminal work, *The Presentation of Self in Everyday Life*, established a basis for the study of how people tacitly present themselves to others, especially in contexts where their contributions are likely to be interpreted as having negative implications. This is nowhere more true than in litigation judgments and arbitration awards, where the writer's primary concern is to argue, justify and persuade the reader to accept their decisions. As Goffman (1971) rightly points out:

> Regardless of the particular objective which the individual has in mind and of his motivation for having this objective, it will be in his interests to control the conduct of others, especially their responsive treatment of him. (Goffman 1971: 3)

Following Goffman (and indeed Garfinkel), it is possible to claim that such control is often achieved by providing systematic and detailed accounts of the writer's argument based on available disciplinary resources to discourage the reader from taking any negative interpretations and implications based on the writer's decision. It can also be argued that such rhetorical contributions are professionally constructed for the benefit of the intended audience and at the same time to maintain their own professional and disciplinary identities. Scott and Lyman (1968: 46), in a similar manner, consider accounts as 'a linguistic device employed whenever an action is subjected to evaluative inquiry'. They report on two kinds of accounts: one as justifications (whereby one accepts responsibility for the act in question, but denies any pejorative quality that may be associated with it) and the other as excuses (whereby one admits that the act in question is bad or wrong, but denies full responsibility). Both types are presented to others to maintain social order. Similarly, Shotter (1984) focuses on how people make their behaviour accountable in a moral world. He describes how people talk about themselves in terms of the social order and socially constructed morality in which they exist, and must account for their experiences in ways that are intelligible and legitimate in their current social context. He further points out that people often account for their experiences in ways that are accessible to their readership and also seen as professionally legitimate in their current social and professional contexts (see Garfinkel and Goffman earlier).

Although legal judgments and arbitration awards are two important legal genres that seem to incorporate, to varying degrees, the writer's accounts, to justify, argue and explain the decision of the court or the arbitration tribunal, as the case may be, there has been no reported work on arbitration awards as accounts. This chapter will make an attempt to take awards as an established specialized genre and discuss the rhetorical structure, use of lexico-grammatical resources, rhetorical strategies and more importantly the invested professional reasoning that the arbitrator makes use of in explaining, justifying, and reasoning the decision arrived at depending upon his functional role as legal expert, fact finder, adjudicator or facilitator. The chapter will explore three interrelated and overlapping issues:

- To what extent do arbitrators make an attempt to 'account' for their decisions leading to specific awards?
- In doing so, how do they construct arguments (reach decisions and provide reasons)?
- In constructing these accounts, do arbitrators appropriate the discourse(s) of litigation?

Underpinning the argument of this chapter is a general concern regarding the tension between *litigation* and *arbitration*, taking the view that arbitration is part of a continuum, with litigation at one pole, and mediation and conciliation at the other, positioned between these poles in relation to the degree of involvement or control of the parties. In doing so, the chapter attempts to investigate the integrity of legal and arbitration discourses, in particular, litigation judgments and arbitration awards.

Data

The awards for analysis are taken from *The ICC International Court of Arbitration Bulletin*, a professional journal which publishes (among other matters) extracts from ICC awards. The 18 award extracts selected include awards from a mix of jurisdictions, divided into awards where the governing law is the civil law of France or Germany (ten awards: 18,986 words) and the common law of the UK (eight awards, 20,886 words). The total corpus is thus 39,872 words long and the extracts range in length from 461 to 6,351 words, with an average length of 2,215 words. They focus on a range of areas in private international law, including contract (nine awards), agency agreement (three), interest (three), insolvency (one), bankruptcy (one) and sale of goods (one). This modest corpus is not intended to provide a representative sample of ICC awards generally, rather it is meant to provide a starting point for an exploratory analysis of awards and the kind of accounts that they present.

Analysis

In his study of professional reasoning, Hafner (2011) comments on the role and importance of reasoning in the award as follows:

> In summary, the interviews and professional guides on award writing highlight the perceived importance of reasoning. The presence of reasoning may serve to secure the parties' compliance with the award: either voluntarily or by enforcement through the courts. However, there is a desire to keep such reasoning to a minimum, both in order to discourage future litigation and to streamline the arbitration process. (Hafner 2011: 121)

In this chapter, we examine the way that arbitrators use the arbitral award in order to present their decisions, along with associated reasoning or account. We focus on four different rhetorical functions represented in the award:

a. deciding an issue of law;
b. deciding an issue of fact;
c. making an order;
d. negotiating procedure.

We argue that the arbitrator's choice of language reflects a range of different roles adopted by the arbitrator in writing the award, and that the discourses inherent in some of these roles are more closely associated with those of litigation than are others.

Deciding an Issue of Law

In order to resolve the dispute at arbitration, an arbitrator may be called upon to decide relevant issues of law. In such cases the arbitrator assumes the role of *legal expert*, identifying relevant issues and subjecting them to a form of legal analysis, as illustrated in Text 1.

Text 1 (Award 8161)

b) Can Article 89b paragraph 3 HGB be varied by agreement between the parties?	Issue
Under German law, an agent's right to receive compensation cannot be varied by agreement between the parties. Article 89b HGB expressly states that the right to receive compensation 'cannot be excluded in advance'. This provision of German law is mandatory in nature and cannot be excluded even in the context of an international agreement.	Reasoning [Law]
The Agreement was executed and negotiated by both [Defendant] and [Claimant]. Either party could have engaged professional advisors in respect of reviewing the provisions of the Agreement under German law, yet, it would appear, that neither party obtained any legal advice before signing the Agreement.	[Facts]
In the present circumstances, in the Arbitrator's opinion, it is irrelevant who initiated the introduction of Article 14 and subjecting the Agreement to German law as both parties entered into the Agreement in full awareness of the clauses contained therein. By selecting German law, [Defendant] accepted the overriding aspect of Article 89b HGB and henceforth [Claimant]'s right (as agent) to compensation on the valid termination of Agreement.	Conclusion

Text 1 follows a generic move structure that can be observed in legal opinions written by judges and lawyers (Maley 1985; Bhatia 1993; Hafner 2010). The arbitrator first states the issue to be decided and then states the law to be applied, citing and quoting from the relevant legislation (here, Article 89b of HGB, the German Commercial Code). In the Facts move, the arbitrator deductively applies the law to the facts of the dispute, by describing the relevant facts. The combination of Law and Facts moves functions to provide a kind of reasoned account, leading to the Conclusion move, where the arbitrator resolves the issue by providing an opinion on the correct legal interpretation. Certain formulaic phrases typical of legal discourse, both legislative and juridical, can be observed in this generic structure, for example: 'Under German law', 'Article 89b HGB expressly states' to refer to the law; 'In the present circumstances' to refer to and discuss the facts of the matter; 'in the arbitrator's opinion' to hedge the opinion. In addition, the tenor of the text is formal and impersonal: the extract is characterized by a lack of personal pronouns, frequent use of nominalizations and passive voice, and frequent use of technical legal lexis, as is typical of written legal discourse, such as judicial opinions or legislative texts.

The sequence of Issue, Law, (application of law to) Facts, Conclusion which we observe in Text 1 is typical of legal reasoning involving the deductive application of law to facts. It is characterized by the explicit identification of an abstract legal rule which is then applied to the facts of the case. An alternative structure that may be observed in the awards is that of the sequence Issue, Conclusion, and Reasoning (Law and/or Facts), as seen in Text 2.

Text 2 (Award 9561)

The Respondent also objects that the Claimant in its summons for payment should at least have stated that the underlying obligations had not been fulfilled and in what respect.	Issue
The objection is however unfounded. As said before, such a declaration, in order to be construed as a pre-requisite for claiming payment, must be expressly provided in the guarantee. No such provision is contained in the text of the guarantees in question.	Conclusion Reasoning [Law + Facts]
On the other hand, the need for such declaration, contrary to the Respondent's opinion, cannot be derived from Art. 20 of the ICC Uniform Rules on Demand Guarantees (ICC Publication No. 458), since these Rules are not applicable to the guarantees in question. As the Claimant has rightly pointed out, for these Rules to be applicable an express reference thereto according to Art. 1 of the Rules would have been necessary. No such reference can be seen in the Letters of Guarantee, which are therefore 'governed in all respects by the laws of France' (paragraph 5 of both guarantee letters).	Conclusion Reasoning

In Text 2 the arbitrator implicitly constructs the issue from the arguments of the parties by representing their position: 'The Respondent also objects'. The arbitrator's conclusion is presented immediately: 'The objection is however unfounded'. This is then followed by reasons in the form of a statement of law and application of law to the facts. In this text, there is less explicit reference to legal provisions and their effect: although references to legal authority and legal principles are still evident, they are woven into the text and are not provided with as much explanatory detail. In Text 2 the arbitrator engages more actively with the arguments of the parties and as a result we see a number of evaluations, which serve to align the arbitrator with the arguments of the Claimant in this case: 'contrary to the Respondent's opinion'; 'As the Claimant has rightly pointed out'.

Such an alignment of views is also possible without provision of any detailed legal reasoning as in the brief extract below, where counsel's argument is presented, and immediately preferred or endorsed.

Text 3 (Award 8593) (emphasis added)

[Defendant's counsel] emphasised the difference between a 'draw on commission' implying some temporary nature to the payment, as an advance payment and the concept of guaranteed minimum commission.	Reasoning
I must say I agree with him on this point.	Conclusion

Deciding an Issue of Fact

Arbitrators may also be called upon to adopt the role of *fact finder* in order to resolve differences about the facts of a particular case. Text 4 illustrates this role, with the arbitrator considering whether, as a matter of fact, the claimant and defendant had chosen Swiss or French law as the governing law of their agreement. In the text, the arbitrator balances the position of the defendant as described in the first paragraph, against the position of the claimant as described in the second paragraph, before reaching a conclusion in the third paragraph.

In this text, both the first and second paragraphs involve the presentation of accounts, but these accounts are simply the reported arguments of the parties, rather than the reasoned account of the arbitrators. The defendant's position is evaluated and dismissed at the beginning of the second paragraph, with the simple phrase 'The Tribunal does not find this view convincing'. However, the arbitrators also indicate some doubt about the claimant's position when they say 'Such an intention is not established' (paragraph 2). Finally, in paragraph 3 the arbitrators align themselves with the position of the claimant although they do not seem to feel obliged to give any further reasons for this preference. It is possible that the purpose of the discussion in paragraphs 1 and 2 is simply to indicate that the positions of both parties have been understood and considered before a conclusion was reached. It is notable that the discourse here adopts an adversarial character, pitting the accounts of the two parties against one another and then deciding in

Text 4 (Award 8177)

Defendant claims that Swiss law was implicitly chosen from the start. The argument rests on the circumstance that in a previous contract between the parties and another previous contract between Defendant and a sister company of Claimant, as well as in a subsequent agreement between the parties, there was an express choice of Swiss law, coupled with the choice of Lausanne as the venue for an JCC arbitration [...] The omission of any reference to Swiss law in the agreement of April 24, 1987 was not explained by Claimant nor noticed by Defendant at the time the contract was concluded. However, Defendant claims that there was a course of dealings between the parties linking arbitration in Lausanne with the choice of Swiss law. It must be assumed that this practice could not be changed without an express choice of a law other than Swiss.	Issue Reasoning
The Tribunal does not find this view convincing. Claimant argues that, on the contrary, the omission of the reference to Swiss law in this agreement reveals its intention not to submit it to that law, due to an alleged different scope of the intermediary's mission. Such an intention is not established, but clearly, the omission in itself can be interpreted a *contrario* as well as *a pari*.	Conclusion Reasoning
2.4 The Tribunal concludes that in the absence of an explicit choice of law in the agreement of April 24, 1987, there has been no implicit choice of Swiss law, but a later explicit choice of French law, resulting from Defendant's referring to the law of that country in their *sommation de payer* and from Claimant's acceptance of that choice in its 'Reply and Answer to the Counter-Claim'.	Conclusion

favour of one of them, with the arbitrators exercising considerable power in their decision.

Making an Order

Ultimately, it is the role of the arbitrator to resolve the dispute by making a final, binding order on the parties. Here the arbitrator acts as *adjudicator* of the dispute. The following extracts, Texts 5 to 8, illustrate the kind of language used in this role.

In Text 5 a highly formalized approach is adopted, with the section headed up 'Order' followed by seven specific awards. Such an Order is typically found at, or near the end of the award extracts examined. The tenor of the text is formal and impersonal, with the use of the passive voice and legal technical lexis such as 'Claimant' and 'Respondent'. The order is couched in the strongest possible terms, using the indicative mood to signal that compliance with the Order is expected, and that the authority of the arbitrator to make the Order is beyond question. The language use is similar to that which one would expect in a legal judgment.

Text 5 (Award 8632)

Order 1. The claims of the Claimant are dismissed. 2. The Claimant is ordered to pay to the Respondent the sum of $ […] as compensatory damages for breach of fiduciary duty and as damages for breach of the Shareholders Agreement. All claims in respect of which damages are not awarded are dismissed. […] 7. The Claimant is ordered to pay to the Respondent simple interest at the statutory rate of interest payable on judgment debts in England at the date of this Award on the sum of $ … being part of the normal legal costs incurred by the Respondent and already paid by him, from the date of this Award until payment'.	Order

No reasoning is evident in this move, as the relevant issues have already been discussed earlier in the award, and the purpose here is simply to summarize the binding orders made.

Text 5 is notable because of the extremely impersonal tone adopted, using the passive voice to remove any trace of the arbitrator/decision-maker from the text. Other Orders are formulated in the active voice, and in these texts the arbitrator is more involved and less distant. Examples are provided in Texts 6 and 7 below, where the arbitrator's involvement is signalled by the phrases 'the Majority Arbitrators decide […] in favour' and 'My judgment is'.

Text 6 (Award 5896) (emphasis added)

Consequently […] the Majority Arbitrators *decide* Issue No. 1.4 *in favour of* the Defendants Nos. 1 and 2. In view of the determinations made by the Arbitrators, this award is a final award *in favour of* all the Defendants.	Order

Text 7 (Award 8593) (emphasis added)

My judgment is that he is entitled to damages equivalent to 9 months' commission (based on his last year of commission income) plus 12 months of his actual lease payments as set out in the Schedule produced at the hearing.	Order

Texts 6 and 7 demonstrate another dimension of possible variation in the degree of arbitrator involvement: the use of technical labels such as 'the Arbitrator(s)' or 'the Tribunal' (for example, Text 6) being more impersonal than the use of personal pronouns such as 'I/we' or 'my/our' (for example, Text 7).

In some instances, the Order incorporates minimal reasoning, either directly or by reference to the account already provided. Examples are provided in Texts 8–10.

Text 8 (Award 8402) (emphasis added)

Taking into account these comments, the different currencies involved in the dispute and the prevailing interest rates during the relevant periods, *the Arbitrator holds* that *interest shall be paid* by [Defendant] at 6 per cent per annum.	Reasoning Order

Text 9 (Award 9594) (emphasis added)

Under these circumstances recovery of losses due to [Claimant]'s alleged breach of quality *is not granted* since the losses were mitigable and could have been contained by [Defendant] through either further negotiation (by accepting [Claimant]'s offer) or by having taken the timely steps required to repair the machinery.	Order Reasoning

Text 10 (Award 8163) (emphasis added)

Having taken in consideration all these aspects the majority of the Arbitral Tribunal was *of the opinion* that it has no jurisdiction over the [Defendants] for this claim and that therefore the claim had to be dismissed as inadmissible [...]	Order

Such references to reasoning can be seen as a kind of boosting strategy (Hyland, 2005) employed in order to add weight to the arbitrator's Order. In particular, in Texts 8 and 10, the arbitrators note that they have taken into consideration relevant arguments, and by so doing seek to boost the authority of the award. Here it seems likely that this strategy is used as a kind of persuasive appeal to the parties, aiming to secure compliance with the award, as suggested earlier. This boosting strategy has also been observed in barrister's opinions (Hafner 2010).

Text 10 also provides an example of hedging in the phrase 'the Arbitral Tribunal was of the opinion that it has no jurisdiction'. The explicit reference to opinion has the effect of qualifying the claim that the tribunal has no jurisdiction. Again, this strategy is common in legal opinions, including judgments.

The language used in all of the examples above highlights the adversarial nature of the award, where the role of the arbitrator is similar to that of a judge in court: namely, to 'decide' issues, 'grant' 'judgment' 'in favour of' one party over another. As with other legal texts (including legislation, agreements, judgments) there is a performative aspect to the Order, in that the text performs a legal act that declares the respective rights and liabilities of the parties. As a result, it is not surprising that the choice of language used in the Order of the award strongly resembles that of a judgment. In Table 9.1, we indicate the range of verbs that are drawn on in this function.

Table 9.1 Verbs used by arbitrators to make an Order

Performative verbs	Non-performative verbs
Grant (remedies)	X is entitled to
Order (a party to pay)	Must
Dismiss (claims)	Shall
Decline to (grant a remedy)	
Decide (that … OR the issue in favour)	
Determine (that … OR the matter, the amount)	
Find (that)	
Hold (that)	
Have no doubt (that)	
Be of the opinion (that)	
Consider (that)	
Note (that)	
Doubt (whether)	

Note that there are two types of performative verbs in the table: verbs such as 'grant' and 'order' which by their utterance have an effect on the legal relationship of the parties; and verbs such as 'consider' and 'doubt' which declare the opinion of the arbitrator. These can be combined with non-performative verbs such as 'must', 'shall' or 'be entitled to' to indicate the obligations of the parties. An example of such a combination is to be found in Text 8: 'the Arbitrator holds that interest shall be paid'.

Negotiating Procedure

As part of the arbitration process, the arbitrator can be called on to act as a *facilitator* who negotiates the dispute resolution procedure with the parties to the dispute. In this role, the arbitrator must maintain a neutral stance and attempt to accommodate the parties, who are supposed to agree on the dispute resolution procedure. Unlike litigation, in arbitration the parties have considerable flexibility in terms of the procedures that they adopt.

In the following example (Text 11), there is evidence of a conflict in the role of the arbitrators, who are caught between the role of neutral facilitator and that of adjudicator of the dispute, as outlined above. The award involves parties who have apparently attempted to resist the arbitration process by refusing to participate, for example in the drafting of the terms of reference of the arbitration. These parties have subsequently come to the arbitration with the intent of submitting claims which lie outside the terms of reference, as established in their absence.

In order to deal with this set of circumstances, the arbitrators present an account that draws on legal sources (paragraphs 1 and 2) as well as on general principles of fairness in arbitration (especially paragraphs 3 and 5). These rules and principles are applied to the particular facts of the case at hand. The award weighs two competing interests against one another: the Respondent's 'opportunity to present

Text 11 (Award 10621)

Article 19 of the ICC Arbitration Rules is explicit about new claims and counterclaims:	Reasoning [Law]
'After the Terms of Reference have been signed, no party shall make new claims or counterclaims which fall outside the limits of the Terms of Reference unless it has been authorized to do so by the Arbitral Tribunal, which shall consider the nature of such new claims or counterclaims, the stage of the arbitration and other relevant circumstances'.	
No good reason has been offered to deviate from this rule. [Respondent 1] and [Respondent 3] had every opportunity to participate in drafting the Terms of Reference, but declined to do so. All Respondents have already been given ample opportunity to present their case, and any additional delay could constitute a denial of Claimant's right to a fair arbitration.	[Facts]
The Tribunal has bent over backward to accommodate [Respondent 1] and [Respondent 3]. All notices and procedural orders were copied to both parties via fax, DHL and registered mail. At the hearings Messrs. [A and B] admitted to having received these communications. In addition to refusing to participate in drafting the Terms of Reference, both Respondents declined to submit pre-hearing briefs or to cooperate in pre-trial discovery.	
These two Respondents' [sic] request new hearings and more time for counterclaims communicated to the Tribunal only at the hearings and in the post-hearing briefs. See [Respondent 1]'s 'resubmitted' briefs on [...] and [Respondent 3]'s submission of ...	
To permit Respondents to ignore proceedings and then ask for more hearings would be grossly unfair to the other parties. The ICC Rules and English arbitration law are both premised on fairness to all parties. The most elementary notions of due process require that arbitrators show respect for the rights of both sides in a dispute. A respondent cannot ignore an arbitration until the last moment, and then expect to be permitted to file new counterclaims that require the other side to begin again almost at ground zero.	Conclusion Reasoning [Law]

their case' and the Claimant's 'right to a fair arbitration' (see paragraph 3). The discourse of the award reveals another side of the arbitrator – party relationship, one which is only seen rarely in the awards under analysis. Unlike judges in litigation, arbitrators derive their authority directly from the parties to the dispute and therefore rely on the cooperation of the parties in a way that judges do not. In Text 11, one senses the frustration of the arbitrators when, in paragraph 4, they break from the generally formal tenor of the award and rely on colloquial language when they say that, 'The Tribunal has bent over backward to accommodate [Respondent 1] and [Respondent 3]'.

Discussion and Conclusions

Most professional communities have at their disposal their own discursive resources which draw on their knowledge of what forms of communication are appropriate to represent their specific professional actions. It is thus expected that arbitrators as professionals have their own discursive resources which will be typical of their profession, and accomplished arbitrators will skilfully exploit such resources to achieve their institutional goals and realize their communicative actions. However, it appears as if the discursive options available to arbitrators are considerably constrained by their institutional membership of the legal community. As such they find it difficult to disassociate and distinguish themselves from their parent profession and perhaps not surprisingly continue to appropriate and make use of those discursive resources which have been an established part of their professional repertoire.

The analysis above offers support to the argument that arbitrators writing awards are called upon to perform similar roles to a judge writing a judgment in the litigation context. They act as legal expert when deciding issues of law, fact finder when deciding issues of fact, adjudicator when making an order and facilitator when negotiating procedure with the parties. Of these four roles, the first three are also strongly associated with judges in the litigation context, while the fourth is perhaps less so. The present study highlights the way that arbitrators draw upon legal discourse structures (raising issues, stating and applying legal rules) in order to account for the decisions and orders that they make. The tenor of the texts analyzed is frequently formal and impersonal, with considerable use of legal technical lexis, particularly where rules are stated or orders are made. Accordingly, we may argue that the awards analyzed here illustrate that arbitrators are significantly influenced in their writing by the forms they are quite used to following in their litigation practice.

Gotti, in this volume, based on his study of Italian arbitration awards, goes even further to claim that Italian awards in his corpus are characterized by excessively long sentences, binomial and multinomial expressions, predominant use of nominalizations, impersonal style, and many other rhetorical features typical of legal discourse. Based on his very comprehensive analysis, he concludes that there is:

> […] a marked influence of legal discourse on these texts (Italian Arbitration Awards). All the main features of legalese (both lexical and syntactic) have been traced in abundance in the arbitration documents taken into consideration. Also the main textual structure of legal judgments has been found to be at the basis of the layout of arbitration awards. In spite of the fact that arbitration is a procedure that is meant to be simpler and quicker than its much more complex and slow counterpart litigation, the language used in awards still presents the complexity that is typical of legal language.

So far as the nature of accounts in awards is concerned, Breeze (also in this volume), using appraisal analysis (Martin and Rose, 2003), focuses on clarity and logic of argument as key values in the discourse of arbitration to realize persuasiveness of arguments or evidence in order to seek positive reaction on the part of the writer. She claims that arbitration awards are essentially dialogic in nature, in that they address readers of various kinds seeking 'to persuade them of the truth, legitimacy or logicality of certain views or arguments, and of the untruth, illegitimacy or illogicality of others'. She further claims that arbitration awards are written 'in reaction to other (previous) texts and with the reader's (future) reaction in mind' (Breeze, in this volume). She points out that 'the text itself is also dialogic in that it contains accounts of different arguments or assertions and the corresponding counter-arguments, so that a great deal of the text is concerned with resolving a conflict between opposing or contradictory moves in a cogent and coherent manner' (Breeze, in this volume).

This dialogic quality of the text of awards was also observed in the present study, where arbitrators employed a strategy of presenting (in an adversarial fashion) the arguments of both parties to the dispute, and then aligning with one side or the other. This strategy serves to show that both sides of the argument have been taken into account before one side is preferred. However, it is possible for arbitrators using this strategy to reach a preference for one side of the argument without providing a reasoned account. At times therefore, there is a relatively weaker effort displayed in arbitrators' accounts in arbitration awards, with less effort employed in explaining, clarifying or justifying their decisions, and perhaps little concern to persuade intended readers to accept their decisions. When some arbitrators were confronted with these observations, they offered at least two main reasons: firstly, any detailed reasoning in an award is likely to expose it for challenge in a court of law; and secondly, providing a reasoned account may involve more expense in terms of time and money, which is dispreferred by most of the parties to the dispute.

In the awards examined, the power and authority of the arbitrator to make a binding award on the parties is clearly visible. This is particularly evident when arbitrators make orders, which they do in terms that are largely similar to legal judgments. It could be argued that arbitrators have more power than their counterparts in litigation: the discursive construction of negotiation of justice represented in arbitration awards is particularly authoritative, in that it cannot be challenged in a court of law, except on procedural grounds. Nevertheless, advocates of international commercial arbitration (ICA) point out that, unlike litigation, arbitration provides parties with greater control and a more flexible dispute resolution process. As a consequence, arbitrators must also be flexible at times, and accommodate to the procedural preferences of the parties in order to facilitate the resolution of the dispute. Thus, the power of the arbitrator is subject to the procedural freedoms that arbitration promises to the parties.

There is a common perception in arbitration circles that arbitration is becoming more like litigation. One expert, interviewed for the purposes of the project, summed it up in the following way:

> [...] my sense is that international arbitration to a considerable extent is looking like litigation, that's a generality, there're a million cases where this is not so, but it's a generality. How that came about, I suspect a lot of causes: American lawyers for one thing are used to a kind of litigation that involves an enormous amount of discovery, depositions, interrogatories, requests [for] document production. American lawyers seem to think that they have to turn every stone before they're ready to do battle at a trial, and to a certain extent I think that state of mind has been carried over to arbitration. Because in the US and around the world, big law firms have developed with arbitration groups of specialists, and often they tend to be peopled by litigation specialists who all of sudden go into arbitration.

Certainly the present study supports the notion that the reasoned accounts presented in awards draw on the discourse of litigation documents such as legal opinions and judgments. They do so both in terms of the rhetorical features that they use and the technical legal language employed. Nevertheless, there is some evidence from the present study to suggest that reasoned accounts in awards are less prominent a feature than they are in litigation genres. The reason for this may be that arbitrators generally feel that extensive justification of or accounting for the final decision will only add to the increasing cost of arbitration. Or, it may be that the arbitration community is relatively small, and cases often get concentrated in few hands, so that writing elaborate accounts will only leave less time for arbitrators to take on more cases. Or, it may be that arbitrators feel that the less elaborate the award, the less the chance of it being challenged. There is also the factor that they are rarely, if ever, used as precedents, and hence arbitrators feel relatively little pressure to account for their decisions. In our view, as ICA matures as an institution and acquires integrity of its own, the need to be more accountable to the stakeholders and to the community at large will grow. Studies of the kind presented in this chapter may provide some evidence to underpin such claims.

References

Bhatia, Vijay K. (1993): *Analysing Genre: Language Use in Professional Settings*, London, Longman.

Breeze, Ruth (2012 [In this volume]): Appraisal Analysis of Dissenting and Concurring Opinions. In Bhatia, Vijay K., Candlin, Christopher N. and Gotti, Maurizio (Eds) *Discourse and Practice in International Commercial Arbitration: Issues, Challenges and Prospects*, Farnham, Ashgate Publishing.

Firkins, Andrew and Candlin, Christopher N. (Submitted and under review): *Child Death Inquiry Reports as Accounts of Institutional Error and Apportionments of Blame.*

Garfinkel, Harold (1956): Conditions of Successful Degradation Ceremonies, *American Journal of Sociology*, Vol. 61, 420–24.

Garfinkel, Harold (1967): Good Organizational Reasons for 'Bad' Clinical Records. In Garfinkel, Harold, *Studies in Ethnomethodology*, Englewood Cliffs, NJ, Prentice-Hall, 186–207.

Goffman, Erving (1959): *The Presentation of Self in Everyday Life*, Garden City, NY, Doubleday-Anchor.

Goffman, Erving (1971): *Relations in Public*, New York, NY, Basic Books.

Gotti, Maurizio (2012 [In this volume]): The Judicialisation of Arbitration Discourse in the Italian Context. In Bhatia, Vijay K., Candlin, Christopher N. and Gotti, Maurizio (Eds) *Discourse and Practice in International Commercial Arbitration: Issues, Challenges and Prospects*, Farnham, Ashgate Publishing.

Hafner, Christoph A. (2010): A Multi-perspective Genre Analysis of the Barrister's Opinion: Writing Context, Generic Structure, and Textualization, *Written Communication*, Vol. 27, No. 4, 410–41.

Hafner, Christoph A. (2011): Professional Reasoning, Legal Cultures, and Arbitral Awards, *World Englishes*, Vol. 30, No.1, 117–28.

Hartland, Nick (1989): Texts and Social Organization, *Journal of Pragmatics*, Vol. 13, 395–405

Heritage, John (1987): Ethnomethodology. In Anthony Giddens and J. Turner, *Social Theory Today*, Cambridge, Polity Press, 224–72.

Hyland, Ken (2005): *Metadiscourse: Exploring Interaction in Writing*, London, Continuum.

Maley, Yon (1985): Judicial Discourse: The Case of the Legal Judgment, *Beitrage zur Phonetic und Linguistik*, Vol. 48, 159–73.

Martin, Jim and Rose, David (2003): *Working with Discourse: Meaning Beyond the Clause*, London, Continuum.

Scott, Michael B. and Lyman, Stanford M. (1968): Accounts, *American Sociological Review*, Vol. 33, 46–62.

Shotter, John (1984): *Social Accountability and Selfhood*, Oxford, Blackwell.

Chapter 10
Cultural Variation in Arbitration Journals: *The International Court of Arbitration Bulletin* and *Arbitration International* Compared

Paola Catenaccio

Background and Aim

Over the last few years, recourse to arbitration as the preferred means for the resolution of commercial disputes has grown considerably, giving rise to what has been called a 'specialized international regime' (Lynch 2003: 84) of international commercial arbitration (ICA). A key role in the creation of this regime has been played by the international community of arbitration scholars and practitioners, who have proven extremely active in furthering the development of arbitration at both the professional and the academic levels.

By virtue of their commonality of intents and sharedness of values and practices, arbitration experts – as highlighted by Lynch (2003) based on Haas (1992) – can be said to constitute an epistemic community, that is, 'a network of professionals with recognized expertise and competence in a particular domain and an authoritative claim to policy-relevant knowledge within that domain or issue-area' (Haas 1992: 2). Among the identifying features of an epistemic community is the fact that the professionals who belong to it share 'a common policy enterprise' (Haas 1992: 3) which encourages them to promote their cause by engaging in policy innovation and diffusion, the latter being carried out most notably through international organizations and their publications (Lynch 2003: 98–9).

The important function ascribed to institution-based communication activities in the development of a culture of arbitration makes arbitration-related publications – and more specifically arbitration journals – a particularly interesting field of inquiry for discourse analysts. As one of the 'mechanisms of intercommunication' (Swales 1990: 25) through which members of the arbitral community develop and maintain professional expertise – not necessarily uncontroversially, but rather reaching consensus through discussion and debate – arbitration journals are privileged loci for the observation of discourse formation and transformation. Indeed, their pivotal role in shaping the arbitration regime is further enhanced by their dual nature as both repositories of information on practice-related issues, and as sources of normative knowledge – quickly becoming orthodoxy – in the consensually regulated field of arbitration. In this domain, the line between scholar and practitioner is often blurred, with leading scholars often working as professional arbitrators and leading arbitrators frequently contributing to the academic debate with academic articles and books; moreover – and perhaps more importantly – owing to the peculiarly limited involvement of lawmakers in this branch of the law, the definition of norms and procedures is left to arbitration scholar-practitioners (Ginsburg 2003: 1340–41), which results in it becoming enshrined in books and journals rather than in legislative instruments.

Starting from these premises, this chapter focuses on aspects of arbitration culture as they are reflected in the discursive features of periodical publications issued by two leading international arbitration institutions, namely the arbitration division of the Paris-based International Chamber of Commerce (ICC), with its semi-annual *Bulletin*, and the London Chamber of International Arbitration (LCIA), with its quarterly *Arbitration International*. More specifically, the aim of the study is to identify similarities and differences in the ways in which the two journals contribute to the construction of the discourse of arbitration, with a view to outlining common concerns and diverging interests (or approaches) in the lines of scholarship pursued. Of course, articles appearing in the two journals cannot be strictly considered textual productions originating within the institutions, nor can they be regarded as official statements, as they are written by a variety of authors who may or may not be aligned with the official positions of the institutions themselves. However, when scholars choose to which journals to contribute they are likely to select those which are most suited to their own research approach. In addition, publishing institutions can be expected to exercise a considerable degree of control on the editorial content of their journals, which are therefore likely to reflect – besides a common core of shared values – 'local' interests and attitudes, thus providing useful material for the linguistic investigation of the domain-internal debate on the nature and future of arbitration.

London Chamber of International Arbitration and International Chamber of Commerce: Shared Values and Competing Interests

The rationale for the selection of journals published respectively by LCIA and ICC as the focus of the comparison rests upon two main pillars. Firstly, the *ICC Bulletin* and the LCIA-published *Arbitration International* are among the journals which enjoy the most widespread diffusion in the field, and can therefore be taken to be representative of the global arbitration scholarship. Secondly, the universally recognized different character and nature of the two organizations – sometimes resulting in outright antagonism – makes their journals an ideal source of information for the study of the discursive articulation of their peculiar features.

The ICC is the world's leading ICA institution.[1] Often referred to as the only truly international organization in the arbitration scenario, it is dominated by business interests. Its international vocation and business-oriented attitude are also reflected in the procedure adopted for the appointment of arbitrators, which is based on recommendations made by a neutral 'national committee', usually a business or similar organization in a specific country.

LCIA is the second most popular arbitration court in Europe. The organization is firmly grounded in the English culture and tradition, although in the last few years it has made substantial efforts to overcome perceptions that it is exclusively English in nature and composition, for instance by appointing non-English presidents. For the appointment of arbitrators, however, LCIA continues to draw largely on the English bar and retired judiciary, particularly in cases governed by English law.

While both are actively engaged in the promotion of arbitration and other forms of alternative dispute resolution, ICC and LCIA also have competing interests and differing attitudes. LCIA can be seen as one of the key representatives of the older pioneer generation of arbitrators – the original elite which first contributed to the creation of an international arbitration culture. More recently, however, with the consolidation and spread of the practice of arbitration, a different type of professionals has developed which is best exemplified in the ICC membership. As Lynch (2003: 102) puts it succinctly:

> the diffusion of new ideas and increased accessibility of arbitration to the public [...] has led to new patterns of behaviour and practice and to a rise to prominence of Anglo-American law firms within the international arbitral regime. While senior members of the epistemic community still exercise influence on the process (mainly through the arbitral institutions they helped create and the academic journals they control), they are overshadowed by the more powerful ICC, which is dominated by business and professional interests.

These differences in approach are obviously most evident in the way in which the core activities of the two institutions are conducted. By virtue of the eminently discursive nature of arbitration such activities are necessarily embedded in textual forms which display, in their linguistic and discursive makeup, features of the legal cultures in which they originate (cf. chapters in Bhatia, Candlin and Gotti 2003).

In addressing the issue of similarities and differences in the discursive outputs of ICC and LCIA, therefore, this study relies on a body of literature which has already yielded interesting results. More specifically, it builds upon previous research (Garzone 2003; Garzone 2007; Garzone and Catenaccio 2008) which has identified considerable and consistent differences in the textual productions

1 For the description of ICC (and that of LCIA that follows) reliance has been placed on Born (2001: 13–14).

of ICC and LCIA, detectable both in legal documents such as the arbitration rules published by the two organizations, and in more informal materials, such as the discursive self-presentation of ICC and LCIA and of their activities in their respective websites. These studies have shown that LCIA texts exhibit several of the typical features of legal English, whereas ICC texts are less imbued with legal language, displaying instead a more direct, business-like and customer-oriented attitude. An additional aim of the research presented in this chapter, therefore, is to verify whether the similarities and differences identified in the journals considered are consistent with the findings of previous research on other discourse types.

Materials and Method

This study has been conducted on a corpus of articles published in the LCIA journal *Arbitration International* and in the *ICC Bulletin* from 2004 to 2008. *Arbitration International* is a peer-reviewed quarterly academic journal; the *ICC Bulletin* (which has an English and a French version) is issued twice a year and includes, besides academic articles, considerable additional materials, most notably excerpts of the awards discussed or referred to in the articles. For comparability purposes, the corpus includes only English articles and awards, with materials in French (very limited in number) being excluded from the analysis even though they were appended to English articles. All the materials were subdivided into two subcorpora, details of which are given in Table 10.1.

As can be seen from Table 10.1 below, the two subcorpora differ quite substantially in size, with *Arbitration International* counting two-and-a-half times as many tokens as the *ICC Bulletin* and displaying greater lexical variety. As the criterion used for corpus compilation was temporal, it was decided not to adjust the subcorpora to make them more comparable sizewise. From a methodological viewpoint, this decision was justified by the approach taken to the analysis, which did not intend to provide generalizable evidence of language use in large corpora, but rather to focus on specific textual and discursive features selected on the basis of preliminary quantitative investigation (using Wordsmith Tools 4.0) and analyzed qualitatively in a discourse-analytical perspective. The perspective adopted is therefore primarily corpus-driven, rather than corpus-based (Sinclair 1991; Tognini Bonelli 2001), with qualitative interpretation being the main aim.

Table 10.1 Corpus composition: *ICC Bulletin* and *Arbitration International*

	Arbitration International	*ICC Bulletin*
Tokens	1,437,882	561,320
Types	26,503	17,398
Standardized TTR	36.46	33.72

Corpus Investigation and Interpretation of Results

As a first step in the investigation, quantitative data were extracted from the corpus using the wordlist and keyword functions of Wordsmith Tools 4.0. The concordance function was then used to examine the context of occurrence of selected lexical items and identify divergences in their textual use.

Wordlist Study

The comparison of the top 100 items in the two subcorpora highlighted elements of convergence as well as divergence. Table 10.2 below shows the most frequent lexical items (included in ranks 1–100, down to a frequency of 0.12 per cent) appearing in both the *ICC Bulletin* and *Arbitration International*. Regardless of differences in the relative frequency of the items, these words can be taken as an

Table 10.2 Lexical items in top 100 most frequent words common to both *ICC Bulletin* and *Arbitration International (LCIA)*

Word	*ICC Bulletin* %	*Arbitration International (LCIA)* %
ARBITRATION	0.92	1.10
PARTY/IES	0.84	0.65
LAW	0.64	0.58
AWARD/S	0.56	0.29
ARBITRAL	0.47	0.31
CASE/S	0.47	0.27
COURT/S	0.46	0.56
ARTICLE	0.41	0.21
TRIBUNAL	0.39	0.36
INTERNATIONAL	0.39	0.56
RULES	0.37	0.26
ARBITRATOR/S	0.35	0.36
CONTRACT	0.28	0.12
STATE/S	0.28	0.31
AGREEMENT	0.26	0.23
DISPUTE	0.24	0.16
SEE	0.21	0.22
CONVENTION	0.20	0.13
PROCEEDINGS	0.16	0.17
NEW	0.24	0.14
DECISION	0.14	0.15
COMMERCIAL	0.13	0.13
LEGAL	0.12	0.12

indication, however general, of the lexical core around which a common discourse of arbitration is constructed and organized. As may have been expected, words such as *party(ies)* and *arbitrator(s)* – which refer to the key actors in arbitral proceedings – but also *law*, *award(s)* and *court(s)* top the list, followed by other no less unsurprising items such as *court(s)*, *contract* and *agreement*. *State(s)* also occurs quite early in the list, with *dispute* and *convention* following soon behind.

A quick check at the concordances for these words confirms that – as suggested by the presence of the above mentioned terms in the top positions in the wordlists – among the common concerns of the two journals are issues relating to state jurisdiction and the validity/enforceability of awards, as well as accounts of arbitration cases and decisions. At a closer look, however, differences start to emerge in the contextual occurrences of each and the same word in the two subcorpora.

While a detailed analysis of all the words included in Table 10.2 lies beyond the scope of this study, a few examples for selected lexical items can provide useful insights into the different discursive foci of the two journals. For instance, the item *law* features similar collocates in the two subcorpora – such as *arbitration law, international law, applicable law, model law* – but in the *ICC Bulletin* corpus expressions such as *applicable law* and *law applicable* are remarkably more frequent than in *Arbitration International*. Moreover, the ICC journal also displays more frequent occurrences of the noun phrase *state law*. By converse, *Arbitration International* displays a considerably higher frequency of the string *[UNCITRAL] model law*. Examples 1–5 below illustrate the wider contexts of occurrence of some of these expressions in the two subcorpora:

1. The Tribunal concludes therefore that it has the power to decide this dispute ex aequo et bono according to Article 17.3 of the ICC Rules and that in using its power it does not have to determine any specific *applicable law*. However, it may refer to the *applicable law* without being bound to apply it. This conclusion and the explanation given above are sufficient to deal with the first issue determined by the Terms of Reference. (*ICC Bulletin*, award excerpt)
2. The fourth case involved an arbitral award made in Switzerland between a Finnish party and a party owned by the Turkish State. The arbitration clause included the following sentence: 'The Board of Arbitration shall take as base the provisions of this Contract and Turkish laws in force'. In the arbitration, the Turkish party argued that this sentence meant that Turkish law applied to both substance and procedure. In the award, the majority of the arbitral tribunal held that '"Turkish laws in force" [should] not be understood as choice of procedural rules'. Having prevailed in the arbitration, the Finnish party sought enforcement in Turkey. The Court of First Instance and the Court of Appeal refused enforcement, holding that the award violated Article V(1)(d) of the Convention. Again, this result

might have been avoided if the arbitration clause had been drafted more carefully, although it is surprising that a court should construe the words 'Turkish laws in force' as referring not only to the substantive *applicable law* but also to the procedural *applicable law*, for it is generally understood that the choice of a place of arbitration (here, Zurich) implies the choice of the arbitration law of that place (that is, Swiss international arbitration law). (*ICC Bulletin*)

3. In those jurisdictions where the threshold conditions to enforcement in Article IV(1)(b) of the Convention are satisfied by providing documents that show an apparent agreement to arbitrate, validity, including the existence of the apparent agreement, is usually regarded as a matter to be dealt with under Article V(1)(a), the relevant law being the law of the alleged agreement or, if not indicated, of the place where the award was made. In such jurisdictions, the enforcing court may, when considering whether the documents provided do show a prima facie agreement to arbitrate, be influenced by decisions concerning the existence of that agreement by the tribunal or the courts at the seat of arbitration, since they will be decisions under the *applicable law*. (*Arbitration International*)
4. The 2006 amendments to the Model Law (ML) included two options for Article 7 on the writing requirement. One option maintains the original structure of Article 7 and specifies what is to be understood by writing in new subsections 3 and 4. In this first option, Article 7(3) explains that the writing requirement is a question of proof of the agreement, and not a prerequisite for its existence. Article 7(4) then lays down how the writing requirement is to be understood. In doing so, it largely follows Article 6(1) of the UNCITRAL ML on Electronic Commerce. Thus, the writing requirement is met by an electronic communication if its content is accessible so as to be usable for subsequent reference. There then follows a non-exhaustive list of examples, including electronic data interchange, electronic mail, telegram, telex and telecopy. (*ICC Bulletin*)
5. The ML's procedural baseline is found in Article 18, entitled 'Equal treatment of parties' which states, 'The parties shall be treated with equality and each party shall be given a full opportunity of presenting his case'. Article 19 of the ML refers to the principle of party autonomy by stating that, 'the parties are free to agree on the procedure to be followed by the arbitral tribunal in conducting the proceedings' with the caveat that the agreed-upon procedure will be 'subject to the provisions of' the ML – in other words, to the principle of equal treatment. (*Arbitration International*)

The excerpts above highlight the differences in the textual and discursive approaches pursued by the ICC and LCIA. Examples 1 and 2 illustrate the context of occurrence of the string *applicable law* in the *ICC Bulletin*. The first one is a passage from a quoted award, and exemplifies an arbitral decision.[2] The second is a commentary on an arbitration case in which the meaning of *applicable law* was – in the opinion of the commentator – unduly stretched to mean something quite different from the generally accepted interpretation of the phrase. Both excerpts refer to actual arbitration cases, and if example 1 cannot be used as evidence of the textual style prevailing in the *ICC Bulletin*, as it belongs to a text which is simply embedded in the journal, it clearly indicates a commitment to discursive inclusiveness, where primary sources play a key role. A demonstration of the preferred style in the *ICC Bulletin* is provided by excerpt 2 – the commentary – which is drafted in an accessible language, with short sentences and the use of clearly flagged cohesive devices that facilitate text processing. By contrast, example 3, which illustrates the dominant style in *Arbitration International*, tackles the issue of the applicable law in much more abstract terms, providing generalizations rather than actual examples. The complex textual structuring of the argument is strongly influenced by the English legal tradition, with extensive left- and right-branching, non-finite secondary clauses, and syntactic discontinuity.

Similar remarks apply to excerpts 4 and 5, which exemplify the contexts of occurrence of the expression *Model Law* in the two journals. Excerpt 4, taken from the *ICC Bulletin*, explains a recent amendment to the ML. It displays the conventional features of the expository text type (Werlich 1979), with a topic-giving introduction ('the amendment [...] included two options'), analytical text structuring ('one option [...]') and the use of both additive and explicatory sequence forms ('then [...] thus [...]'). Excerpt 5, from *Arbitration International*, also provides an explanation of an article of the ML, but does so primarily through paraphrase and quotation, with little additional explication and in a manner which suggests a greater concern for the statement of principles rather than for the illustration of their application.

These examples, however limited, lend themselves to a number of considerations, both in respect of the discursive approaches of the two journals to (only apparently) similar topics, and to the textual realizations of such approaches. The *ICC Bulletin* tends to focus on individual cases and on solutions to specific problems; even when tackling issues of principles (as in the explanation of an article of the UNCITRAL ML) the main concern is for their practical application. *Arbitration International*, on the other hand, displays a greater speculative tendency, with issues of applicability being addressed mainly in theoretical terms and only rarely with reference to actual cases. These different approaches are also reflected in the linguistic organization of the articles in the two journals: the *ICC Bulletin* favours an expository style which appears to be particularly suited to an audience of professional arbitrators, while *Arbitration International* draws on

2 Examples of this kind are common, as the *ICC Bulletin* corpus includes numerous award excerpts which usually comprise the first part of the award, where applicability decisions are stated.

linguistic strategies which are typical of legal discourse, with the doctrine, rather than the practice, of arbitration being the main focus.

The considerations put forth above are further supported by the analysis of the collocates of the term *award*. Both the *ICC Bulletin* and *Arbitration International* count among the most frequent strings including the word *award* phrases such as *final award, arbitral award, enforcement of an/the award* and *award rendered*. Here as well, the contexts of occurrence are remarkably different, as shown in examples 6 and 7 below:

6. In terms of numbers, refusals of enforcement may seem to be within an acceptable range. Some 1,400 court decisions have been reported on the interpretation and application of the New York Convention in the 32 volumes of the Yearbook Commercial Arbitration. Approximately half of these decisions concern the *enforcement of arbitral awards* (the other half deal with enforcement of arbitration agreements under Article II(3) of the Convention). There were thus around 700 enforcement decisions, out of which some 70 refused enforcement of the award. A score of 10 per cent can be considered to be a successful achievement for an international convention. (*ICC Bulletin*)
7. Article 36(1)(a)(v) of the ML differs from Article V(1)(e) of the Convention in the substitution of 'court' for 'competent authority'. In Article 36(2) of the ML, the phrase 'to provide appropriate security' is substituted for the phrase 'give suitable security'. Whereas the Convention refers to an adjournment of 'the decision on the enforcement of the award' the ML simply refers to an adjournment of 'its decision'. Article 36(2) of the ML states:

   If an application for setting aside or suspending an award has been made to a court referred to in paragraph (1)(a)(v) of this article, the court where recognition or enforcement is sought may, if it considers it proper, adjourn its decision and may also, on the application of the party claiming recognition or enforcement of the award, order the other party to provide appropriate security. (*Arbitration International*)

For the word *award* the LCIA journal also features collocates such as *foreign, international* and *jurisdiction* (in the phrase *award on jurisdiction*), the latter always occurring in contexts in which principled discussions of applicability are reported in the legal style customary to the publication, as shown in example 8 below:

8. The UNCITRAL ML adopts an intermediate approach on this issue. Under Article 16(2) of the ML, a party who wishes to contest the jurisdiction of an arbitral tribunal must raise his objection no later than the submission of his statement of defence, or be deemed to have waived his objection. Under Article 16(3) of the ML, the arbitrators, faced with a timely challenge to

> their jurisdiction, may, if they choose, decide the question of jurisdiction as a preliminary question and render a partial *award on jurisdiction.* If the tribunal holds that it has jurisdiction, and if a party objects to the tribunal's ruling, he may go at once to court to challenge the ruling. While the matter is before the court, however, the arbitrators may, if they choose, continue with the arbitration up to and including the rendering of an award.

Finally, another collocate of *award* in the ICC corpus is the verb *see,* which often occurs in the formula *see award.* This expression is interesting because it points to a feature which is typical of the *ICC Bulletin,* namely the provision of extensive additional material – typically excerpts from awards rendered – which is used to substantiate claims and arguments put forth in the academic articles themselves.

Such use confirms the hands-on attitude to much of the journal's contents. The custom of providing award excerpts to illustrate the issues discussed in the articles also explains the frequency of words such as *claimant* and *respondent* in the *ICC Bulletin* corpus, which is reported in Table 10.3 below.

Table 10.3 lists lexical items which are frequent in the ICC corpus, but not in the LCIA one. Besides *claimant* and *respondent,* other words included in the list refer to specific practical issues which appear to concern the ICC readership, but not the LCIA audience. For instance, *interest* and *rate* often co-occur in the expression *interest rate,* and refer to issues of compensation to be granted upon rendering an award. Similarly, *time* and *terms [of reference]* also occur in commentaries on awards or in award excerpts, and are related to the discussion of matters relating to the conduct of proceedings, or to substantive issues in the final settlement.

Table 10.3 Lexical items occurring in the top 100 positions in the *ICC Bulletin* wordlist which do not appear among the top 100 words in the *Arbitration International* corpus

ICC Bulletin	
Word	**%**
CLAIMANT	0.26
INTEREST	0.24
RESPONDENT	0.21
REFERENCE	0.15
CLAIM	0.15
ENFORCEMENT	0.13
CLAUSE	0.13
TERMS	0.12
RATE	0.12
APPLICABLE	0.12
TIME	0.12

Table 10.4 Lexical items occurring in the top 100 positions in the *Arbitration International* wordlist which do not appear among the top 100 words in the *ICC Bulletin* corpus

Arbitration International (LCIA)	
Word	**%**
ACT	0.15
JURISDICTION	0.14
EVIDENCE	0.13
ISSUE	0.12

By contrast, the *Arbitration International* wordlist features journal-specific items which appear to be less concerned with exemplifications and more focused on the establishment of principles (see Table 10.4).

Excerpt 9, which includes both *act* and *jurisdiction*, is an example of this principled approach:

9. Under Swedish law it follows from s. 27 of the Arbitration *Act* that a tribunal denying *jurisdiction* has to do so in the form of an award. Section 27 provides that any decision which terminates the proceedings without determining the substantive issues referred to the tribunal shall take the form of an award. Furthermore, s. 36 of the Arbitration Act allows for recourse against such a decision. (*Arbitration International*)

Similar remarks apply to the word *issue*. This is often used to refer to the topic of discussion, which is thereby framed as a 'problem' to be dissected and analyzed:

10. Applicable Law. Especially in the international context, the *issue* is further complicated by the question of the law applicable to determining whether the non-signatory is bound to arbitrate. 'From a methodological point of view, it seems that in many cases, the arbitral tribunal determines separately the law applicable to the various contracts, even if it reaches the conclusion that the applicable law is the same for all of them'. (*Arbitration International*)

Finally, (also) the term *evidence*, when considered in its context of occurrence, is also shown to refer to the still underdetermined issue of the acquisition of evidence:

11. In international arbitration, as in municipal law, direct *evidence* is generally preferred over indirect *evidence*. However, international tribunals often make presumptions or draw inferences on the basis of indirect evidence when the direct evidence is not sufficient to decide the matter. International tribunals also take judicial notice of facts which are so well known or so

> easily verified as to make proof superfluous, as well as of the applicable law. (*Arbitration International*)

The examples provided in the above discussion, though not exhaustive, paint a picture of arbitration discourse as one characterized by considerable thematic consistency which is nonetheless accompanied by significant divergences in approach. The *ICC Bulletin* appears to be concerned with substantive issues, which it discusses with frequent recourse to examples drawn from awards in an effort to provide guidelines for the development of professional expertise. *Arbitration International*, on the other hand, tends to tackle topics which are subject to controversy or which are still in need of definition and/or specification. This suggests a speculative, theory-oriented attitude, in line with the more markedly academic composition of the LCIA membership.

Keyword Study

While wordlists provide information on the absolute frequency of lexical items, further insights into the lexical peculiarities of a corpus can be gained through the study of keywords, that is, lexical items which – though not necessarily very frequent in absolute terms – are relatively more frequent in one corpus compared to another. In the case of the two subcorpora under investigation, the lists of keywords extracted (displayed in Tables 10.4 and 10.5) offer particularly interesting data which confirm the preliminary conclusions drawn at the end of the previous paragraph:

As can be observed, nearly all the words which occur with a significantly higher relative frequency in the *ICC Bulletin* are related to substantive issues or practical concerns linked to the conduct of arbitration. By contrast, the *Arbitration International* keywords include mostly abstract or general terms, validating the hypothesis of a more practical focus of ICC compared to LCIA, which also appears concerned with framing the domain arbitration, pitching it against *litigation* and *mediation*.

Another interesting feature is the presence, in the *Arbitration International* keyword list, of the terms *witness* and *discovery*: taken together with *evidence* – discussed above, and with which they tend to co-occur – they confirm the journal's interest for this topical issue in arbitration scholarship.

But the most surprising element is the presence in the *Arbitration International* list of keywords of such items as the first and second person pronouns and adjectives *I*, *me*, *my*, *we*, *you* and *your*. Usually taken as indicators of interpersonal focus, their presence would appear at first sight to be poorly suited to the highly formal style which is a defining feature of the LCIA journal. Thus, a closer look at the concordances for the personal pronouns is required to shed light on their textual functions.

With a few exceptions, occurrences of *I* and *you* appear to be split among two main types of discourse, both of which involve the extensive use of direct

Table 10.5 *ICC Bulletin* keywords (compared to *Arbitration International*)

ICC Bulletin keywords	
Keyword	**Keyness**
INTEREST	1.232.02
CLAIMANT	1.118.69
RATE	1.055.83
RESPONDENT	840.53
PAYMENT	739.31
REFERENCE	630.07
AMIABLE	506.37
CONTRACT	505.57
DATE	500.29
REFEREE	470.08
ARTICLE	447.14
DEFENDANT	394.06
BOARD	366.79
PARTIES	344.10
ALTERNATE	332.99
CLAIMANT'S	299.11
BOARDS	296.81
AMOUNT	284.37
IMMUNITY	282.49
COURT'S	281.17
GUARANTEE	276.35
TERMS	275.02
EXTRACT	274.58
BANK	272.41

Table 10.6 *Arbitration International* keywords (compared to *ICC Bulletin*)

Arbitration International keywords	
Keyword	**Keyness**
YOU	1.075.27
I	543.33
WE	426.7
ACT	341.51
EVIDENCE	309.48
NAFTA	292.41
THINK	280.98
MEDIATION	249.78
TREATY	238.56
INVESTMENT	222.33
INTERNATIONAL	219.25
MODEL	214.69
MY	204.17
YOUR	176.00
PRIVILEGE	161.42
PROTECTION	157.07
INVESTOR	155.91
LITIGATION	142.26
WITNESS	135.31
TREATMENT	130.84
PROCESS	128.47
AMICUS	125.38
DISCOVERY	121.96
ME	117.27

speech. The first one is the exemplification of witness testimony, which, besides being discussed in abstract terms, is also presented in the form of transcripts of arbitration moots which are then commented on by experienced arbitrators. The second is the publication of interviews with leading arbitrators who share their views on a variety of topics, all of them relating to the management of arbitration proceedings. The interpersonally-oriented approach signalled by the use of first- and second-person indicators is therefore a feature of embedded texts which, regardless of their different nature, serve the common purpose of providing materials and information useful for the development of professional expertise. The presence of these texts is particularly interesting because it indicates that

LCIA also considers training a priority, but approaches the topic in a mediated manner in the form of simulations and expert commentaries.

In contrast with the first-person singular pronoun, which almost invariably appears in quotes, the first-person plural *we* occurs in the articles with two main functions. On the one hand, it is used to put forth opinions which are presented as shared by the LCIA community, or at least by those scholars within it who have the authority to establish orthodoxy, as in example 12 below:

12. […] the Court of Appeal of Paris concluded that the referee was not acting in the capacity of an arbitrator, that therefore his decisions were not arbitral awards and, accordingly, that they could not be subject to an action to set aside.

Overall, we do not necessarily disagree with the result reached by the Paris Court of Appeal, which denies the characterization as an award, even though we would have welcomed more detailed reasons supporting it. The brevity of these reasons, admittedly familiar to French courts, has led to criticisms. In other cases, it is used to indicate membership to a wider arbitration community or even society in general:

13. We now have (thanks to the ingenuity of the legal fraternity) a 'rule of law' regime in which investors in foreign countries, through the instrumentality of bilateral treaties, can exercise direct rights of action against the state entity in which the investment is made without contractual relations with it.

At other times still, the first person plural is used as a rhetorical device to guide the reader through a process of learning and persuasion – yet another example which confirms the variety of uses to which the pronoun *we* lends itself, and which highlights the need to interpret its meaning and function in context:

14. It may be thought that these are weighty arguments against encouraging – and perhaps even against allowing – dissenting opinions in ICA. Yet we have to face reality. As Sir Gerald Fitzmaurice appreciated: 'there are questions of realism'. The reality is that, so far as ICA is concerned, the dissenting opinion is here to stay. But then, may we not distinguish between dissenting opinions which are 'good', in the sense that they are unobjectionable in their tone and content, and the rest?

The latter use is particularly interesting because it suggests self-framing of the writer (in this case a renowned scholar in the field) as a teacher and mentor, an authoritative figure who can steer the less experienced scholar and the professional in need of guidance to the safe harbour of orthodoxy and expertise.

Conclusions

This study has highlighted a common core of the discourse of arbitration shared by the two journals, with a focus on themes such as the enforceability of awards, applicable law, and the relationship between state/domestic laws and UNCITRAL. As expected, there are, however, differences in approach which are manifested both at the level of discourse organization and of text structuring.

As far as topic selection and discourse organization are concerned, the *ICC Bulletin* displays a greater concern for substantive issues, with frequent recourse to exemplifications in the form of excerpts from awards. The *Arbitration Journal*, on the contrary, has a more theoretical and speculative focus, and displays a greater concern for topical issues still in need of theoretical and conceptual codification, such as the collection of evidence.

At the textual and linguistic level, the two institutions are characterized by distinctly different styles. ICC opts for mainly expository texts drafted in accessible language and characterized by processing ease. LCIA, by contrast, is obviously steeped in the tradition of legal English, which results in much more complex syntactic structures and a markedly abstract style.

These results confirm the findings of earlier research which had shown the discursive styles of ICC and LCIA to differ precisely along these lines. In her study of arbitration rules across legal cultures Garzone (2003) showed that the LCIA rules are characterized by a drafting style which is typical of the English legal tradition, with its customary complexity and high degree of explicitation. By contrast, the ICC rules were found to be inspired by the French arbitration legislation and to have adopted the drafting style typical of the civil law tradition, more oriented towards clarity and broad outlines. In a later study of the rhetorical strategies of self-presentation deployed by LCIA and ICC in their websites (Garzone and Catenaccio 2008), LCIA was found to remain steeped in legal discourse even while promoting itself, whereas ICC proved much more inclined to adopt a business-like approach to communication.

The fact that the differences between ICC and LCIA are also carried on in their journals suggests that the two organizations are characterized by different cultures whose approaches to the development of arbitration scholarship also differs. If scholarship dominates the concerns of LCIA, with issues of training and application descending from principled discussions of theory and concepts, the main interests of ICC are practical and empirical aspects of arbitration. The abundant reference material provided by ICC in the form of award excerpt goes precisely in this direction: readers are encouraged to look at precedents not so much so as to be able to rely on them for future decisions, but rather in order to develop a professional expertise on the basis of empirical evidence. By contrast, the attitude to training and practice which emerges from the LCIA journal is based on the commentary of simulations and on the provision of expert opinions, with scholars and leading arbitrators remaining the authoritative source of knowledge and expertise.

These differences, however, should not be interpreted as an indication of the existence of conflicting discourses within the domain of arbitration. Rather, they should be seen as signs of the vitality and dynamism – and continual evolution – of a multifaceted global arbitration discourse.

References

Bhatia, Vijay K., Candlin, Christopher N. and Gotti, Maurizio (Eds) (2003): *Legal Discourse in Multilingual and Multicultural Contexts: Arbitration Texts in Europe*, Bern, Peter Lang.

Born, Gary (2001): *International Commercial Arbitration: Commentary and Materials*, The Hague, Kluwer Law International.

Garzone, Giuliana (2003): Arbitration Rules Across Legal Cultures: An Intercultural Approach. In Bhatia, Vijay K., Candlin, Christopher N. and Gotti, Maurizio (Eds) *Legal Discourse in Multilingual and Multicultural Contexts: Arbitration texts in Europe*, Bern, Peter Lang, 177–220.

Garzone, Giuliana (2007): Arbitrato Commerciale Internazionale e Culture Giuridiche: Osservazioni contrastivo-comparative. In Preite, Chiara, Soliman, Luciana T. and Vecchiato, Sara (Eds) *Esempi di Multilinguismo in Europa: Inglese lingua franca e italiano lingua straniera, la contrastività nella codificazione*, Milano, EGEA, 107–31.

Garzone, Giuliana and Catenaccio, Paola (2008): *The Discourses of Arbitration and Mediation: A Comparative Analysis*. Presented at the symposium Interdiscursive Colonization of Arbitration Practices in a Changing World, convened by Vijay K. Bhatia and Maurizio Gotti at the AILA Conference, Essen, 25–28 August 2008.

Ginsburg, Tim (2003): The Culture of Arbitration, *Vanderbilt Journal of Translational Law*, Vol. 36, 1335–45.

Haas, Peter M. (1992): Introduction: Epistemic Communities and International Policy Coordination, *International Organization*, Vol. 46, No. 1, 1–35.

Lynch, Katherine (2003): *The Forces of Economic Globalization: Challenges to the Regime of International Commercial Arbitration*, The Hague, Kluwer Law International.

Sinclair, John (1991): *Corpus, Concordance, Collocation*, Oxford, Oxford University Press.

Swales, John (1990): *Genre Analysis*, Cambridge, Cambridge University Press.

Tognini Bonelli, Elena (2001): *Corpus Linguistics at Work*, Amsterdam, John Benjamins.

Werlich, Egon (1979): *A Text Grammar of English*, Heidelberg, Quelle and Meyer.

Chapter 11

Voices in Arbitration Awards: Polyphony and Language Reports*

Giuliana Garzone and Chiara Degano

Introduction

One of the most distinctive traits awards share with court judgments is that they largely consist of what Thompson (1994, 1996) – in order to avoid the confusion between 'reported speech' and 'indirect speech' – calls 'language reports'. This massive presence of reported language events is inherent in this text genre: in making their final decision arbitrators have to summarize facts about the case at hand, and in doing so they quote excerpts from the contract from which the dispute arose and from any text exchanged between disputants to illustrate each parties' stances and submissions, report testimonies' declarations, occasionally refer to normative texts (Conventions, statutes) and previous similar cases, and finally give their own opinion. Also the argumentative process that underlies decisions is inherently dialogic or polyphonic (for example, Amossy 2000; with specific reference to judgments cf. Mazzi 2007a: 114ff., 2007b, 2008),[1] so in arbitrators' discourses there are various other 'voices' and views echoing and intertwining with their own opinions and with strands of argumentation leading to the final decision.

In syntactic terms this renders the texts of awards rather intricate, if only because there are substantial stretches of text that are in a position of syntactic dependency on reporting verbs or nouns. A further element to be considered is that the insertion of language reports involves not only the transposition of direct into indirect speech or the verbatim quotation of excerpts from statements and

* This chapter is based on a research conducted within the framework of the national research project *Tension and Change in English Domain-Specific Genres* funded by the Italian Ministry of Education, University and Research (COFIN Grant nr. 2007JCY9Y9). While both authors are responsible for the general design of this study and for its conclusions, Giuliana Garzone has authored the first two sections and Chiara Degano has authored the other two sections

1 As regards legal discourse, to our knowledge the notion of polyphony has rarely and only recently been used as a research tool, and as part of a diversified methodological framework (cf., for example, Mazzi 2007a, 2007b on judicial argumentation, Azuelos-Atias 2010 on proofs of criminal intent, and Yovel 2010 on polyphony in lay litigants' submissions).

documents, that is, the use of reporting verbs followed by reported clauses, but a whole range of ways in which one's, and others', views and statements are more or less overtly interwoven into discourse (cf. Ducrot 1984: 171).

Background, Aim and Scope

It has been observed more than once that the meaning of the construct of polyphony is not at all unequivocal, as every scholar using it tends to start from a slightly different definition (cf., for example, Nølke, Fløttum and Norén 2004: 13; Dendale 2006: 3). Originally introduced by Mikhail Bakhtin (1929/1984) with regard to the novel and later expanded to embrace all forms of linguistic communication (Bakhtin 1981), it postulates the presence of different 'voices' in all 'speech utterances' (in Bakhtin's terminology). The notion was taken up and elaborated by various scholars in linguistics, and in particular Oswald Ducrot (cf. Ducrot 1984), the Scandinavian ScaPoLine group (Nølke, Fløttum and Norėn 2004) and by Bres and Nowakowska (Bres 1998, 1999; Bres and Nowakoska 2005), who place themselves in the area of 'praxematics' (Barbéris et al. 2003).

The definition of polyphony on which this study is based is that provided by Ducrot, who sees it as the quality of a text in which 'the utterance signals, in its enunciation, the superimposition of several voices' ('l'enoncé signale, dans son enunciation, la superimposition de plusieurs voix';[2] Ducrot 1984: 183). Thus, in a polyphonic utterance 'there is a multiplicity of points of view that juxtapose, superpose or respond to each other' ('il y a multiplicité de pdv [points de vue] qui se juxtaposent, se superposent ou se répondent'; Ducrot 1986: 26).

In examining the inherent internal property of discourse to incorporate multiple layers of other discourses, researchers have proposed various classifications, each containing a multiplication of discursive entities (or 'enunciative entities': cf. Nølke 2006) and points of view that are identified as co-present in discourse, even when this is not immediately apparent (as for instance, in negation).[3]

This chapter focuses on one of the most manifest forms of polyphony, that is, that obtained through the insertion of language reports in the text, which Thompson (1996: 506) calls 'signalled voices in the text', while Fairclough (1992: 117–18) uses the expression 'discourse representation' and sees it as one among several forms of 'manifest intertextuality', that is, 'the case where specific other texts are overtly drawn upon within a text'.[4] With specific reference to English, the use and realization of language reports has been studied in fiction (for example,

2 If not otherwise indicated, all translations from French are ours.

3 For polyphony in negation, cf. Ducrot 1984: 217ff. For a list of linguistic indicators of polyphony or dialogism cf. Bres 1998 and 1999, systematized in Dendale 2006: 28. For a discussion of 'signals of dialogic text' in the Anglophone tradition cf. Thompson 2001: 65ff.

4 The other forms of manifest intertextuality described by Fairclough are presupposition, negation, metadiscourse and irony (see Fairclough 1992: 117–23).

Table 11.1 Corpus characteristics

Tokens used for word list	445,383
Types (distinct words)	10,372
Standardized TTR	33.24

Leech and Short 1981; Hickman 1993) and, quite extensively, in academic texts (Thompson 1996, 2001). In legal discourse, language reporting has been dealt with only marginally by Mazzi (2007b, 2008) as part of his research on judicial argumentation, while it has hardly been investigated with regard to arbitration awards.

This chapter will focus specifically on this aspect, exploring the deployment of various forms of language reporting and the choice of reporting verbs/expressions used in each case. The aim is to identify regularities, if any, and to retrieve those textual and contextual variables with which they may be connected, for example, the participants involved, the way argumentation is constructed in text, the use to which quotations are put in subsequent text, and so on.

The analysis is based on a corpus of 74 awards of the Paris International Chamber of Commerce (ICC) rendered between 1984 and 2003, extracted from the Kluwer Bank[5] (see: http://www.kluwerarbitration.com),[6] for a total amount of about 445,000 words (see Table 11.1).

A qualitative analysis of the corpus has been carried out in a discourse-analytical framework, relying in particular on instruments specifically developed for the analysis of language reports and dialogism, which are illustrated below. Recourse has also been made to corpus linguistic tools – and specifically Wordsmith Tools 4.0 (Scott 2004) – so as to confirm qualitative insights, especially by means of concordancing.

Analytical Tools: Categorization of Language Reports and Reporting Verbs

Language Reports

The first crucial element is the identification and description of the different types of syntactic arrangements used in language reports so that subsequently such

5 It is to be noted that the awards available from the Kluwer Bank, and originally published in the *Yearbook Commercial Arbitration* are abridged. However, considering that their structure and all the important passages are retained (in the 'Note General Editor' preceding each volume the awards are declared to be 'full text', cf., for example, Vol. XXX, 2005: 11), that all awards have been abridged on the basis of uniform criteria, and that our research takes an essentially qualitative approach, this fact does not affect the validity of the findings presented in this study.

6 Unless otherwise indicated, all websites were accessed on 1 November 2010.

description may be drawn on in the analysis and categorization of this type of structures in arbitration awards.

As Thompson (1996) points out in his fundamental study of language reports in academic discourse, the last few decades have seen several studies which have departed from traditional grammatical accounts of reported speech based on grammatical transformations (for example, Quirk et al. 1985: 1020–33), in order to produce semantically-based – and, it is argued, more accurate – descriptions (see Halliday 1994: 250–73). Several studies have also appeared which take a discursive perspective, and as such go beyond the traditional categories of direct/indirect speech to include various other less canonical options (see Leech and Short 1981, partially drawn from Thompson 1996; Hickman 1993; see also Gülich 1978; Mortara Garavelli 1985; Calsamiglia and López Ferrero 2003; Calaresu 2004, which focus on texts in languages different from English).

In these works, authors attempt to account for all the various forms of language reporting, even the least apparent ones, by means of either a comprehensive repertoire of categories (as in Leech/Short 1981 and Mortara Garavelli 1985) or a list of dimensions combining reciprocally (as in Gülich 1978; Thompson 1996; Calaresu 2004).

The categorization used in this chapter to explore the distribution of various forms of language reports in arbitration awards partly relies, for its starting point, on the model set forth in Thompson (1996),[7] but with modifications so as to make the various categories more intuitively recognizable:

a. 'Quote' (Thompson 1996: 511–13): a direct quotation, that is, one where the language event is represented as being quoted verbatim, so the quotation is a separate enunciation,[8] maintains its own deictic centre, and the discontinuity between the two autonomous discourses involved is signalled by specific punctuation, such as colon, inverted commas and dash. This form of quotation is lexico-grammatical in nature, as it formally claims to reproduce the exact *wording* of the statement (Halliday 1994: 252).[9] In the following example from an arbitration award, quote is used to report excerpts from a normative text that is relevant to the case:

7 Thompson's (1996) model is considerably complex, including several functional options for language report (cf. the synoptic table on page 524) in four 'dimensions of choice' – voice, message, signal, attitude – but for the purposes of this discussion it will suffice to examine the options regarding the message.

8 Many authors have dealt with direct quotations in depth, among them – apart from Thompson (1996) – are Halliday (1994: 250–52); Mortara Garavelli (1985: 51–7); Li (1986: 30–33); Calaresu (2004: 94–5); Calsamiglia and López Ferrero (2003: 155).

9 Although Thompson (1996) considers Free Direct Speech as a special case of Quote and includes it in this category, we prefer to classify it separately as, 'Free Quote', as it differs from Quote significantly because of the absence of reporting signals.

(1) Moreover under the title 'Correctness of Information' such duty is explicitly provided in Sect. 7.20 MA *which reads*:

> All information disclosed to the Buyer up to the date of this Agreement or included in the Disclosure Letter or to be given to the Buyer in the course of Buyer's due diligence investigation is or, when given, will be complete and accurate in all respect. (Award 2003–2: 133)[10]

It is usually taken for granted that quotes carry with them a 'verbatim stipulation', but this stipulation has been shown to be purely fictive in many types of discourse (cf. among others Sternberg 1982; Tannen 1988; Mayes 1990). This is certainly the case in conversation, in journalism and in fiction, all the more so as often the cited language event does not encode speech or text, but thought. This probably applies much less to arbitration discourse, where quotes often refer to important points in relevant texts (for example, Statutes or Arbitration Clauses, as in example (1) above), which are reproduced literally.

b. 'Free Quote': this form of language report is of the type traditionally classified as Free Direct Speech, as it has all the characteristics of a quote, but the discontinuity between the main discourse and the reported discourse is not signalled by specialized punctuation. In most cases the reporting verb does not appear at the beginning of the enunciation, but at the end or in the middle, so that the reader is not immediately aware of the reported nature of the discourse. The 'verbatim presumption' it carries seems to be much less strict than in the quote proper. Very popular in journalism, free quotes seem to be relatively infrequent in awards. See the following example:

(2) The award sought by the claimant, *it alleges*, would prevent the respondents from changing the status quo in a way that would cause irreparable harm to the claimant and/or aggravate the existing disputes. (Award 2001–3:86)

c. 'Partial Quote':[11] (it) consists in an integrated language report, and may appear in a paraphrase or in a summary with segments of the original language event – of greater or lesser extension – signaled as being cited

10 Awards are referred to by means of the year when they were issued and the number that has been assigned to them for classification in the corpus. Unless otherwise indicated, in all examples emphasis is added.

11 Also in this case Thompson (1996: 512–13) does not have a separate category, but deals with this form of language reports as a subcategory within direct quotes. Here Partial Quote is treated separately as in our view its discursive impact is different from that of Quote, as it is tightly interwoven in the text in which it is embedded.

literally by means of inverted commas or other clear graphic marking, and permitting the mixing of the syntactic traits of direct and indirect style. It corresponds to what Calsamiglia and López Ferrero (2003: 155) categorize as 'integrated citations', also called 'scare quotes' in common parlance.

(3) According to respondent, the application of the CISG to the assessment of the correctness of the Agreement's termination derives from the parties' will, and 'a different approach would violate the contract and the parties' original intention, which the arbitrator is required to enforce'. (Award 2003–1: 152)

(4) Pursuant to Sect. 7.13.1 MA respondent would under all circumstances only have to 'give reasonable (zumutbare) assistance ... to Buyer'. (Award 2003–2: 134)

d. 'Paraphrase' (Thompson 1996: 515–17): corresponds to the traditional category of Indirect Speech. The deictic centre of the reported discourse is the same as that of the main discourse, because the language report is realized in a subordinate clause governed by a reporting verb, as in (5) below, or a de-verbal noun, as in (6). Because of the re-elaborated nature of this type of language report, in which 'it is *meaning* that is recoded to become a wording', Halliday (1994: 253) sees the resulting statement as 'twice cooked'.

(5) *Respondent argued that* claimant had waived the right to arbitration. (Award 2002–1: 95)

(6) *It is our opinion that* claimant was released from the three-month obligation and could have requested arbitration by November 1999. (Award 2002–1: 111)

e. 'Free Paraphrase': corresponds to the traditional category of Free Indirect Speech. Mortara Garavelli (1985) uses the expression Implicit(ly) Indirect Speech (*Discorso Indiretto Implicito*), and Thompson (1996) calls it Echo – a denomination that is not adopted here because considered not sufficiently intuitive. While in narrative – and sometimes in everyday conversation – it is used to obtain special communicative effects, in non-literary texts it is often utilized when a paraphrase, a summary or an insertion (see below) is continued without repeating the reporting signal (cf. Leech and Short 1981:326). This happens occasionally also in arbitration awards, as in the following example where the claimant's views are reported:

(7) [22] [...] Claimant states that the Agreement only provides for two grounds for termination of the Agreement: failure to reach a sales

> quota (Art. 3.4.3), and bankruptcy of either party (Art. 10). Albeit the letter of credit is mentioned under Art. 3.6.3 as the preferred method for payment, the Agreement provides for no sanction or penalty for failure to issue the document. The only remedy provided for in the contract for failure to open a letter of credit, where it amounts to failure to pay the price for delivered goods, is interest, not termination of the Agreement.
> [23] The Arbitrator does not share this view. […] (Award 2003–1: 156)

Here the first sentence consists of a paraphrase introduced by the verb 'to state'. The sentences that follow are grammatically independent, but still report the claimant's arguments, thus qualifying as free paraphrases. This is confirmed by the fact that in the subsequent paragraph reference is made anaphorically to the three sentences together (from 'Claimant states' to 'termination of the Agreement') as 'this view' ('The Arbitrator does not share *this view*').

f. Summary (Thompson 1996: 517): describes the action more than the message reported, being followed by a noun group or a prepositional phrase, and corresponds to what Leech and Short (1981: 324) call 'Narrative Report of Speech Act' or 'NRSA'. This is an example:

> (8) By letter of July 1996, *the charterer categorically rejected the termination of the contract* on alleged reasons of force majeure, pointing out that it was the owner's duty under the contract to avoid that the vessels be arrested and to procure that the arrest be revoked. (Award 1999–6: 172)

g. Insertion: cited words or sentences are included in the main discourse by means of markers such as 'in the words of X', 'according to X', which have the function of assigning explicit words to a particular agent (literal or non-literal, depending on whether or not graphic signs of quotation are used) without any communicative verb. Insertion corresponds to Calsamiglia and López's 'inserted citation':

> (9) *According to claimant*, Art. 152 does not require to file a lawsuit that includes the substantial issues of the dispute but simply one that addresses the problem from the angle of procedural law. (Award 2002–1: 95, emphasis added)

> (10) Thus, *in the opinion of the sole arbitrator*, both defendants are bound by the arbitration clause in the contract and may be claimed as parties to these proceedings by the claimant. (Award 2001–2: 50)

These are the categories that will be applied in this work as regards types of language reports.

Reporting Verbs and Nouns

A further element that needs to be examined is that of reporting verbs, and associated de-verbal nouns.

Reporting verbs have been extensively studied in academic writing. Thompson and Yiyun (1991) propose a complex classification which they summarize in a useful scheme (1991: 371). Although their categorization is strictly tailored for academic discourse, their argument is more generally applicable, namely that reporting verbs and nouns are hardly ever neutral, but rather evaluative, conveying as they do either the reported author's attitude toward the information in his/her original statement or the reporting writers' (that is, the arbitrators') view of such statement and the pragmatic/rhetoric role they assign to the language report in their reasoning.

As regards arbitral awards, rather than referring to non-evaluative and evaluative reporting verbs (or nouns) in the manner of Thompson and Yiyun, we deem it more accurate to distinguish between verbs that have a purely locutionary value, that is, they simply cite or report someone's declarations with no further additions or implications, and verbs and nouns that do incorporate an illocutionary component, as they not only report statements or views, but also indicate the purpose that the subject intends them to serve, that is, the type of illocution they convey or that the reporter attributes to them.

Verbs with a purely locutionary value used in awards include common verbs like *say* and *state*, and more specialized verbs like *submit* and *testify*. For example:

> (11) *Mr K says* his employment was unlawfully terminated. (Award 1999–1: 46)

> (12) *The claimant*, in its Application for Interim Measures of Protection, *submitted that* an Award on interim measures was necessary in addition to a procedural Order, to ensure the chances of enforcement of the arbitrators' decision in the country of the respondents, i.e., India, if necessary. (Award 2001–3: 87–8)

Verbs and nouns endowed with an illocutionary value, like *argue*, *contend*, *assert*, *agree*, *object*, which account for the majority of reporting signals in arbitration awards, for the most part introduce views, stances or decisions:

> (13) *The sole arbitrator therefore finds* that there has not been an assignment of the contract from shipping company A to shipping company D. (Award 2001–2: 49)

(14) *The claimant concludes* that by such conduct, the respondents are estopped from claiming that the Agreement has been repudiated. (Award 2001–3: 86)

While in examples (11)–(14) the verb forms are active, it is important to note that many reporting devices are in effect impersonal in tone, even where they are used to express a clear stance or to announce a decision (and in particular that of the arbitrators). Among the grammatical forms used for this purpose are agentless passives:

(15) *It is in this context noted that* according to general principles of contract law, including Russian, in particular a debtor may not assign a debt without the approval of the creditor. (Award 2001–2: 48)

(16) *It can therefore be concluded that* the purported breached obligation, upon which termination was justified, is the obligation to pay the price of the goods. (Award 2003–1: 155)

(17) *It has also been decided that* the claimant's debit for overdue charter fees be set-off against its major credit for damages. (Award 1999–6: 179)

Another form used for this purpose is that of reported predication (Sinclair 1986), that is, a recourse to expressions starting with anticipatory *it* (cf. Quirk et al. 1985: 955–6) whose impersonal character contributes to presenting the content of the language report as universally shared, thus reducing the arbitrators' responsibility towards the truth value of their statements.[12] In the corpus the most common forms are '*it is clear that*' and '*it is obvious that*', which express certainty based on evidence:

(18) *It is clear and undisputed that* the contract does not contain any explicit stipulation concerning the choice of law. (Award 2001–2: 51)

(19) *But it is obvious that* the same pattern must apply if seller warrants correct and complete information. (Award 2003–2: 137)

12 Analyzing academic discourse, Lukka and Markkanen (1997) classify impersonal forms as forms of hedging in that they relieve the writer from taking responsibility for the content of the text. In arbitral awards this is much less evident than in academic discourse, but it is certainly the case that the use of impersonal expressions serves to avoid setting forth propositions as if they derived from the arbitrators' personal point of view, presenting them instead as generally shared.

It is evident that in these examples recourse to reported predication is intended to express unattributed mental and verbal processes, thus presenting information as objective and unbiased.

In concluding this introductory discussion we may say that the primary distinction to be made is that based on the presence/absence of a component of illocutionary force in the verbs and nouns used to introduce language reports; the second variable to be considered concerns the arbitrators' voice and consists in the preference for personal or impersonal grammatical expression.

Voices in Awards

We begin the discussion of language reports in arbitration awards by identifying and describing the voices, that is, the discursive entities, that are active in this text genre. These reveal the different and interconnected views, claims and counterclaims involved in the arbitration process, and serve to carry forward various strands of argumentation.

How extensively recourse to projected text occurs in awards emerges already clearly in the abstract ('Facts') that precedes each of them in the *Yearbooks* where they are published. This is a result of the degree of textual condensation required for abstracts, which makes the recurrence and frequency of reported speech more visible. The textual structure of the abstract is intrinsically interactional, organized as it is as a chain of actions and counteractions – mostly verbal – referring to exchanges of various types of oral and written texts between the parties (statements, arrangements, agreements, e-mails, orders, contracts, letters, facsimiles).

For instance, the abstract of Award 2000–2 has a total of 1,119 words of which 1,102 words (91.4 per cent) fall within the scope of one of the language report forms classified above. The scheme in Table 11.2 exemplifies the chain of actions and counteractions reported in the first two paragraphs of this abstract:

It is noteworthy that virtually all actions mentioned in this scheme are performed verbally and carry with them a language report. This means that there is little in the abstract that is not 'discourse representation' (Fairclough 1992: 118). The analysis of a section of the abstract shows this clearly:

> (20) Early the following year, [1] D filed a request with the ICC for arbitration, relying on the arbitration clause in the contract [2] which provided for arbitration in Geneva. [3] S contested the validity of the contract containing the arbitration clause and [4] requested that the sole arbitrator render a preliminary award [5] holding, inter alia, 'that there was no binding arbitration agreement'. [6] The sole arbitrator in his Procedural Order No. 2, decided that the further examination of the case would not be limited to the preliminary issues. (Award abstract 2000–2)

Table 11.2 Structure of Award 2000–2 (based on Abstract ['Facts'])

Buyer (S)	Seller (D)
Buyer approached seller for the purchase of x.	Seller confirmed by fax the sale of X. The stipulated condition of payment was 'by irrevocable L/C at 90 days B/L date'. M of seller D also stated in the fax that 'our official order confirmation will follow shortly'.
Mr A, president of S, wrote by hand on the fax, under the payment conditions, 'E. O. remissa diretta' [sic] (translation: 'and/or directly payment 90 days').	M of seller D faxed S a contract in the form of an 'Order Confirmation' [...] asking S to send it back 'duly countersigned for acceptance'. The Order Confirmation provided for a letter of credit as a condition of payment as follows: by irrevocable letter of credit payable at 90 days [...] and to be payable against presentation of the following documents ....
The Order Confirmation was returned countersigned by the president of S, Mr A, who had signed above the words 'for acceptance'.	On 9 September, Mr P, on behalf of D, sent by courier two originals of the contract that had been previously faxed, inviting S to 'revert with one duly countersigned original for our reference'.
On 13 October, S's legal counsel wrote to D stating that the offer for the supply of the goods had been modified in respect of the condition of payment which, under Italian law, was to be considered as a new offer to which his client had not agreed.	On 14 October, D informed S by fax that the goods were ready at the port of loading [...] and on 16 October, D's legal counsel wrote to S, asking S to confirm that it was ready to perform its obligations under the contract. On 26 October, D's lawyers informed S that D was taking measures to mitigate its loss as a result of S having failed to take delivery of the goods, and on 18 November, D sold the goods to a Filipino client at a reduced price.

In this short passage there are as many as six different language reports, of which three are summaries ([1], [2] and [3]), and three are paraphrases ([4] and [6]), in one case [5] combined with a partial quote, the voices involved being the parties ([1], [3], [4], [5]), the arbitrator ([6]) and a text, that is, the arbitration clause ([3]).

Returning to the analysis of awards, even from a superficial investigation it is evident that the leading voice that 'governs' the text and is responsible for reporting all other voices is that of the arbitrator or of the tribunal. In consequence, its presence could be expected to be largely implicit, but this is seldom the case. It tends to be made explicit at points where actual findings and decisions are announced, as in the following example where the arbitrators refer to themselves in the third person, a usage that is largely present in all the awards included in the corpus:

> (21) *The sole arbitrator therefore finds* that there has not been an assignment of the contract from shipping company A to shipping company D. (Award 2001–2: 49)

> (22) *The Arbitral Tribunal holds that*: The Arbitral Tribunal lacks jurisdiction to decide the merits of the dispute between claimant and respondent. (Award 2002–1: 114)

While (21) and (22) report the tribunal's final decision, the arbitrator's voice is frequently made explicit also in the course of the reasoning, and in this case too third person reference is often used:

> (23) *The arbitral tribunal is of the opinion that* the Russian text clearly excludes the competence of the common courts. (Award 2001–1: 16)

> (24) Regarding the disputed scope of SA *the Arbitral Tribunal comes to the conclusion that* the claims for representations and warranties as raised by claimants are not covered by the SA. (Award 2003–2: 133)

A confirmation of the frequency of recourse to third person reference to make the arbitrator's voice felt, and of the great variety of reporting signals used in combination with it, can be found in the concordances for the words 'arbitrator/s' and 'tribunal'. Representative samples are shown in Figures 11.1 and 11.2.

Occasionally arbitrators also use the first person plural to refer to themselves:

> (25) *It is our opinion that* claimant was released from the three-month obligation and could have requested arbitration by November 1999. (Award 2002–1: 111)

Or, make use of an impersonal statement, which nonetheless clearly expresses the arbitrators' views:

> (26) In light of the testimonies given by Mr A and Mr P and based on the description they gave on their exchanges and communications, *there can be no doubt that* Mr A was aware that the Licences might cause a problem. (Award 2003–2: 140).

As anticipated above, however, there are also many cases in which the arbitrators' voice is signalled in statements that do not indicate any explicit illocutionary act

1	years from anticipated startup. The	arbitrators	accept the argument of the defen
2	The proper law of the contract. The	arbitrators	are convinced that the rules
3	the dismissed manager … The	arbitrator	believes that the physical
4	First buyer or claimant? [34] The	arbitrators	come to the conclusion that
5	port of destination … [51] The sole	arbitrator	concludes that the wording of
6	[68] As a matter of law, the	arbitrator	considers that claimant took
7	the CSCD Decision, the minority	arbitrator	continues, the Decision has
8	place of payment… Accordingly, the	arbitrators	decide in their discretion that
9	last objection is rejected and the	arbitrator	declares having jurisdiction to
10	. For this reason the sole	arbitrator	deems it appropriate to award
11	courts of that state. [65] The sole	arbitrator	deems the rule of Sect. 27(b)
12	(indemnité de procédure). The Sole	arbitrator	denied both claimants' claim
13	arbitration and therefore the sole	arbitrator	determines that the Swedish
14	over a period of three years. The	arbitrator	does not doubt that, if
15	payment. In this case the sole	arbitrator	finds it reasonable that the
15	claim for "other damages", the sole	arbitrator	held as follows: [59] "Finally
17	that it would not be the case. The	arbitrator	holds that under Art. 177(2) of
18	as well as of their defence. The	arbitrator	is of the opinion that the fact
19	hardly ascertainable. However, the	arbitrator	is of the view that
20	of the contract. [64] The sole	arbitrator	also notes that the claimant was
21	itration clause is void. [27] The	arbitrator	notes that the parties, pursuant
22	Petition of 2 May 1986. [15] The	arbitrator	observed that by filing the
23	present value amount of … [39] The	arbitrators	recognize that the claimed lost
24	the Spanish company. The sole	arbitrator	rejected both contentions for
25	arbitration proceedings. The sole	arbitrator	ruled that the validity of the
26	true in this matter should the	arbitrator	state, as example, a lack of
27	the position of which the Sole	arbitrator	summarizes in the following way
28	in French Francs (…) [64] The sole	arbitrator	takes notice that both parties

Figure 11.1 Concordance 1: 'Arbitrator' (lines containing reporting signals)

Note: Concordance 1 shows instances of the reporting signals that appear in the concordances of 'arbitrator*' (which includes 738 lines in all). One example is given for each verb or expression.

1	ctory phrase of Art. 2.1.2., the	tribunal	accepts that the more natural
2	[15] The majority of the Tribunal	tribunal	acknowledges that this is a close
3	erits of this claim, the arbitral	tribunal	admits the main claim; indeed, th
4	the water treatment, the arbitral	tribunal	agrees that it was delivered on t
5	the documents from 1971 on. The	tribunal	appreciates that the parties have
6	of the given case whether the	tribunal	assumes that one or the other way
7	defendant. For two reasons the	tribunal	believes that the second of these
8	be completed. Thus, the arbitral	tribunal	cannot but conclude that this fai
9	dispute scope of SA the arbitral	tribunal	come to the conclusion that the
10	than may at first appear. The	tribunal	concludes that their existence
11	account. To conclude the Arbitral	Tribunal	considers that obviously there is
12	Eastern Country. Therefore the	tribunal	concludes that the place of payme
13	of the sub-charter. The arbitral	tribunal	unanimously decides that the
14	the case at issue, the Arbitral	Tribunal	deems that the claimant was not
15	of proof, heavy as it is. The	tribunal	determines that claimant knew or
16	claims or relationships. The	tribunal	emphasizes, however, that such an
17	which sumbmitted an offer, the	tribunal	estimates that the Portuguese
18	purchaser in February 1990 … The	tribunal	feels that the situation was
19	that connection. But the arbitral	tribunal	finds that this is not the sort
20	for these reasons the arbitral	tribunal	holds that it has jurisdiction to
21	of the Agreement. The Arbitral	tribunal	is of the opinion that the most
22	rench). In addition, the arbitral	tribunal	is of the view that the removal
23	pursuant to that statute. The	tribunal	notes that the contractual relati
24	and cause. [38] Nevertheless, the	Tribunal	observes that: (1) art. 1261cc is
25	are concerned, the arbitral	tribunal	points out that, regardless of t
26	eller Otherwise shall agree'. The	tribunal	recognizes that it might rule
27	of the environment. The arbitral	tribunal	rejects this claim. as noted by
28	Fast-track procedure. [17] The	tribunal	rules that, by virtue of express
29	completeness of that the Arbitral	Tribunal	states that it also does not shar
30	For this case [60] Sect. 18: The	tribunal	takes the view that the loss of p
31	of the Guarantee. The arbitral	tribunal	underlines that the case against
32	of assets. [20] The arbitral	tribunal	understands that, without giving

Figure 11.2 Concordance 2: 'Tribunal' (lines containing reporting signals)

Note: Concordance 2 shows instances of the reporting signals that appear in the concordance of 'tribunal' (which includes 1,920 lines in all). One example is given for each of the verbs or expressions featuring in the concordance lines.

but rather have a metatextual, that is, a merely locutionary value, using verbs like 'to note' to bring in a new element or thread of argumentation.

> (27) *The sole arbitrator notes that* the defendants have not contested the fact that the contract exists but only which parties there are to the contract. (Award 2001–2: 48)

(28) *It may be noted that* the sequence of events as to the negotiation and performance of the contractual obligations under the contract and as evidenced by the parties' arguments and evidence submitted in these proceedings, are undisputed. (2001–2: 56)

(29) *It should therefore be considered that* claimant has not been released by respondent from its obligation to pay the goods by means of a letter of credit. (Award 2003–1: 159)

The other two main voices in awards are those of the claimant and the respondent, both of which are continuously invoked, in keeping with the nature of the arbitration process where the arbitrator stands between two (or more) disputants and in taking their arguments into consideration decides in favour of one of them.

The selection of concordance lines presented in Concordances 5 to 7 offer an overview of the verbs of saying which typically collocate with 'claimant' and 'defendant'/'respondent' as subjects. As can be seen, they are for the most part related to argumentative speech acts through which the point of view of each party is reported.

```
1   e to such effect, be considered that the claimant accepted that shipping company
2    brief claimant reduces its claim.… Thus claimant admits that an agreement was r
3   , thus falling under Art. 19(2) CISG.(4) Claimant adds that in any event the 'or
4   ially, and communicated it to defendant. Claimant admits that legal and fiscal a
5   signed under duress. [6] "On the merits, claimant acknowledges that respondent d
6   ses are highly speculative. Furthermore, claimant advised the tribunal that the
7   rs made by its competitors. Furthermore, claimant affirms that its task was, thr
8   e general waiver of the Protocol in that claimant agrees by Art. d.4 to waive 'a
9   enter in the United States. By so doing, claimant alleges, defendant committed a
10  y period was thus extended until [date], claimant argues. Since the tests and as
11  lies that such use be stopped. [10] "The claimant asks for damages in the amount
12  he contract. [33] "Having done this, the claimant asserted the lack of the agree
13  at it has been induced by fraud or dolo. Claimant asserts that defendant failed
14  sserts that claimant accepted the goods. Claimant challenges this assertion. Cla
15  table relief. IV. Equitable Relief [39] "Claimant claims that first defendant ha
16  added). Defendant itself, in a letter to claimant confirmed that defendant was o
17   which it asserts will happen by [date]. Claimant considers that at least one mo
18  respect to [the system]. This issue, the claimant contends, is controlled by the
19  ee of charge from defendant to supplier. Claimant contests this allegation. [29]
20  ed shall be deemed to have been waived. [Claimant] declares that it has no claim
21  suant to the Agreement. (....) [58] "The claimant demands 10% interest on the du
22   not apply in the case at hand. Further, claimant denies a violation of Sect. 8.
23   Agreement. In its closing statement ... claimant emphasized that Art. 6.1 of th
24   16 March 1987, addressed to respondent, claimant gave notice of default (...),
25  ol of systematic interpretation: Whereas claimant holds the view that 'the calcu
26  ities of the expertise. At that hearing, claimant informed the envisaged expert
27  ecommending [product B]. (....)"70" 27. "Claimant maintains that a major failure
28  te X who are nationals of the State. The claimant objects that State X's law is
29   in Procedural Ordinance No. 3. However, claimant proposed to produce the bankin
30   Tercier, op. cit., Chap. 3489, p. 430). Claimant repeated this complaint by let
31  as a real conflict of interest for ABCD; claimant replied that they were not wil
32  ctual acceptance not having taken place, claimant requested an expert opinion fr
33  rrespondingly reduced." III. Costs [35] "Claimant requests reimbursement for all
34  was no longer manufacturing the product. Claimant responded that it had a bindin
35  could be met within the stipulated time, claimant stated: 'we in no way waive ou
```

Figure 11.3 Concordance 3: 'Claimant'

Note: Concordance 3 shows instances of the reporting signals that appear in the concordance of 'claimant' (which includes 4,000 lines in all). Only one example is given for each verb or expression. The synonym 'plaintiff' also appears in the corpus, but with only 42 hits (for 'plaintiff/s'), so it has not been deemed necessary to show its concordance lines. It can however be specified that the reporting verbs the word 'plaintiff/s' collocates with are 'show', 'request', 'proved', 'concur', know', all occurring once, except 'know' that occurs twice; it also collocates once with the deverbal noun 'claim' ('the plaintiff's claim').

The selection of concordance lines featuring in Concordance 3 depicts the range of verbs collocating with 'claimant', irrespectively of their frequency. However, if the whole concordance output is considered, the verbs recurring most

```
1    the Law of Michigan. In its reply, first defendant accepted the choice of Michig
2    emed fully effective, either because the defendant acknowledged in accord with t
3    e and from making such deductions. First defendant admits that said documentatio
4    endant on 4 December 1991. In this telex defendant agrees to the terms of the co
5     thirty-year statute of limitations. The defendant agues that the effort to 'ini
6     Even if there were a consideration, the defendant alleges, it would have been i
7     be waived by the parties to a contract. Defendant argues that a substantial num
8    istent with the seller's ownership; ...' Defendant asserts that claimant accepte
9    ystem? [51] "As in section A, supra, the defendant challenged the claimant's rig
10   dditional Installations (....) [60] "The defendant claims that an additional lic
11   nt]'. From the fact of being copied, the defendant concludes '[the president] an
12   o was in charge of the project for first defendant, confirmed the receipt of sev
13   ments were ambiguous as to whether first defendant consented to the joinder of s
14   itrable under Egyptian law'. Implicitly, defendant considers that Egyptian law s
15    its contractual services. That refusal, defendant contends, either justified th
16    (....) V. Services Rendered [23] "First defendant contests the claimant's right
17   arrier seeking to be paid for the goods. Defendant counterclaimed costs and dama
18   t EIC benefits were to accrue to the JV. Defendant countered that mandatory prov
19   In its aforementioned letter to the ICC, defendant declared that it did not even
20   justifiable conditions. Furthermore, the defendant denies that claimant was ever
21    juncture, it need only be recalled that defendant emphasizes that clause Q(d) o
22   No. 2 is invalid. In September 1997, the defendant informed the arbitral tribuna
23   y with regard to its internal documents, defendant maintains that claimant used
24   nnot be disregarded in the present case. Defendant maintains that claimant, whic
25    in relation to some of these claims the defendant makes two additional points:
26   the entry into force of this Law.' [15] "Defendant mentions in this context Art.
27   igned. In its submission in defence ..., defendant notes that this document 'has
28   t section of the Agreement. [64] "Second defendant objected that neither claiman
29   quired a substantial Interim Award. [9] "Defendant opposes this application and
30   ing in the Interim Award, and generally, defendant points out that claimant's or
31   t continues to have standing to sue. The defendant questions the applicability o
32   less 'variable costs'. (....)"172" [33] "Defendant raises a number of defences t
33   ity of the effluents." 2. Defendant [3] "Defendant requests that the claims be r
34    is not subject to the arbitrator. First defendant says it never consented to ar
35   pending arbitration. The Motion of first defendant states:  'The contract contai
36   uses inFIDIC [3] "Under this heading the defendant submits that all the other cl
```

Figure 11.4 Concordance 4: 'Defendant'

Note: Concordance 4 shows instances of the reporting signals that appear in the concordance of 'defendant' (which includes 2,735 lines in all). One example is given for each verb or expression.

```
1    t has waived its right to arbitrate, and respondent accepted claimant's waiver.
2    e payment without a letter of credit and respondent acknowledged that fact. Such
3    bribery. For some specific contracts ... respondent admitted that no bribes were
4    ed its issuance. After the announcement, respondent agreed to pay the costs of t
5    nvince the tribunal. [28] "(i) As far as respondent alleges never to have seen t
6    en signing the development agreement the respondent approved 'the execution draw
7    re covered by the Settlement Agreement', respondent argues that if those claims
8    ated 10 July 1986 addressed to [agents], respondent asked to carry the first del
9    7] "According to the Terms of Reference, respondents assert: A. Assignment and l
10   Formation of Contracts [10] "Even though respondent challenges the jurisdiction
11   . 205 et seq.). (....)" X. Set-off [52] "Respondent claims that it should be all
12   ompt any reaction from claimant thereon. Respondent concludes on the basis of th
13   imant the original contract duly signed, respondent considers that there is no c
14   s committed himself to deliver them. The respondents contend that by reason of t
15   ver from the claimants in respect of the respondents' counterclaims the sums of
16   - Prior to the agreement of 9 June 1986, respondent declared as follows in a let
17   o 2000 (Y2K-problem or -phenomenon). The respondent denied the legal and factual
18   e of a contract between the parties [3] "Respondent explains that, as a matter o
19   e case at hand it was not necessary that respondent expressed its consent by sen
20   for the respondents. On 18 May 1984, the respondents gave notice to the Main Con
21   y, there is no written document by which respondent informed claimant that the L
22   been vague and often contradictory. [7] "Respondent insists also on the fact tha
23   ys had not yet elapsed. On this date the respondent made clear by his telex that
24   wsuit proving the claimed right …'. [7] "Respondent maintains that although Art.
25    any document. [34] "As a matter of law, respondent opposes the requirements for
26   ice Reduction [45] "In the contract, the respondent promised to 'place at the co
27   ntil such special form is complied with. Respondent raises therefore the issue o
28    (....) B. Appointment of Expert [5] The respondent requested the arbitral tribu
29   laimant waived its right to arbitration. Respondent says that it definitely did
30   egarding them.' [63] "On the other side, respondent stated: … by filing the same
```

Figure 11.5 Concordance 5: 'Respondent'

Note: Concordance 5 shows instances of the reporting signals that appear in the concordance of 'respondent' (which includes 1,109 lines in all). One example is given for each verb or expression.

often are 'assert'[13] (26 occurrences), 'argue' (22), 'allege' (20), 'maintain' (19), 'claim' (18) and 'contend' (16). Concordances 4 and 5 refer to 'defendant' and 'respondent' respectively:

If we consider the two synonyms together, the most frequent verbs collocating with defendant/respondent are 'argue' (33 hits), 'allege' (26 hits), 'contend' (15 hits), once again verbs with a strongly argumentative force. These same verbs also feature among the most frequent ones collocating with 'claimant' (cf. Concordance 3).

We may conclude that, as was shown to be the case for the abstract, a large part of award texts consist in the disputants' reported voices, which are often juxtaposed in continuous textual sequences (cf. example 30 below), and are sometimes reported together, referring to them as 'the parties', as in (31):

> (30) [35] *Respondent claims that* its reasoning is supported by a number of decisions by the Jordanian Court of Cassation […]
> b. Claimant's allegations
> [36] *Claimant is at issue with all of respondent's allegations. Claimant argues that* it filed its application with a Jordanian court as the jurisdiction of the Jordanian courts was stipulated in the bank guarantees and stated that the request dealt exclusively with the prevention of the calling of the guarantees and had nothing to do with the construction Contract and the claims arising from it. (Award 2002–1: 105)

> (31) *In the instant case, the parties have agreed that* the CISG would apply to the Agreement. As a matter of fact, Art. 11.2 of the Agreement provides that: 'The Arbitrator shall apply the 1980 UN Convention on the International Sale of Goods for what is not expressly or implicitly provided for under the contract'. (Award 2003–1: 152)

In the first example, the disputants' views – notably the respondent's counterclaims and the claimant's response to them – are reported, while in the second example the two parties are conflated into the same subject as there is no disagreement between them on the specific point being considered. The subsequent sentence ('As a matter of fact, Art. 11.2 of the Agreement provides that […]') indicates the reasons why the parties agree on this point by making reference to the relevant Article of the Agreement at issue, and thus introduces a further voice that is present in awards, that is, that of the texts arbitrators rely on in order to support their argumentation, be they arbitration clauses, statutes, international Conventions or simply statements exchanged in writing by the parties. In the example just

13 Here and in the following comments the figures refer to the lemma considered in all its forms (for example, the entries asserts, asserted, asserting all taken together, as members of the lemma 'assert').

discussed the text relied on is an article of the Settlement Agreement from which the dispute originated.

In 19 of the awards witnesses' and testimonies' voices also appear, the item 'witness'[14] occurring 108 times in the corpus, and 'testimony' 51 times. The way they are treated discursively is exemplified in the following extract:

> (32) In light of *the testimonies* given by Mr A and Mr P and based on *the description they gave* on their exchanges and communications, *there can be no doubt that Mr A was aware that* the Licences might cause a problem. *Mr A testified that* he had reported that the problem 'was an open issue and that nothing was filed in the due diligence data room'. (Award 2003–2: 140)

In this example, initially Mr A's and Mr P's testimonies are only reported in the form of vague summaries ('testimonies', 'description') and synthesized evaluatively by the arbitrators ('*there can be no doubt that* Mr A was aware that [...]'), but then a paraphrase of part of the testimony follows.

To sum up the observations put forth so far in this overview of the voices represented in arbitration awards, it can be stated that many of the combinations of subjects and verb forms utilized as reporting signals are used irrespectively for arbitrator/s or tribunal and claimant/respondent: *accept, acknowledge, admit, affirm, agree, believe, conclude, confirm, consider, continue, declare, deem, emphasize, estimate, hold, say, state, underline.* In contrast, some other verb forms are used only to describe actions performed by the arbitrator or tribunal, essentially where there is reference to the arbitrators' views about the issue at hand (*assume, be convinced, be of the opinion, be of the view, deem, (not) doubt, feel, find reasonable*), or to steps in the reasoning process through which the dispute is sorted out (*come to the conclusion, summarize, take notice, understand*), or where the final decision is reported (*decide, determine, reject, rule*). On the other hand, there are several verbs that collocate only with 'claimant(s)/defendant(s)', some simply indicating their contribution to the debate (*add, explain, insist, invoke, maintain, remark, question, reply, say, submit*), but most of them indicating a specific illocutionary point (*allege, argue, assert, aver, claim, contend, contest, disagree, object, request, urge*) of a typically argumentative nature, with few verbs reserved exclusively for the defendant (*challenge, counter*) which specifically depict actions of rebuttal. The verbs used for witnesses (107 hits) are in part the same used for claimant and respondent (*explain* and *state*) and in part are 'dedicated' verbs, such as *testify*. In line with their role within the arbitration procedure, the verbs associated with these actors lack the argumentative illocutionary force presented by the verbs which most frequently collocate with the denominations of the parties.

---

14 Here and whenever a search word has multiple inflections, the form quoted in the text is to be taken as a lemma. Concordances have been extracted for all the inflected forms.

The overview provided so far has offered a systematization of the repertoire of reporting forms used in arbitration awards while at the same time paying attention to their functional distribution in relation to participants and their respective roles. To this point, our observations have utilized the corpus to identify regularities occurring at a local level without considering their realizations discursively. In the next section of the chapter we integrate the insights thus obtained with a close reading analysis of an award so as to extend our investigation of the interaction between formal and functional aspects of language reporting in awards. Such an approach will allow us to consider the use to which different types of quotations are put discursively, taking into account a broader context than is afforded by a corpus-based analysis.

Close Reading Analysis

The text chosen for detailed discursive analysis is Award 2000–2, the abstract of which was already used in the previous section as a means of exemplifying the introduction of the main voices present in this genre. This award refers to a dispute between a Swiss seller (D) and an Italian buyer (S) of industrial products about a sales contract exchanged by fax, whose uncertain validity as well as ambiguity concerning the means of payment had caused the buyer's refusal to take delivery of the goods, allegedly causing a substantial loss to the seller.

As far as the overall distribution of the forms of language reports utilized in this text are concerned, it is immediately clear that there is a prevalence of indirect forms and, in particular, paraphrases taking the prototypical form 'subject + reporting verb + reported content', although it should be noted that this does not imply any exclusive use; on the contrary, all other types of language reports are found in our corpus. The following examples will illustrate the variety of reporting forms as well as the richness of voices featuring in the particular award analyzed in this section:

> (33) Respondent had requested at the outset of this arbitration that the proceedings be limited to the examination of preliminary issues that should be disposed by way of a partial award. In Procedural Order No. 2 the arbitrator dealt with these procedural questions and answered negatively for the first part thereof, while reserving his decision as for the second part. (Award 2000–2: 111)

In (33), the inception features a request by the respondent, to be followed by the arbitrator's considerations and reply, thus establishing a typically dialogic question-and-answer pattern. The respondent's voice – rendered through a paraphrase – is introduced by the verb form 'had *requested*' and the arbitrator's decision is reported simply in the form of a summary: '*answered* negatively for the first part thereof'. With regard to the respondent's reported voice, it is to be noted that the use of the subjunctive (*be limited*) is dependent exclusively on the reporting verb 'to request', which makes the illocutionary function of the utterance explicit. In the next example, another typical pattern is represented, in which one of the parties, namely the respondent, supports his/her claim (in this case the non-existence of a valid arbitration agreement) making recourse to three strands of argumentation:

> (34) Respondent's submissions in this respect are threefold: first of all, respondent submits that a contract has never been entered into between the parties; secondly, it argues that claimant's representatives who intervened in this matter and eventually sent documents to respondent had no valid powers to bind their principal, i.e., claimant; thirdly, respondent submits that in case the arbitrator would retain jurisdiction over the matter, an arbitral award would not be enforceable due to the lack of a valid arbitration clause by application of the Convention on the Recognition and Enforcement of Foreign Arbitral Awards signed in New York (USA) on 10 June 1958 (hereinafter referred to as the New York Convention). (Award 2000–2: 111)

For the sake of textual coherence, the respondent's arguments are first subsumed under the deverbal noun 'submissions', having recourse to what Werlich (1976/1982: 155) calls a numerical introduction ('respondent's submissions in this respect are *threefold*'), to be then addressed singularly by means of paraphrases. On the basis of our categorization of reporting signals (section 'Language Reports' above) only one of the verbs used – 'argues' – carries an explicit illocutionary point, signalling the argumentative force of the respondent's words. However, the structural parallelism achieved through the combination of sequence forms ('first of all', 'secondly' and 'thirdly') and the repetition of the pattern 'subject + reporting verb + that' confers an argumentative value also on the otherwise neutral verb 'submits'.

The use of argumentative verbs of saying associated with the respondent, but also with the claimant, is a recurrent pattern, as revealed by quantitative analysis. As anticipated in our review of reporting verbs, and confirmed by the concordance lines featuring in Concordance 1, verbs range from neutral signals of reported language, with merely locutionary value (*submits*, *asserts*, *affirms* ...) to forms that essentially provide an interpretation of the original speech act, with respect to the function it performed within the context of discourse (*argue*, *contends*, *objects* ...). The following example further illustrates this point:

> (35) Respondent *explains that*, as a matter of fact, it returned by fax claimant's fax of 18 August whereby it had *expressed the will* to have the 'E/O remissa diretta' payment clause inserted in the Contract and, also by fax, the 20 August 'order confirmation' without understanding it but with its signature.

> Respondent also *points out that* no letter of credit has ever been opened by 14 September according to the terms of the Contract, which did not prompt any reaction from claimant thereon. Respondent *concludes* on the basis of these factual elements, together with the additional fact that it did not return duly signed the original Contract received from claimant by courier of 9 September, that no contract has ever been entered into between the parties and, as a result, no arbitration agreement was ever agreed upon. (Award 2000–2: 112)

The verbs 'explains', 'expressed [the will]' 'points out' and 'concludes' provide an interpretation of the function of the respective utterances, presenting their content as part of the respondent's defence of his/her argument that no valid arbitration agreement exists: the verbs 'explain' and 'point out' signal that what follows has to be interpreted as the grounds for his/her conclusion, which is also presented explicitly by the use of the verb 'concludes'. The case of 'expressed the will that ...' is even more indicative of how such 'interpretive' reporting verbs can serve for the reader as a guide for a clearer understanding of the text, compared to more neutral renderings. This emerges clearly if one compares this formulation with the way the same circumstance is reported in the abstract preceding this award, as is shown below:

> (36) S, as buyer, approached D, as seller for the purchase of a quantity of a industrial product. On 18 August, D confirmed by fax to S, the sale of a quantity of the product, according to the specifications and conditions mentioned in the fax. The stipulated condition of payment was 'by irrevocable L/C at 90 days B/L date'. [...] *Mr A, president of S, wrote by hand on the fax, under the payment conditions 'E. O. remissa diretta'* [sic] (translation: 'and/or directly payment 90 days'), countersigned the fax and sent it back to D on 18 August or shortly after that date. (Award 2000–2: 107)

The reference to the phrase 'E.O. remissa diretta' that the respondent added to the fax establishing the conditions of the purchase at issue is a faithful rendering of the original communicative exchange, with no attempt at mediation or interpretation on the part of the drafter: 'Mr A, president of S, *wrote by hand on the fax*, under the payment conditions 'E.O. remissa diretta''. If this is compared with the reporting strategy used in excerpt (35) ('it had *expressed the will* to have the 'E/O remissa diretta' payment clause inserted in the Contract'), it becomes evident that excerpt (35) is much clearer, thanks to a greater extent of mediation on the part of the drafter. Here the act of writing by hand the expression 'E/O remissa diretta' under the payment conditions is interpreted in light of the intention of the original author, who added that phrase to the contract in order to modify it. Excerpt (35) is also quite representative of the complexity of voice overlaps in awards, as three layers of voices can be identified: the first one is the level of the arbitrator drafting the award, who offers an account of the facts (referring to the claimant and respondents in the third person); the second level is that of the parties' reports of the facts (on which the arbitrator draws for his/her own account), as well as their claims and counterclaims, and the third level is represented by the original agreement between the parties – in this case the contract, the mention of which is embedded in the reported voice of the respondent himself ('Respondent also points out that no letter of credit has ever been opened by 14 September *according to the terms of the Contract*').

The qualitative in-depth analysis conducted so far, inevitably briefly, has shown that indirect forms of reported speech (and in particular paraphrase and summary) prevail in the award. This preference can be accounted for by the fact that these forms are more easily embedded in the flow of the arbitrator's discourse, pivoting on its same deictic centre. At the same time, these forms have the advantage of allowing the writer to add an interpretation of the illocutionary force of the original words, so as to orientate the reader to the intended understanding of the text. This said, arbitration awards also evidence forms of direct reporting, especially partial quotes, as illustrated in the excerpts below:

> (37) Respondent points out the contents of Sect. 17 of the Contract which provides, among others, that 'this contract has been drawn in English language in two originals'. (Award 2000–2: 125–6)

Partial quotes are generally used to signal that words are reported verbatim, but also to attribute the responsibility for the reported fragment of text to someone else, and at the same time serve to increase the impression of precision in the formulation of the language report. In arbitration awards both uses can be found: the verbatim function is adopted when specific parts of previous documents are reported, as for example the partial citation of Sect. 17 of the contract in excerpt (37) above. In this case the respondent quotes verbatim from the contract to support his/her claim that no binding contract exists between himself and the claimant: the fact that in Sect. 17 reference is made to that contract as 'the original' (by saying that '*two originals* have been drawn') is used by the respondent to support his/her view that since s/he never returned it duly countersigned, s/he did not legally enter into the contract.

In (38) below the partial quotes report excerpts of the correspondence between claimant and respondent:

> (38) 'Later on claimant, "following [its] previous fax dated 18 Augut and [its] previous phone-conv", sent the Contract by fax of 21 August to respondent, asking the latter to "sign it and send back to [respondent] duly countersigned for acceptance'. (Award 2000–2: 127)

Here the use of partial quotes seems to be justified by the arbitrator's intention to refer faithfully to a document the buyer has countersigned (the contract sent by fax prior to the paper version sent by courier), so as to hold him/her accountable for what s/he had accepted.

The distancing function of partial quotes, on the other hand, seems to prevail in the following excerpt:

> (39) In the instant case one can easily state that an arbitration agreement results (i) from the fax sent out by claimant to respondent on 21 August to which the '*order confirmation*' was attached and which reproduced the text of said arbitration agreement, as confirmation of a buying order made by respondent on 18 August 1998, and (ii) from the fact that said fax was then returned by respondent to claimant, bearing its signature above the terms 'for acceptance'. [...] It does not matter that respondent did not return duly countersigned the '*original*' contract attached to claimant's letter of 9 September couriered to respondent which, in any case, was nothing but the '*order confirmation*' referred to above, to be forwarded again to claimant for its '*reference*' only. (Award 2000–2: 124)

In this case partial quotes are used to mention two controversial aspects of the dispute, namely the 'order confirmation' and the validity of the contract. With regard to the former, the arbitrator appears to distance him/herself from the denomination 'order confirmation' chosen by the parties – and functional to the respondent's defense – for a document that s/he would rather call 'a contract' – as suggested by the following statement featuring in the abstract:

> (40) On 21 August, Mr M of seller D faxed S *a contract in the form of an 'Order Confirmation'* for the specified quantity of the product, asking S to send it back 'duly countersigned for acceptance'. (Award 2000–2: 108)

By means of inverted commas the expression 'order confirmation' is attributed to the parties, whereas the word 'contract' is endorsed by the arbitrator who, also in a subsequent remark, takes the opportunity of underlining that the parties themselves sometimes refer to the order confirmation as 'the contract' ('The Order Confirmation (also sometimes referred to by the parties as the contract) was dated 20 August and signed for D by Mr K').

With regard to the second controversial aspect in (39), the arbitrator uses scare quotes for the word 'original' referred to the contract, to indicate that s/he does not endorse the connotation of 'sole binding document' attached to the adjective, which is only attributable to the respondent. In fact, what the respondent deems to be the original contract (which s/he did not sign) is not seen as such by the arbitrator, in whose view the countersigned fax already possessed legal validity.

While it is quite natural to find the parties' voices 'speaking' in the awards in the form of language reports, as their contentions are at the basis of the arbitrator's discourse, the arbitrator's own voice sometimes goes unsignalled, as we mentioned above, without any attributing device introducing it. This is obviously tacitly assumed to be the narrating/governing voice throughout the text. This is the case in the following examples:

(41) [Here] it suffices therefore for the arbitration agreement to be valid on the substance that it conform to Swiss law [...]. (Award 2000–2: 114)

(42) Accordingly, respondent has not demonstrated that the validity of the contract at stake was dependent upon the compliance of the written form. The related objection is therefore rejected. (Award 2000–2)

In other cases impersonal forms are used (section 'Reporting Verbs and Nouns' above) which implicitly attribute the reported voice to the arbitrator. In the examples below recourse is made to anticipatory-*it* constructions in (43) and (44), agentless passive in (45) and impersonal subject 'one' in (46):

(43) *It is worth mentioning* in passing *that* the parties, in their respective pleadings, have argued this issue in application to that law. (Award 2000–2: 118)

(44) To sum up, *it suffices to say that* all communications sent by claimant's representatives to respondent should be considered as having been ratified by claimant. (Award 2000–2: 125)

(45) In effect, *it may be considered that*, by 16 October at the very latest, claimant had ratified the Contract when, through its lawyers *whose authority is not questioned*, it had sought performance of the contract in granting respondent a certain time-limit to perform its own obligations. (Award 2000–2: 120)

(46) In the instant case *one can easily state that* an arbitration agreement results (i) from the fax sent out by claimant to respondent on 21 August to which the 'order confirmation' was attached and which reproduced the text of said arbitration agreement, as confirmation of a buying order made by respondent on 18 August 1998, and (ii) from the fact that said fax was then returned by respondent to claimant, bearing its signature above the terms 'for acceptance'. (Award 2000–2: 116)

There are, however, also cases where the arbitrator's voice is explicitly signalled as such, as in the examples below:

(47) *The arbitrator considers* therefore *that* this particular issue does not affect the validity of the arbitration agreement and only needs to be examined with the merits of the case. (Award 2000–2: 115)

(48) However, *the arbitrator is of the view that* it is appropriate to apply the presumption formulated by one of the leading legal scholars: [...] (Award 2000–2: 125)

(49) *In the arbitrator's view*, the terms 'E/O R.D. 90 DS' added by respondent under the payment condition on claimant's fax of 18 August did alter the offer because it is understood from respondent's President's oral statement, that he made it clear, at least initially, that it did not want to have the letter of credit as sole means of payment. Therefore, respondent's reply to claimant's fax of 18 August cannot be considered as an acceptance within the meaning of the above-mentioned provisions. (Award 2000–2: 1275)

In examples (47)–(49) the arbitrator is explicitly presented as the source of the reported voice, which is either conveyed through indirect speech ('considers that', 'is of the view that') or inserted citation ('in the arbitrator's view'), a reporting device which is used quite frequently in different forms ('in the arbitrator's opinion', 'according to claimant', 'according to Art. 6', and so on).

Irrespectively of the form used, what is worth noting in all these examples is that although they are discursively presented as reported speech, most are not really reported. While the words of the parties inserted in the awards were originally uttered in another context (preliminary agreements between the parties, oral hearing preceding the final drafting of the award ...), the arbitrator's considerations arise within the award itself and are not in fact 'twice cooked' (Halliday 1994: 253), that is, they are not the result of a re-elaboration. In these cases devices which normally have a reporting function are used metadiscursively to introduce a statement, namely to frame what follows as the decision of the judge. In this way a discontinuity is created in the arbitrator's voice, which up to that point was directed at setting out facts, and which thereafter shifts to one of deliberation.

Concluding Remarks

This chapter contributes to identifying the nexus of voices that are present in arbitration awards, examining in particular language reports. The analysis, carried out on a corpus of international arbitration awards, confirms the high degree of polyphony which characterizes this text genre, and highlights a massive presence of reported language.

Our analysis has systematically investigated language reporting as a distinctive discursive feature, exploring it both extensively, through recourse to corpus analysis, and intensively, through in-depth analysis of a specific award chosen as a representative example. While the corpus approach allowed us to gain an overview of the most typical realizations of language reports in this text genre, also shedding light on the pervasiveness of voices in the textual construction of awards, in-depth close reading has permitted us to observe the intricate texture of voices within a meaningful context, paying attention to their function as well as to their formal realization.

In light of the analysis thus carried out, some observations can be put forth. Firstly, all the different techniques of reporting identified in literary and academic genres are also found in arbitration awards. Paraphrases are by far the most recurrent forms, to the point that they can be considered the unmarked language reporting strategy in awards, probably thanks to their suitability to accommodate several layers of voices within the arbitrator's discourse, without shifting its deictic centre. However, also summaries, quotes and partial quotes are quite regularly used, and even free paraphrase and free quote – normally rarer and more readily associated with literary or journalistic writing – do occasionally occur. Recourse to quotes is generally made either to refer to a section of a statute or any other legal sources which are brought to bear on a specific case, or to documents drafted and/or agreed upon by the parties before the controversy arose, to hold them accountable for their original commitment. In either case the use of verbatim quotations seems aimed at supporting the arbitrator's reasoning and the ensuing decision.

Secondly, regularities have been observed in the distribution of these forms: parties' submissions are generally introduced by means of reporting verbs in the active form, often giving preference to verbs with a specific illocutionary value; even when purely locutionary verbs are used, they often occur in contexts which confer an argumentative force on them. This obviously reflects the litigative stance of the parties involved in an arbitration. As regards the arbitrator's or the tribunal's voice, when it is explicitly signalled as such, it tends to be reported in the form of a paraphrase, occasionally continuing into a free paraphrase, and is generally signalled by illocutionary verbs, expressing stances, views and decisions, although this is mitigated by frequent recourse to impersonal forms.

Thirdly, with regard to the distinction between locutionary and illocutionary verbs, while verbatim reports introduced by a neutral reporting verb could be expected to convey the original message more clearly as it reduces the chances for distortion to a minimum, our analysis suggests that in actual fact this might not be the case. Considering the complexity of the nexus of voices nested in awards, the faithful verbatim reproduction of the original language event does not necessarily favour comprehension, while a heavier interpretive intervention on the part of the arbitrator such as summaries or paraphrases, especially if associated with illocutionary verbs, can favour comprehension and enhance readability, being more synthetic and at the same time more explicative.

References

Amossy, Ruth (2000): L'Argumentation dans le Discourse. Discours Politique, Littérature d'Idées, Diction, Paris, Nathan.

Azuelos-Atias, Sol (2010): *A Pragmatic Analysis of Legal Proofs of Criminal Intent*, Amsterdam, John Benjamins.

Bakhtin, Mikhail M. (1929/1984): *Problems of Dostoevsky's Poetics*, edited by Caryl Emerson, Minneapolis, MN, University of Minnesota Press.

Bakhtin, Mikhail M. (1981): *The Dialogic Imagination: Four Essays*, edited by Michael Holquist, translated by Caryl Emerson and Michael Holquist, Austin, TX, University of Texas Press.

Barbéris, Jeanne-Marie, Bres, Jacques, Lafont, Robert and Siblot, Paul (2003): Praxematics: A Linguistics of the Social Production of Meaning, *International Journal of the Sociology of Language*, No. 160, 81–104.

Bres, Jacques (1998): Entendre des Voix: de quelques marqueurs dialogiques en français [Hearing Voices: About some dialogic markers in French]. In Bres, Jacques, Legrand Réé, Madray, Françoise and Siblot, Paul (Eds) *L'Autre en Discours* [*The Others in Discource*], 191–212.

Bres, Jacques (1999): 'Vous les Entendez?' Analyse du Discourse et Dialogisme ['Can you Hear it?' Discourse Analysis and Dialogism], *Modèles Linguistiques*, Vol. 20, No. 2, 71–86.

Bres, Jacques and Nowakowska, Alexandra (2005): Dis Moi avec qui tu 'Dialogues', je te Dirai qui tu est … De la Pertinence de la Notion de Dialogisme pour l'Analyse du Discours [Tell Me Who You 'Dialogise' With, I'll Tell You Who You Are … About the Relevance of the Notion of Dialogism for Discourse Analysis], *Marges Linguistiques*, No. 9, 137–53. Online at <http://www.revue-texto.net/Parutions/Marges/00–ml092005.pdf>, accessed 10 October 2011.

Calaresu, Emilia (2004): *Testuali Parole. La Dimensione Pragmatica e Testuale del Discorso Riportato* [*The Very Words. The Pragmatic and Textual Dimension of Reported Speech*], Milano, Franco Angeli.

Calsamiglia, Helena and López Ferrero, Carmen (2003): Role and Position of Scientific Voices: Reported Speech in the Media, *Discourse Studies*, Vol. 5, No. 2, 147–73.

Dendale, Patrick (2006): Three Linguistic Theories of Polyphony/Dialogism: An External Point of View and Comparison, *Sprogli Polyphony Arbeitspapiren*, Vol. 5, February, Roskilde, Institut for Sprog og Kultur, Roskilde Universitetscenter. Online at <http://webh01.ua.ac.be/dendale/Articles/Dendale2006Polyphony Roskilde.pdf>, accessed 10 November 2010.

Ducrot, Oswald (1984): *Le Dire et le Dit* [*Saying and Said*], Paris, Les Éditions de Minuit.

Ducrot, Oswald (1986): Charles Bally et la Pragmatique [Charles Bally and Pragmatics], *Cahiers Ferdinand Saussure*, No. 40, 13–37.

Fairclough, Norman (1992): *Discourse and Social Change*, Cambridge, Polity Press.

Gülich, Elisabeth (1978): Redewiedergabe im Französischen. Beschreibungsmöglichkeiten im Rahmen einer Sprechakttheorie [Reported Discourse in French. Description Options within the Framework of Speech Act Theory]. In Meyer-Hermann, Reinhard (Ed.) *Sprechen-Handeln-Interaktion* [*Speech, Negotiation, Interaction*], Tübingen, Max Niemeyer, 49–101.

Halliday, Michael A.K. (1994): *An Introduction to Functional Grammar*, London, Edward Arnold.

Hickman, Maya (1993): The Boundaries of Reported Speech in Narrative Discourse: Some Developmental Aspects. In Lucy, John A. (Ed.) *Reflexive Language: Reported Speech and Metapragmatics*, Cambridge, Cambridge University Press, 63–90.

Leech, Geoffrey N. and Short, Mick (1981): *Style in Fiction*, London, Longman.

Li, Charles N. (1986): Direct Speech and Indirect Speech. In Coulmas, Florian (Ed.) *Direct and Indirect Speech*, Berlin, Mouton de Gruyter, 29–45.

Lukka, MinnaRiita and Markkanen, Raija (1997): Impersonalization as a Form of Hedging. In Markkanen, Raija and Schröder, Hartmut (Eds) *Hedging and Discourse: Approaches to the Analysis of a Pragmatic Phenomenon in Academic Texts*, Berlin, Walter de Gruyter, 168–87.

Mazzi, Davide (2007a): *The Linguistic Study of Judicial Argumentation: Theoretical Perspectives Analytical Insights*, Modena, Edizioni Il Fiorino.

Mazzi, Davide (2007b) Reporting Verbs: A Tool for a Polyphonic Analysis of Judgements. In Echlich, K. and Heller, Dorothée (Eds) *Studien zur Rechtskommunikation*, Bern, Peter Lang, 31–55.

Mazzi, Davide (2008): La Sentenza come Genere Argomentativo: Una riflessione linguistica [The Judgement as an Argumentative Genre: Linguistic Reflections]. In Garzone, Giuliana and Santulli, Francesca, Il linguaggio Giuridico, *Prospettive Interdisciplinari* [*Legal Language. Interdisciplinary Perspectives*], Milano, Giuffré Editore, 239–62.

Mayes, Patricia (1990): Quotation in Spoken English, *Studies in Language*, Vol. 14, No. 2, 325–63.

Mortara Garavelli, Bice (1985): *La Parola d'Altri* [*Other People's Words*], Palermo, Sellerio.

Nølke, Henning (2006): Pour une Théorie Linguistique de la Polyphonie: Problèmes, avantages, perspectives [For a Linguistic Theory of Polyphony: Problems, advantages, perspectives]. In Perrin, Laurent (Ed.) *Le Sens et Ses Voix. Dialogism et Polyphonie en Langue et en Discours* [*Meaning and its Voices. Dialogism and Polyphony in Language and Discourse*], Mets, Université Paul Verlaine, 243–69.

Nølke, Henning, Fløttum, Kjersti and Norén, Coco (2004): *ScaPoLine. La Théorie Scandinave de la Polyphonie Linguistique* [*ScaPoLine. The Scandinavia Theory of Linguistic Polyphony*], Paris, Editions Kimé.

Quirk, Randolph, Greenbaum, Sidney, Leech, Geoffrey and Svartvik, Jan (1985): *A Comprehensive Grammar of the English Language*, London, Longman.

Scott, Mike (2004) *Wordsmith Tools 4.0*, Oxford, Oxford University Press.

Sinclair, John (1986): Fictional Worlds. In Coulthard, Malcolm (Ed.) *Talking About Text: Studies Presented to David Brazil on his Retirement*, Birmingham, English Language Research, University of Birmingham, 43–60.

Sternberg, Meir (1982): Point of View and the Indirections of Direct Speech, *Language and Style*, Vol. 15, No. 2, 67–117.

Tannen, Deborah (1988): Hearing Voices in Conversation, Fiction and Mixed Genres. In Tannen, Deborah (Ed.) *Linguistics in Context: Connecting Observation and Understanding*, Norwood, NJ, Ablex, 89–113.

Thompson, Geoff (1994): Reporting. *Collins COBUILD English Guides 5*, Birmingham, Collins COBUILD.

Thompson, Geoff (1996): Voices in Text: Discourse Perspectives on Language Reports, *Applied Linguistics*, Vol. 17, No. 4, 501–30.

Thompson, Geoff (2001): Interaction in Academic Writing: Learning to Argue with the Reader, *Applied Linguistics*, Vol. 22, No. 1, 58–78.

Thompson, Geoff and Yiyun, Ye (1991): Evaluation in the Reporting Verbs Used in Academic Papers, *Applied Linguistics*, Vol. 12, No. 4, 365–82.

Werlich, Egon (1976/1982): *A Text Grammar of English*, Heidelberg, Quelle und Meyer.

Yovel, Jonathan (2010): *Language and Power in a Place of Contingencies: Law and the Polyphony of Lay Argumentation.* Yale Law School Faculty Scholarship Series, Paper 32. Online at <http://digitalcommons.law.yale.edu/fss_papers/32>, accessed 10 November 2010.

Awards Quoted

1999–1. Final award in case no. 10060 of 1999. *Yearbook Commercial Arbitration*, A.J. van den Berg (ed.), Vol. XXX (2005), 42–65.

1999–6. Final award in case no. 9466 of 1999. *Yearbook Commercial Arbitration*, A.J. van den Berg (ed.), Vol. XXVII (2002), 170–80.

2000–2. Final award in case no. 10329 of 2000. *Yearbook Commercial Arbitration*, A.J. van den Berg (ed.), Vol. XXIX (2004), 108–32

2001–1. Final award in case no. 9762 of 2001. *Yearbook Commercial Arbitration*, A.J. van den Berg (ed.), Vol. XXIX (2004), 26–45

2001–2. Final award in case no. 9771 of 2001. *Yearbook Commercial Arbitration*, A.J. van den Berg (ed.), Vol. XXIX (2004), 46–65

2001–3. Award by consent in case no. 11443 of 2001. *Yearbook Commercial Arbitration*, A.J. van den Berg (ed.), Vol. XXX (2005), 85–9.

2002–1. Final award on jurisdiction in case no. 10904 of 2002. *Yearbook Commercial Arbitration*, A.J. van den Berg (ed.) Vol. XXXI (2006), 95–116.
2003–2. Final award in case no. 11440 of 2003. *Yearbook Commercial Arbitration*, A.J. van den Berg (ed.) Vol. XXXI (2006), 127–47
2003–1. Final award in case no. 11849 of 2003. *Yearbook Commercial Arbitration*, A.J. van den Berg (ed.) Vol. XXXI (2006), 148–71.

Chapter 12
A Comparison between American and Italian Online Dispute Resolution Systems

Larissa D'Angelo

Introduction

With the acronym 'ADR' (alternative dispute resolution) we designate all those procedures employed for settling controversies without resorting to ordinary justice. Arbitration and mediation are an example of ADR instruments, in which different techniques emerge. These models are now employed in many countries and they have become an integral part of the judicial system.

Many reasons have inspired the birth and the spread of these alternative procedures, which are different and peculiar depending on the nation. For example, in the USA, ADR was originally thought of as a tool to defend the rights of all those subjects that, for economic or ethnic reasons, could not afford the expensive and long justice of the courts (Maggipinto 2006).

A fundamental reason for concern in Italy has been the crisis of ordinary justice that was not able to provide effective and timely solutions to controversies, particularly with regard to electronic commerce. With the advent of computer technologies, and of the Internet in particular, we have seen the birth of procedures to resolve disputes totally, or partly, online. This new phenomenon, which has developed widely in the US, and in the last few years also in Europe, is known by the acronym of 'ODR' (online disputes resolution). The traditional methods of resolution of the controversies do not satisfy the need for rapidity and efficiency that is at the base of the new economy. The internationality of commercial transactions and the slow and time-consuming development of court cases and the elevated costs of traditional justice have led the market and the operators themselves to rely on alternative systems, which are more economic, fast and often more efficient.

The first experiments took place in the US, at first within universities or non-profit organizations. Subsequently, the new models of online resolution of the controversies have had wide diffusion in all sectors of the market and particularly in the virtual one. Today, in fact, the ODR service most used in the world is offered by SquareTrade, an American society that manages the procedures of resolution of the quarrels on behalf of eBay. Thanks to a mutual symbiosis, SquareTrade has grown quickly and in only five years it has managed more than a million and a half disputes, resolving more than 200,000 of them (Maggipinto 2006).

In Italy, although the number of people relying on ODR is still low, its diffusion is in continuous and positive growth. In the last few years this phenomenon has become more and more popular. In particular, in the years 2000–2003 there was a rapid growth of online sites set up for promoting the resolution of disputes online through the ODR system. When it appeared, some people considered ODR to be too innovative, destined to disappear in a short time; instead others believed it was suitable only for certain instances (Sali 2003). However, despite this criticism, ODR has developed constantly, gaining more and more attention from Italian users. Nonetheless, although it is considered a faster and cheaper tool able to overcome geographical barriers, Italian consumers still seem to prefer the traditional mediation and arbitration practice (Katsh and Wing 2006). The experts think this is mainly for cultural reasons and of the fact that, because ODR only uses written language, authority is more difficult to be established (Conley and Raines 2006; Hattotuwa 2006). Moreover, ODR requires a certain familiarity with long-distance communication instruments.

In the context of this situation the present chapter analyzes the evolution from ADR to ODR and focuses on ODR practice in Italy and the US, comparing it with traditional forms of arbitration, litigation and mediation. While focusing on critical moments in the ODR process, particular attention is devoted to the relevant cultural as well as semiotic characteristics of this phenomenon.

From Alternative Dispute Resolution to Online Dispute Resolution

In the last few decades in the US, as well as in Europe, there has been a strong and widespread increment in the use of ADR. This mainly includes the following methods: arbitration, mediation and conciliation.

If in Europe ADR is now becoming more and more widespread, it is in the US that the techniques of alternative resolution of the controversies have given life to a real 'juridical cultural movement' (Bruni 2006).

Already in 1887, the American Federal Government promoted mediation in commerce with the *Interstate Commerce Act*, a law that regulated commerce among states and founded a mechanism that managed trade union controversies between the railway companies and their employees.[1] In 1925 the Congress approved the *Federal Arbitration Act*, a law that governed the arbitration of controversies on commercial contracts. More recently, the federal courts have imposed arbitration as a means to solve trade union conflicts, violations of civil rights, retirement frauds and anti-trust cases.

1 Traditionally, there is the tendency to tie the birth of ADRs in America with a conference in 1906 of the American Bar Association, during which Roscoe Pound presented a talk entitled 'The Causes of Popular Dissatisfaction with the Administration of Justice'. See <http://www.law.du.edu/sterling/Content/ALH/pound.pdf>.

It is however in the second post-war period, and most of all at the beginning of the 1960s, that mediation and arbitration greatly developed in North America. This constant growth of cases resolved through these procedures has also been promoted in 1998, when Title 28° of the Bill of the Rights (regarding the resolution of conflicts) was changed, establishing that ADR tools must be used first, before relying on traditional court justice. Influenced by such a success, the European Union and several other countries have also drafted ad hoc legislative interventions, regulating the principal characteristics of ADR procedures (Bruni 2005).

In Italy, mediation and arbitration are the most widely used ADR instruments, and are becoming increasingly popular among users as they have proved to meet different functional needs. Arbitration, the classic dispute resolution system for companies, represents a strong alternative to ordinary court cases. This procedure results in an arbitration award, which is as binding as the decision of a judge of first instance. The dispute resolution system has been particularly appreciated by small or medium enterprises (Sali 2003). Yet, as formal arbitration is mirroring litigation in both time and expense, commercial mediation, which instead implies a negotiated agreement between the parties, is becoming the most attractive ADR option. In this procedure agreement is reached by the parties through the work of a neutral party, the mediator, who helps them explore and analyze the true interests involved in the dispute. He/she also identifies the differences implied in the parties' respective positions, leading them towards a resolution of the dispute, without imposing any decision.

The terms mediation and conciliation are often used as synonyms of the same concept, that is, an informal cooperation towards the solution of a controversy thanks to the neutral participation of a third and neutral participant. In reality, mediation and conciliation have their own specific fields of application deriving from the professional characteristics of these two instruments, the techniques and the tactics they employ and from the theoretical developments of the experts working in each field. The term 'conciliation' should be employed for civil, commercial and employment matters, whereas the term 'mediation' is better suited for procedures involving family disputes as well as social matters (Uzqueda and Frediani 2002).

In the USA, ADR instruments also include various hybrid forms of arbitration and mediation, such as: *Facilitative Mediation*, *Evaluative Mediation*, *Med-Arb*, *Med-then-Arb*, *Quick Arbitration*, *High-Low Arbitration*, *Baseball-Last-Offer-Arbitration*, *Rent-a-Judge*, *Private Judging*, *Small Claims Resolution*, *Dispute Review Board*, *Early Neutral Evaluation*, *Partnering Dialogue*, *Summary Jury Trial* and *Mini-trial* (Katsh 2000).

One of the reasons for the relatively recent development and spread of ADR systems in the USA and in Italy is that they are able to free courts from the burden of generally small cases that inevitably slow down the judicial process. The access to a traditional judicial process is also discouraged by the quantity, the complexity and the technical nature of legislative texts. In particular, as regards the Italian context, this problematic situation is the consequence of a number of correlated factors, such as: the enormous amount of material that each process accumulates; the insufficient structures available and the limited familiarity with a computerized management of disputes. In sum, the great amount of judicial work still to be processed inevitably hampers the Italian judicial system.

The complexity of the judicial system is particularly problematic in small to medium patrimonial controversies, where single consumers are involved; the average time needed to carry out a civil process and the costs of a lawyer often do not compensate for the benefits deriving from a favourable verdict. The consumer therefore often prefers renouncing his or her own rights. Negative consequences also derive from litigation between parties belonging to the same partnership or involved in a positive economic relationship; reverting to a judge might lead to a breakdown in the economic relationship, something that is less likely to happen in an extrajudicial resolution of the controversy.

Within this problematic context, ADR instruments have proved to play an important complementary role as they are not simply an alternative to litigation, but are often more suitable for certain types of controversies. Moreover, in ADR, parties can choose the method of resolution, playing a more active role in the procedure. This consensual approach increases the parties' possibility of maintaining a commercial relationship once the issue has been settled.

In particular, ADR instruments have proved to be able to respond positively to the needs of medium to small disputes, such as those in business to business (B2B) and business to consumer (B2C) transactions over the Internet. E-commerce transactions are spreading quickly, with each of them potentially triggering a dispute (Hart 1999). Therefore, the growth of e-commerce greatly depends on the possibility of providing consumers with easy access to justice and also of taking advantage of the opportunities provided by the online environment and by ODR in particular.

Besides being the easiest and most innovative way of resolving problems deriving from transactions generated on the World Wide Web, ODR is also becoming popular as a means of resolving off-line disputes. The reason for this is that the ODR service is simple and easy to carry out as it allows users to overcome time and space barriers, offering them the possibility to communicate easily. In its relatively brief history, the ODR system has already been applied not only to the B2B and B2C market, but also to consumer-to-consumer (C2C) transactions (Del Ninno 2008). All these are environments where both consumers and businesses need faster and more reliable instruments to solve disputes.

The main functions performed by ODR are the following:

- Assisted negotiation: Two parties exchange monetary offers, following an automatic system offered by a provider of ODR services. In this case no neutral party, intended to help the participants solve the controversy, is present.

- Online conciliation or mediation: The participants communicate by e-mail or on a chat line, with the presence of a third party, the mediator, who helps them reach an agreement. This model is the one which most faithfully resembles the traditional mode of face-to-face mediation.
- Online arbitration: The participants rely on the decisions of an arbitrator, who not only helps them reach an agreement, but who also produces an award. This procedure is carried out exchanging all the relative documents by Internet. In essence, if online mediation is based on the dialogue between the participants, in online arbitration the parties mainly exchange documents online.

The next section of the chapter provides a panorama of the most interesting innovations and experiences concerning ODR. In particular, the analysis will illustrate, evaluate and compare the new procedures and ODR providers available to Italian and American consumers and businesses.

Online Dispute Resolution in the USA

Online mediation is said to have begun in the USA in early July 1996. A Kansas computer hobbyist had set up a website and was publishing local news, drawing information from radio, television and the local newspaper. Some words and phrases he used were copied from news stories that had appeared in the local paper. One day in the spring of 1996, an editor of the local print media contacted him and accused him of copyright infringement. The hobbyist temporarily took down his site but because he felt within his rights, he sought legal advice. After a series of inconsistent and unsatisfactory answers, he contacted the Online Ombuds Office (OOO), an academic ODR pilot project established a few months earlier by the University of Massachusetts Center of Information Technology and Dispute Resolution, in Amherst. Ethan Katsh and Janet Rifkin, co-founders of the OOO, served as mediators in the dispute.

Communicating with the hobbyist and the editor mostly by e-mail, they assisted them in reaching an agreement. A little later, the newspaper launched its own website and the hobbyist had its own site online again, cohabiting in cyberspace peacefully. From filing to agreement, the process had barely taken a month and it can be considered as the first ODR case ever settled.

By 1999 a variety of Internet entrepreneurs had realized that there were commercial opportunities in ODR and a number of activities and experimentations by existing online ADR were initiated. There was great variety among these efforts but they shared a common understanding, namely that while cyberspace may be an interesting place, and for some a lucrative place, it is not likely to be a harmonious place.

The earliest online ADR projects were generally university-related projects. The most well-known project was the Virtual Magistrate project, originally located at Villanova University. It was set up in 1996 to arbitrate disputes between Internet service providers and subscribers. The OOO received initial support from the National Center for Automated Information Research. Other early projects included eResolution, originally called Cybertribunal, and Resolution Forum. These non-profit projects have been joined by several other ventures, some of which are still active today (Table 12.1). Except for Internet Neutral, all were created in 1999 and all were inspired by a realization that connecting people and machines via a network opened up some intriguing conflict intervention applications. For example: CyberSettle, ClicknSettle and SettleOnline rely on the ability of parties connected by a network to submit electronic settlement offers to a machine, and use software to compare the confidential bids submitted by disputants. If the offers are within a certain range, the machine will end the dispute by splitting the difference. When the offers are far apart, the machine keeps the offers secret and negotiations can continue without anything having been given up by the parties. This process is based on an extraordinarily simple set of calculations but it can also be especially useful, particularly in some disputing arenas, such as insurance company/claimant disputes, where the disagreement is over money and where settlement out of court has always been expected. Since August 1988, according to co-founder James Burchetta, more than 5,000 disputes involving more than $20 million worth of claims have been settled in this manner by CyberSettle.

I-Courthouse was founded by a trial lawyer who understood that groups of people can work together online even if they are separated by distance. Trial lawyers are specifically interested in the decisions of groups known as juries, but assembling mock juries can be difficult and expensive. I-Courthouse is premised on assembling online juries. For disputes that are filed, the jury can provide the parties with feedback on the merits of the different positions. For lawyers who might be preparing for trial, I-Courthouse can provide low-cost opportunities to evaluate one's case before a panel in advance of the trial.

SquareTrade (see: http://www.squaretrade.com) was founded in mid-1999 and has used ODR in over 800,000 disputes in over 120 countries. It was founded by three former McKinsey and Co. consultants and Harvard Business School graduates. SquareTrade first partnered with the world's largest online marketplace, eBay, to handle disputes between buyers and sellers around the world and has been the American ODR provider with the largest caseload. In May 2008, squaretrade.com announced it would no longer accept filings of ODR disputes and is currently no longer available as an ODR provider.[2]

OnlineMediators.com was started by the founders of the highly-used Mediation Information and Resource Center (see: http://www.mediate.com) and WebMediate.com is a new venture launched by several Harvard Law School students.

CyberSettle and ClicknSettle have resolved many cases involving insurance companies and claimants.

---

2 See <http://www.squaretrade.com/pages/odr-discontinued>.

Table 12.1 American online alternative dispute resolution providers

Website	URL	Level of automation	ADR instrument
ClicknSettle	clicknsettle.com	High	Assisted Negotiation
CyberSettle	cybersettle.com	High	Assisted Negotiation
Disputes.org	disputes.org	Low	Arbitration
eResolution	eresolution.org	Medium	Mediation/Arbitration
I-Courthouse	i-courthouse.com	Medium	Online Litigation
Internet Neutral	internetneutral.com	Low	Mediation
National Arbitration Forum	arbforum.com/domains	Medium	Mediation
Online Mediators	onlinemediators.com	Low	Mediation
Online Ombuds Office	ombuds.org	Low	Mediation
Resolution Forum	resolutionforum.org	Medium	Arbitration/Mediation
SAVIOMM	aadrol.com	High	Mediation
SettleOnline	settleonline.com	High	Assisted Negotiation
SquareTrade	squaretrade	High	Arbitration/Mediation
Transecure	transecure.com	Medium	Arbitration/Mediation
World Intellectual Property Organization	wipo.int	Medium	Arbitration

Online Dispute Resolution in Italy

In Italy, ODR has been developed by the Milan Arbitration Chamber (cf. website at http://www.risolvionline.it). This procedure has been defined as an 'open model' (Sali 2003: 3) because it aims to favour a direct exchange of communication between participants; it is the mediator's duty to help parties discuss openly and find – through dialogue – a satisfactory solution to their dispute.

In the traditional model of non-virtual mediation, to overcome the mistrust and the disagreements of the parties the mediator draws on a range of psychological techniques that allow him or her to interpret the non-verbal language of the participants, as well as their attitudes, their emotions and their immediate reactions. Obviously, the reproduction of this model online is meeting some difficulties, at least in relation to the present state of computer techniques. Indeed, the online mediation systems inspired by this open model are particularly limited by the limited 'communicativeness' of the software now available. E-mail communication or chat-room conferences are the only means which can be used to recreate, as far as possible, the typical situation of a hearing of conciliation in a virtual environment. As a real arbitration institution would do, the supplier of the mediation service makes available to the parties a virtual meeting place (resolution room) as well as an experienced and qualified mediator.

To begin the procedure, the provider presents a form on the webpage to be compiled by the participants, asking for contact details of the company or the person initiating the mediation and the contact details of the person/company that will receive the mediation request. This form can also be submitted by the lawyer representing a consumer or an enterprise. There are no limits as to value: all the controversies can be submitted to the service, independent of their economic value. The party that intends to institute an attempt at conciliation compiles and sends the submission form online. Besides providing personal data, the claimant must also briefly describe the controversial matter from his or her point of view, adding any necessary attachments and describing the nature and the value of the controversy. At the beginning of the mediation process the claimant must also indicate his or her credit card number, because the procedure fee must be paid in advance. After having received the compiled form by e-mail, the supplier contacts the counterpart and sends him or her another form, asking once again for the contact details of the counterpart and a brief summary of the problem to be solved.

Online mediation is voluntary in nature; where the counterpart contacted by the manager of the service does not agree to participate, the mediation attempt will not take place. If he or she does agree, a mediator is named, a time and date for a meeting is set, and a reserved communication line is created (that only the parties and the mediator can access using personal passwords), by means of which the procedure develops.

At the date and time arranged beforehand, the participants and the mediator connect themselves to the website (see: http://www.camera-arbitrale.com/conciliazione/) and insert the code of the mediation case, the passwords and the usernames assigned by RisolviOnline. Once the virtual contact between the parties and the mediator is established, the procedure reproduces the traditional scheme of nonvirtual conciliation. The mediator introduces himself or herself and asks the parties to do the same; afterwards, each party will be asked to give his or her own version of the facts. The mediator may then ask for further explanations and subsequently will identify the controversial matters, and draft a resolution proposal. The system is designed in such a way as to allow the parties to choose the type of negotiation that they prefer: an exclusive conversation with the mediator (using the available 'reply' command), or all the participants (using the command 'reply to all').

As happens in traditional mediation, this system also allows the mediator to interact separately with each party, to discuss in private the most delicate and confidential aspects of the controversy. As in traditional mediation, the virtual system must be able to guarantee confidentiality in the procedure, assuring privacy in the negotiation and guaranteeing inaccessibility of all communications by third parties.

At the end of the meeting, if the result is positive, the mediator sends the participants the Online Mediation Agreement by mail. Two copies of the Agreement must be printed, signed and sent to RisolviOnline by fax. The service keeps a copy of the document and makes sure that each participant receives a copy signed by the other party. This last operation is necessary to make the online agreement binding, thus conferring on it the nature of a real contract enforceable by law.

The Future of Online Dispute Resolution in the USA

Although the emergence of ODR as a sub-category or type of ADR is providing a viable 'alternative to ADR', ODR has been until now relatively sidelined by technological limitations, which have generally restricted ODR to e-mail and chat-based systems or methods. However, in the case of mediation of litigated cases, these e-mail and chat-based asynchronous methods seem to be less than competitive for a variety of reasons when compared to live, face-to-face mediations.

In the typical e-mail or chat-based version of online mediation, the user makes a mediation request by e-mail that a mediation be set up, whereupon a mediation file is opened, but the method does not immediately begin the mediation process or put the user in immediate visual or audio contact with the mediator and other participants. Rather, the user first waits for the online mediation service to set up a file, and respond, again by e-mail, or via some other means of communication, so as to inform the user of the results of his request. The user must then go through additional stages of preparation before setting up an asynchronous, sequential mediation accomplished by the posting of e-mail exchanges. The user then fills out and submits a request by clicking a submit button, after which the user waits for an indeterminate time to learn what the result of his/her request is, and then waits a further indeterminate time to engage in mediation. Mediations begun in this type of online mediation typically are conducted by e-mail exchanges. However, as is the case with RisolviOnline, they may also feature real time 'chat' areas, computer-sharing graphical presentations, and other types of graphical, non-verbal communications. While this type of online mediation allows online requests for mediation to be made, and non-verbal, asynchronous, sequential negotiations to occur, the user is not able to quickly and efficiently request, commence and conclude a mediation expeditiously online, as can be done in a face-to-face mediation, mainly due to the absence of a fully synchronous audio and video connection of all mediation participants. Additionally, this type of online mediation also leaves a user waiting for information about whether the process has commenced. The user then must also wait for a mediator to be assigned and commence e-mail exchanges or face-to-face meetings.

In view of the shortcomings of the early text-based, and later chat-based, asynchronous online mediations, many scholars and commentators forecast a variety of changes for ODR. IN response to ODR shortcomings is the patent pending SAVIOMM method, which was put into commercial operation in January 2008 by AADROL Inc. This innovative ODR provider represents the future of ODR because of the advanced, yet affordable technology it uses. The world's first online synchronous audiovisual mediation of a civil lawsuit occurred on 8 January 2008.

SAVIOMM provides a dramatically improved, online mediation method. It enables the mediator and all other mediation participants to use a computer, audio and visual communication means and a broadband Internet connection to request and participate seamlessly in a live, synchronous audio/visual online mediation proceeding. This proceeding occurs before professional mediators who are 'on duty' during normal business hours. It integrates video and audio connections into a seamless, real-time online mediation where all participants can see and hear each other synchronously. All participants can also view synchronously any evidentiary materials, documents and audio–video presentations online. SAVIOMM is thus functionally equivalent in usefulness, impact and immediacy to a face-to-face, traditional mediation.

A person desiring to commence a synchronous audio–visual immediate online mediation through SAVIOMM must connect his or her computer and monitor equipped with a webcam to the World Wide Web by cable, DSL, T1 or equivalent Internet connection. The user then navigates to the SAVIOMM website and clicks on a button to access the website's synchronous audio–visual immediate online mediation reservation/order form page. The user inputs onto this page mediation order information, agrees to terms and conditions of the service, authorizes payment by a major credit card for mediation fees, and such payment and information are processed immediately as soon as the user submits the form online.

Upon approval of the order, the user is immediately notified by e-mail of the acceptance of the mediation order and the service provider's 'on duty' mediator is notified by e-mail of the reserved mediation. He or she promptly proceeds to notify the mediation participants of the imminent synchronous audio/visual online mediation. The mediator communicates to each participant the URL to be typed into the web browser in order to proceed immediately to the online mediation conference. The mediator also provides a common telephone number for a backup synchronized audio conference connection.

All participants in the mediation can see and hear each other synchronously and may conduct audio communications simultaneously by means of Voice Over Internet Provider (VOIP) on line as well as telephone. The telephone audio connection is available in case of any problem with the use of VOIP service. The mediation is commenced when participants have connected with the mediator. The method uses a main virtual 'conference room', as well as multiple, additional, separate virtual 'caucus rooms', where the mediator may meet separately with any participant to facilitate negotiations in the mediation, and then shuttle between parties and/or rejoin all participants again. This shuttling and rejoining can be undertaken as many times as necessary without interrupting the synchronous audio/visual online mediation connections.

In the future it should even be possible to advance to face-to-face holographic audio–visual mediations, which will replace the current Flash video modality. This future technology ought ultimately to make ODR virtually analogous to in person face-to-face mediation and potentially lead ODR in becoming the predominant form of ADR (Sharp 2008).

As happens with RisolviOnline, although in a much more automatic and immediate way, if an agreement is reached the mediator is able to draft the mediation agreement online. This can be done on the spot, can be seen by all participants, and can be edited live.

Similarly, a final mediation agreement is stipulated and signed. Thanks to electronic signatures, there is no need to print and exchange documents by fax, as happens with the Italian ODR provider.

The Future of Online Dispute Resolution in Italy

The service provided by the Arbitration Chamber of Milan offers several advantages: the use of e-mail and fax allows participants who are not able to, or do not want to meet in person, the chance to communicate rapidly without incurring in excessive costs. The system also allows the supplier of the service to name experienced and prepared mediators without worrying about travel distances and expenses, as well as with renting a facility to conduct the mediation (Bordone 1998). Consequently, an important aspect of ODR is that international commercial relations are enhanced because the solution of a controversy between international parties is not slowed down or impeded by long distances. As far as RisolviOnline is concerned, 45 per cent of mediation requests have been initiated by foreign parties, thus demonstrating the international scope of the ODR instrument. Lawyers' fees are perhaps the greatest expense in traditional litigation, and even at times in traditional mediation, whereas in cyber-mediation parties are able to reduce costs, as hiring an attorney is often unnecessary (Lan 2001).

There are also several benefits that stem from the asynchronous nature of e-mail communication. Messages are not transmitted live, but can be written and sent later. Since e-mail and web posting can be written, posted and responded to at any time, taking part in cyber-mediation is very convenient. The scheduling difficulties that can arise in traditional mediation do not appear in ODR; parties are able to engage in the negotiation when they are ready and at convenient times. The mediator can contact either or both of the parties privately, without affecting the flow of the mediation. The idle time that disputants experience is similarly reduced because, in contrast to traditional mediation, the mediator can devote time to one party without wasting the time of the other party. As Melamed (2002) explains:

> Experienced mediators are well aware of the benefits of asynchrony. This is a big part of the reason that many mediators 'caucus' (meet separately) with participants. Mediators want to slow the process down and assist participants to craft more capable contributions. This concept of slowing the process down and allowing participants to safely craft their contributions is at the heart of caucusing. Surely, the Internet works capably as an extension of individual party caucus and is remarkably convenient and affordable. Internet communications take less time to read and clients do not hear a professional fee meter clicking. When the Internet is utilized for caucus, the 'non-caucusing participant' does not need to sit in the waiting room or library reading *Time* magazine or growing resentful at being ignored.

It may also be argued that more thoughtful, well-crafted contributions result from the ability of the parties to edit messages before sending them: 'Asynchronous Internet communications have the advantage of being edited "best" communications sometimes in contrast to "first" (often impulsive) responses that can take place in real time face-to-face mediation discussions' (Melamed 2002). On the other hand, synchronous communications such as the ones offered by the American ODR provider allow all mediation participants to hear and see each other live, as in a face-to-face meeting. This advantage greatly improves communications and interaction, including access to important verbal, 'body language' and emotion-related cues or observations lacking in other forms of ODR methods.

Many of the cyber-mediation mechanisms, such as the fully automated cyber-mediation websites discussed above, are available all-day long, every day of the year. Disputants can therefore proceed to negotiate the settlement of disputes immediately, rather than waiting lengthy periods to go to trial. The cost of the service is also proportional to the value of the controversy. Although a payment is necessary to start the mediating process, in case the counterpart refuses to participate, the sum will be refunded entirely.

The Italian system nevertheless has some drawbacks when compared with traditional mediation or the new online mediation system applied by SAVIOMM. Indeed, the practice of mediation cannot easily be reproduced in the online environment because cyberspace is not a 'mirror image' of the physical world. Virtual communication – at least as it is now – is not especially 'communicative' from an emotional and nonverbal point of view. Negotiations are certainly more effective when parties are able to communicate freely facing one another. For example, helping parties to listen and understand concerns, empathize with each other, vent feelings and confront emotions is considered an important art in mediation:

> For many participants, mediation is about the 'venting' of feelings and emotions that they would be unable to express in a more formal setting such as a courtroom. The opportunity to tell one's version of the case directly to the opposing party and to express accompanying emotions can be cathartic for mediation participants. (D'Zurilla 1997: 1323)

Substituting e-mail for dialogue, for example, makes it difficult to give any weight to emotion in mediation. Additionally, communication online without a video and audio communication system (webcam) does not express the variable tone, pitch and volume of the participants and cannot convey personality traits or physical cues. It is therefore more difficult to evaluate the flexibility of a particular party, or the strength of a party's feelings or confidence on a particular issue. Consequently, some authors (Katsh et al. 2000) have argued that the lack of personal presence in cyber-mediation can make it more difficult for the mediator to maintain effective control over the negotiating parties:

> The online medium, at least the e-mail environment, makes it difficult for the mediator to manage or temper the tone of the interactions without sounding controlling and judgmental. The mediator, at least in the beginning, is a disembodied voice and cannot use her own physical 'personhood' to set the parties at ease and create an environment for sustained problem-solving. Similarly, absent the physical presence of the disputants, the mediator has difficulty using the intuitive cues of body language, facial expression, and verbal tonality that are part of face-to- face mediation processes. (2000: 714)

Experts in this sector agree in considering this model inadequate and believe that new efforts to improve the level of virtual communication, such as the ones that are emerging in the USA, are necessary. Although the effects of a highly automated ODR system such as SAVIOMM are yet to be analyzed, some improvement can certainly derive from a greater diffusion of video and audio communication systems that make long-distance visual communication possible between the participants and the mediator. Another important issue discussed by Katsh (1996: 971), is the concern over the protection of confidential material in ODR. While traditional mediation does not necessarily create a physical record, online mediation does create such a record. This could potentially enable a party to easily print out and distribute e-mail communications without the knowledge of the other party. This may hinder the development of open and honest exchanges in cyber-mediation. Finally, familiarity of Italian users with IT technologies will become fundamental when the Internet becomes the main vehicle through which mediation takes place. To take advantage of ODR, a user must be able to manage the software and hardware necessary to chat online, send e-mails and faxes, and at times, even to use a webcam.

For all these reasons, the RisolviOnline service provided by the Arbitration Chamber of Milan has had a difficult beginning and is only now receiving positive feedback from consumers and firms. In the first few years, many requests for online mediation that were submitted to RisolviOnline were not all related to its scope. This was probably due to the fact that this innovative service was clearly explained and also that Italian world wide web users were not familiar with its scope, nature and modalities. According to the RisolviOnline Statistics Report published online,[3] 117 new requests for online mediation services were filed in 2007. This is an impressive result when compared to the 16 requests filed in 2003. On the other hand, if we consider the latest statistics available from the Arbitration Chamber of Milan, we see that of the 117 requests filed in 2007, only eight parties have agreed to participate in an ODR while 31 have decided to find an agreement outside this procedure. Although the overall number of requests is constantly rising and ODR is becoming more and more known to the public, one cannot help notice that the service is still in its early phase, even if RisolviOnline has been active since 2002.

---

3 See <http://www.camera-arbitrale.com/consulta.php?sez_id=4&lng_id=7>.

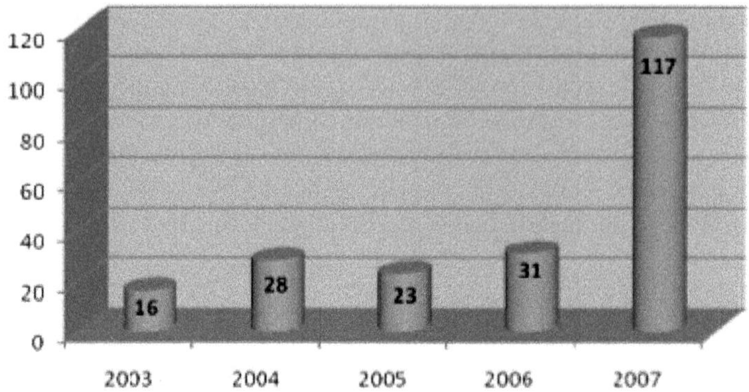

Figure 12.1 RisolviOnline mediation requests (2003–2007)

Conclusions

The data and commentary provided in this chapter show that ODR systems both in Italy as well as in the USA offer several advantages: they allow participants who are not able to,or do not want to meet in person, may communicate rapidly without incurring excessive costs. Both systems also allow the supplier of the service to name experienced and prepared mediators without worrying about travel distances and expenses, and without having to rent a facility to conduct the mediation proceedings. International commercial relations are enhanced, since the solution of a controversy between international parties is not slowed down or impeded by long distances. The advantages of this instrument are clear both in terms of relationships between firms, as well as those between consumers and businesses. ODR does not merely translate traditional ADR instruments to be used on the web; rather, if ADR responds to the need to facilitate access to the instruments of justice, especially from an economic point of view, ODR responds to the ever-increasing need of businesses and consumers to solve economic disputes, taking advantage of the rapidity and convenience of the online instrument.

The Italian system nevertheless has some drawbacks when compared to SAVIOMM, one of the most popular virtual systems in use in the USA. Virtual communication in Italy – at least as it is now – is not very 'communicative' from an emotional and non-verbal point of view because of the lack of webcams. Negotiations are certainly more effective when parties are able to communicate freely facing one another. For example, helping parties to listen and understand concerns, empathize with each other, vent feelings and confront emotions is considered an important art in mediation. In a virtual environment such as the one used by RisolviOnline it is therefore more difficult to evaluate the flexibility of a particular party, or the strength of a party's feelings or confidence on a particular issue. Consequently, the lack of personal presence in cyber-mediation can make it more difficult for the mediator to maintain effective control over the negotiating parties. Finally, the familiarity of Italian users with IT technologies becomes fundamental when the Internet becomes the main vehicle through which mediation takes place. To take advantage of ODR, Italian users must be able to manage the software and hardware necessary to chat online and use a webcam (Conley and Raines 2006; Hattotuwa 2006), a knowledge that unfortunately still seems to be generally lacking (D'Angelo 2010).

In the USA, new efforts have been made to improve the level of virtual communication. The main improvement certainly derives from the adoption and diffusion of a video and audio communication system, which makes long-distance visual communication possible between the participants and the mediator. In this way, synchronous communication and chat-room conferences allow all mediation participants to hear and see each other live, as in a face-to-face meeting, and may thus be used to recreate as far as possible the typical situation of a hearing of mediation in a virtual environment. This advantage greatly improves communication and interaction, including access to important verbal, 'body language' and emotion-related cues or observations lacking in the Italian form of ODR method.

Although cyber-mediation has been criticized because of its impersonal nature, it is likely to become more popular and better suited to resolving disputes as technology advances. Online mediation will probably be fully developed when videoconferencing becomes commonplace, where video cameras and microphones are built into every computer, videoconferencing software is easily accessible and modems are fast enough.[4] When this becomes a common reality, ODR will reach consumers on a wider scale, and users will become more familiarized with the many advantages offered by this virtual procedure.

References

Arbitration Chamber of Milan. *RisolviOnline Statistics Report 2002–2007*. Online at <http://www.camera-arbitrale.com/consulta.php?sez_id=4&lng_id=7>, accessed 15 June 2011.

Bordone, Robert C. (1998): Electronic Online Dispute Resolution: A Systems Approach – Potential Problems and a Proposal, *Harvard Negotiation Law Review*, Vol. 175, No. 3, 190–91.

Bruni, Alessandro (2006): *I Metodi di A.D.R. nell'Esperienza Americana – Risoluzione Alternativa delle Controversie*. Online at <http://www.overlex.com/leggiarticolo.asp?id=974>, accessed 15 June 2011.

Bruni, Alessandro (2005): Dossier del Mediatore, *Mediares*, Vol. 5, 163–87,

4 The important role played by technology is strongly emphasized by Katsh and Wing, who consider it a 'fourth party' in ODR able to serve as 'a tool for the third party by aiding, assisting, and enhancing the third party's information management activities' (2006: 113).

Conley Tyler, Melissa and Raines, Susan (2006): The Human Face of Online Dispute Resolution (Introduction to Special Issue), *Conflict Resolution Quarterly*, Vol. 23, No. 3, 333–42.

D'Angelo Larissa (2010): Online Dispute Resolution in Italy. In Bhatia, Vijay K., Candlin, Christopher N. and Gotti, Maurizio (Eds) (2003): *Legal Discourse in Multilingual and Multicultural Contexts: Arbitration Texts in Europe*, Bern, Peter Lang.

Del Ninno, Alessandro (2008): *Procedure Alternative di Risoluzione delle Controversie: Conciliazione ed arbitrato*. Online at <http://www.leggiweb.it/articoli/A5061696/Conciliazioneedarbitratoonline.html>, accessed 15 June 2011.

D'Zurilla, William (1997): Alternative Dispute Resolution, 45 LA. B.J. LA. B.J. 352.

Hart, Christine (1999): *Online Dispute Resolution and Avoidance in Electronic Commerce*, Draft Report. Online at <http://www.law.ualberta.ca/alri/ulc/current/hart.htm>, accessed 15 June 2011.

Hattotuwa, Sanjana (2006): Transforming Landscapes: Forging New ODR Systems with a Human Face, *Conflict Resolution Quarterly*, Vol. 23, No. 3, 371–82

Katsh, Ethan (1996): Dispute Resolution in Cyberspace, *Connecticut Law Review*, Vol. 28, 953–71.

Katsh, Ethan and Wing, Leah (2006): Ten Years of Online Dispute Resolution (ODR): Looking at the Past and Constructing the Future. In Symposium On Enhancing Worldwide Understanding Through Online Dispute Resolution, *The University of Toledo Law Review*, Vol. 38, No.1, 19–46.

Katsh, Ethan, Rifkin, Janet and Gaitenby, Alan (2000): E-Commerce, E-Disputes, and E-Dispute Resolution: In the Shadow of 'eBay Law', *Ohio State Journal on Dispute Resolution*, Vol. 15, Issue 3, 705–714.

Katsh, Ethan (2000): The New Frontier: Online ADR Becoming a Global Priority, *Dispute Resolution Magazine*, 2000, Winter, 6–9.

Lan, Hang (2001): Online Dispute Resolution Systems: The Future of Cyberspace Law, *Santa Clara Law Review*, Vol. 41, 837–55.

Maggipinto, Andrea (2006): Un Alleato dell E-commerce, *Computer BUSINESS Review Italy*, Vol. 3, No. 8.

Melamed, Jim (2002): *The Internet and Divorce Mediation*. Online at <http://www.mediate.com/articles/melamed9.cfm>, accessed 15 June 2011.

Sali, Rinaldo (2003): *RisolviOnline Experience: A New ODR Approach for Consumers and Companies*, Proceedings of the UNECE Forum on ODR 2003.

Sharp, Geoff (2008): What's New: Meeting f2f Holographically, mediate.com.

Uzqueda, Ana and Frediani, Paolo (2002): *La Conciliazione: Guida per la Soluzione Negoziale delle Controversie*, Milano, Giuffrè.

Chapter 13

Arbitration in Action: The Display of Arbitrators' Neutrality in Witness Hearings[1]

Stefania Maria Maci

Introduction

In 2006, the Italian Government promoted a reform of arbitration under Legislative Decree 40/2006, in line with the United Nations Commission on International Trade Law (UNCITRAL) Model Law (ML). International commercial arbitration (ICA) in Italy is now ruled by Art. 806-832 of the Code of Civil Procedure (CCP) and is a highly standardized legal procedure; arbitration is regarded as an alternative form of dispute resolution, commonly known as ADR. The term *alternative* does not refer to the fact that it is an alternative to legal processes, since 'arbitration is an extra-judicial method of dispute resolution',[2] and therefore a *private* (that is, *confidential*) *extra-judicial process* and, as such, an alternative to the *public judicial process* held in the court of law. In other words, arbitration is an *extra-judicial process* resolved *privately* and *outside* the ordinary court of justice; this is why its final product, the award, has the same legal effects as a judgment pronounced by a judge (Maci 2007, 2008). There are therefore legal aspects within commercial arbitration which make arbitral procedures dependent on legal social practices and discourse.

ICA, as a form of colonization or transition, confirms what has been pointed out by academic research (Bhatia 2004; Fairclough 2007): not only are global dynamics and universal regulations mediated by local configurations of resources and ideas which are context-dependent, but they also give rise to a complex process of blending of professional cultures when applied to professional practices. The

1 The research on which this chapter is based is part of an international research project funded by the Research Grants Council of the Government of HKSAR [Project No. 9041191 (CityU 1501/06H)] entitled *International Commercial Arbitration Practices: A Discourse Analytical Study* (see <http://www.english.cityu.edu.hk/arbitration/>). It also contributes to the National Research Programme *Tension and Change in Domain-specific Genres* directed by Prof. Maurizio Gotti of the University of Bergamo, funded by the Italian Ministry of University (COFIN Grant No. 2007JCY9Y9).

2 See <http://www.camera-arbitrale.it/show.jsp?page=118303>, accessed 15 June 2011.

result of these social/professional practices in discursive and generic terms is to maintain the formality and constraints imposed by the professional community. Yet such a result is represented through a text in which social variations and tensions coexist. Indeed, as Bhatia (2009) has indicated, the doctrine of ICA interacts with (international) arbitration laws, the (national) institutional rules of application and the (local) specific rules of the seat of arbitration.

The tendency of expert members of a discourse community to adopt lexico-grammatical, rhetorical and discoursal generic conventions deriving from a particular genre in the realization of another in order to communicate their private intentions results in the 'colonization of one genre by the other by invading its integrity' (Bhatia 2004: 87). Generic integrity can be defined both by text-internal (contextual, textual and intertextual) and text-external features (discursive practices, discursive procedures, disciplinary culture) and is 'flexible, negotiable or sometimes contexted' (Bhatia 2004: 123). When conventions or resources associated with other genres are appropriated by some domains, expert professional members resort to interdiscursivity, one of the important functions of text-external generic resources across professional genres (Bhatia 2007: 393). This has created a gap between the ideal and the real, between the actuality of written discourse in academic, professional and institutional contexts and its idealistic representation in genre analysis. Indeed, genres are characterized by conventionalized features but in their realization in social practices are dialectically dynamic as they develop and change (Bhatia 2004).

In the formal realization of arbitral awards, there is indeed a change as the whole procedural discourse goes through various stages: from facts to generalizations, from generalizations to norms and from norms to formal knowledge (Iedema 1999: 50). The internal equilibrium represented by the interrelation between the elements characterizing this social practice of detecting facts is therefore rearranged and recontextualized as a formal organizational meaning which the aspect of the award takes on. In arbitral proceedings, the development from facts to pronouncements is highly regulated by provisions. In Italy, for instance, the arbitration process entails the gathering of the information required by the arbitral panel in order to have a clear view of what happened so as to be able to apply legal norms to the parties' behaviour and reach an objective and neutral award. This recontextualization occurs through discursive practices and through various aspects of arbitration stages, processes and procedures. In one of these stages, witness examination may be required. Here, strategies are employed to transform social practices and structures and are expressed through discourse and narratives which 'connect the present with the past with predictive or perspective imaginaries for the future' (Fairclough 2007: 12). In other words, not only do people act and interact; they also interpret and represent to others what they or others did through discourse (Fairclough 2001: 236). When these strategies are put into practice, discourses become *operational*, that is, expressions of new institutions, new procedures and the relations between them. Such discursive operationality requires new forms of communicative interaction, that is, new forms of dialogue representing relations between genres (Fairclough 2005).

The gathering of information in Italian arbitration can be preceded by a pre-trial process in which arbitrators try to reach a conciliation agreement between the parties. Such an attempt is usually realized as a witness hearing, where the parties, their counsels and the arbitrator panel officially meet. Witness hearing is a special case of institutionalized interaction. Recent conversation analysis (CA) studies have investigated issues of person reference in interaction (Enfield and Stivers 2007), aspects of interactional sequence organization (Schegloff 2007) and, in pedagogical terms, CA applied to Languages for Specific Purposes (LSP) (Bowles and Seedhouse 2009). The importance of context in CA has been investigated by a Special Issue of the *Journal of Pragmatics* (McHoul 2008) in more general terms. Our in-depth investigation derives from the study of interaction in legal contexts, with particular regard to witness testimony and cross examination (Harris 2001; Hobbs 2003). The exploration of witness examination in ICA has recently been carried out by Bhatia (2009) and Anesa (2009), who have described the processes of arbitral hearings and the writing of minutes. Such CA investigation into arbitration processes invites further exploration.

It is the purpose of this chapter to investigate the extent to which such social practices as witness hearings within arbitral proceedings are managed by the arbitral panel in order to analyze the way in which arbitrators display neutrality and/or mitigation as well as the way they engage in various conversational strategies so as to establish fairness. Specifically, this study seeks to identify and describe the conversational devices that arbitrators use in order to display their neutrality.

Background and Methodological Approach

Broadly speaking, the code of arbitrators' conduct explicitly states that the arbitrator must remain impartial and independent with respect to competing positions and to the reasons for any disagreement (see also Art. 18 of the UNCITRAL ML and Art. 809-815 of the Italian CCP). Indeed, arbitrators commonly try to ascertain that both parties have equal opportunities to give their own stories, or that neither party is coerced into agreement. According to the official ideal of neutrality, they must resist the impulse to agree or disagree with one or the other party, to refute and support positions, to challenge and contradict, or to bolster and confirm; such a stance, as stated by Jacobs (2002: 1406), is difficult to maintain, especially in witness hearings.

According to Bhatia (2009), witness examination in arbitration is usually replaced by a detailed written statement in order to reduce costs and times and to provide for what in legal terms is indicated as *discovery* or *disclosure*. In common law countries, witness examination for *disclosure* is not very common but is allowed according to the discretion of the arbitral panel, whereas it is unfamiliar in civil law jurisdictions. The frequent use of written evidence in ICA reflects the influence of civil law tradition whereas recourse to questioning – which is conducted by the court and never by the counsel – mirrors the bias of common law jurisdictions. ICA, therefore, echoes the balance between common law and civil law practices and traditions. Yet the system is evolving towards a common law process favouring the adversarial process as shown by witness hearings.

In Italy, the recent reform of arbitration, while aligning Italian arbitration to international law, has made it clear that ADR has a core legal format[3] in the sense that the arbitral panel has the same rights and powers as a judge and the final award has the same legal effects as a judgment. Therefore, not only do arbitrators apply the Italian CCP in arbitral practice, they also follow Art. 816-ter of CCP dealing with witness hearings in arbitral procedures which states that witness hearings are generally oral (though witnesses can present written answers if so decided by the president of the arbitral panel). According to Art. 420 of the Italian CCP, judges can opt for a pre-trial interrogation of the parties which is conducted in order to gather information about the facts (that is, the *discovery*).[4] The final decision of the judge cannot be conditional upon this type of examination, as the judgment is based on reasoning which reflects the judge's interpretation of the law applied to the case under discussion. According to Art. 422 of the Italian CCP, the deposition can be recorded. The transcript of any recorded depositions has to be sent to the parties for the formulation of their deductions and counter-deductions (Art. 423).[5]

The investigation carried out in this chapter involves the identification of the sequential and interactional features found in talk through an examination of the transcripts of the recordings of two different arbitral hearings, obtained from one arbitrator in Milan,[6] who has followed the provisions under Articles 816-ter and 420-422 of the CCP. The recordings of the witness examination last one hour and twenty minutes and one hour and 40 minutes respectively. The analysis is based on the official transcripts of the arbitral panel sent to the parties' counsels. Transcript no. 1 contains 6,050 words and comprises 77 turns, whereas Transcript no. 2 consists of 6,058 words and 87 turns. In both hearings, the arbitral tribunal was composed of three members: two arbitrators appointed by the parties plus the president. In the first case (Transcript no. 1) the president of the arbitral panel

3 As to the development of Italian arbitration, see Maci (2007 and 2008).

4 Although in Italy, as in any other civil law country, *discovery* does not exist (de Franchis 1986), the recent reform of the Italian CCP (in force as from 15 July 2009) seems to indicate the existence of a form of *discovery*.

5 See also Art. 22 of the UNCITRAL ML which states that 'Subject to any contrary agreement by the parties, the arbitral tribunal shall decide whether to hold oral hearings for the presentation of evidence or for oral argument, or whether the proceedings shall be conducted on the basis of documents and other materials'. Cf. also Art. 806 of the Italian CCP.

6 The transcript of recording no. 1 was made in 2008; in this recording, the arbitrator was the president of the arbitral panel. The transcript of recording no. 2 was made in 2004; in this recording, the arbitrator was chosen by one of the parties. For privacy reasons, all sensitive data has been omitted in the present chapter and replaced by an asterisk.

was appointed by the Milan Bar Association; in the second case (Transcript no. 2) the president of the arbitral panel was appointed by the arbitrators chosen by the parties. Such a difference in appointment derives from the arbitral clause included in the contract.

Results and Discussion

Transcript No. 1: The Kindergarten Case

In Transcript no. 1 (T1) the plaintiff claims that the defendant performed a breach of contract regarding an agreement with the management of a private kindergarten. The transcript is preceded by its official record in which the following elements occur:

a. identification of the parties, their counsels and the arbitrators;
b. exact indication of when (date and time) and where (place) the hearing starts;
c. description of the formal method of questioning (first the arbitral panel's and then counsels' questions);
d. statement that the recording and its transcript supplements the written minutes;
e. definition that all pre-trial documentation has to be regarded as final evidence;
f. designation of the final decision by arbitral award should conciliation be impossible;
g. request of the parties' briefs;
h. indication of the time at which the hearing ends;
i. signatures of all participants.

Since the very beginning of the transcript, the issue of neutrality is made clear by the way in which the president carries out the task of interviewing the two parties (turn 1, excerpt no. 1):

(1) PRESIDENTE – Chiedo anzitutto alle parti di voler rendere una dichiarazione in cui possono evidenziare quali a loro avviso sono i fatti determinanti e cruciali che stanno alla base del presente arbitrato. Allora, cominciamo anzitutto seguendo l'ordine prima uno e poi l'altro, dalla *. [PRESIDENT – First of all I ask the parties to make a statement in which they can outline the main and crucial facts which, in their opinion, are at the basis of these arbitral proceedings. So, let us begin by following this order, first one party then the other, beginning with *.] *T1*

Although neutrality is neither defined nor explicitly expressed by the president, it can be inferred in the sense that this declaration makes sure that the chair is not taking either side. Not only do these statements serve to clarify practical operationality, they also emphasize the president's impartial role. The hearing pattern established by the chair is followed throughout the examination (including a total of eight questions).[7] Each question is put to both litigants. Usually, the first statement is made by the plaintiff. The president then turns to the defendant inviting her/him to answer (turn 3, excerpt no. 2):

> (2) PRESIDENTE – Grazie. Rivolgo la medesima richiesta di rendere le proprie dichiarazioni alla Cooperativa * [PRESIDENT – Thank you. Cooperative * is requested to produce their statements in a similar way.] *T1*

In these arbitral proceedings, the defendant is represented by a person who has very recently been appointed by the firm. Such a representative has little information about the facts and is not able to answer. Even when it is clear that the defendant cannot make any statement at all, the president always turns to her/him (turns 35–36, excerpt no. 3):

> (3) PRESIDENTE – La Parte * sulla medesima domanda?
> SIG. * – Non so cosa dire.
> [PRESIDENT – Can the defendant * answer the same question?
> Mr * – I don't know what to say.] *T1*

In addition, the order of questioning, as indicated in the official record accompanying the transcript, is followed by an explicit invitation by the president to the other arbitrators and the parties' counsels to formulate questions (turn 9, excerpt no. 4):

> (4) PRESIDENTE – Gli Arbitri hanno qualche domanda? I Difensori? Passiamo alla seconda domanda.
> [PRESIDENT – Have the arbitrators any questions? Counsels? Let's proceed to the second question.] *T1*

Furthermore, when either arbitrators or counsels do have questions, they never direct them to the litigants but to the president who accepts or rejects the questions.

---

7 Although lawyers in court are advised to use questions which allow the examiner to remain in control of the proceedings (see Hyams, Campbell and Evans 1998: 88–9), the questions in these arbitral proceedings are submitted entirely to the witness, which clearly indicates the need to gather information as discussed in the background section above. The opening question is about the clarifying statement of the parties; five questions tend to reveal the reasons why the facts occurred; two questions have the purpose of informing the arbitral tribunal whether the litigants were aware of some crucial elements or not.

If witness examination is granted by the president to the arbitrators or counsels, the president can reformulate the question or better clarify certain points, as indicated below (turns 38–39, excerpt no. 5):

(5) AVV. * – Siccome ha affermato che sarebbe stato * a contattare la Cooperativa per scopi poco commendevoli pare di capire, ma nell'atto iniziale si dice in realtà che è la Cooperativa che si è proposta a * attraverso contatti io vorrei che si spiegasse questo.
PRESIDENTE – Va bene. la domanda è ammessa, sempre con la precisazione che la Signora * risponda sulla base di quello che è a sua conoscenza e specifichi se è conoscenza diretta o indiretta. Grazie.
[COUNSEL * – Since she claimed that * might have been the one to contact Cooperative * for somewhat dishonest purposes (or so it would seem), but at the opening of the statement, on the contrary, Cooperative * is actually said to have got in touch with *, I would like this point to be explained further.
PRESIDENT – Ok. The question is allowed provided that Mrs * will base her answer on what she knows and will declare whether this knowledge is direct or indirect. Thank you.] *T1*

This pattern indicates that the hearing is highly institutionalized: participants cannot take the floor whenever they want to, as they have to follow the rules established by the president of the arbitral panel who controls the interaction and exercises her/his power over it.

What is evident here is the particular reference to people in the interaction: the chair uses the first person singular pronoun when asking the questions and refers to a third person pronoun when referring to one of the parties. As Gotti (2008: 101) states, the use of the first person pronoun appears in specialized texts when the stress is on 'authorial autonomy within the discipline'. Although the hearing cannot be regarded as a specialized text (as witnesses can be laypeople rather than professionals), the way in which the president manages the examination is indeed professional and expresses the chair's active role as agent – calling for responsibility in action – and her/his authority in the proceedings. The use of third person pronouns when referring to the present litigant is not an impolite form but is very formal in professional settings and, at the same time, implicitly indicates personal detachment. There is also the occurrence of the first person plural pronoun, as indicated below (turn 39, excerpt no. 6; see also excerpt no. 4 above):

(6) PRESIDENTE – Passiamo alla domanda successiva.
[PRESIDENT – Let's proceed to the next question.] *T1*

The president introduces each question with a formulaic expression in which, by using the imperative plural form *let's*, he or she expresses the viewpoint of the group involved in the arbitral proceedings. The use of *us* enhances neutrality when compared to the expression of the president's personal perspective as indicated in the first turn (excerpt no. 1 above). The chair refers to and includes both disputing parties as he or she prefaces the question and shows no bias towards one party or the other as the terms of agreement are still to be reached[8].

Transcript No. 2: The Estate Agency Case

Transcript no. 2 (T2) is very different from T1. The arbitral proceedings are about a conflict between two firms which in the hearing are represented by their counsels only – no managers or key figures ever appear in the whole arbitral process. The hearing proceedings, therefore, are between legal professionals. In this case the plaintiff claims that the defendant is charged with a breach of contract in delaying the construction of a building in a town in North Italy.

The fact that the hearing is between the four counsels and the three arbitrators seems to influence the conventional and institutionalized layout of witness examination in commercial arbitration. As can be seen from the president's introduction, no official procedure has to be followed (turns 1 and 14, excerpts nos 7 and 8):

(7) PRESIDENTE – Vorrei richiamare la vostra attenzione su questo documento 21 mi pare [...] ma quell'arco di tempo e quelle varianti in quell'arco di tempo non sono coperte da questa scrittura, ma giocano un ruolo chiave all'interno dei rapporti tra le parti?
[President – I would like to draw your attention to this document, no. 21, I think [...] yet aren't this time span and those variations in that time span covered by this agreement or rather, do they play a key role within the parties' relationship?] *T2*

(8) PRESIDENTE – Volevo anche chiedervi se la proroga al 28 giugno, che mi pare pacifica dal 31 maggio al 28 giugno, è stata accompagnata anche da una proroga delle polizze di assicurazione. Perché credo fossero delle polizze al 31 maggio [...] Ho un appunto, può darsi che sia un mio appunto che non [...].
[PRESIDENT – I would also like to ask you if the June 28th contract renewal – which, I think, had clearly been valid from May 31st to June 28th – is accompanied by a renewal of the insurance policies. Actually, I think they were policies expiring on May 31st [...] I have a note, it may be my own which doesn't [...].] *T2*

It is worth noting the presidential introductory negative question in excerpt no. 7. Negative questions are quite commonly treated as accomplishing assertions

8 On this point cf. also Heisterkamp 2006.

of viewpoints rather than questioning (Heritage 2002). By employing negative interrogatives, the president is suggesting how counsels should look at the case and trying to offer the best solution to the case as envisaged by her/him by constructing the rhetorical background supporting her/his legal reasoning in the case. The construction of negative interrogatives seems to be a strategy commonly employed by the president, as we find them again in turn 35 (excerpt no. 9):

> (9) PRESIDENT – Ecco, su questo Piano, non credete che si possano magari svincolare per non aggravare poi richieste dell'una o dell'altra parte? [PRESIDENT – Well, as far as this Plan is concerned, don't you think that maybe they can be released in order not to aggravate the requests by one or the other party?] *T2*

The president is leading the interaction and subtly persuading counsels of the correctness of her/his reasoning. Indeed, the question is not a question at all. The opening 'non credete che [...] [don't you think that [...]?]' is not questioning the meaning of the second part of the sentence: 'si possono magari svincolare [...] [maybe they can be released [...].]'. It is of course mitigated by the use of the impersonal form 'si [one]' which conveys detachment and not personal involvement (the sense being referred to is unagentive responsibility for the case in question), by the epistemic 'possono [can]' and 'magari [maybe]' which add an idea of possibility not yet taken into consideration. Thus, from the start, it seems that the president of the arbitral tribunal has an idea in mind which is implicitly revealed rather than explicitly expressed.

From the opening question onwards, the atmosphere, although professional, seems relaxed. The president refers to her/his colleagues by using the second person plural pronoun 'voi [you]', indicating a less formal context and at the same time emphasizing that both (the defendant's and the plaintiff's) counsels are equally treated in this case and indistinctively represented as a group. This plural form gives way to the second person singular 'tu [you]', which in Italian is used in informal settings (turn 51, excerpt no. 10):

> (10) PRESIDENT – Intendi il 17 settembre?
> [PRESIDENT – Do you mean September 17th?] *T2*

At turn 76 there is an interesting development in the interaction: for more than an hour, the interaction was between 'io [I]' v. 'tu/voi [you]'; suddenly, the president of the arbitral tribunal begins to use the pronoun *we* (excerpt no. 11):

> (11) PRESIDENTE – Non riusciamo a rispondere, *, perché su questa posizione qua bisogna che siano chiari, il professore ha dichiarato una certa cosa, che riguarda tra l'altro intese tra avvocati, quindi se tu ritieni di confermarlo [...].

[PRESIDENT – We cannot answer, *, because on this issue they must be clear, the professor has declared one thing, which, incidentally, deals with agreements between lawyers, so if you think you can confirm it […].]
T2

The choice of the inclusive *we* refers to the arbitral panel only. Indeed, at turns 68 and 71 the arbitrator chosen by the defendant, who has been silent throughout the hearing, takes the floor by asking the plaintiff a question which reveals the arbitrator's conflicting position with the president. The chair of the arbitral panel is therefore signalling the necessity for the panel to be united and not to disagree – which however, is not an expression of neutrality but of mitigation of the disagreement within the panel. At the same time, the president seems to look for a justification regarding the arbitrator's question. The president's expression 'non riusciamo a rispondere [we cannot answer]' does not express any criticism of the *dissenting* arbitrator, but it rather acknowledges that the arbitral panel works as a group and that the inability to find a satisfactory solution for everybody is to be attributed to the plaintiff, who has not taken any position as to the issue under examination. It seems that in that passage neutrality is directed at the arbitral panel as a group rather than the single litigants.

Throughout the hearing, the president asks for confirmation of her/his reasoning, which apparently suggests tentativeness. The interaction is not regulated, although each question asked by the president is answered by the counsels in turn – without any requests elicited by the chair. Looking at how interaction typically develops between the president and the counsels, neutrality seems to be hindered (turns 17–20, excerpt 12):

(12) PRESIDENTE – […] purtroppo l'art. 38 non fornisce gli strumenti necessari e, quindi, si procede attraverso una sorta di simulazione. Ho inteso bene? […] Dice: il contratto di appalto all'art. 38 prevede una detrazione, questa clausola però non è applicabile. E' pacifico tra di voi che non è applicabile?
AVV. *– Certamente no, la invoco in tutti i miei atti, questa è un'opinione dei lavori che francamente per me rimane sua. Non è neanche parte del contratto, per cui […]
AVV.* – naturalmente l'opinione del Direttore dei lavori è l'unica opinione possibile perché non ci possono essere altre interpretazioni.
PRESIDENTE – Ma non credo che questo giochi a favore dell'una o dell'altra parte, perché il Direttore […].
[PRESIDENT – […] unfortunately Art. 38 does not provide the necessary tools and therefore a sort of simulation is carried out. Am I correct? […] It says: according to Art. 38 of the procurement contract an allowance is possible but this provision cannot be applied. Do you agree that it is not applicable?

COUNSEL * – Of course not! I quote it in all my documents, this is an opinion of the Building Director and only his. It is not even in the contract, so [...]
COUNSEL * – Obviously the Building Director's opinion is the only possible opinion because there cannot be any other interpretations.
PRESIDENT – Yet I don't think this favours either one or the other party because the Director [...].]

Once again, the arbitral chair asks for confirmation of a hypothesis and its possible interpretations. The president is not questioning but rather looking for the assertion of an opinion. Both counsels freely take their turn and are not interrupted by the president, who, instead, while listening to them, corroborates her/his personal interpretation of the case. Elsewhere, the president of the arbitral panel is not afraid of expressing what he or she thinks, which seems to weaken her/his role as regards not only neutrality but also arbitral competence (turn 23, excerpt no. 13):

(13) PRESIDENTE – Questi documenti francamente sono di quelli che sono in lingua greca per noi arbitri e avvocati, quindi bisognerà poi rivederli [...].
[PRESIDENT – Frankly, these documents belong to that category of papers which are all Greek to us arbitrators and lawyers, and therefore they need to be examined again [...].] *T2*

The fact that neutrality is not maintained is evident in turn 26 (excerpt no. 14) and is confirmed in the president's concluding remarks at the end of the hearing (turn 87, excerpt no. 15):

(14) PRESIDENTE – Questo non per anticipare nessun giudizio, ma perché siamo tra avvocati e quindi è inutile fare come il giudice che sta muto ecc. La mia opinione è, a meno che poi voi mi dimostriate che è sbagliata, che l'insegnamento più recente della Cassazione sembrerebbe non applicare neppure all'Arbitrato rituale queste scansioni dolenti del processo civile.
[PRESIDENT – What I am going to say does not anticipate any judgment, but since we are among lawyers and therefore there is no point in behaving like a judge who doesn't open her/his mouth, etc. My opinion is – unless you can demonstrate that it's wrong – that it may seem that even the most recent lesson learnt from the Court of Cassation does not apply these deceitful interpretations of the civil process.] *T2*
PRESIDENTE – Vorrei poi segnalarvi alcune decisioni sulle quali io poi mi soffermerò, ma perché in questa vostra memoria eventualmente voi possiate considerarle, anche se non è rituale forse dare queste indicazioni, ma è inutile giocare a carte coperte[...].
[PRESIDENT – I would like to express some decisions and will elaborate on these, so that in your brief you might take these into consideration, even

> though it is not standard procedure to point out such issues, but it's pointless not to be outspoken [...].] *T2*

Conclusions

In our analysis we have seen that witness hearings in arbitral proceedings follow the same structure: the president takes the floor and explains how the hearing will be conducted, questions are asked and answered both by the plaintiff and the defendant. Arbitrators and counsels are allowed to ask questions. Indeed, arbitral examinations are a form of discourse that represents

a. a social activity, in the sense that they constitute a genre;
b. a social representation (of strategies, for instance), where they constitute texts;
c. a social construction of identity, where they constitute style (Fairclough 2001: 232–3), as the different behaviour maintained by the two presidents seems to suggest.

Arbitral hearings realize a form of discourse which has a fundamental role in social transition because it is endowed with performative power so as to bring into being the very (recontextualized) realities it claims to describe. It goes without saying that such discourse order is not a rigid system but an open one susceptible to change. As revealed by the analysis of the transcripts, T1 represents a very institutionalized interaction where the relation between all the parties involved in the arbitral proceedings is characterized by a different distribution of power between them. The president's discursive intervention is perceived as neutral because equal opportunities are offered to everyone taking part in the hearing. The president's footing in T1 is precise: the use of the first person singular pronoun signals authority, the use of the third person singular to refer to the litigants indicates the president's personal detachment from the case; the use of the first person plural underlines the role of the participants as a group in seeking a final solution leading to either conciliation or arbitral award. The president never provides litigants with information and never expresses her/his affiliation or disaffiliation to one or other of the parties. Neutrality seems therefore to be maintained throughout the hearing.

In T2, things are different. A change occurs in the interaction, which seems to suggest an absence of neutrality in the way in which the president of the arbitral panel conducts the hearing. Although equal opportunities are offered to all the participants in the case, the maintenance of neutrality seems impossible. The apparent informal context on the one hand seems to create a positive atmosphere in which arbitrators and counsels work *together* and in a team: turns are taken following the usual procedure as indicated above, but they are elicited by the president. On the other hand, the informal context allows the president to express her/his reasoning aloud. In addition he or she creates a contextual setting which favours persuasion: the use of negative interrogatives, as we have seen, does not question the issue but is rather a strategy used by the president to assert her/his opinion.

The diversity between T1 and T2 lies in the different social relations existing between all the parties involved in the hearing. As Fairclough states (2007), social practices are established forms of social activities in which various social moments[9] interact. These moments are not discrete: each of them internalizes in itself other moments without being reducible to them. If the relation between them varies, *change* occurs in the internal equilibrium characterizing the social practice. Different power relations result in distinct political and economic decisions and strategic choices. This may give rise to unpredictable results because what varies is the way in which discourse interprets and represents the social transitions people witness as well as the way in which discourse is appropriated and recontextualized in different domains.

What changes here is the relationship between the participants: in T1 we have professionals (the arbitral panel and the counsels) and lay people (the defendant and the plaintiff); in T2 we have only professionals (the arbitral panel, the counsels and the lawyers acting as legal representatives of the defendant and the plaintiff). Therefore, in T1 the most important thing is to construe neutrality in a very formal context where the plaintiff and the defendant must perceive the importance of the witness examination practice as having a precise legal effect, whereas in T2 the most relevant element of the hearing is the formulation of a satisfactory solution to be realized as an award.

References

Anesa, Patrizia (2009): Arbitral Hearing and the writing of minutes. Paper presented at the international conference on *Researching Language and the Law: Intercultural Perspectives* held in Bergamo on 18–20 June 2009.

Bhatia, Vijay (2004): *Worlds of Written Discourse*, London, Continuum.

Bhatia, Vijay (2007): Interdiscursivity in Critical Genre Analysis. *Proceedings of the 4th International Symposium on Genre Studies*. Online at <http://www3.unisul.br/paginas/ ensino/pos/linguagem/cd/English/36i.pdf>, accessed on 31 July 2009.

Bhatia, Vijay (2009): Witness Examination in International Commercial Arbitration. Plenary paper presented at the international conference on *Researching Language and the Law: Intercultural Perspectives* held in Bergamo on 18–20 June 2009.

Bowles, Hugo and Seedhouse, Paul (Eds) (2009): *Conversation Analysis and Language for Specific Purposes*, 2nd edition, Bern, Peter Lang.

9 Fairclough (2007: 12) identifies the following moments which are dialectically related in a social process: discourse, power, beliefs, values, desires, social relations, institutions and ritual, other practices.

De Franchis, Francesco (1996): *Dizionario Giuridico. Italiano-Inglese*, Milano, Giuffre.

Enfield, Nicholas J. and Stivers, Tanya (2007): *Person Reference in Interaction: Linguistic, Cultural and Social Perspectives*, Cambridge, Cambridge University Press.

Foto d'archivio.

Fairclough, Norman (2001): The Dialectics of Discourse, *Textus*, Vol. 19, No. 2, 231–42.

Fairclough, Norman (2005): *Governance, Partnership and Participation: Cooperation and Conflict*. Unpublished paper given at the conference of the International Association for Dialogue Analysis, Bucharest. Online at <http://www.ling.lancs.ac.uk/profiles/263>, accessed 27 April 2009.

Fairclough, Norman (2007): Introduction. In Cortese, Giuseppina, Fairclough, Norman and Ardizzone, Patrizia (Eds) *Discourse and Contemporary Social Change*, Bern, Peter Lang, 9–14.

Gotti, Maurizio (2008): *Investigating Specialized Discourse*, 2nd edition, Bern, Peter Lang.

Harris, Sandra (2001): Fragmented Narratives and Multiple Tellers: Witness and Defendant Accounts in Trials, *Discourse Studies*, Vol. 3, No. 1, 53–74.

Heisterkamp, Brian L. (2006): Conversational Displays of Mediator Neutrality in a Court-based Program, *Journal of Pragmatics*, Vol. 38, No. 12, 2051–64.

Heritage, John (2002): The Limits of Questioning: Negative Interrogatives and Hostile Question Content, *Journal of Pragmatics*, Vol. 34, Nos 10–11, 1427–46.

Hobbs, Pamela (2003): 'You Must Say it for Him': Reformulating a Witness' Testimony on Cross-examination at Trial, *Text*, Vol. 23, No. 4, 477–511.

Hyams, Ross, Campbell, Susan and Evans, Adrian (1998): *Practical Legal Skills*, Oxford, Oxford University Press.

Iedema, Rick (1999): Formalizing Organizational Meaning, *Discourse Society*, Vol. 10, No. 1, 49–65.

Jacobs, Scott (2002): Maintaining Neutrality in Dispute Mediation: Managing Disagreement While Managing Not to Disagree, *Journal of Pragmatics*, Vol. 34, Nos 10–11, 1403–26.

Maci, Stefania M. (2007): *Arbitration in Italy: Litigation Procedures in Arbitral Practice*. Paper presented at the International Conference on 'Issues of Identity in and Across Cultures and Professional Worlds', Rome, 25–27 October 2007.

Maci, Stefania M. (2008): *Litigation Procedures in Italian Arbitral Practice*. Paper presented at the International Workshop 'Linguistic and Discursive Aspects of International Arbitration', University of Milan, Italy, 22–23 September 2008.

McHoul, Alec (Ed.) (2008): Questions of Context in Studies of Talk and Interaction – Ethnomethodology and Conversation Analysis, Special Issue of *Journal of Pragmatics*, Vol. 40, No. 5, 840–62.

Schegloff, Emanuel A. (2007): *Sequence Organization in Interaction: A Primer in Conversation Analysis*, Volume 1, Cambridge, Cambridge University Press.

Chapter 14
Arbitration in Italy: A Two-headed Janus?

Ulisse Belotti

> Solanio:
> Not in love neither? Then let us say you are sad,
> Because you are not merry: and 'twere as easy
> For you to laugh and leap and say you are merry,
> Because you are not sad. Now, by the two-headed Janus,
> Nature hath framed strange fellows in her time:
> Some that will evermore peep through their eyes
> And laugh like parrots at a bag-piper,
> And other of such vinegar aspect
> That they'll not show their teeth in way of smile,
> Though Nestor swear the jest be laughable.
>
> (W. Shakespeare, *The Merchant of Venice*, Act 1, Scene 1)

Introduction

In the first act of the comedy, Solanio mentions the two-headed Janus *(Janus bifrons)*, the deity of ancient Rome who was considered the father, *Ianus pater*,[1] of all Gods. In those times, the temples dedicated to Janus were very simple and consisted of a long corridor having an entrance and an exit. The entrance and the exit symbolize the acts of entering life and passing away respectively while the two-faced head of Janus, located above the entrance door, represents the flowing of life from one stage to another, from birth to death. In more recent times, the myth of Janus has been used to convey different meanings and the expression 'two-faced Janus' may be used to refer to someone who says something and then says something totally different, that is, showing two different faces according to interlocutors and circumstances.[2]

The concept of two-faced reality may well be applied to other facets of human behaviour such as, for example, the resolution of disputes between parties. In theory, a dispute may be resolved in two totally different ways. One may decide

1 This deity was also named *Ianus Cerus* (creator) and *Ianus Consivius* (procreator) which testifies how important Janus was in the Roman Pantheon.

2 In the Italian culture Janus is often associated with the idea of falsehood and duplicity. For example, one of the definitions of 'Janus' reads 'Persona falsa, ipocrita' (False, hypocritical person. My translation), *Grande Dizionario della Lingua Italiana* (Battaglia 1961, Vol. VI: 767).

to take a legal action against the counterpart and leave the whole matter to the decision of a judge or one may decide to settle the dispute through alternative forms of dispute resolutions, be they conciliation, mediation or arbitration. Furthermore, a party may decide to try some forms of amicable settlement before resorting to arbitration and then, if this proves to be unsatisfactory, to opt for litigation. The two-headed Janus can then be taken as a metaphor of dispute resolutions; one face may be arbitration and the other one litigation. For the purpose of this study, mediation and conciliation will not be considered while we will focus on arbitration with particular reference to the Italian situation.

Arbitigation

> In the Hamlyn Lectures on *Commercial Law in the Next Millennium* (1997), Professor Roy Goode drew attention to the fact that initially it was the delays and expense associated with litigation that had led to the growth of commercial arbitration, which was expected to be 'fast, flexible, informal, private, relatively inexpensive and conducive to finality'. Whilst the expectation had come true in commodity arbitrations, commercial arbitrations took a life of their own, acquiring the pejorative sobriquet: *arbitigation.* (Nariman 2000: 264)

Nariman's lecture, the tenth annual Goff Arbitration Lecture in honour of Lord Goff of Chievely, was delivered in Hong Kong on 17 February 2000. The last word in the excerpt *arbitigation*, which Narinam calls a sobriquet, suggests the idea that arbitration and litigation, two procedures which are deemed to belong to two different worlds, have now become an indistinguishable entity which encompasses features of both. This study, drawing on Nariman's idea of *arbitigation*, sets out to answer two main research questions:

1. How and to what extent has arbitration become similar to litigation, as far as the Italian situation is concerned?
2. When talking about arbitration, what kind of linguistic realizations do Italian arbitration practitioners employ in their narratives?

Data and Methods

This study is based on 14 interviews with professionals involved in arbitration practice, covering a time span of five months, from October 2008 to February 2009. The interviews were made on the basis of a questionnaire[3] comprising 13 sections covering various aspects of arbitration practice. Additional questions were asked to better clarify the content of specific answers.The respondents were

3 The questionnaire was drawn up by the research project main investigators.

11 law-firm professionals, based in Milan and Rome, mainly acting as either counsels to the parties or arbitrators in arbitration proceedings, two professionals (non-lawyers) acting as arbitrators and a chairperson of an arbitration institution. As far as gender is concerned, 12 interviewees were males and two females. Respondents were all non-native speakers of English except one native speaker (AE) and they all agreed that interviews would be conducted in English. All interviewees were informed that they would be recorded and permission was asked in order to include the recordings in the corpus. A copy of the questionnaire and a description of the project outlining the main objectives were e-mailed to each interviewee. All interviews were then transcribed (288,648 words) using SoundScriber (2004) and the transcriptions were mailed to interviewees for proofreading, together with a copy of the audio file of the interview. All interviewees' feedback confirmed that the transcriptions were accurate and no complaints were made. Even though the number of interviews is limited, it seems worth pointing out that interviewees account for one-third of all Italian arbitrators listed in the 2008/2009 issue of the *Practical Law Company* (Dispute Resolution Handbook, Volume 1, 2008, Practical Law Company Ltd. London: 410–12). The corpus comprises 14 audio files amounting to 9 hours 40 minutes of recorded interviews.

Discourse Community

Research has increasingly come to emphasize the importance of discourse communities as groups of people who share the same conventions and communicate with other members in order to achieve specific goals. For example, Swales (1990) lists six criteria for defining a discourse community: common goals, participatory mechanisms, information exchange, community-specific genres, highly specialized terminology and a high level of expertise even though these discourse community traits refer to written communication only. However, in 1998 he revisited the question and differentiated between discourse communities and 'place discourse communities' in which both written and spoken communication was taken into consideration. Indeed, one of the issues which has not been well defined yet is about 'how large (or small) a discourse community might be' (Borg 2004: 399). In actual fact, people may belong to different discourse communities at the same time. As far as our corpus is concerned, the vast majority of interviewees (11 out of 14) belong to the discourse community of legal practitioners whose native language is Italian (NS). At the same time, as they speak English (ELS) when involved in international commercial arbitration (ICA), they are members of the larger transnational discourse community of advocates and arbitrators who use English in their profession. Moreover, if we consider that these legal practitioners may be hired as either counsels to the parties or arbitrators, we may conclude that they belong to a net of discourse communities (see Figure 14.1), that is, counsels speaking Italian and/or English, arbitrators speaking Italian and/or English, whose unifying traits seem to be the conventions and the technical language that they use. One additional element which characterizes these particular discourse communities or 'communities of practice' (Wenger 1998: 78) is the highly specialized language that they use which serves the function of communicating efficiently (Bhatia 2004) with the other members belonging to the same community.

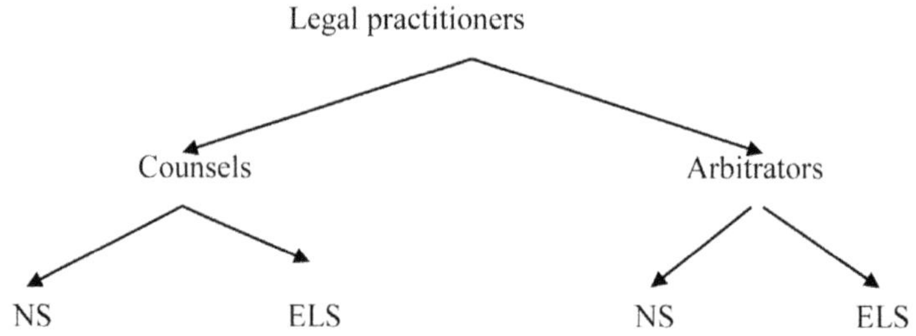

Figure 14.1 Net of discourse communities
Source: Author.

Specialized Language

One of the most striking and distinctive features of legal language is the use of Latin words and expressions (Mellinkoff 1963) which are employed mainly because they are easily recognizable technical terms, shared in the community of those who work with legal terminology (Crystal and Davy 1969). Although Latin words and expressions are quite commonly used in both written legal and arbitration language (Belotti 2003), it is quite surprising that they are used in spoken language. In our corpus 19 occurrences have been detected and these occurrences belong to three different patterns. Some expressions, such as *ex aequo et bono* and *de facto*, are formulaic in nature and serve the purpose of conveying well-established legal concepts in a limited number of words. Others are short forms of more elaborate expressions, such as *dies a quo* (CERG[4] 2008: I1) which, in its full form, reads *dies a quo non computatur in termino, dies ad quem computatur*. In this case, the Latin phrase is used not to deliver a different concept but to underline what has already been expressed in English. In other cases, respondents have used full expressions as in the following excerpt.

4 Throughout this chapter CERG refers to the interviews based on the project questionnaire administered to arbitration practitioners; the numbers refer to the individual interviews.

(1) R: (.)[5] respectful (.) thank you (.) of the law (.). should make business sense so that is (.) what is amicable meaning (.) (subvocalizing) cannot be (.) summum ius (.) fiat justitia et pereat mundus eh (.) again the law must not be forgotten eh. you cannot (.) issue an award which is eh (.) plainly illegal but you must go to the real tracks of the matter understand what is the eh (.) business problem which has emerged and how it can be solved in a business like situation eh (.) let's see the rest of the. lawyers (chuckle) (2.3) of course (.) lawyers bring ehm (.) to arbitration their ehm (.) mental structure of going to court where they argue on points of law and of course (subvocalizing) as arbitrators we often are (.) confronted with lawyers or things to be in courts (.) they want just writs (.) split the legal hair into sixteen parts whilst it it is not really the (.) really the idea and the aim of the original arbitration. (CERG 2008: I 2)

Here the respondent, talking about how awards are rendered, maintains that the panel's decisions should be consistent with the nature of disputes between entities which have been doing business for a period of time and that settlements should not be made at any cost. In actual fact, the Latin phrase means 'the extreme law is the greatest injustice' which seems to suggest the idea that arbitrators should apply the law but *cum grano salis*. From a pragmatic point of view, the Latin maxim, which is embedded in a sentence uttered in English, is used without any explanation which assumes a shared knowledge on the part of the interlocutor. The same applies for all Latin phrases and expressions in the corpus which seem to convey the idea that Latin phrases are so deeply rooted in the legal language that no explanations are needed. Moreover, respondents not only used Latin expressions normally employed in legal language but also expressions which are typical of arbitration language. For example, one of the interviewees, talking about intervention from national laws and courts said that:

(2) […] mm (.) Italian tribunals are quite rigorous in the interpretation of the Kompetenz-Kompetenz principle and ehm (.) (CERG 2008: I 4)

The speaker mentions the Kompetenz–Kompetenz principle which is about the ability of the arbitral tribunal to rule on the question of whether it has jurisdiction. The principle of Kompetenz–Kompetenz is well established in international arbitration, and is accepted in many national laws. In English law, for example, it is given statutory force by section 30 of the *Arbitration Act 1996*. It seems worth pointing out that no explanation about the meaning of the principle is provided which implies shared knowledge on the part of the interlocutor.

5 See Appendix 2 for the list of conventions that have been used for the transcription of the audio recorded material.

Positive and Negative Aspects of Arbitration

This section will concentrate on issues connected to arbitration practice which are of particular salience, such as the participation in the selection of arbitrators, flexibility and informality of processes and procedures, confidentiality and privacy in arbitration proceedings and costs of arbitration.

Respondents were asked to rate (1 the most important and 10 the least important) aspects and considerations for preferring arbitration to litigation in ICA and then rate areas of concern which, in their view, were likely to make ICA less attractive as an instrument of alternative dispute resolution (ADR) (see Appendix 1). Tables 14.1 and 14.2 show how Italian arbitration practitioners rated these aspects of the arbitration procedure. All interviews were single, except for the ones marked with an asterisk in which two practitioners belonging to the same law-firm took part in the interview.

Participation in the Selection of Arbitrators

Participation in the selection of arbitrators seems to be the most important reason why respondents prefer arbitration to litigation, since the vast majority of them agrees on indicating that the selection of arbitrators is crucial to making the whole arbitration procedure effective. If we compare this with the figures in Table 14.2 for the same issue, we see that data show that this issue is not considered relevant in terms of 'concern' as it is probably felt as 'taken for granted'. Interviewees rated 'Flexibility and informality of processes and procedures' (3.2) as the second reason for preferring arbitration to litigation, even though 50 per cent of all respondents rated this reason as first. In Table 14.2, the same reason was rated 7.5 meaning that it is not seen as particularly relevant as 'concern'.

It is interesting to note that one of the respondents who rated 4 this particular issue argued that:

> (3) Well (2.5) eh (2.4) what happens normally is that arbitrators tend to follow the path eh (.) established (.) the procedural path established for a state court litigation and this has eh (.) in the view of arbitrators a number of advantages (.) eh (.) well (.) first of all eh (.) it makes the management of the procedure a bit more eh (.) predictable. (CERG 2008: I 7)

Here, both the flexibility and the informality normally associated with the arbitration procedure are valued less important than the predictability of court litigation offering a 'procedural path' which is deemed to be easier to follow. In other words, arbitration is associated with unpredictability while the 'procedural path' followed by court litigation offers a more secure route. One of the interviewees (R2) from the same legal firm, after rating 5 this particular issue, added that:

Table 14.1 Reasons for preferring arbitration to litigation

	I 1	I 2	I 3	I 4	I 5	I 6*	I 7*	I 8	I 9	I 10	I 11	I 12	Av.
Flexibility and informality of processes and procedures	1	1	6	3	6	5	4	3	7	1	1	1	3.2
Enforceability of arbitration awards	5	6	2	10	4	7	1	5	3	6	8	7	5.3
Confidentiality and privacy in arbitration proceedings	3	5	9	4	7	6	2	6	5	4	7	4	5.1
Participation in the selection of arbitrators	2	2	3	1	2	8	3	4	1	2	2	2	2.5
Relatively lower costs as compared with litigation	9	7	4	9	3	1	9	7	6	8	5	9	6.5
Relative speed of completion of arbitration proceedings	10	4	1	5	8	2	5	1	2	3	4	5	4.1
Freedom in the choice of venue of arbitration	4	3	5	2	1	3	6	2	4	5	3	5	3.5
Costs of arbitration	6	10	7	8	9	4	10	8	10	7	6	8	7.7
Challenge to arbitration awards. Interference from national laws and courts	7	8	8	6	5	9	7	9	9	9	9	10	8.0
Appeal system within the arbitration framework	8	9	10	7	10	10	8	10	8	10	10	6	8.6

Table 14.2 Areas of concern in international commercial arbitration

	I 1	I 2	I 3	I 4	I 5	I 6*	I 7*	I 8	I 9	I 10	I 11	I 12	Av.
Flexibility and informality of processes and procedures	7	9	4	8	5	5	6	7	10	8	9	10	7.5
Enforceability of arbitration awards	4	4	5	3	7	7	9	2	7	9	2	2	5.0
Confidentiality and privacy in arbitration proceedings	8	8	8	6	8	8	8	6	9	6	4	7	7.1
Participation in the selection of arbitrators	6	2	6	9	6	1	7	5	4	4	8	9	5.8
Relatively lower costs as compared with litigation	9	7	7	5	9	6	3	3	8	5	5	3	5.9
Relative speed of completion of arbitration proceedings	5	6	1	2	4	4	5	4	6	3	6	6	4.1
Freedom in the choice of venue of arbitration	10	3	2	7	3	9	4	8	5	7	7	8	6.0
Costs of arbitration	1	10	3	1	1	2	1	1	2	1	1	4	2.3
Challenge to arbitration awards. Interference from national laws and courts	2	5	10	4	2	3	2	9	3	2	3	1	3.8
Appeal system within the arbitration framework	3	1	9	10	10	10	10	10	1	10	10	5	7.5

(4) R2: It was inevitable that it would become similar because it is substitute for decisions by the courts and the courts have developed the law and procedures over the centuries to deal with disputes and the course of the countries with good court systems are actually very good systems for solving disputes and so it was natural that arbitration would tend to follow that pattern because what is the alternative? They are obviously not deciding on the basis of friendship or on the basis of who pays the judges more or ehm (2.1) so what is it that makes people tend to follow law and the law is going to be largely written in decisions that are laid down by judges because of the jurisprudence. (CERG 2008: I 6)

In this case the respondent highlights the fact that courts have developed a system which seems to be better equipped to solve disputes than arbitration and as a consequence it is not surprising that arbitration follows the pattern established by courts. It is worth noting that the quote begins with the verbal phrase 'it was inevitable that' which conveys the idea that arbitration is inevitably bound to resemble litigation.

Italian arbitrators seem to have different opinions regarding the nature of arbitration proceedings compared to the more formal practice of court litigation, as exemplified in the following excerpts.

(5) […] I'm somehow concerned in seeing it as a tendency to have more and more rules of procedure regulating the proceedings and somehow limiting the ehm (1.7) discretionality (discretion. My emphasis) of the arbitrator and of the parties. (CERG 2008: I 4)

(6) […] the liberty of forms eh (2.1) eh (1.8) in arbitration is still one of the key issues eh (2.2) and it's the reason for which eh (2.2) you also expect arbitration (.) arbitrators always to go to the very (.) to the kernel of (.) of the matter and therefore I would say that eh (2.3) informality is still is still a key (1.4) a key feature… (CERG 2008: I 11)

(7) […] one Chinese party (.).one English party eh (1.4) the (2.0) applicable law (.) they sign a contract (.) the applicable is the Italian law eh (.) but they don't want to litigate either in China nor in England nor in Italy so (.) arbitration in Switzerland (.) applicable law the Italian with three arbitrators that by chance are two Italian and one Swiss (.) conducting in English (1.8) it's (1.7) you you understand the (.) the (.) this situation would never be so (1.7) balanced (.) managed as in arbitration before a state court eh (1.8) system. (CERG 2008)

(8) […] I am strong believer that the procedure is fundamental in any dispute (.) so I personally dislike the informality of arbitration proceedings. (CERG 2008: I 6)

In (5) the speaker highlights the fact that arbitration itself is strongly affected by rules. This may result in limiting the freedom of both arbitrators and parties which should be allowed to exercise their own discretion in choosing how the arbitration procedure is to be conducted. From a linguistic point of view, it is interesting to note the use of the downtoner (Hyland 2000) *somehow* which, used twice as a pre-modifier, serves the purpose of conveying semantic indeterminacy to the verbal phrases. The informal nature of arbitration proceedings seems to be closely connected to the notion of flexibility, as exemplified in (6). Here the respondent, by using the noun phrase *the liberty of forms*, alludes to arbitration procedures which are perceived as being different from those of litigation. The issue of flexibility is clearly synthesized in (7) in which the speaker mentions a situation which could hardly be managed by a State court while in (8) the speaker states that an arbitration procedure should not be too informal thus supporting the idea that court-like procedures are likely to be more efficient. Here, the indefinite determiner *any*, in the noun phrase *in any dispute*, belongs to a class of words which Janney (2002: 470) calls 'overinclusive'. This boosting device conveys the idea that all disputes should be dealt with according to well-established procedures.

Confidentiality and Privacy in Arbitration Proceedings

Confidentiality in arbitration procedures has been a debated issue for a long time. To (2008) and Ong (2005), for example, after examining decisions made by British and Australian courts, come to the conclusion that even though the two countries belong to the same legal system, they display wide divergence on this particular issue. Kouris (2005) suggests that, as confidentiality still represents a major benefit, it should be given its original position in both national legislations and arbitral institution rules. On the one hand, given the controversial nature of this particular aspect of arbitration, Misra and Jordans (2006) maintain that confidentiality must be subject to exceptions ranging from the involvement of third-party witnesses, reliance on arbitral awards to enforce rights against third parties to the very general issue of public interest considerations. On the other hand, Trackman (2002: 8) argues that confidentiality clauses are not normally included in arbitration agreements and that in most leading commercial law systems the issue of confidentiality is not even mentioned. An interesting issue is raised by Buys (2003) who observes that all parties involved in arbitration procedures should carefully ponder both benefits and costs of confidentiality before presuming the existence of a general duty of confidentiality or enforcing such a duty.

As far as the Italian situation is concerned, the section of the Italian Code of Civil Procedure regulating arbitration is silent on the matter.[6] On the other hand,

6 Italian Code of Civil Procedure, Book IV – Title VIII – Arbitration amended by Legislative Decree of 2 February 2006, n. 40. Online at <http://www.camera-arbitrale.it/Documenti/synoptic_chart_cpc.pdf>, accessed 15 June 2011.

the Arbitration Rules of the Arbitration Chamber of Milan (the leading arbitral body in Italy) updated as from 1 January 2004, still contain a specific article on confidentiality.[7] In addition, the Members of the Milan Club of Arbitrators, a group of influential arbitrators operating in collaboration with the Milan Arbitration Chamber, have repeatedly expressed 'their support for the general principle of confidentiality in international commercial arbitration' (Coppo 2008: 606). Indeed, our data show that none of the respondents thinks that this is a particularly relevant aspect of arbitration since all interviewees rate it between 5 and 9. In addition, data in Table 14.2 shows that the average rate for this issue is 7.1 which means that the level of concern for this aspect of arbitration is quite low. On the other hand, it is interesting to note that this aspect of arbitration seems to be quite controversial since only five out of 12 interviewees think that confidentiality still plays a relevant role in arbitration proceedings. The comments from those who support the idea of confidentiality as a positive aspect range from very general considerations to more specific reasons.

(9) […] it is eh (.) definitely an advantage of arbitration proceedings and the parties do perceive this as a (.) an advantage. (CERG 2008. I 4)

(10) […] in that case eh (.) they (1.4) there is a particular need for confidentiality (1.6) they want absolutely to avoid eh (.) publicity and so arbitration is the preferred choice. (CERG 2008. I 10)

(11) […] Well (1.8) much to my surprise eh (2.1) I (.) I (.) much to my surprise it's still VERY (.) VERY (.) a very strong argument in favour of arbitration. (CERG 2008. I 12)

(12) […] with arbitration ya (.) there is all this talk about confidentiality but at the end of the day what happens if you disclose it (.) nothing happens so (1.8) a it's a paper tiger whereas court order confidentiality is the real thing. (CERG 2008. I 6)

(13) […] so if you want to know about that arbitration you can find probably over fifty pages of details on it if you just read XXX's[8] reports eh (.) so that

---

7 Article 8:

1. The Chamber of Arbitration, the Arbitral Tribunal and the expert witnesses shall keep all information relating to the proceedings confidential.
2. The award may be published only with the prior written consent of the parties to the Chamber of Arbitration.

Online at <http://www.camera-arbitrale.it/consulta.php?sez_id=178&lng_id=14>, accessed 15 June 2011.

8 The letters XXX stand for the name of the company which is not mentioned for the sake of privacy.

proceeding was less or certainly not more confidential than if we had been in a court. (CERG 2008. I 6)

(14) [...] so far I have never seen one of my clients choosing eh (1.8) the arbitration instead of ordinary jurisdiction just because of (1.4. of the confidentiality (.) so I do not think it is any more that important or (.) for the specific target that I have (.) commercial and international corporations I do not see confidentiality is a major (1.5) major issue. (CERG 2008: I 10)

(15) [...] confidentiality is e (.) mm (.) maybe (1.3) clashes with certain duties of disclosure ehm (.) so it has been (.) when we (.) if I may say so (1.6) we mmm (.) present arbitration in seminars or so (.) confidentiality is one of the things one says (.) one mentions (.) well eh (.) it is somewhat overrated. (CERG 2008: I 2)

In excerpts (9), (10) and (11), confidentiality is seen as a positive feature of arbitration. In (9) the noun *advantage* has been used twice in order to highlight the fact that confidentiality is seen as a good quality of the whole arbitration procedure. In the same excerpt, the speaker used the verbal phrase *do perceive* in order to stress the positive perception that the parties have with regard to confidentiality. In (10) confidentiality is considered particularly important for intra-group disputes in which a high level of confidentiality is required and the use of the pre-modifying adverb *absolutely* conveys the idea that any type of publicity is to be avoided at any cost. In (11) the grammatical parallelism *much to my surprise* serves the function of conveying the idea that confidentiality is unexpectedly seen as a central motive for choosing arbitration. The same pattern is used in the following sentence in which the adjective *very* is repeated three times with the intent to strengthen the illocutionary force of the adjective *strong*. On the other hand, while admitting that confidentiality is still considered when parties decide to have recourse to arbitration, most interviewees strongly assert that confidentiality is not as important as it used to be in the past. For example, in (12) the principle of confidentiality in arbitration is deemed to be less important than confidentiality orders decided by courts. Here confidentiality is seen as a *paper tiger* meaning that, at least in the Italian legal context, disclosure of what should be kept reserved is not seen as a serious matter. Excerpt (13) exemplifies another issue concerning the fact that confidentiality may be by-passed just by closely looking at a company's quarter or half-year reports. The diminished importance of confidentiality is confirmed in (14) and (15) in which other respondents highlight the fact that the confidentiality, far from being a relevant feature in arbitration, seems to be worth some consideration outside arbitration practice itself.

Costs of Arbitration

As far as arbitration costs are concerned, two respondents out of 12 think that arbitration costs are lower than those connected with litigation. The majority of interviewees (seven out of 12) argue that arbitration costs are the main area of concern among arbitrators. Arbitration proceedings often take years and are therefore expensive and this is mainly due to the fact that parties often agree to extend time-limits set by institutional arbitration rules. In other cases, parties which find themselves in a weaker position than expected tend to produce complex presentations on points of fact or law in order to prolong procedures. The vast majority of interviewees agree on the fact that arbitration is getting more and more expensive in small cases but the reasons are not the same. One aspect, which has received little attention, concerns the decisions made by arbitrators themselves not to be appointed in cases in which the prospective remuneration is not worth the effort.

> (16) We see very often that reputable famous lawyers do not accept to act as arbitrators if for instance the amount of the dispute is not big enough because they make a calculation and they say (.) the maximum I can get from this case is this and (subvocalizing) perhaps it is not convenient and wait for a bigger case to come. (CERG 2008: I 5)

In (16) the respondent clearly mentions decisions made by prospective members of arbitration panels not to be appointed arbitrators in cases which are likely to be unrewarding. As far as linguistic realizations are concerned, it is interesting to note the use of direct speech which seems to serve the function of conveying the idea that the speaker is emotionally involved in what he is saying. In addition, the reported speech *and they say the maximum I can get from this case is this* is not a verbatim reproduction of direct speech acts, which were uttered in Italian. Indeed, reporting has surely involved significant reshaping and reworking of the original speech acts. In actual fact, these reported speech acts, mostly embedded in the narratives, seem to serve not only the primary functions of demonstrating the validity or the likeliness of what is being reported but they have also been used to intensify the reported events themselves by animating different characters (arbitrators, counsels, entrepreneurs).

Other respondents have highlighted the role played by arbitral institutions in keeping costs under control, mainly because the costs in arbitrations conducted under the rules of arbitration institutions are more likely to be foreseen, as indicated in the following excerpt.

> (17) If you really draft a good arbitration clause (.) if you pick up the right arbitral institution and for example you adopt a sole arbitrator clause with an institution that is not too expensive (.) (throat clearing) you have some

> ... way to (.) to keep costs under control that it's still eh (1.6) less expensive than any (.) any litigation. (CERG 2008: I 12)

Why has Arbitration Become Similar to Litigation?

According to interviewees, arbitration is undoubtedly becoming similar to litigation and the reasons provided may be summarized as follows:

- poor or insufficient knowledge of arbitration as a method of resolving disputes;
- the nature of arbitration itself which is considered another form of litigation;
- litigation is preferred because it seems better equipped to resolve disputes;
- amicability has nothing to do with arbitration.

Poor or Insufficient Knowledge of Arbitration as a Method of Resolving Disputes

The specialist background of arbitrators seems to be one of the aspects that has greatly affected the way in which arbitration is conducted. Bautista (2008: 9) observes that:

> Due to their unfamiliarity and lack of experience with international arbitration, some local lawyers would prefer to remain within their comfort zones and recommend domestic litigation even if against the interest of the client.

One aspect of particular salience is expressed by the verbal phrase *to remain within their comfort zones* which seems to refer to those litigation procedures which lawyers are particularly confident with, as in the following excerpt.

> (18) Ya (.) it happens when (.) the arbitration clause makes reference to the rules provided for in civil procedural eh (.) code (.) or when arbitrators are not eh (.) expert in arbitration and they of course feel more comfortable in applying the the usual mmm procedural provisions. (CERG 2008: I 3)

In (18) it seems that two reasons are provided. The first deals with the fact that some arbitration clauses are drafted according to the civil code and the second makes reference to the fact that lawyers are sometimes appointed arbitrators even though they lack specialist background in arbitration. This results in situations in which these legal practitioners, having to act as arbitrators, tend to use the *procedural provisions* with which they are more familiar. This also applies to those counsels to the parties who are not trained in arbitration procedures. If we imagine an arbitration procedure in which both arbitrators and counsels to the parties have no significant experience in arbitration, we can easily conclude that the arbitration itself will be conducted according to the rules and conventions of litigation, as exemplified by another respondent.

(19) Yes (1.6) well ehm (1.8) I (.) I have to confirm that I (.) I have this perception indeed that there is more and more formality coming into arbitration as well (small intake of breath) ehm (2.2) again sometimes the process is led by the parties not necessarily by the arbitrators ehm (1.8) it is also a problem when the (.) counsels do not have a significant experience in (.) in arbitration they may be litigators as (.) as a basis (.) and then eh (.) they would be in fact eh (.) leading (chuckle) ah (1.6) the process to become more proceduralized. (CERG 2008: I 4)

ICA has become a big business and competition is getting harder and harder, that is, competition between arbitral institution, between arbitrators themselves and between law firms (Bautista 2008). Things have changed considerably in the past 30 years. The shift from arbitration being mainly conducted by a limited group of well-known 'Grand Old Men' to what Dezalay and Garth (1996: 54) call the 'American lobby' has marked the introduction of a new style which a US arbitrator (quoted in Dezalay and Garth 1996: 55) summarizes as follows:

> [...] A lawyer comes with a team – more attention to fact, motions, objections, delays. Beginning to look more like litigation.

This quote highlights some of the reasons why arbitration has become similar to litigation. First, the new arbitration practitioners are members of large law firms offering their clients arbitration as part of a more complex set of options, litigation included. Second, these law firm practitioners, being trained as litigators, that is, to win a good result for their clients, tend to behave in the same way in arbitration proceedings and this often results in procedural tactics which are deliberately employed to get that particular result. Reference to 'Grand Old Men' (Dezalay and Garth 1996: 57) is also made by one the interviewees when he states that:

(20) [...] because if you picture the situation now compared to twenty years ago (.) thirty years ago when it was a smaller market where the arbitrators were few (1.4) very high standard eh (.) very competent people (.) prestigious people (.) they were a kind of artists and they (1.5) they were really eh (.) top people (1.5) few cases (2.3) big cases (.) so it was gentlemen were around still eh(1.8) so it was (1.7) probably not necessary to have guarantees (.) procedural guarantees for example (.) now that is a wider phenomenon that is a (.) a (1.4) also a more popular phenomenon ehm (.). there are new eh (1.6) commerce (1.4) there are new arbitrators (2.5) there are (2.7) that sometimes the level is lower (.) that's again (.) that's normal I mean if you have different numbers you have to accept also different qualities of the (.) the players (.) players I mean counsels and

> arbitrators (2.4) the qualities getting lower and so the reaction is to find I think guarantees (.) parachutes like (.) ok so I want the right to be heard (.) I want to use the RIGHT to be heard (.) I want the right to give you so this is (throat clearing) probably the noble reason of this processualizzazione (Judicialization. My translation) then there is also a less noble reason that is eh (2.4) the Anglo-Saxon influence on international arbitration that is more (1.8) stronger and stronger and as you know the Anglo-Saxon approach to a trial to a process is different than our continental approach. (CERG 2008: I 10)

In (20) the respondent focuses on the problems connected to the increasing number of ICA which has had, on the one hand, the positive effect of involving more and more legal practitioners in arbitration practice but on the other hand has had the negative effect of lowering the quality of what he calls *the players*, that is, arbitrators and counsels. Here it is underlined that when arbitration procedures were conducted by few, well-known and highly valued arbitrators (prestigious *people/kind of artists/top people*), there was no need for procedural guarantees and this is what contributed to make arbitration different from litigation. Things have changed radically and rapidly when the number of arbitrators has increased in order to cope with the growing popularity of arbitration as a means of resolving disputes. From a linguistic point of view, this excerpt provides an interesting example of direct speech within the narrative in which the respondent plays the part of a counsel to the parties *I want the right to be heard, I want to use the right to be heard. I want the right to give you.* By using the direct speech format, the respondent reformulates what counsels to the parties might have said to arbitrators. As we do not have access to any original utterances from the counsels involved in the arbitration procedure, we see that direct speech reporting is used as rhetorical device. From a pragmatic viewpoint, this pattern serves the functions of both developing argumentation (Baynham 1996) and exemplifying how procedural rules have been inserted into the arbitration procedure. As far as linguistic realizations are concerned, it seems worth noting that the verbal phrase *I want the right*, slightly modified into *I want to use the right*, has been repeated three times. This grammatical parallelism conveys the idea that the 'rights' fit in a 'litigative' process rather than an arbitration procedure. It is also interesting to note that the pronoun *I* is clearly anchored 'in the context of the reported situation and not in the context of the current reporting situation' (Bolden 2004: 1091). In addition, we see that the verbal tense used, that is, the simple present, is consistent with the flow of narration as it refers to actions occurring at the time of the reported events.

Arbitration as Another Form of Litigation

In recent times, arbitration awards in Italy could be challenged for a number of reasons including mistakes made by the arbitrators in applying the law. After the

2006 reform, the grounds on which parties can challenge an award have been reduced and this has contributed to making arbitration awards more final. It is also apparent that the losing party is likely to do anything in order to avoid enforcement of the award. As far as finality of the award is concerned, opinions are once again divergent. Some respondents stated that the challenge of arbitration awards is on the increase and see this as

(21) [...] a symptom of the fact that arbitration is more and more conceived as a form of litigation (.) the culture and practice of arbitration are therefore changing as well leading to a higher degree of non-compliance. (CERG 2008: I 4)

One of the aspects which has been underlined by interviewees is that in many cases, arbitrators tend to conduct the whole arbitration procedure as if they were in a court because this is what they have been trained for. The following excerpt provides an example of such behaviour.

(22) R: Yes I (.) I (.) believe that ehm (1.8) based on my experience I have seen many arbitrators managing the arbitration process in the same way eh (1.9) they (2.4)they they (1.8) the ordinary courts manage the the ordinary eh (.) proceeding and (.) and I think that this is the most eh (.) the most important challenge for for arbitration trying to (1.5) ehm (.) to to.

I: not to be colonized by litigation (.) is that what you mean.

R: (.) ya (1.5) because basically as I mentioned before many arbitrators tend to eh (.) eh (.) regulate (.) eh (1.7) managing the the proceeding applying eh (1.6) civil procedural (.) provisions (.) and (subvocalizing) it sounds not a good (.) a good approach.

I: as if they were in a court

R: (.) as if they were in a court (.) ya ya. (CERG 2008: I 3)

Litigation is Preferred because it Seems to be Better Equipped to Resolve Disputes

A further reason why arbitration is becoming more and more similar to litigation is that litigation seems to be better equipped to solve disputes than arbitration.

(23) It was inevitable that it would become similar because it is substitute for decisions by the courts and the courts have developed the law and procedures over the centuries to deal with disputes and the course of the countries with good court systems are actually very good systems for solving disputes and so it was natural that arbitration would tend to follow

that pattern because what is the alternative? They are obviously not deciding on the basis of friendship or on the basis of who pays the judges more or ehm (1.4) so what is it that makes people tend to follow law and the law is going to be largely written in decisions that are laid down by judges because of the jurisprudence. (CERG 2008:I 6)

Here, the respondent focuses on the fact that the court system has developed procedures which have proved to be very effective in dispute resolution. The speaker defines arbitration awards as *substitute for decisions by the courts* suggesting the idea that the court system is much more reliable than arbitration.

As far as the appointment of lawyers as arbitrators is concerned, the majority of respondents stated that lawyers have played a significant role in making arbitration effective.

(24) […] have a (1.8) specific experience and can make a prior estimation of what could be the real outcome of the case and mmm (1.7) and so on (1.8) are all elements that should help in eh (1.7) finding a settlement. (CERG 2008: I 10)

(25) […] is absolutely (.) I would say (1.4) necessary because eh (1.7) at the end of the day you expect eh (1.9) an amicable judgment by someone who is grounded in (.) in law […] (CERG 2008: I 11)

The fact that arbitrators should be grounded in the law seems to be one of the main characteristics that Italian arbitrators attach to the profession itself. It seems to be undisputed that an arbitrator, to be a good arbitrator, has to be a lawyer even though with some caution, as indicated by one of the respondents when she maintains that:

(26) […] lawyers do indeed eh (1.7) successfully add value to the dispute provided that they are qualified lawyers and so if if (.) lawyers actually do the arbitrations sector or are litigators and they don't have in their background the willingness to to (.) ehm (1.8) to lead the parties to a settlement and again not to play according to formal rules then that can very much spoil the whole exercise. (CERG 2008: I 4)

Amicability has Nothing to do with Arbitration

Talking about the functions performed by an arbitrator (Nariman 2000: 267) maintains that, 'An arbitrator, is an arbitrator, is an arbitrator, whose function it is, not merely to adjudicate the dispute, but also to help resolve it amicably with the co-operation of the parties'.

One of the aspects that was covered in the answers to this question concerns a preliminary observation on the meaning of the sentence, 'The original aim of arbitration was to help resolve disputes "amicably"'. Most respondents observed that arbitration, having a *per se* adjudicatory nature, has nothing to do with the amicable settlement of disputes. For example one arbitrator said that:

> (27) Eh (.) well (.) ehm (.) in my opinion and based on my experience there is eh (.) there isn't amicability in arbitration ehm (1.8) arbitration is still an adjudicative proceeding eh (.) if parties want to enter into an amicable dispute resolution proceeding, well mediators are ready to provide such a different (2.3) such a different service. (CERG 2008: I 3)

In another case the respondent disagreed with the statement itself and argued that:

> (28) I I don't I don't agree with the main statement I mean eh (.) you find sometimes arbitration clauses that say before resorting to arbitration the parties must make an effort to settle in an amicable way before as a condition to arbitration but once you are in an arbitration by definition you are in a situation where the parties are one against the other and they have to fight a battle which is a legal battle so they need lawyers ehm [...] (CERG 2008: I 5)

Here the speaker argues that arbitration is another form of litigation and his view is supported by the lexical items suggesting that a legal battle is about to start. For example, he said that the parties are *one against the other* or that *they have to fight a battle* and as consequence parties are better equipped if they hire lawyers. Even the assumption that arbitrators should help resolve a dispute amicably and with the active cooperation of the parties becomes questionable because:

> (29) [...] if a a party thinks because it has chosen arbitration then it's going to be a friendly way of settling (.) that's wrong (.) one should have told that party this is not true (.) it's a litigation process (.) it's a process to solve a dispute (.) a legal dispute so (1.7).

The interviewee goes on explaining that:

> [...] but if you have a breach of a contract or a difficulty in (.) in the interpretation of a contract which is a legal document at the end you need a judge or you need a lawyer sitting as an arbitrator. (CERG 2008: I 5)

Here the respondent seems to behave just like a two-headed Janus. It is true that arbitration may be chosen as a method of resolving disputes (Janus wears the mask of an arbitrator) but it is also true that this way of dispute resolution is neither friendly nor speedy. To the contrary, it is a litigation process whose aim is to solve a legal dispute which is so complicated that only a judge or a lawyer sitting as an arbitrator can arrive at a solution (Janus wears the mask of a litigator).

Talking about rewards being produced without the control of judges, one of the interviewees utters two long sentences packed with critical claims belonging to different classes, mainly adjectives and adverbs.

(30) [...] the absence of any effective control by judges of the process means that arbitrations produce an endless stream of artfully written bad decisions with hundreds of pages of utterly useless recapitulation of the proceedings and there in the hundreds of pages is a little pirouette by which a completely illogical resolve is obtained but which is essentially an exercise in impunity by the party arbitrators (.) if they don't have spring courts to tell them they have done a bad job and I find quite frustrating this (.) the fact that in reality the arbitrators are answerable only to their own conscience which unfortunately too often means only answerable to their friends. (CERG 2008: I 6)

In the first sentence, the object of the verbal phrase *arbitrations produce* is represented by a long noun phrase, which contains 17 words. Here it is interesting to note that adverbs have been intensively used as pre-modifiers (***artfully*** *written bad decisions*; ***utterly*** *useless recapitulation*; ***completely*** *illogical resolve*) in noun phrases delivering overt critical claims. In addition, the sentence above shows that the speaker makes use of other linguistic devices to convey criticism such as adjectives (***endless***, ***bad***, ***useless***, ***illogical***) and nouns (***absence***, ***pirouette***, ***impunity***). It seems worth mentioning the fact that the word *pirouette* has been used as a metaphor of something which has been rapidly modified in order to suit the needs of one of the parties. Quite unexpectedly, this stretch of spoken language does not contain any instance of hedges which seems to signal the fact that the speaker's criticism towards certain awards is the main pragmatic goal. In the final section criticism focuses on one of the most important aspects of arbitration itself, that is, the arbitrator's independence and impartiality. Here the respondent argues that arbitrators, as a category, instead of acting independently and impartially, seem to adjudicate disputes according to criteria which have set aside any moral obligation.

Conclusions

Interviewing is undoubtedly one of the most poorly investigated domains of pragmatic enquiry (Briggs 1995) and interviews with arbitration practitioners are no exception. One reason for the scarcity of research into arbitration practice involving interviews and narratives may be found in the profession itself. Arbitration practitioners are busy people and it is very difficult, if not impossible, to schedule an interview with them. In spite of that, we have collected a small corpus of interviews with Italian arbitration practitioners with the aim of exploring facets of arbitration practices. In particular, we have identified some of the reasons why these practitioners prefer arbitration to litigation and the areas of concern in ICA.

As for the reasons why arbitration has become similar to litigation, respondents have identified four main reasons, that is, the poor or insufficient knowledge of arbitration as a method of resolving disputes, the nature of arbitration itself which is deemed to be another form of litigation, the perception that litigation and not arbitration is better equipped to resolve disputes and the idea that amicability has little or nothing to do with arbitration.

As far as the linguistic realizations are concerned, the corpus comprises instances of direct speech acts embedded into narratives serving the purpose of both demonstrating the validity/likeness of what was reported and animating the different characters involved in arbitration procedures. From a lexical point of view, respondents have used a number of Latin phrases and expressions normally used in legal language. Though the results do not allow to draw definitive conclusions, it seems that Italian legal practitioners are so deeply involved in litigation that when narrating their personal experiences in arbitration, they tend to use pragmatic devices and lexical items which are typical of litigation.

Acknowledgements

This chapter has been undertaken within the framework of an international research network: *International Commercial Arbitration Practices: A Discourse Analytical Study*, supported by the Hong Kong Research Grants Council CERG Fund (Project No.9041191). Details of the project and the collaborative network are available at the website (see: http://enweb.cityu.edu.hk/arbitrationpractice/index.html).

I would like to gratefully acknowledge the cooperation of both the project main investigator, Professor Vijay K. Bhatia and the Italian Coordinator, Professor Maurizio Gotti. I am also very grateful to the following advocates, scholars and arbitration experts whose precious collaboration has made this study possible.

Advocate Stefano Azzali
Professor Massimo Benedettelli
Advocate Gabriele Bonivento
Advocate Giovanni De Berti
Advocate Cecilia Carrara
Advocate Roberto Casati
Advocate Paolo Gnignati
Professor Angelo Lucchini
Advocate William McGurn
Advocate Stefano Modenesi
Advocate Micael Montinari
Advocate Alberto Nanni

Advocate Cristina Pagni
Dr Stefano Pavletič

References

Battaglia, Salvatore (1961): *Grande Dizionario della Lingua Italiana*, Torino, UTET.
Baynham, Mike (1996): Direct Speech: What's it Doing in Non-narrative Discourse? *Journal of Pragmatics*, Vol. 25, Issue 1, 61–81.
Bautista, Jun (2008): *International Arbitration – Past, Present and Future*. Paper presented at 'The International Arbitration Conference Brunei' and 2nd RAIF Conference, Brunei, 16–17 August 2008, 7–10.
Belotti, Ulisse (2003): Generic Integrity in Italian Arbitration Rules. In Bhatia, Vijay K., Candlin, Christopher N. and Gotti, Maurizio (Eds) *Legal Discourse in Multilingual and Multicultural Contexts*, Bern, Peter Lang, 19–40
Bhatia, Vijay K. (2004): *Worlds of Written Discourse: A Genre-based View*, London, Continuum.
Bolden, Galina (2004): The Quote and Beyond: Defining Boundaries of Reported Speech in Conversational Russian, *Journal of Pragmatics*, Vol. 36, Issue 6, 1071–118.
Borg, Erik (2004): Discourse Community, *ELT Journal*, Vol. 57, No. 4, 398–400.
Briggs, Charles (1995): Interview, *Handbook of Pragmatics Manual*, Amsterdam, John Benjamins Publishing Company. Online at <http://www.benjamins.com>, accessed 15 June 2011.
Buys, Cindy G. (2003): The Tensions between Confidentiality and Transparency in International Arbitration, *American Review of International Arbitration*, Vol. 14, No. 121, 121–38.
Coppo, Benedetta (2008): Riservatezza vs Trasparenza nell'Arbitrato Internazionale e nei Lavori di Revisione del Regolamento UNCITRAL. La posizione del Club of Arbitrators di Milano, *Arbitraje. Revista de arbitraje comercial y de inversiones*, Vol. I, No. 2, 605–8.
Crystal, David and Davy, Derek (1969): *Investigating English Style*, London, Longman.
Dezalay, Yves and Garth, Bryant G. (1996): *Dealing in Virtue*, Chicago, IL, University of Chicago Press.
Hyland, Ken (2000): *Disciplinary Discourses*: *Social Interaction in Academic Writing*, London, Longman.
Janey, Richard W. (2002) Cotext as Context: Vague Answers in Court, *Language & Communication*, Vol. 22, No. 4, 457–75.
Kouris, Steven (2005): Confidentiality: Is International Arbitration Losing One of its Major Benefits?, *Journal of International Arbitration*, Vol. 22, No.2, 127–40.
Mellinkoff, David (1963): *The Language of the Law*, Boston, Little Brown & Co.

Misra, Jordan and Jordans, Roman (2006): Confidentiality in International Arbitration, *Journal of International Arbitration*, Vol. 23, No.1, 39–48.

Nariman, Fali S. (2000): The Spirit of Arbitration, *Arbitration International*, Vol. 16, No. 3, 261–78.

Ong, Colin Y.C. (2005): Confidentiality of Arbitral Awards and the Advantage for Arbitral Institutions to Maintain a Repository of Awards, *Asian International Arbitration Journal*, Vol. 1, No. 2, 169–80.

SoundScriber (2004): Regents of the University of Michigan. Online at <http://www-personal.umich.edu/~ebreck/sscriber.html>, accessed 15 June 2011.

Swales, John (1990): *Genre Analysis: English in Academic and Research Settings*, Cambridge, Cambridge University Press.

To, Cristopher (2008): *Confidentiality in Arbitrations*. In Bhatia, Vijay K., Candlin, Christopher N. and Engberg, Jan (Eds) *Legal Discourse across Cultures and Systems*, Hong Kong, Hong Kong University Press, 75–108.

Trakman, Leon E. (2002): Confidentiality in International Commercial Arbitration, *Arbitration International*, Vol. 18, No. 1, 1–18.

Wenger, Etienne (1998): *Communities of Practice: Learning, Meaning, and Identity*, Cambridge, Cambridge University Press.

Appendix 1

Section 11 (Advantages of International Commercial Arbitration)

Please rate the following aspects and considerations for preferring arbitration to litigation in international commercial contexts. (Identify the most important by #1 and then follow with (#2, #3 etc) in order of decreasing importance.

Reasons for Preferring Arbitration Over Litigation

- Flexibility and informality of processes and procedures, encouraging active participation of the parties in most areas of decision-making
- Confidentiality and privacy in arbitration proceedings
- Participation in the selection of arbitrators
- Relatively lower costs as compared with litigation
- Enforceability of awards
- Relative speed of completion of arbitration proceedings
- Freedom in the choice of venue of arbitration (neutrality of venue, preferred legal system)
- Costs of arbitration
- Challenge to arbitration awards-Interference from national laws and courts
- Appeal system within the arbitration framework

Section 12 (Areas of 'Concern' in International Commercial Arbitration)

Please rate the following as areas of concern in international commercial arbitration, which, in your view, are likely to make it less attractive as an instrument of ADR: (Please identify the most important by #1 and then follow with (#2, #3 etc) in order of decreasing importance)

- Flexibility and informality of processes and procedures, encouraging active participation of the parties in most areas of decision-making
- Confidentiality and privacy in arbitration proceedings
- Participation in the selection of arbitrators
- Relatively lower costs as compared with litigation
- Enforceability of awards
- Relative speed of completion of arbitration proceedings
- Freedom in the choice of venue of arbitration (neutrality of venue, preferred legal system)
- Costs of arbitration
- Challenge to arbitration awards-Interference from national laws and courts
- Appeal system within the arbitration framework

Appendix 2

Transcription conventions

The audio recorded materials in the corpus have been transcribed according to the following conventions.

Symbol	Represents
(.)	Micro-pause (< 0.2 seconds)
(1.8)	Timed pause
< ? >	Unintelligible speech
a::nd	Colons represent lengthened vowel sound
RIGHT	Underlined, capitalized word shows emphatic stress, enunciated louder than surrounding speech.
?	Indicates rising intonation
↑↓	Indicate rising/falling intonation
< >	false start
o </>	incomplete word (complete of)
Items in brackets indicate non-transcribable vocalizations or other actions	(chuckle) (slight intake of breath) (breath intake) (throat clearing) (subvocalizing)

Chapter 15
Is Arbitration Being Colonized by Litigation? – Practitioners' Views in the Singapore Context[1]

Sujata Kathpalia

Background

Singapore is an international business centre attracting multinational companies from all over the world. This has led to an increase in commercial activity in Singapore as well as a number of disputes among these companies. In the past, these disputes were resolved by the Singapore judicial system but recently arbitration, which offers an alternative method of dispute resolution, is increasingly becoming popular in Singapore. To support the demand for arbitration, the Singapore International Arbitration Centre[2] (SIAC) was set up in July 1991, with financial support from the Economic Development Board (EDB) and Trade Development Board (TDB) of Singapore. Since then it has grown in reputation and is rated third as an independent and neutral third-country venue, with over 1,500 arbitration cases handled to date (ibid). The centre has state-of-the-art facilities as well as technological and legal expertise for arbitration proceedings.

Singapore has adopted the United Nations Commission on International Trade Law (UNCITRAL) Model Law (ML) on Arbitration 1985, and has two systems of arbitration law applied to international and domestic arbitrations (Merkin and Hjalmarsson 2009). The international arbitration law is based on the ML with local adaptations and does not permit judicial intervention whereas the domestic arbitration law allows for intervention in some cases, particularly in cases where one party is weaker than the other (ibid.). The dual track makes Singapore an attractive option for international arbitration activity, and SIAC functions as the central institution for arbitrations as it performs important statutory roles approved by legislation.

Arbitration is one type of alternative dispute resolution (ADR) method among others, such as conciliation and mediation. The main distinction between these

1 The work described in this chapter was supported by a grant from the Research Grants Council of the Government of HKSAR [Project No. 9041191 (CityU 1501/06H)] on *International Commercial Arbitration Practice: A Discourse Analytical Study*.

2 See website of SIAC <http://www.siac.org.sg>, accessed 20 June 2011.

three forms of dispute resolution methods and litigation is that they are not supposed to be adversarial (Tan and Lee-Patridge 2000). Comparing arbitration and litigation, the former is a private out-of-court settlement between two parties who have agreed to accept the decision of an appointed arbitrator, whereas in the latter, the dispute is resolved by the court. According to Tay (1998), the two processes that distinguish arbitration from litigation are the fact that it is private and consensual. As for the process, arbitration has five distinct phases, consisting of Initiation, Constitution of the Tribunal, Pre-hearing, Hearing and Enforcement (Lim, Tan and Woo 1993/1994; Buhring-Uhle 2006). Once the disputing parties have committed to an arbitration agreement in writing in the initiation phase and the tribunal has been established, the pre-hearing phase proceeds to determine the procedural details and document the issues of dispute. In the hearing phase, the documents submitted by both parties are examined and proofs/arguments are presented to the tribunal. The decision is conveyed through an arbitral award which is final and binding in any international commercial arbitration (ICA) and can be enforced in all 140 countries that have acceded to the 1958 New York Convention Convention on the Recognition and Enforcement of Foreign Abitral Awards (Moses 2008).

International arbitrations in Singapore are captured by the *International Arbitration Act 1994*, Act 23 of 1994 which was revised in 1995 and amended before being published in 2002 (Cap. 143A) (Merkin and Hjalmarsson 2009). As for domestic arbitrations, the *Arbitration Act 2001* (Cap. 37) applies in its revised form of *Arbitration Act 2002* (Cap. 10). This distinction between international and domestic arbitration has made Singapore a popular venue for international arbitrations. The fact that foreign lawyers can be involved in international arbitrations held in Singapore has further strengthened Singapore's reputation as an international arbitration centre. For minimum standards of arbitration, UNCITRAL drafted the ML which ensures 'party autonomy over the arbitration proceedings, the absence of any appeal procedure, the restriction of judicial intervention in the proceedings to default powers, and the free enforceability of the award other than in cases of want of jurisdiction or clear unfairness in the procedure' (Merkin and Hjalmarsson 2009: 2). The introduction and amendment of these acts for ICA has raised the attractiveness of arbitration as an alternative and more popular form of dispute resolution in comparison to litigation.

Advantages and Disadvantages of Arbitration

Arbitration is preferred in the commercial world as it offers many advantages over litigation. According to the findings of a recent survey conducted by PricewaterhouseCoopers (2008) based on 82 corporate counsels, international arbitration is not only the preferred dispute resolution method for cross-border disputes but is considered to be effective in practice, particularly in the enforcement of awards. The main advantages are that of speedy resolution of dispute and cost-effectiveness of arbitration; freedom in choice of adjudicator; flexibility of time, date, venue and rules; confidentiality of the proceedings; conducive environment; and enforceability of the arbitral award (Lim, Tan and Woo 1993/1994; Moses 2008; Tay 1998). From the theoretical perspective, arbitration is considered to be a better alternative to litigation in the business world but it is not clear whether the advantages of the former hold in practice, especially in relation to speed and cost of arbitration. It has been claimed that arbitration also has certain disadvantages when compared to litigation. From the perspective of a legal expert, arbitrators lack the power held by judges, they are not required to provide reasons for the awards unlike reasoned court judgments, they do not have recourse to past arbitration proceedings due to the confidential nature of the proceedings, and if they are not trained lawyers, they may lack the legal expertise to deal with complex cases (Lim, Tan and Woo 1993/1994; Moses 2008; Tay 1998). On the other hand, these disadvantages could be perceived as empowering arbitrators as arbitration tribunals enjoy more freedom since they are not bound by the rules of court, have almost unlimited flexibility in deciding procedures and their awards can be written in any form, without any fear of being challenged. Some of the key advantages and disadvantages of arbitration will be examined in the following sub-sections.

Advantages of Arbitration

Arbitration is faster and cheaper mainly due to the flexibility of the arbitration procedure. Parties in the arbitration process are not bound by national procedural laws (Paulsson et al., 1999) and have the freedom to decide on procedures and time frame. In addition, appeals against awards which often delay court decisions are not allowed in arbitrations by law and/or agreement between the parties. This not only shortens the proceedings but reduces the cost as charges are based on the nature, number and length of hearings. According to Tay (1998), arbitration can be cheaper than litigation in certain circumstances such as when disputes are resolved on a documents-only basis rather than through court proceedings and arbitration is conducted by a technical arbitrator in place of lawyers. However, if specialist lawyers are involved and proceedings mirror litigation with full-scale hearings, the cost will escalate unless the arbitrators and lawyers make a concerted effort to save time by narrowing the issues of dispute before the hearings. With the growing popularity of international arbitration as a dispute resolution option, the SIAC updated their rules in 2010 to encourage speedier and more cost effective resolution of commercial disputes through arbitration in Singapore. Some of these changes include an expedited arbitration or 'fast-track' procedure for amounts up to S$5 millions and the award can be issued within six months from the constitution of the tribunal.

Another major advantage of arbitration over litigation is that parties can appoint members of the arbitration tribunal of their own choice based on professional qualifications, experience, personality and cost (Lim, Tan and Woo, 1993/94; Tay,

1998; Paulsson et al. 1999). Judges appointed by the court may not necessarily have the technical background or experience in a particular field of business in comparison to expert arbitrators who are familiar with a specific industry and its related problems. As insiders, they would be able to arrive at innovative solutions and formulate quality awards that depart from legal interpretations of fairness and justice. A judge, on the other hand, would be forced to enforce the law strictly as the court does not allow for personal interpretations in judgments. Apart from their technical expertise, arbitrators tend to generate more trust and confidence as they are selected and empowered by the parties concerned, leading to more amicable conflict resolution. Moreover, many legal experts are overcommitted and hence take a longer time than is necessary or desirable. In order to rectify the situation, the SIAC has recently updated the rules to make it possible for the chairman of the SIAC to consider if the arbitrator being considered for appointment has sufficient availability to undertake the case in a prompt and efficient manner; the main objective is to prevent unnecessary delay due to the non-availability of the tribunal.

Flexibility in the choice of location, date and rules in arbitration proceedings gives it a definite advantage over litigation which has to be conducted in the courtroom at a time and date specified by the court, following specific court procedures. Arbitrators, in agreement with the disputing parties, can design their own set of customized procedures within the acceptable rules of the specific seat of arbitration where proceedings are likely to take place. For instance, they can choose between the documents-only or the inquisitorial approach depending on the circumstances and they may even proceed with arbitration in the absence of a party as the SIAC rules allow this to avoid delay in the proceedings (Tay 1998).

Finally, confidentiality of the proceedings, a conducive environment, and enforcement of arbitral awards make arbitration an attractive alternative to litigation. As the proceedings are held in private and in a setting that is not shrouded by the formality of a courtroom, disputing parties are able to resolve their differences without undue public exposure and preserve their business relationship without a negative impact on their businesses (Lim, Tan and Woo 1993/1994; Tay 1998). As for the outcome of such proceedings, the arbitral award can be enforced as a judgment of the court and this applies to all countries that have signed the New York Convention. While court proceedings are subject to appeals, arbitration awards are final and binding with little likelihood of a judicial review (Paulsson et al. 1999).

Disadvantages of Arbitration

Although arbitration is associated with many advantages, it is not completely devoid of problems in relation to the arbitrators' lack of power, legal expertise and recourse to case studies. In litigation, power is bestowed upon the judges by the courts and the State but arbitrators do not have any legal authority over third parties involved in the dispute. In such cases, they have to seek the assistance of national courts for third-party injunctions and sanctions related to the case (Paulsson et al.

1999). Coupled with this is the issue of legal expertise that arbitrators may lack even though they have technical expertise in the area of the dispute. According to Tay (1998: 20), 'An expert lacking a judicial approach is worse than any non-technical judge'. The final point of concern in arbitration is that arbitrators do not have recourse to past proceedings due to the private nature of these, resulting in their inability to predict the likely outcome of the arbitration (Lim, Tan and Woo 1993/1994).

From the theoretical perspective, it seems like the merits of arbitration outweigh the limitations in terms of importance but it remains to be seen whether practitioners in Singapore endorse these viewpoints based on their practical experience in arbitration.

Objective of the Study

To gain more insights into the relationship between arbitration and litigation, this small-scale survey-based study examines the perceptions of practicing arbitrators in Singapore, specifically to determine the extent to which the integrity of arbitration principles is maintained in arbitration practice, as an alternative to litigation practice. To meet this objective, a questionnaire (see Appendix for the questionnaire) was designed and distributed to arbitrators and legal practitioners in Singapore, and also internationally as part of the international initiative to study *International Commercial Arbitration Practices*.[3] In addition, the proceedings at the 20th AIFA Symposium Singapore on 23 January 2010 on arbitration provided another source of data, as many of the issues at the symposium were related to the questionnaire designed for the present study. The structure of the symposium was defined by the format of the handout which was circulated prior to the symposium. It consisted of blurbs on particular arbitral and legal issues with a list of related questions. These issues and questions were discussed item-by-item at the symposium, providing a rich source of data and enabling a focussed discussion of these issues between legal experts at the symposium as well as between legal and arbitration experts and other attendees during tea breaks. Some of these discussions have been incorporated into the following sections to substantiate the survey findings.

Methodology

As mentioned earlier, the main method of data collection for this study was through specially designed questionnaires. In addition, the survey findings

3 For more details about this international research project entitled *International Commercial Arbitration Practices: A Discourse Analytical Study* headed by Professor Vijay K. Bhatia of the City University of Hong Kong, see the website <http://www.english.cityu.edu.hk/arbitration/>, accessed 15 June 2011.

were substantiated by means of information gathered from the target group and participants of the 20th AIFA Symposium. In addition, the findings were also substantiated through specialist research interviews conducted by the main project. Details on the design of the questionnaire, profile of respondents and symposium handout are presented in this section.

Design of Questionnaire

The survey questionnaire had three main sections. The opening section described the purpose of the questionnaire which was to gather expert opinion from arbitration practitioners on ICA. The questionnaire was centrally designed by the project entitled *International Commercial Arbitration Practice: A Discourse Analytical Study*, funded by the Research Grants Council HKSAR, and based at the City University of Hong Kong. Other aspects of the study highlighted were the objectives of the study, which was to determine the extent to which the integrity of arbitration principles is maintained in arbitration practice as an alternative to litigation practice, and usefulness of the study, that is, to facilitate better understanding of arbitral proceedings and practices. The second part of the questionnaire was designed to gather information on the respondents' personal particulars related to their education, profession, designation and experience as arbitrators. The third part consisted of 20 close-ended (Yes–No, multiple choice, Likert scale, ranking questions) and two open-ended questions on various issues related to arbitration and its relation to litigation and other types of resolution such as conciliation and mediation.

Profile of Respondents

The questionnaire was distributed to several lawyers residing in Singapore, in both hard copy and soft copy versions. Only eight questionnaires were duly completed and returned. The respondents of the survey were all from the legal profession, with six lawyers and two advocates/solicitors. Four of them are currently partners, two are associates, one is a professor of law and one is a counsel. Their qualifications vary from LLB (five), LLM (two) to PhD (one) and they have all had experience in arbitration, with half having handled one to 15 cases and the other half 50 to 100 cases.

Symposium Topics and Questions

The format of the symposium was such that the discussions focused on a set of questions that had been submitted by the participants prior to the session and printed in the form of a handout. Each discussion topic in the handout consisted of background information on the topic and a list of questions related to that topic. Therefore the discussions had a recurrent three-part structure of Topic^Question^Discussion, simulating an actual interview format. Detailed notes were recorded of the entire proceedings but only those discussion topics relevant to the present study are incorporated into this chapter. As mentioned earlier, the views and perspectives published as well as gathered through research interviews from established scholars and practitioners have also been considered as valid evidence for making claims.

Findings and Discussion

The survey questions were grouped according to related categories for ease of analysis. These included the respondents' reasons for preferring arbitration over litigation; concerns regarding arbitration such as cost, court appeals and enforceability of the awards; language, style and method adopted for arbitration proceedings and, finally, comparison between different methods of dispute resolution, particularly between arbitration and litigation. The findings and discussions related to these are presented below.

Reasons for Preferring Arbitration

In response to the question on whether arbitration will continue to be the preferred method of resolving cross-border commercial disputes, a high 88 per cent of the respondents indicated that they strongly agree (50 per cent) or agree (38 per cent) with the statement. According to the survey findings, the three top reasons for preferring arbitration over litigation included confidentiality and flexibility/freedom of choice to parties, enforcement of awards, and being a relatively expeditious process, in the order of mention. The remaining two reasons dealing with informality of the procedure and value for money were not rated high. The responses to this question matched those of a similar question in the questionnaire where enforceability of arbitration awards and freedom in the choice of venue of arbitration were chosen as the top reasons for preferring arbitration over litigation. Following in second place were reasons such as flexibility of processes and procedures, encouraging active participation of the parties in most areas of decision-making as well as confidentiality and privacy in arbitration proceedings. The third reason for preferring arbitration over litigation was the possibility of participating in the selection of arbitrators. The findings are similar to the PricewaterhouseCoopers survey (2008) in which 86 per cent of the corporate counsels indicated that they were satisfied with international arbitration. Even their reasons for preferring arbitration mirror those of the present study, with enforceability of arbitral awards, flexibility of the procedure and freedom to select experienced arbitrators being prioritized in their responses.

It is not surprising that so much emphasis is placed on enforceability of awards, confidentiality of the proceedings and flexibility in conducting proceedings as these factors apply distinctively to arbitration and make this process more attractive in international commercial disputes. Whereas court judgments can only be imposed domestically, arbitral awards can be enforced in all countries that are signatories of the New York Convention (Moses 2008; Tay 1998). As arbitration awards do not allow for appeals and the proceedings are less formal than litigation, time is saved by the elimination of the appeal process and the adoption of procedural shortcuts (Lim, Tan and Woo 1993/1994). Confidentiality is another factor that plays a predominant role in the decision to choose arbitration over litigation as companies are concerned about their image and do not want to make public their disputes with other commercial organizations due to fear of tarnishing their reputation (Moses 2008; Tay 1998). Finally, flexibility in the choice of arbitrators or in the selection of venues and dates of hearing gives more control to the parties in dispute when compared to litigation where no such choice is available. Not surprisingly, the choices of the respondents are consistent with the importance placed on these factors by other legal experts on this topic.

Concerns Regarding Arbitration

On the issue of concerns related to ICA that would make arbitration less attractive in comparison to other methods of dispute resolution, many respondents raised the issues of cost, appeals and enforceability of arbitration awards. While a significant number of respondents (63 per cent) agreed that ICA is as expensive as transnational litigation for medium/smaller cases but better value for more complex cases, the majority (88 per cent) indicated that the recent escalation of costs is a major concern for the disputing parties. These concerns of increased costs and delays in proceedings were also mentioned in the PricewaterhouseCooper survey (2008) by a small percentage (5 per cent) of the counsels who were disappointed with arbitration.

Regarding enforceability of awards and appeals, respondents felt that applications challenging the finality of arbitration awards would compromise the integrity of the arbitration process greatly (63 per cent) or somewhat (25 per cent). As for their views on whether parties at dispute would prefer an appeal system within the framework of arbitration, half of them felt that they would not, but one of them commented that it would depend on the situation such that if one of the parties is related to the jurisdiction where the appellate court is located, it may give rise to fear of partiality. Another respondent pointed out that in Singapore, the preference might be for the intervention of national courts due to the speed with which cases are handled by local courts. However, he elaborated that national courts in Singapore have a hands-off attitude towards arbitration proceedings and prefer not to interfere. There is a trade-off between allowing appeals and cost/speed of the arbitration process. Making allowance for appeals within the arbitration process would definitely have an impact on the cost and speed of the proceedings, making it as lengthy as litigation proceedings, which routinely permit such appeals. This point has also been raised by other legal experts in the field (Moses 2008; Tay 1998).

On the issue of awards, the global survey conducted by PricewaterhouseCooper (2008) provides an interesting comparison to the findings of the present study. When questioned about compliance with arbitral awards, a high degree of compliance was noted in the former study, with 84 per cent of respondents indicating that awards were honoured in full by opposing parties to preserve business relationships. Moreover, it revealed that majority (92 per cent) of arbitration cases are successfully resolved during some point of the arbitral proceedings and the main reasons for settlement are to preserve business relationships, avoid high costs and excessive delay, and a weak case (ibid.). The small percentage of awards (11 per cent) that had to be enforced was mainly due to the circumstances of the award debtor rather than to shortcomings in the arbitral proceedings.

As for the issue of time, there was an interesting discussion during the 20th AFIA Symposium on the stop-clock or time-limited hearings in the western world and the possibility of implementing these in the Asian region for better management of time. The arbitration rules of the major arbitral institutions in the Asian region (SIAC, Hong Kong International Arbitration Centre (HKIAC), Kuala Lumpur Regional Center for Arbitration (KLRCA), Japan Commercial Arbitration Association (JCAA) and China International Economic and Trade Arbitration Commission (CIETAC) provide for flexibility in the conduct of arbitrations and in some cases for expedited procedures. But they make no explicit reference to stop-clock (or time-limited) hearing procedures. It was suggested that time-limited hearings could take the form of setting a time of 50 hours per party over a 20-day period in the local context. Some participants felt that the stop-clock procedure is not necessary and that it may be better to have a proper hearing timetable. The danger about time-limited hearings is that if enough time is not given to parties to explain themselves, the end result could be a delay in the award. In response to this, it was suggested that it might be better to equalize time given to the two parties rather than setting a definite time of 50 hours for each. For instance, the solution would be to give half an hour per cross-examination to one party and follow it up by half an hour to the other party. It should be up to the tribunal, without being offensive, to tell the counsels that a particular matter has been investigated enough and they should therefore move on to the next. However, in actual practice, it may not be possible. In one of the cases, the project researcher had an opportunity to observe, it was found that a particular witness was cross-examined for more than two full days, without much intervention from the arbitration panel.

The PricewaterhouseCoopers study (2008) found that the average time for recognizing, enforcing and executing awards is less than one year, with 57 per cent of participants reporting settlement within a year and 44 per cent usually recovering the full amount. According to most of the subjects, the reason for the high success rate of settlement is the 1958 New York Convention and the failure for full recovery is mainly due to the lack of assets of the non-prevailing party (ibid.). These figures are promising but a more detailed study will have to be designed to find out whether a similar trend exits in the Singapore exist.

Method, Style and Language of Arbitration

English being the international language of trade and commerce is the predominant language used in arbitration and this was confirmed by all the respondents of our survey. They (excluding two respondents) also confirmed that there are generally no guidelines provided on language policy in arbitration. In hearings, cross-examination seems to be a popular mode of obtaining clarificatory or contradictory information from witnesses, if the direct testimony is admitted in the form of written witness statements. This also seems to be the case where the arbitration panel is dominated by experts from civil law jurisdictions, who often disprefer any form of elaborate direct or even cross-examination. Bhatia (2011: 109), also points out:

> The heavy use of written evidence in international arbitration reflects the distinct influence of civil law tradition, whereas discovery is seen as a distinct American practice. In the civil law tradition, evidence is often presented in written form, and the questioning of witnesses is conducted not by the legal counsel, but rather by the judge. Direct examination of witnesses is generally not permitted in arbitration, if the tribunal is dominated by specialists from the civil law jurisdictions.

From the respondents' choices in the present study, it appears that some (50 per cent) confine it to the scope of the written statements made by witnesses, others (38 per cent) go beyond these statements and the remaining claim that most of the testimony is adduced through cross-examination rather than through previously submitted written statements. Although it is possible to base an arbitral award on written evidence, this is rarely the case as in most arbitration cases at least one meeting is held for parties to present their proofs and oral arguments to the tribunal (Buhring-Uhle 2006). As for the cross-examination of witnesses, it seems that arbitrators follow different methods, with some restricting it to written statements but others preferring further exploration of the issues.

The topic of cross-examination was also discussed during the 20th AFIA Symposium held in Singapore. In the ensuing discussion, it was felt that a witness should be allowed to tell a story and the cross-examination should be in the form of 'friendly' questions in arbitration. The opposing view is that witness statements and stories should not be allowed as these are not statements of witnesses but those drafted by their lawyers, and moreover, they extend the time taken for hearings. However, an established arbitration practitioner and trainer from common law background, when asked during the project specialist interview about arbitration as adversarial practice, asserted:

> You must remember that your client who is paying you money is sitting behind you or even at the same table, and they want you to do your very best for them

> [...] and therefore I find that it is definitely an adversarial process. If I am involved in it, I use it as an adversarial process.

However, there seemed to be some consensus among the participants that there should be a middle ground, perhaps a witness conferencing process or a credible way to evaluate witnesses' evidence to separate his/her opinions from that of his/her lawyer's coaching. This issue of identity and voice in written statements has also been raised and discussed at length in Bhatia (2011: 110) where he claims:

> In courtroom examination, particularly in common law jurisdictions, there is a perception that defendants have no voice of their own and their identity is often manipulated by legal counsels. The issue in common law jurisdictions is 'how much of a witness's testimony is presented by the witness, and how much by the counsel?' If this is really so, the valid question to raise then is, 'whose narrative is unfolded in the court?' which presupposes that the witness, and not counsel, is the real presenter of evidence. In ICA, therefore, one may also legitimately ask, 'who is responsible for written statements?' Often the witness provides the facts and the counsel constructs a statement based on the submitted facts. Written narratives from witnesses thus often become repetitive accounts of their factual positions, thereby removing in the process individual identities of the witnesses almost in every statement.

When questioned about the type of language forms used in cross-examining, most survey respondents chose a combination of closed-ended questions and direct questions (63 per cent) or only direct questions (25 per cent). As for the style of the language, there were varied responses with 63 per cent choosing friendly, normal and a combination of normal and focused. However, 25 per cent chose a combination of negative (for example, hostile, loud, insistent and long-winded) and positive (for example, friendly, normal, flexible and focused) styles, stressing the fact that the style depended on the type of case and the style that would work best in a particular situation. Surprisingly, a majority of them (88 per cent) did not fully support the statement that disputes were meant to be amicably resolved by active participation of the parties in the dispute. The same percentage of respondents (88 per cent) denied that the amicability of the arbitration process was destroyed due to the frequent appointment of lawyers as arbitrators. The findings seem to indicate that there is no particular style that fits all cases and that cross-examiners have to adjust their method and tone depending upon whom they are dealing with. Given this feedback, it is difficult to reconcile the findings with the fact that arbitration was never meant to be adversarial and amicability is the feature that distinguishes it from litigation.

On the issue of 'voices' and command of language, the participants of the symposium believed that the chair and members of the tribunal play an important role. They were particularly concerned about mild-mannered versus dominant counsels as they feared that the one with the louder voice would be more persuasive. It was also emphasized that the cultural aspect needs to be taken into consideration in hearings. Tribunals may have to play a dominant role in cases where there is a non-native speaker of English versus a native speaker with better command of English (for example, a Chinese versus an Australian witness). The tribunal should be well prepared and know all the facts so they can ask the right questions and keep the arguments on track, not letting any party dominate due to better command of language. Therefore, it was concluded that the tribunal should play a key role in ensuring that things do not go off the rail and the chair should control the proceedings judiciously.

Influence of Litigation on Arbitration

The general impression of arbitration practice is that litigation is increasingly influencing arbitration, making it similar to litigation, which it was originally intended to supplant (Nariman 2000). A significant number of respondents (63 per cent) supported this statement and in response to a later question in the questionnaire, all of them agreed that to some extent the informal nature of arbitration processes and procedures is giving way to more technical ones found in litigation. They elaborated on this further in the open-ended question that dealt with the issue of arbitration practice being colonized by the processes of litigation. When asked to pinpoint those aspects of contemporary arbitration that make it similar to litigation, the following points were raised:

- Common law procedures such as pleadings, discovery of documents and cross-examination of witnesses.
- Involvement of lawyers and tendency for parties to appoint retired judges as arbitrators who in all probability are likely to follow court procedures in arbitrations.
- The process has become more like litigation due to the adversarial method utilized by lawyers.
- Minimal difference between costs of running an arbitration and litigation.
- Time delays in scheduling hearings due to unavailability or pre-commitments of arbitrators.

Despite all these similarities between arbitration and litigation, one respondent claimed that confidentiality, ease of cross-border enforcements and minimal interference from the courts still made arbitration more attractive than litigation.

Alternative Dispute Resolutions

Apart from litigation and arbitration, there are other forms of dispute resolutions such as conciliation and mediation (Tan and Lee-Patridge 2000; Buhring-Uhle 2006). One of the open-ended questions posed to the respondents was the possibility of these alternatives supplanting arbitration in the future. There was consensus among the respondents that arbitration will not be replaced by conciliation and mediation as the three forms are complementary rather than mutually exclusive alternatives. The preference of one over the other would depend on the level and degree of the dispute and the relationship among the parties. Therefore, in cases where the disputes are complex and involve questions of law, parties prefer adjudication as the possibility of a resolution through mutual consent is low. Although the respondents unanimously felt that one form cannot be replaced by another, some of the respondents highlighted that there is an increasing tendency to draft multi-tier dispute resolution clauses requiring conciliation and mediation as a precursor to arbitration. One of the respondents indicated that dissatisfaction with certain aspects of arbitration procedures has led to innovations such as the ARB-MED and MED-ARB procedures to facilitate the arbitration process. These are a combination of arbitration and mediation processes (MED-ARB) and have given rise to many possibilities of dispute resolution such as pre-arbitration mediation and post-arbitral mediation among others (Buhring-Uhle 2006).

There is overwhelming support for ICA and ADR over litigation among corporations in the findings of the PricewaterhouseCoopers survey (2008). In fact in some industries such as insurance, energy, oil and gas, and shipping, ICA is used as a default resolution method, with 88 per cent of these corporations confirming that they have used it at least once (ibid.). When asked about the type of dispute resolution mechanisms they had used to resolve their international disputes, it was found that 44 per cent mostly used ICA, 41 per cent used transnational litigation and 15 per cent used other ADR mechanisms as an alternative to traditional court proceedings (ibid.). This trend is reflected in the present study through responses to the open-ended questions.

Conclusion

It is clear from this survey-based study that arbitration is not likely to be supplanted by litigation even though it is being influenced by litigation. According to our respondents, all of whom have had some experience in arbitration proceedings, arbitration practice is here to stay and performs a niche function that is different from other forms of dispute resolution, whether litigation, conciliation or mediation. To quote one of the respondents in this study:

> I practice both litigation and arbitration and it may appear that a lot of practitioners treat both as the same and therefore apply the same treatment. However, as the practice of arbitration becomes more and more specialized, I am beginning to see a lot of creative and informal procedures being applied to arbitration so as to make the process more efficient. This is the advantage of arbitration as the parties and the arbitrators are at liberty to modify and mould the procedures in such a way as they fit the disputes being resolved.

The shape of arbitration proceedings is in the hands of the practitioners and it is hoped that with more practice in this type of dispute resolution, they can improvise their skills and make arbitration into a distinct form that has little in common with litigation. At the same time, the fact that arbitration procedures incorporate multi-tier dispute resolution clauses from conciliation and mediation will enable it to preserve its initial goal of being an amiable and friendly form of dispute resolution. In addition, some of its original goals of being a cost-efficient and expeditious method need to be restored by minimizing judicial interventions, curtailing appeals and reformulating the language and style of cross-examinations. A concerted effort to apply a combination of these corrective measures will ensure the future integrity of arbitration practice as distinct from other forms of dispute resolution.

References

Bhatia, Vijay K. (2011): Witness Examination as Interdiscursive Practice, *World Englishes*, Vol. 30, No. 1, 106–16.

Buhring-Uhle, Christian (2006): *Arbitration and Mediation in International Business*, 2nd edition, edited by Kirchhoff, Lars and Scherer, Gabriele, The Netherlands, Kluwer Law International.

Lim, T.Y., Tan, Catherine L.H. and Woo, S.L. (1993/1994): *Arbitration versus Litigation*, Final Year Project, School of Accountancy and Business, Nanyang Technological University.

Merkin, Rob and Hjalmarsson, Johanna (2009): *Singapore Arbitration Legislation Annotated*, London, informa.

Moses, Margaret L. (2008): *The Principles and Practice of International Commercial Arbitration*, New York, NY, Cambridge University Press.

Nariman, Fali S. (2000): The Spirit of Arbitration: The Tenth Annual Goff Lecture, *Arbitration International*, Vol. 16, No. 3, 261–78.

Paulsson, Jan, Rawding, Nigel, Reed, Lucy, and Schwartz, Eric (1999): *The Freshfields Guide to Arbitration and ADR: Clauses in International Contracts*, 2nd revised edition, The Hague, The Netherlands, Kluwer Law International.

PricewaterhouseCoopers (2008): *International Arbitration: Corporate Attitudes and Practices*, London, University of London, School of International Arbitration.

Singapore International Arbitration Centre (2010): Online at <http://www.siac.org.sg/cms/>, accessed 12 August 2010.

Tay, Catherine T.S. (1998): *Resolving Disputes by Arbitration: What You Need to Know*, Singapore, Singapore University Press.

Tan, Ngoh Tiong and Lee-Patridge, Joo Eng (2000): *Alternative Dispute Resolution. In Business, Family and Community: Multidisciplinary Perspectives*, Singapore, Pagesetters Services.

Appendix

Questionnaire for Project on *International Commercial Arbitration Practice: A Discourse Analytical Study*

Thank you for participating in this survey. This questionnaire is designed to gather your expert opinion as arbitration practitioners/legal experts on international commercial arbitration for the project entitled 'International Commercial Arbitration Practice: A Discourse Analytical Study', an international project funded by the Research Grants Council HKSAR, City University of Hong Kong. The results of this survey will be used to study the extent to which:

- the integrity of arbitration principles is maintained in arbitration practice, as alternative to litigation practice; and
- legal knowledge, expertise and experience is necessary in international commercial arbitration practice.

The findings of the survey, we hope, will facilitate a better understanding of arbitral proceedings and practices and lead to publications in international arbitration journals. However, information about respondents will be kept strictly confidential.

Personal Particulars:

What is your educational qualification?
What is your profession?
What is your current designation?
Have you had experience as an arbitration practitioner?
How many arbitration cases have you handled until now?

Survey Questions on Arbitration:

1. The general impression of arbitration practice we have is that litigation is increasingly influencing arbitration, making it similar to litigation, which it was originally intended to supplant. Please indicate the most appropriate response below.

Strongly agree	Agree	Not sure	Disagree	Strongly disagree

2. What, according to you, are the main reasons for preferring arbitration over litigation in international commercial disputes? Please rank the reasons in order of importance (1 = Most important, 6 = Least important).

[ ] Confidentiality	[ ] Flexibility and freedom of choice to parties
[ ] Informality	[ ] Enforcement of awards
[ ] Relatively expeditious process	[ ] Value for money

3. To what extent do you think it is the case that the informal nature of arbitration processes and procedures is giving way to more technical ones often similar to those found in litigation?

Very much	Much	Sometimes	Rarely	Never

4. International commercial arbitration is as expensive as trans-national litigation for medium/smaller cases but better value for money in more complex cases.

[ ] Yes [ ] No

5. Recent escalation of costs in international arbitration is a concern for parties.

[ ] Yes [ ] No

6. Parties at dispute prefer an appeal system within the framework of arbitration proceeding to the one within the system of national courts.

[ ] Yes [ ] No
[ ] Depends on situation (Specify) ____________________

7. To what extent do such interventions through national laws and courts tend to compromise the integrity of arbitration processes and procedures?

Very much	Much	Sometimes	Rarely	Never

8. In the arbitration process, are disputes meant to be resolved 'amicably' by active co-operation of the parties in the dispute?

Very much	Much	Sometimes	Rarely	Never

9. The frequent appointment of lawyers as arbitrators has affected the '*amicability*' of the whole arbitration procedure.

[ ] Yes [ ] No

10. In your opinion, what would be the key attributes that an arbitrator should possess?

[ ] Expert/specialist knowledge [ ] Practical experience
[ ] Friendly personality [ ] Flexibility
[ ] Cross-examination skills [ ] Good command of language
[ ] Any other attributes: ___________________________

11. Would you consider applications challenging the finality of arbitration awards as compromising the integrity of the arbitration process?

[ ] Yes [ ] No

12. How important is the role of cross-examination in International Commercial Arbitration practice?

Very important	Somewhat important	Neither important nor unimportant	Somewhat unimportant	Not important at all

13. In what ways is the process of cross-examination different in arbitration and litigation? Tick the statements below that apply to arbitration.

[ ] Cross-examination is confined to the scope of the statements made by the witnesses.
[ ] Cross-examination goes beyond the written statements provided by the witnesses.
[ ] Most of the testimony is adduced through cross-examination rather than through previously submitted written statements.
[ ] Documents are presented by the counsel for the first time in cross-examination.
[ ] Witnesses are prepared for cross-examination.

14. Are there any guidelines provided on language policy in arbitration?

[ ] Yes [ ] No

15. Is English usually preferred in arbitration even if it is not the first language of the parties?

[ ] Yes [ ] No

16. What type of language forms are used in such cross-examinations?

[ ] Closed-ended questions (yes–no questions) [ ] Open-ended questions
[ ] Direct questions [ ] Coercive questions

17. Indicate the style of language used by civil law lawyers and arbitrators in international arbitration proceedings?

[ ] Hostile [ ] Friendly
[ ] Loud [ ] Normal
[ ] Insistent [ ] Flexible
[ ] Long-winded [ ] Focussed

18. Please select and rank the top 5 reasons for preferring arbitration to litigation in international commercial contexts (1= Most important, 5 = Least Important).

[ ] Flexibility and informality of processes and procedures, encouraging active participation of the parties in most areas of decision-making
[ ] Enforceability of arbitration awards
[ ] Confidentiality and privacy in arbitration proceedings
[ ] Participation in the selection of arbitrators
[ ] Relatively lower costs as compared with litigation
[ ] Relative speed of completion of arbitration proceedings
[ ] Freedom in the choice of venue of arbitration (neutrality of venue, preferred legal system)
[ ] Costs of arbitration
[ ] Challenge to arbitration awards – interference from national laws and courts
[ ] Appeal system within the arbitration framework

19. Please rank the 5 areas of concern in international commercial arbitration, which, in your view, are likely to make it less attractive as an instrument of alternative dispute resolution (1= Most important, 5 = Least Important).

[ ] Enforceability of arbitration awards
[ ] Quality of arbitrators
[ ] Duration of arbitrations
[ ] Costs of arbitration
[ ] Challenge to arbitration awards – interference from national laws and courts

20. Do you believe that arbitration will continue to be the preferred method for resolving cross border commercial disputes?

Strongly agree	Agree	Not sure	Disagree	Strongly disagree

21. In your view, to what extent, and in which particular ways, are other forms of dispute resolution (e.g. conciliation and mediation) are likely to supplant arbitration procedures?

22. In the views of at least some arbitrators, arbitration practice seems to be being 'colonized' by the processes of litigation, in that it has become very similar to litigation. In your experience, what aspects of the contemporary arbitration process make it similar to litigation?

Thank you for completing this questionnaire!

Chapter 16
Confidentiality v. Publicity: The Impact of International Arbitration in the Media

Isabel Corona

Introduction

In the last 20 years the notion of confidentiality in international arbitration has undergone an important transformation. Until the 1990s there was a belief that arbitration proceedings were both private and confidential, and that the duty of confidentiality arose from the very nature of arbitration. Confidentiality had thus been listed as one clear advantage of arbitration over litigation to resolve international disputes.

However, there were a number of cases held during the 1990s (see, for example, Fortier 1999; Dundas 2004) in which the issue of inherent confidentiality was seriously challenged. In 1999 Fortier warned that, in dealing with confidentiality 'nothing should be taken for granted' any longer. After two decades of much analysis in an attempt to bring some clarity to the issue and much debate for and against confidentiality, Beechey (2009) has reached the same conclusion, that 'parties and arbitrators cannot afford to overlook, much less take for granted, the issues raised by the question of confidentiality in international arbitration proceedings'.

How confidentiality is currently understood and applied depends on the law of the seat of arbitration, the rules of the arbitral institution and the contractual provisions made by the parties. There appear to be two approaches to the same principle in the national courts: while in England, France and New Zealand the general approach has been to take an implied duty of confidentiality, the Australian, American and Swedish courts have proved to be more reluctant to an implied duty of confidentiality, unless the applicable arbitration rules and the parties had provided otherwise.

As for arbitral institutions, as Berwin and Baruti (2009) observe, they tend to preserve privacy of hearings and of internal operations of the arbitral tribunal rather than confidentiality of the proceedings.

The view from within the professional practice seems to develop in two main trends. First, there appears to be a general call for an international consensus, and second, as Thomson (2007) summarizes, a general feeling that, 'because of the legal inconsistencies across jurisdictions and different treatment by institutional arbitration rules, parties to arbitration should not assume that the existence of an arbitration, the evidence and the award would be kept confidential'. This current ambiguity is leading practitioners to warn users of arbitral services that 'generic' arbitration clauses rarely deal with the issue of confidentiality and therefore are advised to devise appropriate confidentiality provisions. If implied confidentiality does not seem to work, practitioners call for making it explicit.

In contrast, confidentiality seems to rank low as the most important attribute of arbitration among corporations (Bhatia et al. 2008). A study carried out by PricewaterhouseCoopers (2008) among corporations reveals that enforceability of awards, flexibility of procedures and expertise of arbitrators are seen as the major advantages of arbitration, while length of time and costs are seen as the disadvantages.

The truth of the matter is that the global demand for information and the new media technologies have reached arbitration and have brought in a new perspective, which has caused what Brown (2001: 971) describes as 'a disconnect between that presumption [of confidentiality] and the frequent realities of disclosure and publicity'. There is an increasing number of voluntary and involuntary disclosures that invite to consider transparency reforms, to make information available and the process more transparent (Beechey 2009) for the benefit of the arbitral community as a whole.

The present chapter deals precisely with one case of disclosure and analyzes the reasons for that disclosure. Furthermore, it will argue, in agreement with Rogers and Cadwallader (quoted by Bhatia 2009), that there might be other reasons than to advance transparency.

The arbitration case under study was filed at the Arbitration Institute of the Stockholm Chamber of Commerce in 2007. The parties involved were UK brewer Scottish & Newcastle, and a consortium – made up for the occasion– of Danish brewer Carlsberg and Dutch brewer Heineken (hereafter the Consortium). The arbitration process was part of a six-month-long takeover battle, from October 2007 until April 2008, when Scottish & Newcastle ceased to exist. Because it was 'prematurely' leaked to the press, it developed as a public dialogue between the parties carried out through the Stock Exchange announcements produced by the two parties and the media coverage of the whole story.

This case shows that arbitration can be seen as a double-edged sword, where publicity of the arbitration process, not confidentiality, is the most effective strategy to achieve other purposes. In other words, there is a tactical use of the arbitration process and its publicity by the parties involved.

I have reconstructed the story tracing the stock exchange announcements produced by both parties, 42 in total, and 30 news items published in national, international, business and financial online newspapers. All the texts allowed free access on the Internet.[1]

1 The announcements made by the two companies can be accessed at their websites: those produced by Carlsberg at <http://www.carlsberggroup.com/media>,

When a company is listed on the London Stock Exchange, they are required to make a formal announcement on any event that has an impact on their business. In general, these announcements report business developments and give notice of key dates such as results announcements and trading updates.

The 42 stock exchange announcements publicized by Scottish & Newcastle and the Consortium were nearly always produced in pairs, to confirm communication and proceed forward. They acted as a conversational interaction system, as an electronically mediated conversation between the parties, displaying a turn-taking structure. They were real sites of engagement where professional practice and business communication – that is, discursive practice – were clearly connected. As the process advanced, the announcements grew more informative – more inclined towards disclosing procedures, as well as more argumentative in order to get their position clear. While following the institutional character of the genre and its conventional rules of conduct – of trading practices and trading parties (Knorr Cetina 2007) – at the same time they incorporated generic resources of mass media genres, that is, news reports, such as quotations from their respective CEOs, who made straightforward declarations (referred to as 'Comments') of their position with respect to their company's standing and the other party's moves. Thus the texts resulted in 'pre-cooked' pieces of news, but, as could not be otherwise, providing their side of the story. In doing so, these public announcements in fact acted as real-time press releases used by the media to cover the process.

With respect to this media coverage, it must be made clear that the media texts collected come from English written media addressed to an English-speaking audience. No evidence has been gathered from news reports published by the Danish press so we should allow for the possibility of a cultural 'spin' in their approach. That would also explain why the British brewer Scottish & Newcastle appears as the main actor in the majority of the news items.

The stories published were mainly based on the announcements, which acted as press releases, and thus followed a news-gathering routine. As the announcements from both parties more often than not appeared in pairs on the same day, one as a response to the other, news reports mostly drew on both inputs. As the companies themselves produced highly elaborated compositions, with comments in direct quotations attributed to high representatives, journalists frequently transferred those declarations into their own texts. Consequently, we can say that the media coverage of the whole process was fairly consistent with the content of the stock exchange announcements. However, and as could not be otherwise, their headlines differed significantly, because they responded to the discursive practices of journalism, that is, they fulfilled their very specific functions of being brief, effective and attention getters. They were rich in wordplay with frequent references to the semantic field of beer making and drinking, where the opportunity of playing with the double meaning of 'brewing' could not be resisted.

---

and those published by Scottish & Newcastle at <http://archive.scottish-newcastle.com/sn_acq/acquisition>.

Scottish & Newcastle v. Carlsberg & Heineken

Scottish & Newcastle (hereafter S&N), which traced its roots back to 1777, was the largest UK-owned brewing company, with top-selling beers Newcastle Brown Ale, Foster's, Kronenbourg 1664 and John Smiths. S&N and Carlsberg had been running Russia's largest brewer, Baltic Beverages Holding (hereafter BBH) as 50/50 joint venture since 2002. For S&N this international business was considered the jewel in the crown. It operated 19 breweries – including Baltika, Russia's leading beer brand – holding top position in the booming Russian and eastern European beverage markets.

The six-month-long process, until S&N shares were delisted from the London Stock Exchange on 28 April 2008, had three distinct phases: a first, tentative approach, when the leak and the first announcements took place; a second, three-month period when the arbitration proceedings were disclosed and tight-holding positioning on both sides was played out in the public eye, and a last, confidential third phase that culminated in the final acquisition of S&N by the Consortium.

In the summer of 2007 S&N said to the media that sales had been affected by poor summer weather in Europe and the new ban on smoking in English pubs.[2] The media duly reproduced this as seen in the following headlines:

> 'S&N profits suffer in the rain' (*Evening Standard*, 7 July)
>
> 'Rain dampens brewer's beer sales' (*BBC News*, 7 August)

However, S&N also said that it had seen sales increase in the region where S&N operated BBH, which it owned with Carlsberg. In September news of Carlsberg's interests leaked out. *The Financial Mail* resorted to background knowledge, the ancient confrontation between the Scots and the Danes, for its headline 'S&N mobilizes to fight Danes' (*Financial Mail*, 9 September). The news item reported that S&N was 'hatching secret plans to fend off a hostile takeover bid from Continental rival Carlsberg', and inserted two statements made by its chairman, that 'the speculation was hyped up', but, most interestingly, that they 'were not going to stand still […]. It is like an army, you don't publicize it until the last moment'.

This media speculation that Carlsberg was planning a break-up bid to take 100 per cent control of BBH prompted the first announcements related to the issue. The first one (see Table 16.1) was a formal Carlsberg response, confirming 'discussions' to form a consortium with rival Heineken to jointly purchase S&N (and consequently take BBH for itself).

S&N's first announcement (see Table 16.2) acted as a response and followed a similar generic structure: a first part which included Acknowledgment of Calsberg's

2 S&N had already expressed its concern for the consequences of the ban, as reported by the *Evening Standard* a few months earlier ('S&N warn of £10m blow from smoking ban' *Evening Standard*, 20 February 2007).

Table 16.1 Carlsberg and Heineken's first stock exchange announcement on 17 October 2007

Headline	CARLSBERG AND HEINEKEN RESPOND TO RECENT SHARE PRICE MOVEMENT OF SCOTTISH & NEWCASTLE PLC
Acknowledgement	Carlsberg A/S and Heineken N.V. **note** the recent share price movement of Scottish & Newcastle plc.
Confirmation/1	Carlsberg A/S and Heineken N.V. **confirm** that they are **in discussions** regarding **the formation of a consortium to make an offer** for the entire issued share capital of Scottish & Newcastle plc.
Confirmation/2	**To date no formal approach has been made to Scottish & Newcastle** and there can be no certainty that an offer for Scottish & Newcastle will ultimately be forthcoming.
Announcement	A further **announcement** will be made in due course.

Table 16.2 Scottish & Newcastle's first stock exchange announcement on 17 October 2007

Headline	SCOTTISH & NEWCASTLE PLC – ANNOUNCEMENT TO THE STOCK EXCHANGE
Acknowledgement	The Board of Scottish & Newcastle **notes today's announcement** by Heineken and Carlsberg regarding the formation of a consortium to make an offer for Scottish & Newcastle
Confirmation	and **confirms** that **the company has received no approach from them**.
Evaluation	**The proposed break-up bid** from Heineken and Carlsberg, the company's joint venture partner in BBH, **is unsolicited and unwelcome.**
Statement	S&N is **confident** in its **future** as an independent group with a combination of strong growth in emerging markets and cash generation in developed markets.
Recommendation	**S&N strongly urges shareholders to take no action at this time**.
Announcement	A further **announcement** will be made if appropriate.

announcement and Confirmation of lack of approach, followed by S&N's standing on the issue: Evaluation of the proposal as 'unsolicited and unwelcome' and a statement to confirm their position as 'confident in its future'.

As we can see, these first public announcements of the parties, both released on 17 October 2007, present very clear and consistent moves in their generic structure. They also show strong intertextuality, as texts that transform the recent past into the present (Candlin and Maley 1997), using the previous text produced by the other party. S&N's announcements were always rounded up by a permanent move of Recommendation, addressed to shareholders.

This first public interaction was reproduced in the media, who considered the move as a bid:

> 'Bid plan for Scottish & Newcastle' (*BBC News*, 17 October)

> 'Scottish & Newcastle approached with bid' (*Evening Standard*, 17 October)

On 23 October, S&N alleged that Carlsberg had acted against the best interests of BBH by misusing confidential information to launch a bid, and was therefore in violation of their joint venture agreement, under which Carlsberg was then obliged to sell its shares in BBH to S&N. Heineken responded that the claim 'had no merit'. Two days later Carlsberg made a first proposal of 720p per share, which was rejected and evaluated as 'unsolicited and derisory' by S&N's chairman. This increasing hostility was duly reproduced in the press:

> 'Row brews over Russian beer pact' (*BBC News*, 24 October)

> 'S&N turns down 'derisory' offer' (*BBC News*, 25 October)

> 'Scottish & Newcastle scorns £7bn offer' (*Evening Standard*, 25 October)

On 31 October, S&N announced initiation of arbitration proceedings. S&N reported that it had requested the arbitration tribunal in the Stockholm Chamber of Commerce to confirm that Carlsberg had breached agreements over its joint venture. S&N was working out a legal case whereby they could gain full control of BBH. Should the arbitration court side with S&N, the Danish brewer would be required to sell up its BBH assets under a 'shotgun mechanism' agreement, which requires either company to offer their shares to their partner if they wish to quit the joint venture. Later that day Carlsberg refuted S&N's claims as 'misguided', arguing that the shotgun mechanism was only applicable should a partner wish to leave the joint venture, and should not therefore be considered in the arbitration case. It received a wide coverage by the media:

> 'Bid target S&N takes Carlsberg to court' (*Evening Standard*, 31 October)

> 'S&N attempts to resolve Carlsberg Russian row. The UK brewer will try to settle the dispute through arbitration but the Danish group dismisses the allegations' (*Times Online*, 31 October)

> 'S&N wouldn't have begun action if they didn't think they had a case' (*The Scotland on Sunday*, 4 November)

The finance website *thisismoney.com* even decided to explain, in its '30-second guides', how arbitration works, with brief answers to four questions: 'What is it?' 'How does it work', 'What happens next?' and finally 'What's the relevance?' to which the answer was: 'Warring Scottish & Newcastle and Carlsberg are set to resolve a spat over their Russian joint venture this way'.[3] Carlsberg's CEO summarized the Consortium's standing:

> S&N's legal claims are spurious, without merit and a distraction to advancing discussions on the 720p proposal the Consortium made to S&N on 25 October.

From then until January 2008, S&N and the Consortium would produce 15 public announcements (seven and eight respectively), maintaining two conflicting positions: S&N would stick to the arbitration case and would urge shareholders 'to take no action', while gradually, the Consortium would increase its offer and urge S&N shareholders to direct the Board of S&N to enter into discussions. Each party's arguments are consistently rejected by the other party. Thus, the three consecutive proposals put forward by the Consortium, presented as 'full and fair' and 'very generous' in their announcements, are dismissed as 'wholly inadequate' by S&N. Similarly, the arbitration case, considered 'strong' and 'robust' by the British brewer, is seen as 'misguided and without merit', 'spurious', 'a smokescreen' and 'a step too far' by the Consortium.

As communication through the announcements grew more and more hostile, the strategy pursued by both parties was to make their arguments openly, by disclosing information. In other words, both the Consortium and S&N went totally public, fully immersed in a media battle: the former with its proposal and the latter with the arbitration case.

The Consortium, arguing that S&N's refusal was due to 'the Board's intransigence' and was 'ill-informed', advocated 'full transparency', because, they said, 'it is important that S&N shareholders are fully informed of the merits of the Increased Proposal':

> Following the S&N Board's cursory dismissal of the Consortium's initial proposal and their refusal to engage in discussions to date, the Consortium has decided to provide details of its increased and full and fair proposal directly to the market.

The announcement took several pages, setting out full details of their offer. In turn, S&N launched a counter-offensive by disclosing the full arbitration claim and the value of winning it in an extensive announcement and at a public presentation to analysts, investors and the media. The announcement even included a link to the company's website displaying a PowerPoint presentation summarizing the key points.[4] A direct quotation from S&N's chief executive stated the company's position:

---

3 See <http://www.thisismoney.co.uk/30-secondguides/article.html?in_article_id=425868&in_page_id=53611>, accessed 15 July 2011.

4 The text read: 'A copy of the slides from the meeting is available on the S&N website, www.scottish-newcastle.com' ('Scottish & Newcastle Plc ('Scottish & Newcastle',

> Carlsberg's desire to terminate the BBH joint venture by circumventing the BBH shareholders' agreement provides a huge opportunity for us to take control of BBH through a successful arbitration process.

Carlsberg's reaction[5] was to dismiss S&N's analysis of the arbitration case, arguing that the claims were 'based on flawed assumptions', for which reason, they asserted,

> Carlsberg is delighted that S&N has finally provided further details of its misguided claims [...] It is now very clear that the claims are frivolous and have absolutely no merit and will now therefore shortly request the arbitration tribunal to dismiss the case for being totally unfounded and to constitute a misuse of the arbitration process.

Furthermore, the Consortium explicitly addressed S&N shareholders, who 'should also be aware that such arbitration proceedings in Sweden typically take in excess of 12 months to reach a final conclusion'. Carlsberg said publicly that length of time is seen as a disadvantage in arbitration; in this case; time delay and consequently uncertainty could be a deadly weapon in the stock exchange.

The media coverage of this phase of the process showed that the arbitration case was considered more newsworthy than the proposals. Of the ten news items collected, published in different media from mid-November to mid-December, only two referred to the bid in their headlines: 'S&N rejects improved bid approach' (*BBC News*, 15 November), and 'Bid for S&N brewer turns hostile' (*BBC News*, 16 November). The rest dealt with the arbitration process, with headlines such as the following:

> 'Swedish official to rule on S&N Carlsberg row' (*Edinburgh Evening News*, 5 December)

> 'A tribunal chairman has been appointed to resolve a dispute between S&N and its possible new owner Carlsberg' (*Times Online*, 5 December)

> 'S&N seeks Russian resolution in Carlsberg war' (*The Times*, 5 December)

> 'Carlsberg warned over BBH data' (*The Times*, 6 December)

'S&N' Or The 'Company') BBH Arbitration Update'. 15 November 2007. Online at <http://archive.scottish-newcastle.com>, accessed 15 July 2011.

5 The Consortium made two announcements on the same day: 'Carlsberg A/S and Heineken N.V. – full and fair proposal made to Scottish & Newcastle PLC'. 15 November 2007, 07:35, and 'Carlsberg A/S ('Carlsberg') and Heineken N.V. ('Heineken') S&N Board's Intransigence Jeopardises Shareholder Value' 15 November 2007, 11:50. Online at <http://www.carlsberggroup.com/media>, accessed 15 July 2011.

The matter also deserved an editorial from *The Times* ('Brewing up nicely', 6 December), where it is described as 'a siege' of S&N by the Consortium, and a feature article on the *Sunday Herald* ('DouBle Agents in a Cold War') whose lead paragraph, referring to the famous detective portrayed by Scottish writer Ian Rankin, is worth quoting in full:

> This is one crime that Rebus would not be able to solve. The Edinburgh detective, quaffing a pint of Deuchars IPA in the Oxford Bar, knew all about human foibles. He knew how greed and jealousy can turn fair-weather friends into sworn enemies.[6]

The author described S&N as being 'in a fight for its survival' and hoped it would still be 'in one piece by the end of the arbitration'. There seemed to be an agreement in all the media that S&N was using the arbitration process to attempt to seize control of BBH, the joint venture. But S&N was adding pressure somewhere else as well. S&N requested a 'put up or shut up' deadline from the UK Takeover Panel, which then ruled that the Consortium had a deadline for any formal bid for S&N. This was published in the tabloid press with the following headline: 'Last orders for brewery bidders' (*The Sun*, 18 December).

On 3 January the two brewers confirmed that the Arbitration Institute of the Stockholm Chamber of Commerce had written to both parties, stating that a decision should be reached early that summer. The media translated the news to their readers:

> 'S&N awaits bid battle verdict' (*Financial Times*, 3 January)
>
> 'UK/DENMARK: Carlsberg, Scottish & Newcastle get arbitration decision date' (just-drinks.com, 3 January)

While both S&N and Carlsberg welcomed the letter, Carlsberg warned shareholders again that 'the standard timetable is routinely extended' and in practice cases of this nature 'typically take' twice as long.

Furthermore, as both parties certainly knew, in the Arbitration Institute of Stockholm the final award is not open to appeal. According to International Legal News:[7]

> The possibility to challenge the award before the national courts in Sweden is limited, and even when they are challenged and successfully submitted to trial

6 Kemp, Kenny. 'Double Agents in a Cold War' *Sunday Herald*, 24 November 2007. Online at <http://www.sundayherald.com/misc/print.php?artid=1857567>, accessed 15 July 2011.

7 *International Legal News*,, 20 June 2006. Online at <http://www.imakenews.com/iln/e_article000602946.cfm?x=b11,0>, accessed 20 July 2011.

> under the Svea Court of Appeal, the appeal court has been proven reluctant to set aside an arbitral award or declare it invalid.

Consequently, the arbitral decision was perceived by both parties to be the key to the future of the bid. Then it was the moment for S&N to add pressure by unveiling the 15-page arbitration claim, which was distributed by *Reuters*, the international news service ('Value to S&N of winning the BBH Arbitration', 8 January). The claims were reworded as 'ambitions' ('S&N detail joint venture arbitration ambitions') on the branch website Beveragedaily.com (9 January 2008).

The Consortium's immediate reaction was to publicize a third 'materially improved proposal' of 780 pence per share, to which S&N responded, in a friendlier tone, that they had considered it 'carefully', but still, 'it failed to reflect the unique strengths of the company' and, in a sudden change of gear, declared to be 'prepared to engage only when a firm proposal of at least 800 pence per share had been made'. As the *Financial Times* summarized:

> 'S&N waits for better offer' (*Financial Times*, 16 January).

On 17 January 2007 what had been a three-month-long public clash made a U-turn when both parties made twin announcements: 'Scottish & Newcastle enters into discussions with Carlsberg and Heineken'. Below the same headline there appeared the same brief statement: 'S&N and the Consortium confirm that they have entered into discussions in relation to a possible recommended offer for S&N at 800 pence per share'. From this date until the acquisition was completed, on 28 April, the 16 announcements (eight each) released from both parties explaining the legal process would be identical.

The media understood that S&N had 'reversed an earlier stand', and had the fact summarized in the headline: 'Scottish & Newcastle in talks on Carlsberg–Heineken takeover' (*London-AFP,* 17 January). At the end of the report there appeared the only reference to arbitration that is to be found from this date, which is described as 'a spat', that is, a short and unimportant argument:

> [...] Thursday's statement gave no update on the ongoing spat between S&N and Carlsberg over their joint Russian venture Baltic Beverages Holding [...]

Once they had reached an agreement, they went confidential. No more updates on the arbitration case, not one single mention to it in the announcements. The case can be said to belong to that 25 per cent of cases which, according to PricewaterhouseCoopers (2008), are settled before an arbitral award is rendered.

Using arbitration, BBH turned into a bargaining counter in S&N's takeover defence. The threat of not winning the arbitration case caused the Consortium to raise and re-raise its offers from the initial 720 pence per share to a 750p, then 780p, and finally to 800p, something that experts say is rather unusual when no other party is involved.

Recapitulation

The offer worked outside the formal framework of the takeover code (as ruled by the London Takeover Panel). The consortium's offer was leaked, and negotiations were then conducted publicly. As Peter Kennerly, S&N's company secretary and general counsel, declared in an interview published by *The Lawyer*, 'It was similar to a risky game of corporate chess, played out in the public eye' (thelawyer.com, 12 May 2008).

Publicity was exploited in two different ways: The Consortium pressed S&N by urging the company's shareholders to take action by disclosing full details of their different proposals and giving a full account of what they thought about the arbitration claims and the Consortium's confidence in their policy. In contrast, S&N based its strategy on the publicity of the arbitration case, giving full details of the proceedings and the benefits of winning the case. Instead of dealing directly with the Consortium, S&N dealt with its lawyers. In both strategies the key issue is publicity in their negotiations. Once the fierce controversy vanished, confidentiality was restored. Confidentiality acted as a tool, not as a principle or a duty. It was purely instrumental.

One question which is rather difficult to answer deals with the choice of jurisdiction in this particular arbitration case: Why the Institute of Stockholm and not the London Court? One interpretation would see it as having something to do with the rules in Sweden. The Rules of the Arbitration Institute of Stockholm only provide that the Institute and the Arbitral Tribunal, rather than the parties, must maintain confidentiality in Arbitration:

> Art. 9: The SCC Institute shall maintain the confidentiality of the arbitration and shall deal with the arbitration in an impartial practical and expeditious manner.

The position in Sweden is that an express agreement of the parties in the matter is essential for a duty of obligation to confidentiality in arbitration proceedings. Furthermore, the disclosure of information about the dispute may be necessary in some circumstances. Thomson and Finn (2007) summarize the cases in which public interest has to be recognized:

> One of the parties may conclude that its commercial interests and the interests of shareholders and potential shareholders would be enhanced by publicly disclosing information about the dispute and any resulting award and that, accordingly, it has a duty to make such disclosure.

There is an antecedent known as the *Bulbank* case. In 2000 the Swedish Supreme Court in *Bulgarian Foreign Trade v. Al Trade Finance* drew a distinction between the privacy of arbitral proceedings and the existence of a separate duty of confidentiality regarding the disclosure of documents and information emanating from arbitration. As Dundas (2004) explains, there is no inherent confidentiality obligation in arbitration in Swedish law particularly when the public's legitimate interest prevails:

> Disclosure to investors of the result but not the substance of the arbitration had been necessary, analogous to disclosure to shareholders in a company if an arbitration had a material impact upon its accounts; there could be no breach of duty in disclosing the fact of commencement of arbitration, the existence of an arbitration or the result of that arbitration where there was any legitimate reason to do so.

Disclosure to shareholders may be necessary if arbitration has a material impact on their accounts. The lack of confidentiality in the present case under study could be seen as fully justified in the interests of S&N shareholders. What is more, the continuous messages of S&N and the Consortium to S&N shareholders in their announcements were not only aimed at complying with transparency requirements but also, and most importantly, to direct their course of action. As Kian Ganz wrote in *The Lawyer*:

> 'Their defence of S&N is likely to live on as a textbook case of maximising shareholder value' (thelawyer.com, 12 May 2008).

A few weeks before S&N shares were delisted, *The Sunday Times* published a feature article where the chief executive of S&N, John Dunsmore, gave his version of the story. The article displayed the following headline: 'How I squeezed Carlsberg dry'. Reproduced below are some extracts of this long interview:

> Dunsmore thinks the key to the defence was an arbitration case on the future ownership of BBH. [...] When the bid battle got underway, Dunsmore admits it was far from clear how crucial it would be. 'We did a presentation on November 20 where we outlined our strategy and if you look at the arbitration case presented then, it doesn't stand up very well', he said. [...] He argues that the battle swung S&N's way because Carlsberg could not take the risk of losing the case because, if it did so, it would cede ownership of any stake in BBH. 'That was not a legitimate risk that any bidder could take'.[8]

The media also followed what we could see as a three-move structure in their coverage of the whole story. First they unveiled a plot that was being hatched, then they reported on every step taken by each party in the process, and eventually, they tried to explain what had happened, when all the dealings were done. They were the hands that opened the floodgates and closed them down.

8 Goodman, Matthew. 'How I squeezed Carlsberg dry', *The Sunday Times*, 6 April 2008.

What is of interest here is the way the reader was presented with arbitration. In terms of its lexicalization, that is, how this legal technique is encapsulated in lexical labels, we can see that the words used also underwent a transformation. It was first referred to, neutrally, as a dispute, to then move on to being described as 'a legal battle', 'a power struggle', 'a row', and, eventually, 'a war', when hostility was at its peak. Once the parties were 'in talks', it became 'a spat'.

In terms of its journalistic functionality as having news value, as soon as it came on stage as the core of the matter, it was consistently foregrounded in the majority of news reports; however, when the parties actually reached an agreement for the acquisition, entered into private discussions and ignored the arbitration process, it was totally excluded from coverage. It was not newsworthy any more. Not even to state that, presumably, it was no longer necessary.

In terms of its functionality as a legal technique, arbitration was not only portrayed in the media as a means to solve a dispute, but also as a key strategy to obtain an advantageous cash offer. The media were perfectly aware of that use of arbitration. What remains uncertain is whether the media ever perceived that they had also been used by the corporations. The media coverage brought pressure to bear on both parties to resolve the situation.

International commercial arbitration (ICA) as we now understand it is a by-product of economic globalization. The global demand for information and the new media technologies have reached ICA, and, in information-rich times, the processes are becoming more and more accessible and hence less difficult to keep confidential. In other words, they are more visible. Despite acknowledging the need of disclosure if required by the public interest, some practitioners have seen this development as 'erosion on the concept of confidentiality' (Blackaby et al. 2009: 143) and, as Dundas (2004) does in this statement, argue against the present trend towards transparency in arbitration and blames the new global communication technology for it:

> The internet has undoubtedly and regrettably played a role in the wider dissemination of material which should properly have remained confidential.

The truth of the matter is that arbitration cannot swim against the tide, and, as Bhatia et al. (2009) point out, 'The general principle of confidentiality is giving way to transparency'. Two consequences may be taken from this inevitable trend: first, that transparency may be *used* for other 'private' intentions and second, the more transparent the process is, the more it is paving the path for a growing concern for its public image and its impact in the public eye.

Acknowledgments

I would like to acknowledge project FFI2009-09792, funded by the Spanish Ministerio de Ciencia e Innovación (Secretaría de Estado de Investigación), and also an international research project funded by the Research Grants Council of the Government of HKSAR [Project No. 9041191 (CityU 1501/06H)] entitled *International Commercial Arbitration Practices: A Discourse Analytical Study* (see <http://www.english.cityu.edu.hk/arbitration/>).

References

Beechey, John (2009): Foreword. Confidentiality in Arbitration, *ICC International Court of Arbitration Bulletin*, Special Supplement.

Berwin, Stanley J. and Baruti, Rukla (2009): *Confidentiality in International Arbitration*. Online at <http://www.lexology.com/library>, accessed 20 July 2011.

Bhatia, Vijay K. (2009): Interdiscursive Colonization of International Commercial Arbitration Practice: Accesibility of Data in Critical Genre Analysis. *5th International Symposium on Genre Studies, SIGET*, Caixas Do Sul, Brazil, 11–14 August 2009.

Bhatia, Vijay K., Candlin, Christopher N. and Engberg, Jan (2008): Concepts, Contexts and Procedures in Arbitration Discourse. In Bhatia, Vijay K., Candlin, Christopher N. and Engberg, Jan (Eds), *Legal Discourse across Cultures and Systems*, Hong Kong, Hong Kong University Press, 3–31.

Bhatia, Vijay K., Candlin, Christopher N. and Sharma, Rajesh (2009): Confidentiality and Integrity in International Commercial Arbitration Practice, *Arbitration*, Vol. 75, 2–13.

Blackaby, Nigel, Partasides, Constantine, Redfern, Alan, and Hunter, Martin (2009): *Redfern and Hunter on International Arbitration*, Oxford, Oxford University Press.

Brown, Alexis C. (2001): Presumption Meets Reality: An Exploration of the Confidentiality Obligation in International Commercial Arbitration, *American University International Law Review*, Vol. 16, No. 4, 969–1025.

Candlin, Christopher N. and Maley, Yon (1997): Intertextuality and Interdiscursivity in the Discourse of Alternative Dispute Resolution. In Gunnarsson, Britte-Louise, Linell, Per and Nordberg Bengt (Eds) *The Construction of Professional Discourse*, London, Longman, 201–22.

Dundas, Hew R. (2004): Confidentiality Rules OK? Recent Developments Affecting the Confidentiality of Arbitrations, *Transnational Dispute Management*, Vol. 1, No. 2. Online at <http://www.transnational-dispute-management.com/samples/freearticles/tv1-2-article24b.htm>, accessed 20 July 2011.

Fortier, Yves L. (1999): The Occasionally Unwarranted Assumption of Confidentiality, *Arbitration International*, Vol. 15, No. 1, 131–40.

Knorr Cetina, Karim (2007): Global Markets as Global Conversations, *Text & Talk*, Vol. 27, No. 5/6, 705–34.

PricewaterhouseCoopers (2008): *International Arbitration: Corporate Attitudes and Practices*, London.

Thomson, Claude R. (2007): Confidentiality in Arbitration: A VALID ASSUMPTION? A PROPOSED SOLUTION! *Dispute Resolution Journal*. Online at <http://findarticles.com/p/articles/mi_qa3923/is_200705/ai_n19435153/>, accessed on 20 July 2011.

PART III
Prospects and Conclusions

Chapter 17

Contested Identities in International Arbitration Practice[1]

Vijay K. Bhatia, Christopher N. Candlin and Maurizio Gotti

Overview

International commercial arbitration (ICA), as proposed by the United Nations Commission on International Trade Law (UNCITRAL), was established by the United Nations General Assembly by its Resolution 2205 (XXI) of 17 December 1966 'to promote the progressive harmonization and unification of international trade law'. The UN commission prepared a model law on ICA, which was adopted by the United Nations General Assembly on 21 June 1985, and was recommended for adoption as the UNCITRAL Model Law (ML) on ICA. Although the ML was not binding, the UN recommended its adoption and incorporation into the domestic law of individual member states. The ML was intended to promote the adoption of arbitration as an alternative to litigation to resolve commercial disputes in cross-border contexts, and was also meant to lead to the integration of the processes and procedures across legal systems. It is interesting to note that participants in most ICA cases often come from different linguistic, ethnic, cultural, jurisdictional and even technical backgrounds, speaking different languages.

Today, international arbitration is one of the most widely used alternative dispute resolution (ADR) methods to resolve commercial disputes. It crucially depends on the parties' agreement to resolve disputes through private adjudication by a single arbitrator, or a tribunal of more than one, appointed in accordance with rules of a specific arbitration institution that the parties themselves have agreed to adopt, usually by including an arbitration clause in their contract. The practice of international arbitration has developed in a manner to resolve the disputes with little interference by the courts.

In arbitration, parties or their representatives, often legal counsels, present a dispute to an impartial arbitrator or a tribunal to resolve it and order a decision, known as award in arbitration, which is legally binding and is generally non-

1 This work is supported by a grant from the RGC (Hong Kong SAR) project No. 9041191 (CityU 1501/06H)] entitled, *International Commercial Arbitration Practice: A Discourse Analytical Study*. For details, see the website: <http://www.english.cityu.edu.hk/ arbitration/>.

appealable in a court of law. In arbitration, the parties at dispute have considerable input in the selection of arbitration tribunal, and also in the choice of procedures they would like the tribunal to follow, including the choice of the seat of arbitration, as well as the arbitration rules in terms of which the resolution is negotiated.

Arbitration is thus the most appropriate form of ADR mechanism when the disputing parties fail to resolve their dispute on their own, and want a third party to suggest the resolution of their dispute, and at the same time, when they would like to avoid the time and expense of litigation over which decision-making process they have absolutely no control. As mentioned earlier, the decision of the arbitration tribunal is enforceable and cannot be challenged in a court of law, except on procedural grounds under a very restricted set of conditions. So, the main advantage of arbitration is that it is like litigation in effect, in that it is decided by a neutral arbitrator or arbitration tribunal, but unlike litigation, it is claimed to be informal, expedient, economical, private and confidential in nature, and at the same time, gives sufficient voice and freedom to disputing parties in the way it is actually conducted. The main benefits of arbitration as an 'alternative to litigation' are seen as the following:

- Speedy resolution of disputes: Disputes through arbitration can be resolved in a matter of weeks or months rather than years, as is often the case in litigation.
- Economy of costs: Disputes through arbitration can be resolved at a small fraction of the cost that such disputes may incur in the court of law.
- Privacy and confidentiality: Disputing parties can be assured that all the details concerning the dispute, such as the documents, the amount of dispute, the testimony of specialists, and even the final outcome of the dispute, that is, the award, will remain confidential. The duty of confidentiality is often taken as given in most dispute-resolving arbitration processes.
- Enforcement of awards: Since arbitration is a form of private adjudication, one may obtain the impression that the final outcome will not have the same power of enforcement that is often associated with a court judgment; however, the fact is that arbitration awards have equal, if not more, enforcement value even across jurisdictional borders. This is one of the most attractive aspects ICA practice.
- Limited interference from courts: Courts have no role to play; in fact, they often are supportive of arbitration as it tends to reduce the heavy load of pending court cases.
- Expertise of arbitrators: In arbitration, one does not need to have any legal qualification to become an arbitrator, so this opens up the possibility of having a specialist in the area of dispute act as arbitrator. For instance, if a dispute is about a shipping matter, one may choose a shipping expert as arbitrator (or one of the arbitrators) rather than a legal expert.
- Flexibility of procedures: Unlike litigation, arbitration allows parties to choose whatever manner in which they want the arbitration process to be

conducted, especially in the choice of arbitrators, the seat of arbitration, the duty of privacy and confidentiality, and the mode of delivery of the final award.

- Party participation: Disputing parties are free to participate in the arbitration process, either directly or through their counsels, in a more informal manner than that which is available through court procedures.
- Freedom to customize arbitration process: This is particularly true of the choice of any language, constitution of the arbitration tribunal, and the number of arbitrators and the rules of arbitration.
- Assistance from arbitration centers: Parties can obtain substantial assistance and advice from arbitration centres in terms of the choice of arbitrators, rules of arbitration, infrastructural requirements, such as the informality of court settings, recording facility, production of documents and so on.

Issues

Although the outcome of arbitration is considered final and enforceable across jurisdictions and regions, parties at dispute often look for opportunities to go to court if and when the outcome is not to their liking. To make this strategically possible, they often choose legal experts as arbitrators, rather than specialists in the area of dispute, (despite the provision indicated above) as they are believed to be likely to be more accomplished in exploiting opportunities to challenge an award. This leads to a large-scale involvement of legal experts as counsels and arbitrators, which tends to make arbitration very much similar to litigation. In this context, Arthur Marriott in his 2005 Clayton UTZ Lecture rightly points out:

> Although the 1996 Act gave arbitrators very considerable power over the running of an arbitration and greater confidence in their autonomy, my sense is that they are not really producing radically new procedures more efficient and prompt than hitherto. The English passive tradition dies hard and self-interest is a dominant factor. The practitioners dominate the arbitral processes in the same way as they have dominated litigation, and to the same end.

Nariman (2000: 262), one of the most well-established international arbitrators, goes even further when he emphasizes that, 'International Commercial Arbitration has become almost indistinguishable from litigation, which it was at one time intended to supplant'. Similarly, Kerr (1997) claims that international arbitration seems to have acquired the pejorative sobriquet, *arbitigation*, which signals large-scale 'judicialization' of arbitration.

This overwhelming influence of litigation over arbitration results in an increasing mixture of discourses and contested professional identities as arbitration becomes, as it were, 'colonized' by litigation practices, threatening to undermine the integrity of arbitration practice, and thus compromising the spirit of arbitration as a non-legal practice. However, there is very little research evidence for such impressions and observations, except the opinions and statements from experts in the field, as indicated in the preceding statements from members of the arbitration community. It is interesting to note that the PricewaterhouseCoopers (2006: 17) study of *International Arbitration: Corporate Attitudes and Practices* reveals the need for 'a wider pool of arbitrators, with specialization or expertise in the subject matter of the dispute', in particular, their specialization in the industry sector, their regional or country experience, and their cross-disciplinary expertise, for example, technical or financial background. The study conclusively claims that arbitrators with these skills will save their corporations time and money. However, in practice, the appropriation of arbitration practice by litigation experts continues, and arbitration, as a non-legal practice, continues to be influenced by litigation practice, a development which seems to be contrary to the spirit of arbitration to resolve disputes outside of the courts.

Contested Identities

Discourses in professional contexts are quite strategically drawn upon to represent and realize a number of different identities, which may include any of the following:

- Corporate Identity
- Organizational and Institutional Identity
- Regional, National, Cultural or Ethnic Identity
- Disciplinary Identity
- Professional Identity
- Jurisdictional Identity
- Individual Identity

However, in the discourse, and particularly in the discursive and professional practice of arbitration in international contexts, we may additionally find various representations of what we would like to call 'jurisdictional' identity. The research on which this chapter is based clearly highlights strong and marked contestations based on various kinds of identities discussed above, which can be narrowed down to professional, disciplinary, jurisdictional and individual, because of the involvement of two rather different though overlapping juridical practices (litigation and arbitration), two or more disciplinary concerns (legal, commercial, and other content areas of disputes), at least two jurisdictions (common law and civil law), and at least two main categories of participant, viz. specialist (lawyers) and lay (witnesses).

In the light of this background, there seems to be a need for an evidence-based investigation of the extent to which arbitration practices are indeed influenced by litigation procedures and practices. The international project funded by the Research Grants Council HKSAR under their Competitive Earmarked Research Grant, entitled *International Commercial Arbitration Practice: A Discourse Analytical Study*, which has been undertaken in collaboration with more than 20 international teams of researchers, drawn both from the legal and arbitration practice, as well as from discourse analysis, is an effort in this direction. One of the key objectives of this project has been to investigate the 'integrity' of the current international arbitration practices by analyzing various sets of complementary textual, narrative and discourse data to investigate the extent to which arbitration practices have been interdiscursively influenced by litigation practices, especially in terms of the intention and purpose of arbitration practice, the processes and procedures that are adopted, and also the shared expertise expected on the part of the participants in specific cases. In order to achieve these objectives, the project has drawn upon a multi-perspectival and multidimensional genre analytical framework (Bhatia 2004, 2010; Candlin 1997, 2006; Candlin and Crichton 2011; Crichton 2010) to integrate analyses of data collected from at least three different sources:

- intertextual and interdiscursive relationships among discursive practices in arbitration;
- narratives of experience of key practitioners as tested against those of other stakeholders;
- analyses of critical moments (Candlin 1987) in the discourses of arbitration practice.

Although the boundaries between arbitration and litigation practices are frequently blurred, it is possible to take advantage of such blurring by reflexively seeking confirmations of the communicative characteristics of the arbitration process by testing practitioner hypotheses against other practitioners' experiences and against the actualities of interaction in 'critical sites of engagement' (Scollon 1998: 27), and perhaps at 'critical moments of interaction' (Candlin 1987). In doing so, we have drawn on Goffman's *dramaturgical* theory (1959) of 'on-stage' and 'off-stage' performance to reconstruct and investigate the extent to which the 'integrity' of arbitration practices is maintained in international commercial contexts. Goffman believed that we perform on the front-stage according to our assigned role in a specific professional context, and this often does not reflect our true self because this role is assigned to us by our profession. On the other hand, we also perform off-stage, which is closer to our true self, as we assume this role by choice (cf. also Roberts and Sarangi 1999, for further discussion). The data used in the project represents both 'on-stage' performance and 'off-stage' perceptions of experienced practitioners in arbitration.

Sites of Contestation

In what follows, we would like to identify and highlight some of the key sites identified in the process of ICA practice in which instances of contested identities and the resulting interdiscursive tensions tend to undermine the integrity of arbitration as a non-legal practice, and discuss the extent to which arbitration is being 'colonized' as it were by litigation. Some of these sites of engagement are the following:

1. discovery procedures;
2. written testimony;
3. witness examination;
4. writing of awards.

Discovery Procedures

One of the most contested sites of engagement in ICA practice is the use (or is it abuse?) of the discovery procedure. It offers an interesting site for the study of an interdiscursive phenomenon across professional, jurisdictional, linguistic and cultural boundaries. It is contentious not only because it is shared across two rather distinct professional practices, that is, litigation and arbitration, bringing together international participants, particularly stakeholders who carry their individual, disciplinary and jurisdictional baggage in the form of different ethnic and cultural backgrounds, languages, as well as interdisciplinary expertise, but also because it brings into focus the tension between two distinct legal systems and cultures, that is, common law culture and the civil law culture.

As pointed out earlier, legal counsels experienced in litigation are being increasingly hired to represent party positions in ICA disputes, and they invariably assume that the discovery process in commercial arbitration will be the same as in litigation, with which they are very familiar. American counsels, for instance, often assume that the discovery and deposition procedures will allow evidence and witnesses to be examined before trial. However, the experienced civil law counsels expect each party to produce a limited range of documents relevant to the case without any need for discovery through direct witness examination. Unfortunately, the outcomes are most often swayed by the legal background of the participants, arbitrators as well as legal counsels, though more often pushing the evidence-gathering processes towards increasing judicialization of arbitration practice. Legal counsels, even arbitrators involved in ICA, tend to follow familiar procedures of litigation to conduct arbitration. Some even assume that arbitration is just another form of litigation, which Walter (2001) refers to as 'private litigation', thus creating conditions for contested disciplinary identities.

In most cases, however, it is generally expected that the parties will prepare for inspection all the documents considered relevant to the issues in a particular arbitration dispute. In cross-jurisdictional arbitration trials, it is expected that the parties will cooperate in the discovery of evidence either by limited examination of the witnesses through oral testimony, or by submission of written documents. Some practitioners, especially those from a common law background, believe that without some form of discovery, however limited, there is a risk that the hearing may not lead to a reasonable conclusion, because they think it important that evidence must be presented to parties before they respond to it. In most cases, however, tribunals discourage lengthy and irrelevant discovery. This and other related issues are generally addressed and negotiated at the preparatory phase of an arbitration trial. Although it is sometimes possible to have some discovery in ICA even within a civil law jurisdiction, a typical American-style discovery in common law tradition is less likely to be allowed. Reed (2010) seems to blame any form of elaborate discovery on the legal counsels, especially those from the US.

> A recent study of the Corporate Counsel International Arbitration Group (CCIAG) found that 100 per cent of the corporate counsel participants believe that international arbitration 'takes too long' (with 56 per cent of those surveyed strongly agreeing) and 'costs too much' (with 69 per cent strongly agreeing). Many people blame it on outside counsel – especially those from the US – for requesting too many documents, making too many motions and generally filing too many pages. Others blame in-house counsel for not using their authority to rein in practices they criticize as inefficient or wasteful. And some blame the arbitral institutions themselves for not constructing a system that reins in everyone.

However, it is possible to discern some sort of consensus emerging in favour of a trend to prefer the use of documents, witness statements, site inspections and expert views, rather than the American-style depositions, which are generally dispreferred, except in exceptional circumstances.

Divergent Practices across Jurisdictions Just as discovery is an unfamiliar practice in civil law jurisdictions, the use of written witness testimony is unnerving for common law practitioners. If parties and counsels from civil law jurisdictions do not feel comfortable with the prospect of discovery in arbitration proceedings, American counsels equally dislike conducting cross-examination based only on written statements. The heavy use of written evidence in international arbitration reflects the distinct influence of civil law tradition, whereas discovery is seen as a distinct American practice. In the civil law tradition, evidence is often presented in written form, and the questioning of witnesses is conducted not by the legal counsel, but rather by the arbitrator or the arbitration tribunal. Direct examination of witnesses is generally not permitted in arbitration, especially if the tribunal is dominated by specialists from the civil law jurisdictions.

Another area of contentious procedures is the view of arbitration as an adversarial or consensual dispute resolution process. The rules and procedures in international arbitration reflect a mixture of common law and civil law norms; however, the system is increasingly evolving in the common law direction that favours the adversarial process. Drawing on her data gathered from Singapore, Kathpalia (this volume) points out the distinction between litigation and other forms of dispute resolution processes in the following terms:

> The main distinction between litigation and these three forms of dispute resolution methods (meaning arbitration, mediation and conciliation) is that they are not supposed to be adversarial (Tan and Lee-Patridge 2000). Comparing arbitration and litigation, the former is a private out-of-court settlement between two parties who have agreed to accept the decision of an appointed arbitrator, whereas in the latter, the dispute is resolved by the court. According to Tay (1998), the two processes that distinguish it from litigation are the fact that it is private and consensual.

The concept of adversarial witness examination is drawn from the common law approach, and requires extensive training and practice, neither of which civil law counsels receive in their legal training. Therefore, arbitrators from the US and the UK are generally at a competitive advantage. Gabriël Moens, a well-known arbitration practitioner and trainer from common law background, when asked about arbitration as adversarial practice in a special interview conducted within the framework of this project, claimed, 'You must remember that your client who is paying you money is sitting behind you or even at the same table, and they want you to do your very best for them […] and therefore I find that it is definitely an adversarial process. If I am involved in it, I use it as an adversarial process'. In spite of consistent efforts on the part of scholars and practitioners in arbitration, the process of discovery and information gathering in ICA still remains contentious across professions and disciplines, on the one hand, and jurisdictions, on the other. Even in written testimonies, we find contested identities, though of a different kind, to which we will now turn.

Written Testimonies

In courtroom examination, particularly in common law jurisdictions, there is a general perception that defendants have no voice of their own because it is often manipulated by legal counsels. The issue thus is 'how much of a witness testimony is presented by the witness, and how much by the counsel?'. If this is really so, then it is necessary to ask, 'whose narrative is unfolded in the court', which presupposes that the witness, and not the counsel, is the real presenter of evidence. In ICA, one may also legitimately ask, 'Who is responsible for written statements?' Often the witness provides the facts and the counsel constructs a statement based on the submitted facts. Written narratives from witnesses thus often become repetitive accounts of their factual positions, thereby removing in the process individual identities of the witnesses almost in every statement. This raises an interesting issue, that is, to what extent the individual identity of the witness is crucial for the maintenance of integrity of witness examination, which is invariably lost in written testimony as it is written by the counsel. One may justify this action by the counsels by arguing that witness statements need to be intertextually referenced to the documents submitted by the parties, and this kind of intertextuality (Bhatia 2004) can be adequately and meaningfully provided by the counsels. One may also argue that oral testimonies by witnesses are likely to be more time consuming than the written testimonies by witnesses, and since legal counsels may have a much better understanding of the issues at stake in a particular dispute, it is time saving then to allow counsels to write witness statements than asking witnesses to do it on their own. This again brings direct witness examination in arbitration and litigation somewhat closer to each other. Another concern that disputing parties have is that the counsels have the ability to take out any weak points to limit unnecessary exposure to negative and hence damaging aspects of their case in cross-examination. Although written testimony drafted by legal counsels can be strategically more useful in avoiding unnecessary cross-examination, there is no doubt that counsel written witness testimonies invariably reflect contesting identities of witnesses and counsels.

Witness Examination

As discussed earlier, cross-examination following written submissions presents unique challenges to arbitrators from common law tradition because they are trained to conduct cross-examination after they have conducted the oral testimony (Rubinstein 2004). Written disclosures are restricted and are carefully constructed by legal counsels, and hence provide limited opportunities for cross-examination. Although ICA does allow parties to choose procedures that best suit a particular case and are agreed to by both the parties, the very flexibility in the choice of procedures and processes itself becomes a challenge for arbitrators as they need to agree on a common strategy acceptable to both the parties at dispute. The real problem is in cases where you have arbitrators or legal counsels from two different jurisdictions, one preferring written testimony and the other arguing, on the contrary, for oral witness examination. Even in cases where all the parties agree to allow written testimonies followed by some witness examination and cross-examination, one is likely to observe the tension between witness examination procedures adopted by counsels and arbitrators not only from different jurisdictions, but also, and perhaps more importantly, by the counsels from the same jurisdiction, especially those from common law backgrounds. Let us now highlight some of the important aspects of tension in witness examination in litigation and international arbitration.

Courtroom examination generally consists of direct examination or what is also called 'examination in chief', cross-examination, re-examination, and also a possible examination by judge for clarification, if required. The direct examination is often viewed as a procedure intended to secure trust of the court. To facilitate this, the counsel for witness often gives an opportunity to his or her own witness for an uninterrupted narrative account of events, even though leading questions are generally not allowed. In cross-examination, on the other hand, witnesses are invariably controlled by the counsel and all forms of coercive questioning strategies are used without any hesitation, unless they are seen to elicit irrelevant and inappropriate testimony. Cross-examination thus is regarded as a crucial weapon in the armoury of the counsel not only to test the accuracy of evidence revealed in direct examination but also, and perhaps more importantly, to challenge the testimony as well as the credibility of the witness (Du Cann 1964). The best-known purpose of cross-examination is testing the credibility of the witness. However, there can be a number of other purposes as well; for example, to provide a more complete story than the edited one presented on direct examination, to explore weakness in the logic of the opponent's case, and to gain concessions about facts (Cymrot 2007), thereby making them irrefutable as far as possible. Cross-examination thus is seen as a strategically powerful resource in litigation as well as in arbitration (Bhatia 2011). A Supreme Court judge once described (as reported in Cymrot 2007) a successful cross-examination as a process to 'ooze out' of the witness the desired testimony 'drop by drop'. As in litigation, cross-examination seeks to destroy the credibility of witnesses in ICA as well. As Schneider (2009: 2) quite appropriately points out:

> Cross-examination, as it is generally practiced in the courts of common law countries, seeks to destroy the witness' credibility, to make the witness confirm propositions of the examiner and often to achieve both these objectives. [...] While counsels in international arbitration often do not apply these techniques in the same manner, their principal objectives generally remain the same.

As a consequence, arbitrators, especially from the common law tradition, feel that, despite the divergent practices across different jurisdictions, good cross-examination techniques are becoming increasingly important. Ong (2007: 2), talking about the importance of cross-examination in ICA claims:

> Due to the emphasis on the written word, good cross-examination techniques are now even more important in assisting counsels to tip the balance between winning and losing a case. [...] Despite the divergence in theories as to the meaning or function of cross-examination, it is now almost universally accepted that the main purpose of cross- examination is to weaken or discredit the evidence that has been given by opposing witnesses.

One of the major differences in courtroom trials and arbitration trials is that the courtroom setting is invariably very formal, where the judge is found in formal robes, and witnesses are separated and systematically constrained on the witness stand. The counsels can freely move about to make witnesses uncomfortable. All these institutionalized features of the courtroom context are deliberately introduced to indicate the seriousness of purpose of courtroom trials. As compared with this, arbitration trials often take place in less formal settings, which may not encourage a rigorous cross-examination (Newman 1999). Moreover, business people are likely to be more comfortable in relatively informally organized conference room settings, in which the positioning of witness in relation to the counsel is less intimidating. However, when it comes to the use of strategies in cross-examination, they tend to remain more or less the same, especially in common law jurisdictions. This raises another important issue, that is, to what extent the legal, arbitration, and business communities have shared perspectives on witness examination in ICA?

As mentioned earlier, the use of written statements in place of direct testimony is often a foreign concept to common law counsels who are trained to rely upon oral testimony for the presentation of evidence (Newman 1999). In contrast, the civil law judicial system does not put as much evidentiary weight on oral testimony (Tallerico and Behrendt 2002). This jurisdictional and cultural background plays an important role in witness examination in ICA, especially in cross-examination, which becomes a potential source of conflict. Under the common law system, especially the American system, cross-examination is considered an important aspect of trial, as it provides a testing ground for oral evidence, whether in the law court or in ICA. The real trust and credibility in the testimony is essentially established in the cross-examination of a particular witness. On the other hand, arbitrators trained in the civil law tradition do not regard oral testimony favourably. It is sometimes seen as 'a process of trickery to confuse witnesses'. Newman (1999: cited in Tallerico and Behrendt (2002: 15)) points out:

> Civil Law system considers the concept of oral testimony with scepticism, and cross-examination with animosity. [...] Within the European context, American and English cross-examination is viewed as a process of trickery designed to confuse witnesses rather than to elicit vital information.

David Wagoner, an experienced arbitrator in a specialist interview, pointed out that like litigation, in arbitration also the witnesses are prepared to testify and some practitioners believe that it is a fair game.

> In the major cases rightly or wrongly, the key witnesses are prepared to testify, and that's accepted now in the international arbitration, it's accepted in litigation. That doesn't mean you tell them how to testify, but you tell them what the issues are so you get them thinking about the issues, what the alternatives are, and then you get them to testify. And that's fair game I think. So in general, I would say there's less cross-examination in international arbitration, but who's going to do it? In my Swiss case, the chair did it all, just as a judge in Switzerland would do, or in Germany. In the US they never do it, almost never.

Since arbitration tribunals have been given considerable flexibility almost in all jurisdictions to decide on procedural matters in consultation with the disputing parties, it is possible for them to rule in favour of or against direct testimony in the form of written statements. A tribunal from common law jurisdiction might go for oral testimony whereas the one from civil law may choose the written statements instead. Whatever the context, one might consider oral face-to-face direct examination of witnesses to elicit a more accurate and truthful witness testimony as compared with the written witness statement, which is more likely to offer a carefully drafted testimony by the legal counsel rather than a truthful and genuine testimony by a witness. It is difficult to preserve the integrity of true witness testimony if legal counsels are involved in the process.

Cross-examination can be time-consuming, in that it can focus on trivial inconsistencies sometimes at the cost of the real issue under consideration, and may even overshadow the role of the arbitrator. On the other hand, cross-examination can expose a lying witness, weakness in logic or inaccuracy in facts, that may not surface when the only means of challenging veracity is by an affidavit or testimony from another witness. Although ICAs will most commonly turn on issues of contractual interpretation as to which written documents may be the most reliable evidence, oral testimony and credibility of witnesses can still be very useful.

Writing of Awards

Most professional communities have at their disposal their own discursive resources which draw on their disciplinary and professional knowledge of what forms of communication are appropriate to represent their specific professional actions. It is thus expected that arbitrators as professionals have their own discursive resources which will be typical of their profession, and any accomplished arbitrator will skilfully exploit such resources to achieve their institutional goals and realize their communicative actions. However, it appears as if the options available to arbitrators are considerably constrained by the fact that most of the arbitrators by virtue of their also being members of the legal community find it difficult to dissociate and distinguish themselves from their parent discipline, that is, litigation. Hence, they continue to appropriate discursive resources that have been part of their professional armoury for a long time, which brings into arbitration discourse, especially awards, a distinct identity which seems to be a reflection of their other identity related to litigation contexts. There is sufficient evidence in the corpus of awards from well-represented international resources that arbitrators, in general, are significantly influenced by what they are quite used to doing in their litigation practice. Their discursive products are not very different from what they write in litigation, except in that they are not as detailed as in their efforts in litigation and that their elaborate arguments and reasoning – extensively supported by references to relevant and applicable legislative sections as well as precedents in the form of references to earlier judgments, which are quite typical of legal judgments – are often not so elaborate in arbitration awards. There is thus a relatively weaker effort displayed in their accounts in arbitration awards, which also may imply that there is relatively little effort employed in explaining, clarifying or justifying their decisions, and even perhaps little concern to persuade intended readers to accept their decisions. When some of the arbitrators were confronted with these observations, they offered at least two main reasons: firstly, any detailed reasoned award is likely to expose it for challenge in the court of law, and secondly, such a challenge may involve more expense in terms of time and money, which is generally dispreferred by parties in dispute. Arbitration awards also appear to give the overall impression of a relatively lower level of formality; however, in all other respects, especially in the use of technical lexico-grammatical and formulaic expressions, impersonal style, and also in the use of expressions indicating power and authority, they are very much similar to what one may find in litigation judgments. Gotti (this volume), based on his study of Italian arbitration awards, goes even further to claim that Italian awards in his corpus were characterized by excessively long sentences, binomial and multinomial expressions, predominant use of nominal izations, impersonal style and many other rhetorical features typical of legal discourse. Based on his very comprehensive analysis, he concludes that there is considerable influence of legal discourse on Italian arbitration awards. He further points out:

> All the main features of legalese (both lexical and syntactic) have been traced in abundance in the arbitration documents taken into consideration. Also the main textual structure of legal judgments has been found to be at the basis of the layout of arbitration awards. In spite of the fact that arbitration is a procedure that is meant to be simpler and quicker than its much more complex and slow counterpart litigation, the language used in awards still presents the complexity that is typical of legal language.

So far as the nature of accounts in awards is concerned, Breeze (this volume), using an appraisal analysis approach (Martin and Rose 2003), focuses on clarity and logic of argument as key values in the discourse of arbitration in order to realize persuasiveness of arguments or evidence so as to seek positive reaction on the part of the writer. She claims that arbitration awards are essentially dialogic in nature, in that they address readers of various kinds seeking 'to persuade them of the truth, legitimacy or logicality of certain views or arguments, and of the untruth, illegitimacy or illogicality of others'. She claims that arbitration awards are written 'in reaction to other (previously written) texts and with the reader's (future) reaction in mind'. She further points out that 'the text itself is also dialogic in that it contains accounts of different arguments or assertions and the corresponding counter-arguments, so that a great deal of the text is concerned with resolving a conflict between opposing or contradictory moves in a cogent and coherent manner'. However, as far as the analysis of awards in the present corpus is concerned, it seems obvious that in spite of some degree of accounting or reasoning, most of the arbitration awards are not as detailed as are their counterparts in litigation. They still continue however to be very similar to litigation judgments, especially in the use of lexico-grammatical and rhetorical resources, thus demonstrating the kind of interdiscursive contestation rarely found in other professional discourses and practices.

Another interesting aspect of contested identities is reflected in the discursive construction and dissemination of justice in arbitration. The arbitrators have immense power, more than their counterparts in litigation, that is, judges in the courtrooms, and hence they are seen as arbiters of right and wrong, capable of ranking issues in terms of their significance or lack of it. The discursive construction of negotiation of justice represented in arbitration awards is quite authoritative, in that it cannot be challenged in a court of law, except on procedural grounds. On the one hand, arbitrators are seen as the source of power and authority, and on the other, they are also viewed as masters of persuasion, who must not only seek truth, but at the same time, make it palatable to its intended audience by adequately accounting for its decisions leading to specific awards in such a way that it becomes difficult for the parties to challenge However, one of the very senior practitioners, when asked about such concerns in a specialist interview conducted in the course of this project claimed:

> No, not really […] I do not want my awards upset, obviously. But it doesn't affect that much, I'm just gonna write it in my own way anyhow probably […] obviously we have an obligation as an arbitrator to write an award that's enforceable […] I assume it's always a possibility that someone will challenge it, and I assume that the award's written in such a way that it won't be challengeable.

On the question of whether ICA is becoming increasingly similar to litigation, one expert in a specialist interview summed it up in the following way:

> […] my sense is that international arbitration to a considerable extent is looking like litigation, that's a generality, there're a million cases where this is not so, but it's a generality. How that came about, I suspect a lot of causes; American lawyers for one thing are used to a kind of litigation that involves an enormous amount of discovery, depositions, interrogatories, requests [for] document production. American lawyers seem to think that they have to turn every stone before they're ready to do battle at a trial, and to a certain extent I think that state of mind has been carried over to arbitration. Because in the US and around the world, big law firms have developed with arbitration groups of specialists, and often they tend to be peopled by litigation specialists who all of a sudden go into arbitration.

However, it is interesting to note that although ICA is becoming increasingly similar to litigation, and there is ample evidence that even arbitration awards are written in a typical legal style, especially in terms of their use of lexico-grammar, these awards seem to be different at least in one respect, that is, in their rhetorical patterning, especially in their the use of legal reasoning and accounts. This may be so because of the following factors: it may be that the arbitrators generally feel that extensive justification of, or accounting for the final decision will only add to the rising cost of arbitration; or, it may be that as the arbitration community is relatively small, with cases often concentrated in few hands, they feel that spending time in writing elaborate accounts will leave less time for them to take on other cases; or, again, it may be that they feel that the less elaborate the award, the fewer the chances of it getting challenged. There may even be yet another possibility that, unlike judges in the courts, arbitrators often have extensive powers in conducting arbitration and hence feel more comfortable taking a decision without having any obligation to justify, argue or account for the decision taken. There is also the factor that arbitration awards are rarely, if ever, used as precedents, and hence arbitrators feel relatively little pressure to account for their decisions. In our view, as ICA matures as an institution and acquires integrity of its own, the need to be more accountable to the stakeholders and to the community at large will grow.

Further, we may expect that this development will gradually bring in changes to the way awards are currently written, making them less legal in their form, style and content, and, as such, more detailed in their reasoning. Looking at the current practice, we are unlikely to see any significant changes in the discursive practices of arbitration practitioners in the near future.

Conclusion

In this chapter we have made an attempt to outline some of the key processes and procedures often adopted in ICA practices. We have focused, in particular, on a number of crucial and contested sites of engagement, drawing on a mixture of processes and procedures typical of litigation, on the one hand, and arbitration, on the other. The supposedly informal and non-judicial settings of ICA trials have been viewed as a site of contested identities across a number of different perspectives which represent essentially intercultural, interdisciplinary, inter-jurisdictional, and most importantly, inter-professional practices. The chapter is based on the assumption that ICA practice has its own integrity, with its own professional culture, which is distinct from its close cousin, litigation. There is also an implicit assumption that unlike litigation, which is essentially adversarial in nature, ICA as a professional practice is consensual, a harmonization of various jurisdictional characteristics, and is, or should be, non-adversarial. However, based on the current practices and perspectives of the members of arbitration community, the chapter claims that although such a harmonization is intensely desirable, this is unlikely to be achieved any time in the near future. This is primarily the case because of the involvement of persons within the litigation community from different jurisdictions, most notably from the common law and that of the civil law, the members of which are so deeply rooted in their individual legal culture and jurisdictional practices that they find it difficult to switch their hat, as it were, when they operate in arbitration. The essential consequence of this is that commercial arbitration practices are drawing increasingly closer to those of litigation in all respects, and as a consequence increasingly being viewed as sites of 'contested identities' whether in terms of discovery procedures, written testimony, witness examination or even writing of awards.

The practice of ICA remains contentious. There is no independent means of establishing the nature of its processes and procedures as the doors for any kind of external critical inquiry are intensely guarded, more often than not completely closed by the invocation of a general duty of privacy and confidentiality, given rather than negotiable, in all arbitration procedures. Unlike courtroom practices and proceedings which are open to the public and which provide court judgments that are readily available in published form, arbitration proceedings are held in private and the procedural details about the trials and their outcomes, including the arbitration awards, remain confidential (Bhatia, Candlin and Sharma 2009). Privacy sometimes aids firms in keeping trade secrets and financial dealings confidential from competitors and the public in general, but the parties never hesitate to bring the dispute and even arbitration decisions into the public domain when they see specific advantages deriving from such publicity (Corona 2011).

Redfern and Hunter (1991) rightly point out that investigating the practice of ICA is like peering into the dark. Very few arbitration awards are published and very little of the procedural decisions are made available. Information mainly comes from tapping the experience of the principal arbitral institutions or by looking at individual cases that come before the courts, either as a result of enforcement proceedings or because an arbitral award is challenged by the losing party. This brings a veil of secrecy and lack of transparency to the whole process of arbitration in international commercial contexts, which, in the long run, works to encourage the vested business interests of the participants, be they lawyers, arbitrators or corporate stakeholders. Such a practice will certainly be detrimental to the development of the ICA as an institution with its own independent culture and integrity in practice.

References

Bhatia, Vijay K. (2004): *Worlds of Written Discourse: A Genre-based View*, London, Continuum.

Bhatia, Vijay K. (2010): Interdiscursivity in Professional Discourse, *Discourse and Communication*, Vol. 4, No. 1, 32–50.

Bhatia, Vijay K. (2011): Witness Examination as Interdiscursive Practice, *World Englishes*, Vol. 30, No. 1, 106–16.

Bhatia, Vijay K., Christopher N. Candlin and Rajesh Sharma (2009): Confidentiality and Integrity in International Commercial Arbitration Practice, *Arbitration*, Vol. 75, 2–13.

Breeze, Ruth (2012 [this volume]): Appraisal Analysis of Dissenting and Concurring Opinions. In Bhatia, Vijay K., Candlin, Christopher N. and Gotti, Maurizio (Eds) *Discourse and Practice in International Commercial Arbitration: Issues, Challenges and Prospects*, Farnham, Ashgate Publishing.

Candlin, Christopher N. (1987): Explaining Moments of Conflict in Discourse. In Steele, Ross and Threadgold, Terry (Eds) *Language Topics Vol 2 Proceedings of the 1987 AILA Congress*, Sydney and Amsterdam, John Benjamins,413–29.

Candlin, Christopher N. (1997): General Editor's Preface. In Gunnarsson, Britt-Louise, Linell, Per and Nordberg, Bengt (Eds) *The Construction of Professional Discourse*, London, Longman, viii–xiv.

Candlin, Christopher N. (2006): Accounting for Interdiscursivity: Challenges to Professional Expertise. In Gotti, Maurizio and Giannoni, Davide (Eds) *New Trends in Specialized Discourse Analysis*, Bern, Peter Lang, 1–24.

Candlin, Christopher N. and Jonathan Crichton (2011): Introduction. In Candlin, Christopher N. and Crichton, Jonathan (Eds) *Discourses of Deficit*, Basingstoke, Palgrave, 1–24.

Candlin, Christopher N. and Jonathan Crichton (2011): Emergent Themes and Research Challenges: Reconceptualising LSP. In Pedersen, Margrethe and Engberg, Jan (Eds) *Current Trends in LSP Research: Aims and Methods*, Bern, Peter Lang.

Crichton, Jonathan (2010): Why a Multi-perspectived Approach to Discourse? In Crichton, Jonathan, *The Discourse of Commercialization*, Basingstoke, Palgrave, 20–48.

Corona, Isabel (2011): From Corporate Argumentation to Media Perception: The Recontextualization of Arbitration in the Public Sphere, *World English*, Vol. 30, No. 1, 129–40.

Cymrot, Mark (2007): Cross-Examination in International Arbitration, *Dispute Resolution Journal*, Vol. 62, No. 1, 52–65.

Du Cann, Richard (1964): *The Art of the Advocate*, Harmondsworth, Penguin.

Goffman, Erving (1959): *The Presentation of Self in Everyday Life*, Garden City, NY, Doubleday-Anchor.

Gotti, Maurizio (2012 [this volume]): The Judicialisation of Arbitration Discourse in the Italian Context. In Bhatia, Vijay K., Candlin, Christopher N. and Gotti, Maurizio (Eds) *Discourse and Practice in International Commercial Arbitration: Issues, Challenges and Prospects*, Farnham, Ashgate Publishing.

Kathpalia, Sujata (2012 [this volume]): Is Arbitration Being Colonized by Litigation? Practitioners' Views in the Singapore Context. In Bhatia, Vijay K., Candlin, Christopher N. and Gotti, Maurizio (Eds) *Discourse and Practice in International Commercial Arbitration: Issues, Challenges and Prospects*, Farnham, Ashgate Publishing.

Kerr, Michael (1997): Concord and Conflict in International Arbitration, *Arbitration International*, Vol. 13, No. 2, 121–44.

Marriott, Arthur (2005): *Litigate, Arbitrate, Mediate – Frustrate? Breaking the Dispute Deadlock*, Clayton UTZ Lecture. Online at <http://www.claytonutz.com/ialecture/2005/transcript_2005.html>, accessed 15 July 2011.

Martin, Jim and Rose, David (2003): *Working with Discourse: Meaning Beyond the Clause*, London, Continuum.

Nariman, Fali S. (2000): The Spirit of Arbitration: The Tenth Annual Goff Lecture, *Arbitration International*, Vol. 16, No. 3, 261–78.

Newman, Lawrence (1999): Evidence in Arbitration, *New York Law Journal*, Vol. 3, 30–31.

Ong, Colin Y.C. (2007): *The Art of Advocacy in International Arbitration*. Paper read at the IBA Annual Conference in Singapore, 15 October 2007.

PricewaterhouseCoopers (2006): *International Arbitration: Corporate Attitudes and Practices*. Published in collaboration with Queen Mary, University of London. Online at <http://www.pwc.com/arbitrationstudy>, accessed 6 June 2010.

Redfern, Alan and Hunter, Martin (1991): *Law and Practice of International Commercial Arbitration*, 2nd edition, London, Sweet & Maxwell.

Reed, Lucy (2010): Comments posted under *More on Corporate Criticism of International Arbitration* on Kluwer Law International blog. Online at <http://kluwerarbitrationblog.com/blog/author/lucyreed/>, accessed 3 March 2011.

Roberts, Celia and Sarangi, Srikant (1999): Hybridity in Gatekeeping Discourse: Issues of Practical Relevance for the Researcher. In Sarangi, Srikant and Roberts, Celia Roberts (Eds) *Talk, Work and Institutional Order: Discourse in Medical, Mediation and Management Settings*, Berlin, Mouton de Gruyter, 473–504.

Rubinstein, Javier H. (2004): International Commercial Arbitration: Reflections at the Crossroads of the Common Law and Civil Law Traditions, *Chicago Journal of International Law*, Vol. 5, No. 1, 303–10, 309.

Schneider, Michael E. (2009): *Twenty-one Theses about Witness Testimony in International Arbitration and Cross-examination*, Geneva, 27 January 2009. Online at <http://www.lalive.ch/documents/Conference_paper.pdf>, accessed 15 July 2011.

Scollon, Ron (1998): *Mediated Discourse as Social Interaction: A Study of News Discourse*, New York, Longman.

Tallerico, Thomas, J. and Behrendt, Adam, J (2002): *The Use of Bifurcation and Direct Testimony Witness Statements in International Commercial Arbitration Proceedings*, published by Bodman, Longley & Dahling LLP, based on the lecture on the use of these tools at the June 2002 Biennial Conference on International Arbitration and ADR, Salzburg. Online at <http://www.bodmanllp.com/publications/articles/UseOfBifurcation.pdf>, accessed 15 June 2011.

Tan, Ngoh T. and Lee-Patridge, Joo Eng (2000): Alternative Dispute Resolution. In *Business, Family and Community: Multidisciplinary Perspectives*, Singapore, Pagesetters Services.

Tay, Catherine T.S. (1998): *Resolving Disputes by Arbitration: What You Need to Know*, Singapore, Singapore University Press.

Walter, Mattli (2001): Private Justice in a Global Economy: From Litigation to Arbitration, *International Organization*, Vol. 55, No. 4, 919–47, the MIT Press Stable. Online at <http://www.jstor.org/stable/3078620>, accessed 20 December 2009.

Index

For Product Safety Concerns and Information please contact our EU representative GPSR@taylorandfrancis.com
Taylor & Francis Verlag GmbH, Kaufingerstraße 24, 80331 München, Germany

www.ingramcontent.com/pod-product-compliance
Ingram Content Group UK Ltd.
Pitfield, Milton Keynes, MK11 3LW, UK
UKHW022009180926
475701UK00003B/276

* 9 7 8 1 1 3 8 2 6 9 3 9 2 *